MAKING STRATEGY

SAGE has been part of the global academic community since 1965, supporting high quality research and learning that transforms society and our understanding of individuals, groups, and cultures. SAGE is the independent, innovative, natural home for authors, editors and societies who share our commitment and passion for the social sciences.

Find out more at: **www.sagepublications.com**

2nd Edition

Fran ACKERMANN & Colin EDEN

MAKING STRATEGY

Mapping Out Strategic Success

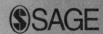

Los Angeles | London | New Delhi
Singapore | Washington DC

First edition published 1998
Reprinted 2000, 2002, 2003, 2004

This second edition published 2011

SAGE Publications Ltd
1 Oliver's Yard
55 City Road
London EC1Y 1SP

SAGE Publications Inc.
2455 Teller Road
Thousand Oaks, California 91320

SAGE Publications India Pvt Ltd
B 1/I 1 Mohan Cooperative Industrial Area
Mathura Road
New Delhi 110 044

SAGE Publications Asia-Pacific Pte Ltd
33 Pekin Street #02-01
Far East Square
Singapore 048763

Library of Congress Control Number: 2010942878

British Library Cataloguing in Publication data

A catalogue record for this book is available from the British Library

ISBN 978-1-84920-119-3
ISBN 978-1-84920-120-9 (pbk)

Typeset by C&M Digitals (P) Ltd, Chennai, India
Printed in India at Replika Press Pvt Ltd
Printed on paper from sustainable resources

SUMMARY OF CONTENTS

CONTENTS

ABOUT THE AUTHORS

Fran Ackermann, BA, PhD

Dr Fran Ackermann is a Professor of Strategy and Management Science at Strathclyde Business School, Glasgow, Scotland. She also is an adjunct Professor at the University of Western Australia Business School. Fran's research interests span a wide set of arenas including: the development and implementation of strategy (with a particular focus on stakeholder management and the identification of distinctive competences), the resolution of messy, complex problems, the role of group decision support systems particularly in the support of group negotiation and the identification and management of systemic risk. She has worked with over 150 companies based around the world (including UK, Australia, France, the US and Italy) in developing strategy that acknowledges the need to attend to both good analysis and social process. She is a keen advocate of linking theory to practice and vice versa.

She is the author of four books, over 20 book chapters and 100 plus refereed papers (in areas such as strategic management, management science, group decision and negotiation and management). Her recent books are: Eden, C. and Ackermann, F. *Making Strategy: The Journey of Strategic Management*. London: Sage, 1998; Bryson, J., Ackermann, F., Eden, C. and Finn, C. *Visible Thinking*: Wiley, 2004; Ackermann, F., Eden, C., with Brown, I. *The Practice of Making Strategy*. London: Sage, 2005.

Colin Eden, BSc (Eng), PhD

Dr Colin Eden is a Vice Dean, and Professor of Strategic Management, of the Strathclyde Business School in Glasgow, Scotland. Colin's major research interests are into the processes of strategy making in senior management teams; the relationship between operational decision making practices and their strategic consequences; the use of group decision support in the analysis and making of strategy; multi-organisational collaboration; and systemic strategic risk. He has worked with over 200 management teams, helping them develop realistic strategies and, in particular develop an understanding of the basis of their competitive advantage, and manage their key stakeholders. The research he has conducted over the past 20 years has been located in the traditions of 'action research' where engagement in the real world is the basis for testing and developing management theory.

He is the author of nine books and over 150 scholarly articles in the fields of management, strategic management and management science. His recent books are Eden, C. and Ackermann, F. *Making Strategy: The Journey of Strategic Management.* London: Sage, 1998; Eden, C. and Spender, J. C. (eds) *Managerial and Organizational Cognition.* London: Sage, 1998; Ackermann, F.; Eden, C. and with Brown, I. *The Practice of Making Strategy.* London: Sage, 2005; Kilgour, M. and Eden, C. (eds) *Handbook for Group Decision and Negotiation.* Dordrecht: Springer, 2010.

ACKNOWLEDGEMENTS

We are grateful to those who have been at the forefront of publishing books that seek to mix theory with practice – for example Bryson, 1995, Nutt and Backoff, 1992, and Rosenhead and Mingers, 2001. In addition we have been used to having around us a number of colleagues who also have a significant commitment to Lewin's belief that 'nothing is as practical as a good theory' (Lewin, 1951: 169). We are indebted, in particular, to the support of Susan Howick and Chris Huxham.

We have now worked with Sage on three books and our editor (now Associate Director) Kiren Shoman has helped and encouraged and cajoled us. She has acted patiently as a sounding board for a variety of possible ways of presenting this book and has shown undue enthusiasm for our sometimes daft ideas. Thank you.

John Bryson, Dave MacKay and Kevin Page have been involved in extended debate about the content and structure of the book and through their contributions the book has been improved enormously. David Andersen, Aime Heene, Anne Huff, Paul Nutt, George Richardson, Olaf Rughase, Ron Sanchez and Mike Schindl have been stimulating company as we tested out ideas and practice.

Karl Weick's research and writing (particularly Weick, 1979; Weick, 1995; Weick, 1999) have been a continual inspiration to our developing thinking and he has always encouraged us to take ideas into practice.

We must also thank the many and varied clients we have worked with over the past 20 years.

INTRODUCTION
THE STRUCTURE AND DESIGN
OF THE BOOK: HOW TO READ
THE BOOK

AIMS

The book aims to address the challenges of how to *build a robust strategy* that *people want to implement*. It presents strategy making as *both an analytical and social process* in a way that differentiates it from most other books. Strategy making is seen as something applicable to managers of departments, divisions, the small and medium enterprises (SMEs), as well as the top management teams of public and for-profit organisations.

Designs for four facilitated strategic conversations are presented. The designs have been used extensively, in a wide range of countries, by management teams in all types of organisation. Each strategic conversation can *deliver usable strategies in three to eight hours*. The conversation is designed as a 'strategy forum' (in some parts of the world this would be called a 'strategy making workshop').

The four strategy forums are presented, both through discussing the original theoretical and conceptual grounding of each forum along with the practical requirements for developing usable strategies. These forums, when taken together, provide a powerful means for agreeing a *negotiated strategy*, and comprise: *strategic issue management*; *agreeing organisational purpose*; *competitiveness from the exploitation and protection of distinctiveness*; and *the strategic management of stakeholders*.

Strategy forums succeed through a focus on the effective facilitation of groups, teams and leaders – *strategy derives from the thinking, conversations, and negotiated agreements within groups*. Thus, the significance of group processes for designing effective strategy is argued. This discussion of strategy making as a social process is therefore accompanied by an exposition on 'how to' facilitate groups.

Making Strategy will appeal to those interested in delivering strategic change – organisational change. Thus, organisational change specialists and management scientists, as well as strategists, are expected to develop a different way of thinking about their theories in practice as well as developing their practice.

Teachers of strategic management might be inclined, or only have enough time, to require students to study only one of the four ways of thinking about, and practising, strategy making. Scholars and researchers might concentrate only on the chapters that present background theories and concepts underpinning strategy making, whereas managers might explore only the chapters dealing with the application of the theories.

Making Strategy: Mapping Out Strategic Success builds off, extends and updates, the two previous books *Making Strategy: The Journey of Strategic Management* (Eden and Ackermann, 1998) and *The Practice of Making Strategy* (Ackermann and Eden with Brown, 2005).

ACCESSIBILITY

Making Strategy: Mapping Out Strategic Success is designed to be accessible to strategic management scholars, practising managers, consultants and students of management (particularly post-experience students – for example those studying for an MBA). It is aimed at those who wish to integrate both the theory and practice of strategy making. It is not necessary to read 'everything' – readers can focus on specific sections of the book because each chapter is written as a stand-alone piece, even though the chapters build up to a holistic interpretation of, and approach to, making strategy. For example, an interest in organisational purpose might mean turning immediately to the exploration of the theories and concepts related to seeing strategy as purpose. Reading this exploration of the concepts about organisational purpose might attract an investigation of the companion chapter on how to decide organisational purpose in practice. Or, vice versa.

The book has been structured so that it is easy to read because the main text is not dominated by academic jargon and references. Where jargon is introduced it is because it is a label that is regarded as helpful, and one that will be often used as a short-hand throughout the book. Endnotes are also used throughout to facilitate (1) reading without the interference of references, (2) a more detailed discussion of some of the concepts, and (3) an indication of useful further reading and reference quotations.

A small number of articles or books are listed at the end of each of the 'theory' chapters as recommended further reading about concepts underlying the particular approach to strategy making.

THEORY AND PRACTICE: CHAPTER PAIRS

Each of the four facilitated strategic conversations (forums) is set out as pairs of chapters. The first chapter of each pair deliberates on the arguments for approaching strategy from a particular stance, develops the theories and concepts, and relates the stance to the work of others. In addition the chapter provides a summary of the practical implications of the stance for the use of the designed social process that is specifically scripted to adhere to the stance taken. Each stance is promoted so that it leads naturally to practical procedures (we call them 'scripts'), and these scripts are presented in the second of the pair of chapters. Although the chapters are closely matched, there are some occasions where the 'how to' presentation does not include absolutely all aspects discussed in the concepts chapter.

Thus the second of each chapter pair is a 'how to do it' presentation. These chapters present a series of carefully designed scripts that when taken together constitute a 'strategy forum' – a practical expression of the stance taken in the first of the pair of chapters. Indeed, these scripts encompass *instructions set out as statements in a bold font*. In each case the timing of each script is indicated as well as the 'deliverable' from a package of scripts. Each forum is designed to take about half a day and typically involves a management team of five to twelve participants. Each strategy forum is designed so that a management team sees progress through a *deliverable ('take-away') within each hour of a forum*. In addition, the overall resource requirements are shown at the beginning of each of these chapters. They are presented so that the chapter could be used independently of the rest of the book.

It is our expectation that one of the management team will be, in effect, a client for, or leader of, the forum. In addition we anticipate that *there will be someone who will act as a facilitator of the forum*. The facilitator may be someone external to the group who takes on the role of facilitator. They may also be a professional facilitator external to the organisation. But, on many occasions they may be one of the managers acting as both facilitator and participant – a difficult role, but often the only way of undertaking a strategy forum. We use the term 'manager-client' throughout as a label for the manager as facilitator and client.

As we suggest above, strategy making is a social process and so a critical chapter pair is dedicated to this topic. The first of these (chapter 2) discusses *the nature and role of groups* and this is paired with a later chapter (chapter 11) which concentrates on providing *guidance to would be facilitators*. These chapters are separated because the role of facilitation is better appreciated following a reading of at least one of the 'how to' chapters.

Finally, the first and last chapters constitute another pair. The first chapter sets out the arguments for approaching strategy from a particular stance and so declares the key assumptions about strategic management. The final chapter shows how *the four forums can be integrated* to increase the robustness of the strategy making. In addition it provides the *follow-through* that is an essential part of delivering and testing the agreements that derive from the four strategy forums. Also it addresses the issues of *closure, monitoring, and the project management* of strategy implementation.

EXAMPLES AND CASE MATERIAL

The chapters provide examples, illustrations and vignettes that aim to bring concepts alive and illustrate strategy making in practice. They are all based on real cases; however, in many instances, the data has been modified to protect confidentiality. In many examples the name of the organisation is revealed, and in these instances permission will have been given. In other instances data in the public domain has been used (rather than client based data), and the source provided.

COMPUTER SOFTWARE AND GROUP SUPPORT

The approach to making strategy is action-oriented and so is concerned with causality – with how to change the world. Thus, networks of causality representing the complexity of strategic change are a crucial part of understanding strategic change – what to do and why to do it. Maps are developed that show the network of causality – a 'causal map' which is a network of phrases and arrows linking them. These causal maps are used as an important vehicle for encouraging effective strategic conversations.

Easy-to-use computer software is employed to help in the display and continual modification of the causal map. The map, publicly displayed, acts as a system to facilitate negotiation. The visual interactive nature of the mapping software acts as a vehicle for representing the continually changing views of the group, and helps manage the complexity of networks of causality.

The software is not essential, but rather it is extremely helpful to making strategy. The software is powerful and so can be used in a sophisticated manner, but it can also be used in a simple but effective way.

The Decision Explorer® software used to facilitate strategy making is available free to those purchasing this book. In addition, a 'quick guide' and a 'video' presenting the use of it in a strategy making environment are all available free to purchasers of this book – instruction for downloading this material are in the Appendix.

1

STRATEGY AS FOCUS

Strategy is about agreeing priorities and then implementing those priorities towards the realisation of organisational purpose.

In this book we address a very simple but powerful definition of strategy. We see strategy as about *agreeing* where to *focus* energy, cash, effort and emotion for long term sustainable success.

We see strategic *management* as about *implementing* the *agreements* about where to *focus* energy, cash, effort and emotion.

Thus, *strategy is about agreeing priorities and then implementing those priorities towards the realisation of organisational purpose.* This means resolving the debate about which issues deserve the most attention; there is always competition across an effective management team for which issues deserve priority attention. Each manager has their own view, and should have their own view, because they have different expertise, a different role with different accountabilities, and they have each experienced the different consequences of not paying attention to their own, let alone others', views. Thus, strategic management can never be anything other than the outcome of negotiation among those with power to create the future of the organisation.

In addition, strategic management requires an acceptance that one person's claim on the future will be seen as operational to others, and others' claims will be seen as too broad and general. Managers who are good strategic thinkers (about what impacts the future success of their organisation) will often be thinking of extensive and sometimes complex ramifications of apparently operational actions but which can have significant strategic implications.

It is also important to negotiate a coherent strategy where:

- Strategy statements do not contradict each other either singly or as meaningful 'chunks' of strategy.
- Strategic action programmes do not contradict each other or the overall strategy statements.

- Operational systems and procedures (costing, remuneration, transfer pricing) – including embedded routines – are not inconsistent with strategic intent and are designed so that they increase the likelihood of the implementation of strategy.
- Personal and organisational reward systems are not inconsistent with strategic intent.
- Actual behaviour of the management team does not contradict the rhetoric of strategy.[1]

Strategic management is coherent when it can be recognised as a holistic phenomenon.

Thus, strategy and strategic management is coherent when it can be recognised as a holistic phenomenon. In this book we present four ways of thinking about and developing strategy (forums) – each are stand-alone but can come together to make a holistic strategy and take account of the above requirements for coherence and where the whole is greater than the sum of the forums (chapter 12).

As implied by the above list, some of the supposedly operational systems can have enormous strategic implications: for example, the costing system, the transfer pricing system, the management information system, and the underlying assumptions about estimating processing time in the manufacture of products and services. However, we must recognise that often these systems will have grown accidentally rather than as an intended support to the delivery of strategy. Where there is internal coherence of this type of organisational system then these systems can become self-fulfilling and self-sustaining as determinants of the strategic future of the organisation – they support and strengthen one another. Similarly, each of the strategy forums can work together as self-fulfilling and self-sustaining determinants of the future.

NEGOTIATING A SUCCESSFUL STRATEGY: THE SOCIAL *PROCESS* OF STRATEGY MAKING

Any organisational change that matters strategically will involve winners and losers.

The main thesis of this book is that the *process* of strategy making is the most important element in realising strategic intent. It is our clear and convinced view that when strategic management fails to manage the real activities of an organisation it is because of the inability of strategy to change the way in which key people in the organisation both *think and act* as managers of its future. Thus, the issue of political feasibility of strategic change will be central to our considerations. Political feasibility implies, at least, building a powerful coalition within which there is enough consensus to deliver coordinated action to create strategic change.[2] To argue that political feasibility is key is not new. What is new is that this book considers the issue in some depth (see particularly chapter 2) – relating it to the theory and practice of managing power, politics, multiple perspectives and the power of emotional as well as analytical commitment to delivering strategy.

It is rare for strategy to promote the status quo. Strategy development will almost always imply changes in the organisation – in its relationship with the environment and in its relationship with itself. Any organisational change that matters strategically will involve winners and losers,[3] and so will involve some managers *seeing themselves* as potential winners and some as potential losers. It follows that any strategy development or thinking about strategy will, without deliberate intention, promote organisational politics. Thus strategy is an instrument of power, and so of change; 'organisations must be seen as tools ... for shaping the world as one wishes it to be shaped. They provide the means for imposing one's definition of the proper affairs of men upon other men'.[4]

A common experience for many managers is that the strategic planning process takes on the form of an 'annual rain dance'. The activity is taken to be important enough to devote some limited time to because the intellectual arguments for doing so are difficult to argue with – 'of course an organisation must have a strategy'. However, often the reality is that the activity will simply result in 'the usual annual budgeting battle' which is focused on short term issues and the retention of the status quo. Some managers will come off badly and others well, but this will be related more to their political clout and negotiating skills than any consideration of the longer term impact of the budgets on the strategic future of the organisation. These budgeting rounds will have a real impact on the strategic future of the organisation as a part of the 'emergent strategising'[5] of the organisation, but not in a thoughtful or designed way.[6] Statements about the strategic future of the organisation will be used, when appropriate, as a part of the negotiation for resources but will not necessarily form part of a coherent whole, or result in action.

When managers begin to realise that the strategy making process might be 'for real' and might actually have some real consequences for their future in the organisation then those participating in the process will begin to make judgements about whether they will gain or lose from the process. This assessment is influenced by their believing that strategic change will shift the balance of power and will value some skills and resources more than others. The surfacing of strategic options carries the concomitant surfacing of anticipated social and political consequences. Any organisational change is seen by many managers as an opportunity for self-aggrandisement and the acquisition of power.[7] The politics that this process of anticipation creates will be the result of each participant's personal understanding of the impact of strategy. This understanding may, or may not, be accurate – what matters is that each participant anticipates and takes action to influence strategic thinking on the basis of these anticipations. 'If men define situations as real, they are real in their consequences'.[8] As this political dynamic unfolds it can be a major contributor to a team being unable to address the fundamental issues, and being diverted to internal coalition building designed to retain the relative security of the status quo.

The communications within a strategic conversation – a strategy forum – can then become dominated by each participant seeking to influence the definition of the situation in ways that anticipate possible changes in status, power, self-image and so on. Most senior managers are very skilled in the process of defining situations in a light favourable to their own aspirations and inclinations. Thus, the way in which situations are defined becomes crucial as it determines the nature of the agendas to be addressed and the processes by which strategic issues are surfaced. The extent to which a management team is able to address the fundamental strategic issues, rather than address only the fears and aspirations of each member of the team, will be a measure of their likelihood for success. We are not suggesting that fears and aspirations of management, or other staff, may not be a legitimate strategic issue, rather we are making a distinction between those issues that directly affect the core activity of the organisation compared with those that facilitate that activity or support particular manager's aspirations.

We must consider the elements of negotiation that increase the probability of it being successful.

As long as we accept that strategic management follows from negotiation among power brokers then we must consider the requirements of negotiation that increase the probability of it being successful. Here we consider five such requirements of successful negotiation of strategy.[9]

- REQUIREMENT 1: managers as leaders are *good strategic thinkers.*
- REQUIREMENT 2: managers can *surface and respect* the thinking of the different perspectives of their staff.
- REQUIREMENT 3: managers can *manage the negotiation* between the different perspectives.
- REQUIREMENT 4: managers can create the best from *combining the wisdom, experience, and different perspectives.*
- REQUIREMENT 5: strategy can, and will, be implemented because it accepts that *operations and strategy are not separable.*

Managers have to devise ways of tricking themselves into regularly thinking about the important rather than the urgent.

A strategy need not be, and rarely should be, a detailed plan, and this book does not assume a plan will be developed.[10] It does assume that a more or less detailed framework for strategic change will be developed. Strategic opportunism[11] is not rejected as inappropriate, but rather thought of as highly appropriate in some organisational contexts. Thus, it may be appropriate to keep many different issues and activities on the go at once, so that chance encounters are likely to be relevant and acted upon with respect to some part of the framework for strategic action. Often there is no time to gather more than a very small amount of the information on most issues; managers have to make use of 'intelligent guesswork' and hunches. There is a strong tendency for 'the urgent to drive out the important', and so many managers have to devise ways of tricking themselves into regularly thinking about the important rather than the urgent. Thus, making strategy must be engaging for those who have to deliver the strategy – strategy should not be made by those without the responsibility and accountability for its implementation.

Strategy making is influenced by the way in which issues are presented,[12] the identification of their significance, their exploration as the group constructs a shared understanding of them, and the point at which a negotiated settlement is likely. Coordination depends on developing, understanding and agreeing processes and procedures that are coherent with each other, analytically sound, objectively workable and designed with respect to the realities of their importance to the organisation. Cooperation depends on good working social relationships as well as on procedures and bureaucracy. Cooperation is crucial to managing strategic futures, because strategic opportunism depends not only on the ability to work together on issues that cannot be dealt with by current procedures, but also on the ability to effectively engage in team work, and pay attention to multiple perspectives. Thus, making and delivering strategy uses experience and wisdom. Strategy making is about a future that does not yet exist and so evidence from the past may be useful but may also be irrelevant.

Strategy making is a creative act that should not be overwhelmed by 'paralysis by analysis'. The process of making strategy needs, therefore, to be a designed process but one that allows experience, wisdom and different perspective to open up the strategic conversation before closing it down and reaching agreements and closure. Active sense making[13] by human beings is more important than 'hard data'. Thus, strategy making is, in this book, seen to be a creative act that must be undertaken by those with the power to make it happen, rather than just an act of analysis by support staff. It is also an 'inside-out' approach to strategic management, where the management team will seek to develop and exploit their uniqueness in serving customers (exploiting the inside of the organisation) and then test, adapt and/or extend this strategy against the outside world. This approach is in contrast to an 'outside-in' way of building strategy, where the organisation seeks to understand the external world and adapt to it.[14]

Effective organisational change relies upon incrementalism, upon many 'small wins', rather than the single 'big win'.

It is possible to incrementally change an organisation over time and achieve the same outcome as what might be expected only with revolutionary change.[15] Effective organisational change relies upon incrementalism, upon many 'small wins', rather than the single 'big win'.[16] Major organisational change is more likely to arise from the systemic and strategic confluence of lots of small wins rather than through a single 'big bang' change programme. Sometimes, of course, incrementalism is not possible,[17] but we are suggesting that it will usually stand a better chance of success.

In this book we discuss in detail four strategic conversations each of which encourage incremental movement towards a successful strategic future.

CHANGING MINDS AND BEHAVIOUR: THE ROLE OF CAUSAL BELIEFS

In this book we are taking commitment to delivering strategy as almost more important than the results of analysis. But, there need not be a conflict, as long as commitment from the power brokers is held to be paramount. The power brokers, possibly a management team, are a social group. Agreeing strategy is thus a social and psychological *negotiation* (changing minds and relationships). Good *analysis must inform* this negotiation where possible. However, managing the negotiation to achieve emotional and thinking (cognitive) commitment drives the process of making effective strategy.

As we have argued above, the designed social *process* is what can determine commitment. *Negotiation* that can lead to consensus, rather than compromise, requires a number of important features:

- Start from 'where each participant is at' – their immediate and personal or role concerns. If these concerns are not addressed then they will inhibit the negotiation in a dysfunctional manner.
- Seek to develop new options rather than fight over 'old' options. Get the group to be creative about pulling together the wisdom of each member of the team.[18]
- Actively engage every member of the team. Use fair processes that ensure that those with the loudest voices are not treated as if they only have the best views[19] (attend to 'procedural justice').[20]
- Use a 'transitional object' – a picture/model that is equivocal (fuzzy but meaningful phrases that have uncertain authorship rather than precise assertions and numbers) and changing, and that facilitates shifting of positions.[21] This is a picture that all of the group jointly construct and change as the designed conversation moves forwards.

The use of natural language – conversation, debate and arguments – as the basis of modelling facilitates a positive role for equivocality. Equivocality in this sense means the provision of sufficient degrees of 'fuzziness' to encourage negotiation. The fuzziness allows for gentle shifts in thinking and positions that are imperceptible to others (and sometimes to the participant themselves). This transitional process is more likely when the modelling process is visually interactive[22] and so the publicly displayed picture becomes a 'transitional object'.[23]

In seeking to find out 'where each participant is at' it is helpful to use the notion of claims – claims that seek to persuade others towards a particular course of action.[24] By getting managers to consider the varying claims and capture these, a more complete picture can be gained ensuring both procedural justice and an easy understanding of why a particular procedure is being followed ('procedural rationality').[25] Separating the proponent from the contribution reinforces equivocality, allows a claim to be viewed in its own right rather than 'claims being offered according to their proponents' leverage',[26] and helps build a more comprehensive and robust understanding.

Pulling together the wisdom of each team member involves understanding their arguments (claims) about how and why to change the world. And, we have argued above, for strategic change being about unravelling causality – expressing the mechanisms for change. Thus the picture developed by the group will be a 'causal map'[27] – a network of causality of argumentation. A causal map is a basis for action and change where actions are those statements that are taken to cause a given outcome.[28] Each action in turn is informed by actions that support them (explanations) placing the former action as an outcome. Therefore, each node on the causal map can be both an action and an outcome depending upon the level of abstraction required.

The causal map, when projected on a public screen, allows participants to have time to 'mentally pause' rather than feeling pressured to respond emotionally to face-to-face and verbal communication. This avoids the 'knee jerk' – often poorly considered – response being made public. For example, a particular perspective being put forward by one participant might fly in the face of the views of another. However, because there is less pressure to respond immediately the member who disagrees is able to listen to the contribution and, as the mapping process reveals the context, appreciate in more depth the contribution and its value. As a result, it might be that the potential antagonist is either persuaded or at least sees merit in the views of the other member. In addition, by not contradicting or arguing publicly the person is able to change their mind imperceptibly and thus avoid the issue of being stuck defending a position that they may no longer subscribe to. They are thus able to listen better. This reduces the likelihood of group members responding physiologically with a solely emotional rather than cognitive response.

CHANGING WAYS OF THINKING AND ACTING: CHANGING THE MEANING OF ACTION

Too often conversations about strategic change never go beyond verbal rhetoric or nice sounding strategy statements that have little meaning in terms of action implications. The statements allow managers to do almost anything and be able to justify it within the framework of the statements in strategy documents. We have argued before that strategy making is about strategic change, and the formation of strategy cannot be divorced from issues of implementation.[29]

One important way in which we can find out whether an organisation has changed is by listening for the changes in the claims. Thus, it follows that any evaluation of strategic change should explore changes in the language of strategic issue management.

It is worth stressing that, in many respects, shared understanding about strategic intent will make things happen differently in the organisation. Most successful strategic change will come from managers viewing their world differently *and so acting differently*. For strategic organisational change we see a continuing process where the conversation itself produces change – expectations and intentions are continually elaborated, and plans are declared as a way of symbolising closure but in fact creating temporary stability. A designed strategic conversation (the forums presented in this book) is expected to promote such changes in thinking and so acting.

STRATEGY MAKING AND STRATEGIC 'PROBLEM SOLVING'

This introductory chapter has presented some of the key assumptions about strategy making that inform the content of the book. In summary, these key assumptions are:

- Strategy is about focus, strategy making is about focusing argument and agreements on what matters.
- Strategy must be practical and politically feasible to be implemented, and so:
  - strategy is negotiated – using wisdom, experience, insight and so different perspectives;
  - strategy making is a social process;
  - strategic management is about organisational change – and so it is about understanding causality;
  - strategy delivery involves changing minds and behaviours.

- Operational decisions, systems and structures are integrally linked to strategic management.

In many respects strategic management and strategic problem solving are, therefore, interlinked. Indeed three of the four strategy making forums presented in this book are just as relevant for tackling strategic problems as they are for making strategy.[30] All strategic problems need to be addressed from the standpoint of: issue management, purpose and stakeholder management, and with exactly the same commitment to gaining ownership, using experience and wisdom, and so group processes. Similarly, and as with strategy making, the problem structuring stage is the crucial forerunner to any more detailed analysis using, for example, operational research techniques – particularly simulation modelling,[31] and spreadsheet modelling.

The four ways of making strategy that are presented in this book are designed to be 'naturalistic' for participants. A participant, and the manager-client, is expected to appreciate each forum as 'an obvious and practical way' of creating a robust strategy, and each step is expected to seem like the next 'obvious step'. Two tests of its voracity are: (1) the extent to which reasonably sophisticated strategy making can happen without any use whatsoever of 'business school jargon', and (2) where strategic management deliverables appear at intervals of one hour or less – where participants can describe the deliverable as an agreement that will guide strategic change. As each hour passes and each forum unfolds, the strategy becomes increasingly more robust, coherent and practical. These requirements are demanding and ambitious, but have been met within the contexts of, at least, several hundred different organisations and facilitated by managers, post-experience manager-students, consultants and the authors.

NOTES

1 'Theories in use' versus 'espoused theories' (Argyris and Schon, 1974).
2 See John Kotter's eight steps to transforming your organisation and the role of forming a powerful coalition (Kotter, 1995).
3 The significance of winners and losers is a key part of considering who to involve in a strategy making team (Ackermann and Eden with Brown, 2005: chapter 2).
4 Perrow (1986: 11).
5 The notion of emergent strategising – allowing strategy to emerge from the patterns of thinking and behaviour embedded in the organisation – is important in this book. We shall refer to the idea in several of the future chapters, particularly in relation to making strategy

through prioritisation and management of key issues (chapters 3) and agreement of purpose (chapter 5).

6   Raimond and Eden (1990).

7   Frost (1987); Mangham (1978); Perrow (1986).

8   Thomas and Thomas (1928: 572).

9   The principle of learning how to approach strategic issues from a number of perspectives has been a matter of interest in the redevelopment of MBA programmes so that they develop critical thinking and leadership – see Datar, Garvin and Cullen (2010).

10 The continuum from deliberate emergent strategising to strategic planning is depicted in Eden and Ackermann (1998: 9).

11 See Isenberg (1987).

12 Dutton and Ashford (1993); Dutton and Ottensmeyer (1987).

13 The work of the authors, over the past 20 years, has been significantly influenced by the writing of Karl Weick and his way of understanding sense making in organisations (of particular note are Bougon, Weick and Binkhorst, 1977; Weick, 1979; Weick, 1983; Weick, 1995).

14 Igor Ansoff was an early proponent of 'gap analysis' (between the external and internal worlds) as the basis for designing a corporate plan (Ansoff, 1965). More recently scenario planning is an example of an outside-in approach (see, for example, van der Heijden, 1996).

15 Balogun and Hope Hailey (2004).

16 Bryson and Roering (1988).

17 Logical incrementalism studied by Quinn (1978) centres strategy development around experimentation and learning from partial commitments.

18 This assertion derives from the Harvard School of *international conciliation* (Fisher and Ury, 1982), and also attends to 'group-think' issues. These aspects of strategy making are considered in more detail in chapter 3.

19 This means considering air-time, anonymity and being listened to. Procedural justice is an important element of good group work in strategy making and it is discussed fully in chapter 2.

20 See chapter 2 for the significance of procedural justice in strategy making.

21 The process of cognitive change involves elaborating a personal construct system (Kelly, 1955; Kelly, 1991), or 'scaffolding' (Vygotsky, 1978).

22 For more information on the use of visual interactive modelling see Ackermann and Eden (1994).

23 De Geus (1988) and Winnicott (1953).

24 Nutt (2002).

25 Procedural rationality is a term introduced by Herbert Simon (Simon, 1976).

26 Nutt (2002: 25).

27 A causal map is a network of causality – a 'directed graph' (Harary, Norman and Cartwright, 1965) that shows phrases (statements/claims) linked to each other by arrows that show the direction of causality. It is a representation of the impact of change, the impact of strategy. In some respect a causal map is akin to a 'cognitive map' – a representation that translates Kelly's theoretical framework (Personal Construct Theory – Kelly, 1955) into a practical tool by acting as a device for representing that part of a person's construct system which they are able and willing to make explicit. Therefore, while Kelly is clear that a construct is not the same as a verbal tag it is nevertheless *useful* to collect verbal tags as if they were constructs. As a result a cognitive/causal map, in practice, is dependent upon the notion that language is a common currency of organisational life and so can be used as the dominant medium for accessing a construct system.

Causal maps and cognitive maps have been at the centre of understanding sensemaking in organisations for the last couple of decades, and before (see, for example, Balogun, Huff and Johnson, 2003; Bougon, 1992; Bougon and Komocar, 1990; Weick and Binkhorst, 1977; Eden and Spender, 1998; Eden, Jones and Sims, 1979; Eden, Jones and Sims, 1983; Huff, 1990; Huff and Eden, 2009; Huff and Jenkins, 2001; Johnson, Daniels and Asch, 1998; Weick and Roberts, 1993). However, in this book they are used as a facilitative, or negotiative, device rather than as a research tool. The maps are developed and worked upon by the participants in strategy making.

See Bryson, Ackermann, Eden and Finn (2004: Resource C) for a history of mapping.

28 Examples of different uses of causal maps for problem solving, strategy making and organisational change can be found in Bryson, Ackermann, Eden and Finn (2004).

29 Simons (1995).

30 See, for example, Ackermann and Eden (2001b); Ackermann, Andersen, Eden and Richardson (2010a); Bryson, Ackermann, Eden and Finn (2004); Eden and Ackermann (2001c); Eden, Ackermann, Bryson, Richardson, Andersen and Finn (2009); Franco (2009); Hindle and Franco (2009); Mingers and Rosenhead (2004); Rosenhead (2006); Rosenhead and Mingers (2001).

31 For example Howick, Ackermann and Andersen (2006); and Howick and Eden (2010).

2

STRATEGIC MANAGEMENT IS A SOCIAL PROCESS

Colin Eden, Fran Ackermann and
Kevin Page[1]

An energetic and committed management team can manage and control their world.

The *process* of strategy making is one of the most important elements in realising strategic intent. It is our clear and convinced view that when strategic management fails to affect the real activities of an organisation it is because of the inability of strategy to change the way in which key people in the organisation both *think and act* as managers of its future. Thus, the issue of ensuring 'political feasibility' for delivering strategic change will be central to any design for supporting strategic conversations. To argue that political feasibility is key is not new. What is new is that we address (both practically and conceptually) the issue in some depth – emphasising the role of group processes in *negotiating* strategy. Addressing political feasibility is not only concerned with managing the process of crafting strategic change, but also with carrying out change that creates coordinated and cooperative action. Using designs that support both a social process and good analysis when making strategy are fundamental to achieving a politically feasible strategy – one that stands a good chance of being implemented. The process must acknowledge that it is a social affair where the nature of social relationships within the group will influence the nature and outcomes of negotiation. In addition it is important to recognise that the social process is a fundamental part of psychological negotiation – changing how people see their world and relate to it.

Any strategic organisational change that matters will involve winners and losers, and so will involve some managers *seeing themselves* as potential winners and some as potential losers. It follows that any strategy development or thinking about strategy will, without deliberate intention, promote organisational politics. Here, we are talking of the organisational politics that derives from different members of a team fighting over competing, but genuinely held, beliefs about what needs to be done to deliver a successful strategic future. This aspect of politics is distinct from the politics that arises from careerism and ambition.

An obvious point to make about strategic change is that the managers and management team in an organisation are the most significant stakeholders. They usually have high levels of autonomy to determine the way the organisation operates and its character. They can withdraw their labour, either physically and move to another organisation, or reduce their commitment. However, this may need to be tempered by the fact that some argue that there is less job security in organisations today, and so greater uncertainty and less power for managers. Nevertheless it is also true that good managers, who are key players in creating strategic futures, are still mobile because they are in demand. Managers (and staff) also have enormous power to 'work to rule' – *their* rules – where their autonomy allows them to *play up* to the demands of senior management but deliberately fail to *live up* to them. It is relatively easy for middle to senior managers to argue that 'we tried our best but it just wouldn't work'.

Thus a focus on the *process of strategy making* is a focus on the way the key people in an organisation both 'think and act'. We expect them, as a result of agreeing strategy, to change their manner of 'thinking things through' and deciding what appropriate strategies to adopt. Their commitment to working together as an effective team capable of implementing their agreements also shifts, thus making strategy can be an important part of team development. The strategy making process leads to changed patterns of doing things – decision making processes, ways of seeing, procedures and reward systems.

Strategic management is about people creating outcomes, not just about outcomes.

It matters that managers in an organisation have a driving energy and wish to manage and control their and their organisation's future. Indeed this commitment may matter more than an analytically 'correct' future they envisage. It suggests that, at one extreme, it is more valuable to do *something* powerfully well, rather than doing nothing to achieve 'rationalistically correct' aspirations. An energetic and committed management team can manage and control their world, whereas an analytically correct strategy will be useless without commitment from the team. Too many books on strategic management concentrate almost solely on strategic analysis and devote scarce attention to how the delivery of strategy is inextricably tied to the critical social processes of strategy negotiation. Strategic management is about people creating outcomes, not just about outcomes.

If strategic management does not change the way organisational members think, and so act, strategy can only have any real impact through coercion. Without changing ways of thinking, organisational members continue to see the same problems as they always did, and they continue to solve these problems using the same beliefs as before. Put more formally, their way of *construing*[2] their occupational world has not changed.

All too often strategy starts from the top with a 'rational analysis' undertaken by support staff. The process is driven by the notion that the world outside is turbulent and the organisation must respond to the imperatives set by the environment. The results are often powerful and logic driven attempts to change the organisation. But they come up hard against the realities of the everyday organisationally embedded logic, a logic built over years by those who are expected to change. The result is little, or temporary, change, and a great deal of frustration on the part of those whose learning and wisdom has been ignored. This is not a plea for a participative approach to strategic management as if it were an end in its own right; it is a practical statement about how to create real strategic change that generates energy and commitment within the organisation. Furthermore, participation is most likely to enable the fullest use of the organisation's knowledge, eliciting distinctiveness, addressing the full range of issues, considering the purpose and thus focus its energy, while at the same time, creating slack through leaving behind that which does not sustain the organisation into its future.

STRATEGY MAKING AND THE NATURE OF GROUPS

Strategy is delivered by real people with social futures together.

The need for a sense of cohesion among members of an organisation is often underestimated. The motivation of a management team to stay together and the sense of attachment members have to the team needs to be high. The extent to which members of a team feel a sense of shared membership and want to work together are important elements in strategy making – ultimately, strategy is delivered by real people with social futures together. However, this raises the question of whether too much deliberate and deliberated strategy, and too much commitment to a strategy, can make an organisation blinkered to strategically important new opportunities – leading to a form of self-confirming '*group think*'.[3] After all, strategy is expected to be a way of helping all staff to act cooperatively with some alignment of action, or at least not in continual conflict with one another. Therefore, while acting in unison is often desirable, it does also carry the risk of it encouraging a sort of systematic blindness to new alternatives. Similarly industry sectors often become too fixated on a standard recipe[4] for success, and these are not questioned through strategy making. Sometimes strategies need to encourage divergence of thinking rather than risk too much cohesion. Similarly, although continual and unintended conflict is not often thought to be helpful, some conflict generates the energy for creativity.[5]

There is always a danger that the group negotiates a strategy that nobody wants and nobody knew the others didn't want it either.

Issues of *balance* between cohesion and divergence are critical to effective strategy making. If there is too much influence by the established social order then there is a risk of the 'realities' of the situation being ignored and group think occurring. There is always a danger that the group negotiates a strategy that nobody wants, and, in addition, nobody knew the others didn't want it. The balancing act, between putting the well-being of the group as the primary consideration (group think) on the one hand and allowing or encouraging divergent but creative behaviour on the other, is an integral part of determining the appropriate strategy making process.

Jerry Harvey neatly describes an example of this phenomenon (known as the 'Abilene Paradox')[6] where a group finishes up taking a bus ride to the town of Abilene, a ride that none of the group wanted. However, if the strategy making process is only dominated by the analysis and the rhetoric of what is good for the organisation (without participants considering their own role in the outcomes) then working relationships between managers and staff may become ambiguous, uncertain and threatening. Participants then turn their attention more fully to resolving these uncertainties in their social affairs. Consequently there is a tendency for the organisation to settle back to the old ways of working as the easiest resolution of ambiguity. The principle of strategy making presented in this book, *facilitating both social and psychological negotiation*, strives to increase the chances of productive enquiry by recognising the importance of providing a greater opportunity for participants genuinely to change their mind as well as develop new rewarding relationships. Indeed, 'with many long term clients, business partners, family members, fellow professionals, government officials, or foreign nations, the ongoing relationship is far more important than the outcome of any particular negotiation'.[7]

A further complication is that a management team is often unable to operate in a way that enables differences in perspective to surface. As a consequence artificial and superficial agreement is often reached. Where this occurs, members of the team who disagree with the decisions being made believe that it is too risky to state their own alternative views:

- They may believe that their view is 'out on a limb' from the rest of the group.
- They may believe they will be subject to ridicule for expressing an alternative view.
- They may think that others have already expressed the view, or thought about it, because it seems so obvious, and that the idea must have been rejected for 'good' reasons.
- They may have 'trading agreements' with others in the group that would be broken if they expressed a view which opposes that of their trading partners – to do so would have consequences for support on other issues.
- To dissent from the view of the group may risk team cohesiveness – threatening the established relationships (group think).
- They might damage or destroys the camaraderie of being a team.
- They may be frightened of reprisals for expressing a particular view that is thought to be counter to the prevailing view of those in power.

When some of the above conditions persist in a group then it is likely that they all finish up with a strategy which no-one supports (the 'Abilene Paradox'). Thus, the social norms of a group can discourage the extent to which the thinking of each of the individuals in the group is used in the group decision making.[8] While each individual has their own view of what is needed to create strategic success, their social processes and existing social relationships encourage only shallow thinking to surface – giving the impression to all of a common view of what needs to be done.

The relationship between analysis and emotion is crucial.

However, ineffective group work can be the result of the strategy making process placing too much emphasis on building emotional commitment without designing processes that reinforce high quality rationality. The relationship between analysis and emotion is crucial. Without emotional commitment to delivering agreements the rationality of the reasoning becomes irrelevant and the balance has swung too far to analysis. The value of high quality thinking is close to zero without a willingness of managers to cooperate in its implementation.[9] Indeed there is a great danger of deliberate sabotage of highly rational decisions that have not taken any account of the social needs of the group.[10] Our emphasis is that the most important analysis be undertaken in a way that helps groups determine 'right' answers *and* builds commitment to achieving them. Choices made must recognise that coordinated and cooperative effort is required to deliver strategy. The social relationships of members of an organisation are mostly expressed through the social order that exists in their ways of working together, their patterns of interaction and their dependencies. Strategy development that is effective will perforce knock these relationships. Strategies that do so are at risk, regardless of their reasoned goodness, because sometimes team members will sabotage them in subtle ways in order to retain social equilibrium. And in delivering strategy a lack of commitment to one part of the strategy will always have repercussions for other parts.[11]

POLITICAL FEASIBILITY

Groups act out habits and patterns of behaviour that are related to assumptions that have been proven to be successful in the past.[12] For example, a group might subscribe to the view that:

we always operate a product based divisional structure here because it's the way our customers like to buy from us. They like to keep it simple too. It's just been easier to hire and train new engineers in this structure than try and get them to understand our whole range all at once. You know, I've never met a customer who's ever bought more than one product from us at a time.

These institutionalised decisions and behaviours provide order, predictability and security – you don't get fired doing what is implicitly expected. The decisions and behaviours become the 'way we do things around here', and over time, people *identify* with the invisible values and beliefs that underpin the ways of thinking and acting that have been shown to be acceptable in the group. This process of identification involves taking on the character and expectations of the group, much in the same way that a favourite sports team can encourage rousing and sometimes *blind* support. Identification with the group, and identity within the group, have strong links with the thinking and emotional commitment needed for successful strategy negotiation.[13]

There is a tendency to describe groups in human terms, such as 'the team is very collegiate and it has a great sense of fun' or 'they're a very aggressive team, they don't take any prisoners'. However, it is often unhelpful to talk about groups as if they are just larger versions of a single person. Groups do create identities for themselves, but groups are also networks of relationships and there are different identities within groups. People may side with one another in particular debates, setting up informal 'trading agreements' to help each other subtly secure certain positions and decisions.

For example, consider a comment from a Marketing Director to a Production Director spoken in a Board meeting:

> I've had some outstanding support from the factory this last month, there are some real troopers on your team that we should all be proud of, without them our new product launch would have bombed.

This comment may be more than, for example, a straightforward acknowledgement of additional production capacity. Depending on how it is phrased and delivered, it may contain subtle political value that is intended to prevent the CEO asking awkward questions about the monthly production cost variances. The Marketing and Production Directors now have an agreement and have an identity all of their own within the group. The reply could be:

> It was a tough one for us. It doesn't matter what we throw at the team, they always get right behind an important launch to take our competitors head on.

The social process of strategy negotiation also has to take account of the networks of relationships within the group, as well as a level of identification with the group, and its habits, values and beliefs. The people that identify most with these habits and beliefs are those that can stand to gain from perpetuating it and lose most from changing it (the anticipated winners and losers). More often than not, these people are the powerful actors: those at the top who have been brought up in, and prospered from, the ways of the organisation. Identifying with the values of the organisation has likely contributed to the progression and promotions that have helped them into key leadership or managerial positions. The 'way we do things around here' is both comforting because it is deeply known and unconsciously familiar, and, crucially, it is associated with positive personal experiences.

However, there is more than a sense of comfort at stake. The leaders that make up the top team of a department, division or organisation have their status in that team to preserve and promote. The same leaders prized for their drive and ambition, place considerable value on their personal status within their group – as well as being effective, they need to be recognised as effective, successful and powerful.

Political feasibility then is a multidimensional concept involving the inspiration and mobilisation of others to undertake considered and collective strategic action – building a powerful coalition with a commitment to act. Political feasibility includes considering the extent a manager needs to identify *with* the group, the network of identifications and relationships *within* the group, and the personal status that group members protect and promote. There is one more factor to consider that complicates the work of the strategy making group even further: the role of the leader.

Leadership is used, in the context of making strategy, to emphasise the informal, influential and inspiring relationship qualities of the person with the most power to sway how a group acts and thinks. In this sense leadership is distinct from the formal authority associated with management. Within the group, leaders have most of the emotional leverage. Studies have shown that it is the leader who talks more than anyone else in the group, is listened to more carefully, and whose comments carry a special weight,[14] which is particularly important in a potentially ambiguous situation such as strategy making.

> *Leading strategy making can be the distinctive and exciting activity that defines the leader–follower relationship.*

Leadership centres on the relationship between leaders and followers. In fact, some argue that it is followers that define leaders, and that without the followers there is, by definition, no leader.[15] Moreover, there is a current trend for leadership not to be described in terms of personality traits such as powerful, driven, charming, energetic or assertive; but in ways defined by this leader–follower relationship. The emphasis on the leader–follower relationship has been developed so far that it is claimed that many, not just the gifted few, can become leaders – provided they do something *distinctive and exciting*, and make their followers feel *significant*.[16] Leading strategy making can be the distinctive and exciting activity that defines the leader–follower relationship.

Within this powerful relationship, followers can *mirror* the leader, taking all their cues about 'being and behaving' from some idealised version of the leader they admire.[17] Consequently, on one hand, the role of the leader exploits this relationship in a positive way – the leader builds commitment, establishes an identity for the group, sells hope and makes sense of a complex world on behalf of their group. On the other hand, the leader can be the grand architect, knowingly or unknowingly, of group think. The political feasibility of strategy then must also acknowledge the powerful role that leaders play in groups.

ENGAGEMENT, FAIRNESS AND COMMITMENT

> *An effective approach to strategy has to simultaneously influence individuals and the group as a whole, while changing power, identity and meaning.*

This perspective on strategy making groups is an altogether more comprehensive and complete one than commonly portrayed in strategic management books. The prize for paying attention to a more comprehensive view of the nature of strategy making groups is more effective implementation of strategy. The combination of several familiar aspects of group processes defines the personal and social aspects of political feasibility. These aspects encompass: the comfort of deep taken-for-granted knowledge; institutionalised identity driven behaviour; benefiting from adopting the organisation's habits; having the dynamic forces of trading agreements and status building playing out within the group. These group processes are all wrapped up within leadership relationships that exert significant inter-personal power. An effective approach to strategy, which we explain in detail, therefore has to simultaneously influence individuals and the group as a whole, while changing power, identity and meaning.

In pragmatic terms, a successful strategy requires a shared sense of what the future means for both the group and its members, and a belief that something matters sufficiently to justify the sacrifice of self-interest in order to prioritise and contribute to this future. These are aspects of cooperative behaviour that have been associated with the field of social psychology known as *'procedural justice'*.[18] Procedural justice is a long established field supported by a substantial body of knowledge that demonstrates clear links between the processes used for decision making and the commitment individuals have to those decisions. Specifically, procedural justice relates *the way that decisions are made and people are treated during decision making* to the sense of fairness they feel, which in turn encourages cooperation, trust and engagement with the group's goals. Our approach to procedural justice, however, is distinctive in that it focuses on how groups work, rather than how individuals behave in isolation. This is an important distinction as we use it in a practical sense to facilitate the development of an effective strategy, and in a way that encourages people to *think and act on behalf of the group.*

Engaging people with the group's future starts with motivation – the pushes and prods that move people to action. Many motivation theories exist and compete for attention but, in broad terms, they can be divided into two camps: extrinsic or intrinsic.[19] Extrinsic motivations are the targets, incentives and deliverables that are tied to the rewards to be had from achieving them. Intrinsic motivations, on the other hand, are based on each individual's internal values, beliefs and attitudes – there is no material reward attached to them and they are done for their own sake.

The use of measures as a means to motivate comes later in the strategy process, at the delivery end rather than creation.

Discretionary behaviour such as committing to a group's strategy and cooperating with others cannot be 'scorecarded' or supervised out of people. By definition discretionary behaviour has to be completely voluntary and given freely. The cooperative behaviour associated with building commitment to act is related to intrinsic motivations and therefore influenced by the social processes in the group. However, the use of extrinsic motivations such as target setting, incentives and the pressures to adhere to rules and agreements are valuable tools for ensuring action. The use of measures as a means to motivate comes later in the strategy process, at the *delivery* end rather than during creation.

Many people will have heard, possibly several times, the phrase 'we need to create a burning platform'. This is used as a shorthand way of saying 'I wish people were motivated to get into the important action round here' or 'why don't people just get on with the job of change'. It is originally an expression from John Kotter[20] (whose emphasis we share) who argues that overcoming complacency is a prerequisite to building an engaged coalition capable of achieving change. Complacency, in this sense, means low levels of urgency, acceptance of the status quo and denial.

The powerful social forces of political feasibility perpetuate the status quo rather than provide the impetus for change. The motivation to change only comes when the group (1) feel discomfort from what they are seeing going on in the organisation, (2) sense their implicit goals are under threat, and (3) see a possibility of solving their issues in relative safety.[21] Our approach

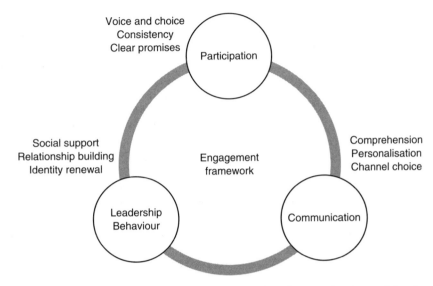

Figure 2.1   The Framework for Integrating Participation, Communication and Leadership Behaviour

to working with groups intentionally increases discomfort through, for example, the process of developing strategy through *issue surfacing* (see chapters 4 and 5), but does this in a socially supportive way using an *engagement framework*.

The engagement framework[22] used here pays attention to the treatment people receive as important decisions are being discussed, and the quality of the processes used to make those decisions. These two factors are not equally weighted, *how people are treated* during decision making is far more significant, in terms of building engagement, than the processes used for making decisions. The approach[23] is a set of activities and processes used to intentionally increase commitment to the strategic future the group intends. This approach to engagement, shown in figure 2.1, integrates participation, communication and leadership behaviour. Individually these are well known to influence engagement,[24] but together they are much stronger and tap directly into the psychology and motivation described earlier.

PARTICIPATION IN STRATEGY MAKING

The motivating effect of giving a 'voice and choice' to participants in a strategy making forum should not be confused with democratising decisions or other aspects of participative management.

In figure 2.1 we present three elements of an engagement framework: participation, communication and leadership behaviour. Each of these elements has a number of aspects supporting it. The three aspects of participation are 'voice and choice', consistency and clear promises.

It sounds obvious but, a prerequisite to engaging people in strategy making is to create a way for them to participate in its development and delivery. This participation is not just about opening dialogue and asking for suggestions. That is only part of it. Participation that builds engagement is about how we manage ongoing relationships with people – seeing them as members of teams that are seeking recognition, trust and a positive sense of their individual worth. Understanding the nature of existing team relationships is crucial for the setup of a strategy making forum and needs to be discussed with the sponsor in advance of the forum (see, in particular, chapter 11 for the discussion of group facilitation).

Effective participation in a strategy making forum is first and foremost an *activity*. It involves and interests those taking part on a matter of importance to the group. This participation builds a person's identification with the group,[25] and through the strategy making process enables the group (and individual) to amend its own identity – its own sense of itself and what is important to it. Participation in the strategy making forum results in a greater awareness of what it means to be a member of the group and a stronger emotional investment in its membership.[26] This increased identification results in members of the group thinking and acting in ways consistent with the goals of the group.[27]

However, the motivating effect of giving a 'voice and choice' to participants in a strategy making forum should not be confused with democratising decisions or other aspects of participative management. Its use here is very clear: to provide the basis of a *negotiation* while attending to the social needs for involvement and identification.

Organisational life is rich in comparison – people in one team instinctively compare their lot with other teams.[28] Achieving consistency, and the appropriate degree of organisational cohesion, is challenging and requires effort that runs counter to the operating premises of local customisation and empowerment. The notion of *engaging* people in a designed strategic conversation requires designing '*consistency*' of process, and 'procedurally rational'[29] processes, into a forum. In addition, consistent treatment of people over time is significant. For example, the contributions of each participant in a strategy making forum need to be treated consistently, having equal value, until the stage of negotiating agreement is reached.

It goes without saying that people will participate only once in a process that does not live up to their expectations. Setting expectations early and clearly, and giving due notice of important decisions and the guidelines for involvement, builds inherent fairness into processes. For example, doing something visible and tangible with the results of the forum is the explication of the clear promise that contributions will be considered. Deliverables created by the group in real time as 'take-aways' facilitate the more likely delivery of '*clear promises*'.

COMMUNICATION IN STRATEGY MAKING

The second element of the engagement framework (figure 2.1) is communication, comprising comprehension, personalisation and the use of suitable channels.

As we suggested in chapter 1, language is the currency of organisational life, and yet a great deal of western communication is based on a 'one-way-street' assumption: *I say and you listen* and I assume you hear what I intended.[30] The communication requirements for groups negotiating strategy demand significantly more than this. In strategy making, it is essential that the meaning of what was intended is conveyed and understood. Thus it is important to avoid thinking in terms of communication, but to think instead in terms of *comprehension*. This means a shift in emphasis away from what has been said, to checking what has been understood and how it relates to other contributions. The role of strategy making forums can provide these check points in a conversation by provoking questions such as: 'What do we mean by such and such a comment?' Responding to this question means someone has to become involved, actively trying to articulate what they understand. This *activity* in itself builds engagement within the group by provoking discussion, eliciting opinions and surfacing possible different interpretations.

Yet it does something else too. It forces people to make sense of things and to *personalise* the discussions within the group for themselves. The expression, 'how do I know what I think until I've said it', explains this personal sense-making.[31] Making time for sense-making by building time for reflection and conversation, and using questions and processes that require people to put things in their own terms supports the *personalisation* component of engagement.

Different communication channels support different information needs and thus are more suitable for certain purposes. People seek accuracy from written communication as it is a *record of agreement*, but derive socially important information such as standing and self-worth from conversations and interactions. In chapter 1 we introduced the central role that a group decision support system and causal mapping can play in strategy making (see figure 2.2 later in this chapter for an example of a causal map). The use of the group support software (Decision Explorer®) to facilitate both procedural justice and procedural rationality, and the causal map as a representation of the interacting views of the group members enables both of these needs to be met.

LEADERSHIP BEHAVIOUR IN STRATEGY MAKING

In figure 2.1 the third element of the engagement framework is leadership behaviour encompassing emotional support, relationship building and identity renewal. These three characteristics go beyond, and extend, our earlier discussion on the role of the leader.

The behaviour of the leader has a disproportionate effect in the group.

Many leaders believe they are good at the behaviours that influence engagement. However, a leader's own assessment of their strengths does not always align with their subordinates' perception.[32] This mismatched perception is especially so in the area of engagement which requires some deft social skills. Compounding this concern about the quality of leaders, people have heightened sensitivity at times when they feel threatened[33] (for example, if they anticipate themselves as losers from the strategy making process) and scrutinise the detail of what they hear and how it is delivered. Courtesy, sincerity, open-mindedness and good listening are the specific behaviours that communicate engagement and help support the political feasibility of strategy. They are the *emotional support components of leadership behaviour* that directly link with the social and personal needs of the group. The reason for emphasising them is that the behaviour of the leader has a disproportionate effect in the group, and determines much of its members' 'emotional register', thus setting the context for thinking and acting.

There is another side of leadership that gets much less attention – the relationships leaders build through the practical support they provide people, especially when working on matters of importance. In a designed strategic conversation, the leader's position is somewhat modified and becomes that of an important *contributing member (and possibly facilitator)*, rather than as someone chairing and controlling the meeting. In this way, the leader demonstrates through word and action that the group and its future matters sufficiently for them to become deeply and productively involved. There is a strong link between the investment a leader is seen to make in both the relationships and the core purpose of a group through its work on strategy, and the commitment a team has for the resultant strategic intent. This *relationship building component of leadership behaviour* can be explained by the phenomenon of social exchange.[34]

In a designed strategic conversation, negotiation happens in real-time, with opinions and perspectives shared and new meanings derived, which enables the group to reach agreements while together. Important agreements related to the identity of the group, what it stands for and what it expects to happen can only be made while working as a group. Here, the leader actively takes part in contributing to the discussion and, through the negotiation process, legitimises and confirms the identity that the group adapts and defines for itself. This is the *identity renewal component of leadership behaviour*.

FACILITATED SUPPORT: THE NATURE OF NEGOTIATION

Given that making strategy is, in this book, taken to be a social process, the role of facilitation of that social process is fundamental, whether the facilitation is carried out by the leader of the group or undertaken by someone in a facilitator-only role. Either way they are facilitating a negotiation and so providing group support. In each of the four ways of making strategy presented in this book the group support is also provided through the use of a group support system that is designed to both help with the management of process – negotiation – *and* provide the basis for analytical support.

Our approach to the design of facilitated support recognises *how* individuals change their mind through a process of social *and* psychological negotiation – changing relationships and changing minds. The 'working documents' – causal maps – used to record and encourage effective conversation must therefore be interactive and changed in real time: they are '*transitional objects*'.[35] The documents used in this book are causal maps – pictures that show the strategy team's causal assertions as a network of interacting statements about what needs to be done and why (helping make sense of the different views).[36] In each of the four approaches to making strategy the map/network is constructed using a set of formalisms enabling the network to be analysed in terms of patterns of goals, strategies, actions, relationships between stakeholders, bases of power, etc. The assertions can be colour coded to show different properties, and the colours can indicate properties of the network that are helpful to the group. These causal maps continuously change through the strategy making forum reflecting the developing conversation and agreements of the group – thus the map or network is in continual transition.

The Role of Equivocality

A degree of fuzziness provides the setting within which face saving can occur.

In strategy making we expect to see a shift in attitude as well as a shift in thinking. Changes in attitude reflect, in part, the role of intuition and hunch[37] which leads to a feeling of comfort about the way forward. Shifts in thinking are about someone 'changing their mind' – involving changed beliefs, changed values and changes in the salience of particular values.

Successful negotiation usually depends upon participants being able to 'save face', as they change their mind and attitudes about possible outcomes and their need to reconcile the stand they now take with their principles and past words and deeds. As such, effective negotiators make their contribution with a degree of *equivocality*, equivocality here being a degree of fuzziness that provides the setting within which face saving can occur. An appropriate level of equivocality or fuzziness, balanced with transparency, is aimed at 'changing minds *and* attitudes', however, this might sometimes mean backing away from clarity as too much clarity begins to emerge.

Our approach to the design of facilitated support must, therefore, recognise the role of equivocality in the causal maps used to record and encourage effective conversation. Causal maps permit an exploration of meaning, but do so within the context of enough equivocality to achieve social and psychological negotiation.

Acknowledgement and Face Saving?

Earlier in this chapter we discussed the significance of procedural justice in attaining political feasibility. Associated with this is the relationship between a statement, and the person who makes the statement. For the sake of justice a person needs to be assured that they have been listened to, which in turn implies that their particular contribution to the conversation must be associated with them. Giving generous credit for acknowledged contributions also increases the contributor's stake in defending these ideas to others outside the group.[38] This is important for promulgation of the agreed strategy. It also, however, gives the person a motivation to defend the idea within the group instead of entertaining the option of changing their mind. This might suggest that giving credit openly for ideas is more appropriate as a group moves towards consensus or agreement, but less helpful earlier. Moreover, credit to individuals will always reward some at the expense of others. Face saving can be made easier if statements can be made, noticed and possibly dismissed, without attribution of those statements to a particular individual. The proponent can change their mind after hearing the debate about their ideas without needing to defend these as 'their own'. In addition, it is often noted that good contributions are not necessarily correlated with the social skills, or the past attributions or the role of the individual making them. Thus, there can be significant benefits to be had from providing some degree of anonymity of contributors at some stages of the strategy making activity. At the very least it facilitates some staff in stating perspectives that they believe may result in punishment as they are contrary from those with power.

Thus our approach to the design of the facilitated support must recognise the role of some degree of anonymity in the causal maps used to record and encourage effective conversation. The approach introduced in this book encompasses this need through the use of computer-based (and manual) methods for understanding, reflecting, negotiating and confirming strategy. Thus, the use of the software (Decision Explorer®) helps establish some level of anonymity, during the early stages of a forum, because it uses typed records rather than handwritten records from self-adhesive labels (such as Post-its®) or 'flip-chart' records where participants believe they can accurately note who said what through recognising the handwriting. In addition, by having the views projected onto a public screen that can be seen by all, using the output from Decision Explorer®, it is also possible to separate the proponent of a contribution from the contribution itself so that, when appropriate, the contributions are judged on their merit alone. We see this activity as significant in managing political feasibility.

The Role of Synthesis

The designed strategic conversation must encourage elaboration rather than early convergence.

Negotiation at the level of shifting ways of thinking is significantly enhanced by a good 'chairperson', sponsor or facilitator, who is able to create a powerful synthesis of the contributions of all participants. The group support software is designed to help in the process of developing effective synthesis through the use of analysis tools that are transparent to the group and can be undertaken with the group – thus, synthesis becomes something that is owned by the group. This synthesis becomes even more valuable if it reveals a new way of looking at the future. It is easier to create a new future when a group generates new options that can be *credited to the group* rather than an individual. Not only is it likely that the options represent the interaction between different causal rationalities but that they significantly provide room for negotiation to take place and lessen the role that designed anonymity needs to play.

Causal maps that represent the content of the arguments about what to change and why to make the changes are the 'transitional objects', or focus, around which negotiation can take place. Causal maps, as models for the group to work with, offer a form of synthesis and a new way of seeing the same data, because meaning is changed by being placed in new contexts with new linkages between the data – new knowledge is created.[39]

Negotiation is more likely to be effective when participants don't attack the position of their colleagues, but rather seek to look beyond it.[40] Rather than asking about their position, the other person is encouraged to elaborate their view. The debate is supportive rather than combative and is typified by 'that's interesting, why do you say that?' as a style of exchange.

The direct implication of this type of exchange as a form of relating is that the designed strategic conversation must encourage elaboration rather than early convergence. The approaches suggested in this book encourage the group to continually seek further elaboration in the early stages of the strategy making. However, one outcome is an increase in complexity. This increase brings with it concerns from the group about the debilitating nature of the complexity generated and also concerns about how the complexity will be managed without it being reduced.[41] It also raises the issue of effective time management – the continual elaboration required to facilitate both psychological and social negotiation, which will change minds, is expensive in terms of the time required for the management of increased complexity.

Thus, our approach to the design of facilitated support must recognise the balance between debilitating complexity and the need to think broadly and deeply with proper management (rather than reduction) of complexity. Paying attention to multiple perspectives is expected to increase an awareness of the complexity of the situation. This complexity can be debilitating for the group:

> the need to take account of intersubjectivity seems overwhelming. It is also clear that the deliberate attempt that it involves to address complexity can appear both to a consultant and members of teams to be a debilitating process, the outcome of which can be potentially destructive to a team. Most particularly an awareness of complexity can sap the desire or felt capacity to act. The world is complicated enough, it may be argued, without seeking to make even more of the complexity explicit and, thus, even more of the difficulties of acting effectively in the world apparent. This is particularly so when whatever one does can be simulated to have both good and bad consequences for somebody in the team. Encouraging members of a team to listen both caringly and analytically to each other is inevitably consuming of both time and energy.[42]

As a result, where increasing complexity can be encouraged it must also be managed. Indeed, the approaches presented in this book encourage multiple perspectives to be surfaced, and so complexity will need to be managed. The management of complexity will partly derive from attention to procedural justice but also from using the software to facilitate both a 'helicopter' view and attention to the detail of the views of all participants.

Creativity

Emotional commitment to any course of action comes partly from having played with the ideas and alternatives.

The synthesis of the ideas of many participants opens up new options and is a form of group creativity. Conflict is resolved not by dealing with the current options of members of the group but rather through the creative generation of new options by the group. Encouraging innovative ideas can help maintain social equilibrium and emotional commitment because of it being fun. 'The more quickly you turn a stranger into someone you know, the easier a negotiation is likely to become'[43] and a faster way for this to occur is to do something enjoyable together. Although provocation is not always fun!

Creativity is not only important for a group but also as an individual process. Attitudinal and psychological commitment to any course of action comes partly from having *played with* the ideas and alternatives.[44]

FACILITATED SUPPORT: THE USE OF A GROUP SUPPORT SYSTEM[45]

When a causal map (such as that shown in figure 2.2 representing a group discussion about strategic goals) is constructed by a group, and displayed so that all members of the group can see the emerging map, it enables members of the group to begin to appreciate how others think (through enhanced appreciation of both the content and the context) and therefore begin to develop a shared understanding.[46] This represents a convergence of understandings as a result of adopting the formal rules associated with the construction of a causal map which demands that not just the statements are captured but also their consequences and explanations.

This shifting from divergence to convergence of understandings typically results in many of the views and options being revised. Convergence moves ownership for views from the individual to the collective.[47] New options emerge as the captured material provides a powerful stepping stone to play with ideas and thus enables creativity. The group support system facilitates the process of creating new options. Moreover, the support system facilitates another of the 'soft' negotiation features – that of encouraging members to change the way they see the situation from their idiosyncratic perspective to a view that encompasses aspects of a number of other perspectives. They have extended their thinking.

The meaning of contributions therefore grows and shifts as the context (statements around them) changes – new explanations and consequences added by others gradually shift the original meaning. Over the course of a forum, the varying 'underdeveloped' and diverse understandings are extended and subtly shifted to a view that is more owned by the entire group. By having the model displayed in front of the group, participants have the time to read the displayed map and reflect on the content rather than having to respond immediately, with associated dangers of inappropriate emotion. Participants are more able to listen – particularly as the process encourages views to be elaborated upon and their meaning clarified. Less stark positions are taken and procedural justice is incorporated. This is notwithstanding the fact that when appropriate, the author of a contribution is able to acknowledge ownership and intervene personally to persuade.

Managing complexity through capturing as many points of view as possible in a *structured* map provides further benefits. For example, the easier it is to listen to what other members think, the greater the likelihood of an increase in understanding of the situation. As views are surfaced and captured, questions regarding their consequences, explanations, constraints and assumptions can

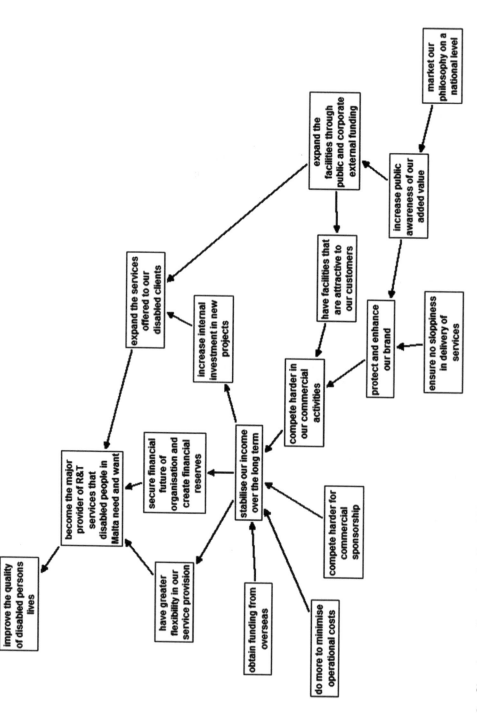

Figure 2.2 Showing an Example of a Causal Map Representing the Early Stages of a Group Discussion About Strategic Goals

be made by naturally developing the causal chains of argument. This type of 'scaffolding'[48] not only provides the means for gaining a better understanding of what is meant by the contribution being made but also assists in the process of integrating the different views together.[49]

THE SIGNIFICANCE OF ATTENTION TO GROUP PROCESSES FOR STRATEGY MAKING

The social process of strategy is thus not something for a leader to eschew because of its apparent complexity; rather it is something to understand how to employ usefully.

The process of making strategy in the way we have described builds a powerful coalition with an emotional and a 'thought-through' commitment to realise its strategic intent. The emotional commitment is derived from the engaging way that the group has negotiated its future, how it has invested in relationships, and how it has positively adapted its identity to guide future actions and decisions. The 'thought-through' commitment develops from the way the group has tested the rationality of the claims about what would be good for the future through the use of causal maps. The use of causal maps as a 'transitional object' captures the meaning and identity of the group in a visual way, taking on symbolic importance for those who participated, and actual importance as a record of the agreements made.

Designed strategic conversations help groups navigate through complex social territory and enable them to make sense of awkward choices and paradoxical situations. Our approach disaggregates the strategy process into two main challenges for a group: *that of building a commitment to act, and acting out commitments.* Developing strategy through issue surfacing and prioritising (chapters 4 and 5) is essentially an attitudinal approach intended to raise the urgency within the group to challenge the status quo. The use of an engagement framework to support the social process of strategy is also directed towards building commitment to act through social identity mechanisms. To ensure that commitments are acted out requires the use of a behavioural change approach, such as changing an organisation's major system, and effective follow-up of the specific agreements reached in the strategy conversation.

There is organisational value created from using this approach to strategy over and above that associated with realising the strategic intent of the group. The approach increases the 'social' capital in the organisation through the use of the engagement framework. Higher levels of social capital, described here as *relationship assets*, are known to increase the ongoing levels of trust in a group, help groups establish new norms and expectations, adapt their identity, and support innovation and higher performance.[50]

The social process of strategy is thus not something for a leader to eschew because of its apparent complexity; rather it is something to understand how to employ usefully. Well understood and used, it enables important decisions to be made quickly, provides strong commitment for action, and further develops important long term capabilities in the organisation.

THE DESIGNED STRATEGIC CONVERSATION AND THE LEARNING ORGANISATION AND ORGANISATIONAL LEARNING

The ability to learn faster than your competitors may be your only sustainable competitive advantage.[51]

Good strategy making is probably the most significant contribution that can be made to developing a learning organisation, and to directly facilitating organisational learning.

The benefits of becoming a learning organisation have been well hyped: for example, 'the ability to learn faster than your competitors may be your only sustainable competitive advantage'.[52] The ideas expressed by writers in this field are plausible and attractive, but often the views of organisational learning are confused with discussion about group or individual learning.

Organisational learning must be such that it belongs to the collectivity, in the sense that it will be valuable only when taken in the strategic organisational context.[53] Thus, knowledge generated through organisational learning will be relatively valueless in impact (as opposed to intellectual value) unless it is used in the context of the organisation. If it is not relatively valueless to the individual outside the specific organisational setting then it is individual learning which travels with the individual, and so is less significant than organisational learning. The individual may, of course, contribute something very special to the organisation, but it is special only when taken in context. Organisational learning cannot simply be just the sum of the views of members of the group (the individual learning); if this were so then it is group learning and the learning can leave the organisation and travel with the group.

This notion of organisational learning being something which has value in context is why strategy making as a social process can be such an important vehicle for creating a learning organisation. The activity of jointly understanding and reflecting on what is and what could be takes place perforce within the strategic context of the organisation. It is driven by the aim of drawing together the wisdom and expertise of individuals and setting them within the context of the culture, stakeholders, environment and aspirations of the particular organisation.

The requirements of organisational learning are exactly those of good strategy making. The strategy making *process* is designed to facilitate learning processes that develop distinctiveness and competitive differentiation which belong to the organisation. However, for the designed strategic conversation to work effectively for strategy making, the learning must also be of enough value to the individual for them to be motivated to join in the learning process. Clearly we expect that the individual may benefit personally from the learning process, but they cannot readily graft the organisational distinctive competence, derived from shared knowledge within a particular strategic context, elsewhere.

In sympathy with other approaches to organisational learning[54] we identify seven key characteristics of organisational learning. These characteristics are key characteristics of good strategy making.

1   A respect for *wisdom* – 'to be wise is not to know particular fads but *to know without excessive confidence or excessive cautiousness*. Wisdom is thus not a belief, a value, a set fact, a corpus of knowledge in some specialised area, or a set of special abilities or skills. Wisdom is an attitude taken by persons toward the beliefs, values, knowledge, information, abilities, and skills that are held, a tendency to doubt that these are necessarily true or valid and to doubt that they are an exhaustive set of those things that could be known'.[55]

2   Appreciation of *systemic properties* in organisations – that systems impact upon each other in complex ways. The appreciation that some patterns are self-sustaining, or reinforcing, through feedback loops – vicious and virtuous circles, and negative (controlling) feedback loops aid learning and management.

3   Respect for *multiple perspectives* on issues. This characteristic demands that organisations respect the actuality of differentiation in expertise, experience and wisdom among individuals in an organisation. Thus, there will be an expectation that there will be different views on what is best for the organisation, and different reasons for those views. There is also a requirement that questioning dominant views is acceptable. These demands are not trivial, for they make very

serious demands on an organisation. Encouraging multiple perspectives will increase the complexity surrounding any issue, and it will also generate more conflict. But it will engender learning.

4   Recognition of the *dilemma of alignment versus differentiation*. Strategy is partly about designing increased alignment of thinking and action, but organisational learning requires some degree of differentiation through multiple perspectives. Part of the outcome from strategy making will be the redesign of structures, procedures and information systems as a source of meanings, reward systems, and so on. These are (re)designed to promote alignment of thinking and action in line with strategic intent. However, multiple perspectives depend on attention to individuality, open communication channels, preparedness to question views, and a management style shifting towards the 'manager as facilitator' and away from management as 'command and control'. The recognition of this dilemma is an important requirement, where balancing conflict with compromise and creativity with standard procedures characterises the dilemma.

5   An ability to *detect key assumptions and 'taken-for-granteds'* that are driving the behaviour of the organisation. Here we are highlighting the role of core assumptions about, for example, how the market works, what motivates the work force, who to take notice of in the environment, learning from failure.[56] These assumptions can often be based on assertions made years ago by senior managers now retired. The ability to detect these assumptions, reflect on their role in creating the future of the organisation, and revisit their validity is a critical task for strategy making and for organisational learning. The use of causal maps to facilitate thinking about strategy provides at least an analytical device for establishing which assumptions are core to an organisation's understanding of its strategic direction – but the assumption must find its way on to the map first.

6   A willingness to *experiment with ideas, thinking and action*. Here there is a cycle that moves from *acting* – testing implications of theories and concepts in new situations to give concrete experiences; to *reasoning* – observation to reflection; to *formation of abstract concepts* and theories to be used in *action*.[57] The implication is that the organisation must have a culture where mistakes are not inappropriately punished. An appropriate degree of psychological safety is required, where staff do not feel as though they must go 'out on a limb' to explore new ways of doing things. Typically this requires *psychological maturity* of the organisation. Encouraging managers to reflect and question develops consciousness and self-knowledge, which is threatening to the power structure of organisations. In a carefully designed strategy making process we seek to promote this psychological safety.

7   Relating to the above, *playfulness* in exploration and reflection is important. Play develops in an intermediate territory extending from the boundaries of the subjective to those of the objectively perceived or shared reality. This is the territory between fantasy and actuality, and is between the subjective and the objective, between the Art and the Science of Management.[58] This is the corollary of encouraging experimentation with ideas, thinking and action. For the experimentation to be effective it must open up the probability of discovery and creativity, and playfulness and fun can promote such outcomes.

Unless an organisation has some aspiration to become a learning organisation then some of the approaches to strategy making we discuss later in this book may be less effective and possibly unhelpful.

THE DESIGNED SOCIAL PROCESS OF STRATEGY MAKING DETERMINES THE SUCCESS OF STRATEGY

In this chapter we described strategic management as a social process, and explained the direct links between how this process is managed and the outcomes that a group can achieve. We introduced the concepts for making sense of the social context for strategy making. The basic premise of the chapter is that strategic intent is only realised when key people in the organisation change the way that they both think and act as managers of its future. This change requires the social affairs of the group to be adapted to suit the envisaged future, and the envisaged future designed to suit the new social affairs of the group – the two are inextricably joined together. The process of achieving a desired future is based on a negotiation between individuals as part of a designed strategic conversation. An energetic and committed management team can manage and control its world to a far greater extent than is anticipated. 'Never doubt that a small group of thoughtful committed citizens can change the world. Indeed, it is the only thing that ever has' (Margaret Mead).

The issues of balance between cohesion and divergence are critical to effective strategy making. Thus, the manager, or facilitator, leading a strategy making group needs to have a keen social sense to 'read' what is happening in the group, in particular to enable members to resolve the tension between staying the same and changing. The concepts introduced in this chapter, and used throughout the rest of this book, provide managers with support to achieve this balance.

Strategic management seen as social process helps identify the human factors that determine the success of strategy implementation. Political feasibility, engagement, fairness and the use of facilitated support are critical areas for the leader of a strategy making group to focus attention on. Political feasibility involves the inspiration and mobilisation of others to undertake considered and collective strategic action – building a powerful coalition with a commitment to act. A successful strategy requires a belief that this collective commitment to act matters sufficiently to justify the sacrifice of self-interest. The engagement framework shown in figure 2.1 helps organise the social process of strategy to achieve this, building individual and collective commitment to a new future through the integration of participation, communication and specific leadership behaviours. One aspect of the framework, participation, provides the basis for negotiation. Negotiation here is the skilful pursuit of agreement, made more effective by using an approach that encompasses the fuzziness of equivocality, appropriate acknowledgement of contribution, the type of synthesis that a good facilitator, or manager-client as facilitator, can provide, and the opportunity for creativity and playing.

We recognise that the fullness of the description given to how groups really work in relation to strategic management may appear daunting. However, what we have described is the social reality of groups of people wrestling with their future, their livelihoods and their reputations, trying to avoid losing, and possibly trying to win. The stakes in these situations can be, and should be, high for individuals, for the group, its wider organisation and its stakeholders. Thus the social process of strategy making justifies a deep exploration – it is crucial for delivering strategic success.

WHAT MIGHT BE WRONG WITH MAKING STRATEGY BY PAYING ATTENTION TO SOCIAL PROCESSES?

Surely the Job of a Management Team Is to Decide the Plan and Make Sure Everyone Else Gets On with It?

Some staff do not appreciate being asked to participate in strategy making – they believe that it is management's job and they expect management to deliver on their responsibility for strategy. This does not mean that staff do not want to know how they fit in to the strategic future of the organisation, but that they prefer to do what they take to be their job while others do their own job.

However, for many managers it is important to feel that they play a role beyond that of ensuring continuing production or service provision at the operational level. They like to feel that their contributions link with the attainment of the vision and that they have the power and ability to play their part. Demonstrating the linking of strategic programmes and lower level responsibilities to grander organisational goals, linking changes in operations to strategic outcomes, and linking rewards for managerial thinking and action to the delivery of strategy is of course difficult. Yet it is only when this can be done that the individual manager can feel more than a 'cog in the wheel'. It is also this relationship between thinking and action that provides the necessary basis for individual, group and organisational learning.

This issue relates to the difficulty in deciding the extent of participation in strategy making.[59] An increase in participation is desirable for the two reasons of a better decision being made and more commitment being gained ('buy-in'). These outcomes offer mutual support to one another: a better decision is likely to gain more commitment (substantive rationality will be recognised and gain cognitive commitment); and an increase in participation in order to raise emotional commitment through a designed social process will, providing social negotiation is designed to support psychological negotiation, also increase substantive rationality. However, there is a third element, the need to consider the efficiency of the procedure. Higher levels of participation in strategy making take time. Determining the cut off point for participation focuses upon the amount of time that elapses during the process, and on the size of the organisation.

Where strategy making requires a lengthy period of time, possibly due to the need to involve stakeholders, or to carry out detailed analysis, then this may suggest that fewer members are involved; there can be disillusionment with the process if nothing appears to be happening following an input. Where the turnaround is relatively short (in one organisation, we were involved in developing a strategy within nine days that involved more than 45 people) it is easy to maintain enthusiasm and commitment. The size of the organisation requires taking a practical viewpoint when deciding on the number of participants.

Business Organisations Are Not a Democracy!

Our view of the need for consideration of participation and empowerment must not be confused with the concerns of those for whom there is a moral crusade about democratising the work place. Some of the process-oriented approaches to strategic problem solving have been heartily criticised by commentators for being conservative and for supporting a managerial ideology.[60] The approaches they criticise may do this, but the proponents and designers of such approaches never declare that they set out to radicalise managerialism in organisations. Similarly while in this book we argue for greater degrees of participation than usual, we do so for reasons that are to do with the nature of the difficulties in achieving strategic organisational change.

There Is Not Enough Time to Pick Through Politics of Strategy Making

There is not enough time not to.[61]

Politics is as much to do with different points of view about how to deliver success[62] as it is to do with careerism and ambition. Working with different perspective is crucial for the development of a robust strategy, and is central to the strategy forums discussed in this book.

Changing 'This Place' Is Impossible – It Doesn't Matter What You Do

There is already much written about how difficult change is to achieve. Many have personal experiences of being on the receiving end of ill-conceived efforts to change an organisation, and some would even own up to conceiving these efforts that thwart and frustrate. The point we emphasise is that strategic change is challenging. However, it is our direct experience of using the approaches we describe in this book, which have a sound theoretical basis refined by practical use in several hundred research settings, that groups can, and do, achieve change. This requires them to change how they see their world, and use language in a way that conveys new shared meanings with others that commit themselves to the goals of the group.

Changing world views and gaining the commitment of the strategy making team is clearly a necessary but not sufficient condition for achieving change. Change has to manifest itself in tangible ways in an organisation for those inside and outside the strategy making team to see the evidence and value of change beyond that captured in language. Changes to, for example, the organisation's major measurement systems such as the costing system (see chapter 12) is evidence of change. The ascent of winners and the demise of losers is again clear evidence that something significant is taking place. Our view is that strategy conceived as a social process has a far greater chance of making important strategic changes happen. If an environment is characterised by 'it doesn't matter what you do', then it is most likely that a social process is the only way to make something happen.

Paying Attention to Social Processes Is a Way of Avoiding the Real World – and Hitting the Numbers

The numbers are most certainly not an irrelevance and strategy making must lead to follow through into budgeting and the development of some form of performance indicators (see chapter 12).

This Is a Way of Getting Commitment to the Wrong Ideas

The dangers of group think are significant – where a group can be in danger of ignoring the real world. Too much attention to the group feeling good about their strategy can risk ignoring rational analysis which evidently shows that a commitment to a strategy is misplaced.

In the four strategy forums presented in this book there is a significant attempt to balance social process issues with good analysis. However, analysis is seen as something that informs strategy as negotiation rather than the other way around. Indeed, in the facilitation chapter (chapter 11) there is a clear acknowledgement of the interplay between managing social process and managing content.

NOTES

1 Dr Kevin Page is Operations Director of the Clydesdale Bank and Visiting Professor at Strathclyde Business School.
2 We see an important distinction between perception and construal. Different people may perceive (see) different things, but what is more important is how people who perceive the same things interpret (construe) them differently.

3   Janis (1972) introduced the idea of 'group think' where the aim of retaining social cohesion in the group overrides the likelihood of important views emerging.

4   For more on 'industry recipes' see Spender (1989).

5   Stafford Beer (1966) introduces the concept of entropy to acknowledge the need for energy in any successful organisation.

6   Harvey (1988).

7   Fisher and Ury (1982).

8   See Walsh (1988); and Walsh, Henderson and Deighton (1988).

9   See Floyd and Woolridge (1992) and Woolridge and Floyd (1990).

10 Guth and MacMillan (1986).

11 Eisenhardt (1989).

12 Edgar Schein defines the culture of a group as a 'pattern of shared basic assumptions that was learned by the group as it solved its problems of external adaption and internal integration, that has worked well enough to be considered valued, and therefore, to be taught to new members as the correct way to perceive, think, and feel in relation to those problems'. See Schein (2004).

13 See Olaf Rughase (Rughase, 2006) whose view of strategy making focuses on the role of identity.

14 Daniel Goleman and his colleagues (Goleman, Boyatzis and McKee, 2002) describe the emotional dimension of leadership in some detail. Of particular interest for the study of power and emotions in groups is the significance of the leadership role – 'everyone watches the boss'.

15 David Collinson (Collinson, 2009) describes the relationship between leaders and followers with an emphasis on understanding the nature of followers.

16 Rob Goffee and Gareth Jones use the title 'Why Should Anyone Be Led By You?' to present their argument that leaders need not conform to the images associated with trait based theories of leadership. Their view is that leadership is about 'being yourself – more – with skill' (Goffee and Jones, 2006).

17 Manfred Kets de Vries has written extensively on leadership from a psychoanalytic perspective. He explores the nature of people in organisations not just as consious and rational beings, but as people subject to contradictory conflicts, fantasies and anxieties. A helpful summary of his position and clinical approach is described in a book chapter entitled 'A Clinical Approach to the Dynamics of Leadership and Executive Transformation' (Kets de Vries and Engellau, 2010).

18 The term 'procedural justice' has been popularised within the field of management studies through the publications of Kim and Mauborgne (Kim and Mauborgne, 1991; Kim and Mauborgne, 1995; Kim and Mauborgne, 1996), their work on gaining commitment to strategy implementation is useful reference. A thorough review of the field is provided in the *Handbook of Organizational Justice* (Colquitt, Greenberg and Zapata-Phelan, 2005).

19 Roger Gill (Gill, 2006) describes motivation in the context of leadership influence and inspiration.

20 Kotter (1995).

21 See Schein (2004: 320).

22 The framework used here is developed using concepts drawn from the literature on group-oriented models, in particular, the Four Component Model of Procedural Justice promoted by Tyler and Blader (2000). This model is based on social identity explanations and emphasises the role of intrinsic motivations that lead members to undertake pro-social helping behaviours (acting in the interests of others) on behalf of their group. The model seeks to explain

pro-social helping behaviours in relation to the Quality of Decision Making Processes and the Quality of Treatment received. Tyler and Blader (2000: 125–131) further elaborate these two components into a four component model to include both formal and informal sources of justice information. The four components are: (1) Formal Quality of Treatment: the overall rules of the group that prescribe how people are to be treated; (2) Informal Quality of Treatment: quality of treatment during personal experiences with supervisors; (3) Formal Quality of Decision Making Processes: traditional justice constructs of quality and accuracy of procedures; and (4) Informal Quality of Decision Making Processes: the implementation of the formal rules by a supervisor, including how rules are interpreted and adapted for local situations.

23 The interdependent nature of behaviour and attitude is demonstrated in several theories in the psychology literature. However, the direction of causality – does attitude lead to behaviour or the other way around – is less understood with research providing support of both directions.

Moreover, the understanding of this causality in organisations appears even less clear, particularly in the strategic change arena. Balogun and Hope Hailey (2004) contrast the approaches suggesting that an attitude approach focuses on individuals, and targets change through individual attitudes on the premise that change in behaviour will follow; while behaviour-led change focuses on the organisation, changing roles, responsibilities and relationships, with the effect that an attitude change will follow. Kotter's eight steps to transforming organisations is a much cited approach to leading change (Kotter, 1995). His term 'burning platform' is well known in corporate settings and essentially is about creating such a sense of discomfort, sometimes through a manufactured crisis, that people start to act, in other words it is an attitudinal-led approach. Denis, Langley and Rouleau (2007) also shun the attitudinal-led approach in favour of the behavioural approach and propose that it is by imposing new roles, responsibilities and relationships that new attitudes and behaviours are 'forced'. There has not been any significant debate in the strategic change literature in attempting to understand and reconcile these opposing positions.

The position adopted here is that the two approaches can be used together. Issue surfacing is essentially an attitudinal approach. The use of an engagement framework to support the social process of strategy is also fundamentally targeting attitude to build commitment to act, though through social identity mechanisms. To ensure that commitments are acted upon requires the use of a behavioural change approach such as changing the organisation's major measurement systems.

24 The selected readings relate to the individual components of the engagement framework presented in figure 2.1: Bies and Moag (1986); Bobocel and Zdaniuk (2005); De Dreu and West (2001); Folger and Bies (1989); Gopinath and Becker (2000); and Kim and Mauborgne (1996).

25 The social anthropologist Fredrik Barth's position is that identification and collectivity is 'generated as emergent by-products of the transactions and negotiations of individuals pursuing their interests' (Jenkins, 2008).

26 See Tajfel (1981).

27 This is the social psychology perspective on the role that social identity plays in influencing behaviour within groups promoted by Henri Tajfel (Tajfel, 1981).

28 The premise of relative deprivation holds that people's reactions to outcomes are related to how they compare those outcomes with others with whom they compare themselves to. The original research on relative deprivation dates from military studies in 1949. A summary is provided in Colquitt, Greenberg and Zapata-Phelan (2005).

29 Procedural rationality implies that the procedure that a group is involved with is not opaque but transparent and seen to be sensible by those participating in it (see also Simon, 1976).

30   See Axley (1984).
31   See Weick (1979).
32   Van Velsor, Taylor and Leslie (1993).
33   The relationship between arousal and behaviour can be traced back to the Yerkes-Dodson law which determined that performance increases with arousal but only to a certain point (Yerkes and Dodson, 1988).
34   Cropanzano and Mitchell (2005).
35   The notion of a 'transitional object' is introduced by de Geus (1988) and Winnicott (1953). Others involved in group model building use the term 'boundary object' (Zagonel, 2002).
36   Eden and Ackermann (2010a) discuss the use of causal maps in the context of group decision making.
37   See Agor (1989).
38   Fisher and Ury (1982).
39   Bryson, Ackermann, Eden and Finn (2004) present a series of cases that demonstrate the impact of mapping within the context of problem solving, strategy making and organisational change.
40   Fisher and Ury (1982).
41   Eden, Jones, Sims and Smithin (1981) discuss the significance of the complexity of many views being accounted for, and the possible debilitating effect of taking these views seriously – managing complexity rather than reducing it.
42   See Eden, Jones, Sims and Smithin (1981: 43).
43   See Fisher and Ury (1982: 38).
44   See Eden (1993).
45   Group support systems have been developed over the past 20 years in order to help the productivity of groups, provide anonymity and facilitate effective problem structuring and resolution. See, for examples, Ackermann and Eden (2001a); Eden and Ackermann (2001a); Kilgour and Eden (2010); Lewis (1993); Lewis (2010); Lewis, Garcia and Hallock (2002).
46   Through the representation of a *socially constructed reality* (Berger and Luckmann, 1966).
47   Ackermann and Eden (2010a) report on the role of group support systems in facilitating negotiation with respect to the propositions from Fisher and Ury (1982).
48   Construct elaboration (Kelly, 1955) or scaffolding (Vygotsky, 1978) suggests a *gradual* shifting in ways of seeing the world.
49   Ackermann and Eden (2010a) report on the use of a group support system to encourage better working across two organisations wrapped into a dysfunctional relationship.
50   There are competing definitions of social capital that are related to its use by individuals, communities and industry networks; see Leana and Van Buren (1999). Essentially it is described as an asset that resides in social relationships. According to Nahapiet and Ghoshal, the term 'social capital' emerged from community studies related to networks of interpersonal relationships that provide the basis for trust, cooperation and collective action. These relationships are seen as a valuable resource for the 'conduct of social affairs'. Nahapiet and Ghoshal's definition is that social capital comprises 'the sum of the actual and potential resources embedded within, available through, and derived from the network of relationships possessed by an individual or social unit' (Nahapiet and Ghoshal, 1998).
51   De Geus (1988).
52   De Geus (1988).
53   Argyris and Schon (1978: 8–29).
54   Dickens and Watkins (1999); Easterby-Smith and Lyles (2003); Galer and van der Heijden (1992); Garrett (1990); Garvin (1993); Hayes, Wheelwright and Clark (1988); Kim and Mauborgne (2005); McGill, Slocum and Lei (1992); Normann (1985); Senge (1992).

55 Meacham and Kuhn (1983).
56 Provera, Montefusco and Canato (2010) have conducted interesting research that shows the significance of learning from failure in high reliability organisations.
57 Kolb's learning cycle (Kolb and Rubin, 1991).
58 Eden (1993).
59 Floyd and Woolridge (1992); Floyd and Woolridge (1994); Floyd and Woolridge (2000); Woolridge and Floyd (1990).
60 See, for example, Rosenhead (1989) and Bryson and Crosby (1992) in relation to not-for-profit strategy making.
61 Graham Allison's book on the Cuban Missile crisis is an interesting exposition on different ways of understanding strategic decision making (Allison, 1971).
62 See Paul Nutt's exposition on the fight over different claims on the future (Nutt, 2002).

Further Reading

Fisher, R. and Ury, W. 1982. *Getting to Yes*. London: Hutchinson.

Harvey, J. 1988. 'The Abilene Paradox: The Management of Agreement'. *Organizational Dynamics*, Summer: 17–34.

Kotter, John 1995. 'Leading Change: Why Transformation Efforts Fail'. *Harvard Business Review*, 73: 59–67.

Nutt, P. C. 2002. *Why Decisions Fail: Avoiding the Blunders and Traps that Lead to Debacles*. San Francisco: Berrett-Koehler Inc.

Tyler, T. R. and Blader, S. L. 2000. *Cooperation in Groups: Procedural Justice, Social Identity, and Behavioural Engagement*. Oxford: Psychology Press.

3

STRATEGY AS THE PRIORITISATION AND MANAGEMENT OF KEY ISSUES

Colin Eden and Fran Ackermann

Unless managers are allowed to debate and argue about these issues, then they will not be engaged by the abstract exercises that are typically at the core of most strategy meetings.

For managers at any level strategy is often seen as irrelevant to their organisational life. It is sometimes seen as a bureaucratic need to have a document called 'the strategy', a method of planning budgets or an 'annual rain-dance'[1] where the management team go away, play golf and become engaged in 'death by flip-chart'.

However, what managers do get engaged with is making claims about what needs to be done to be successful.[2] Every manager has their own view about what is most important for a successful organisational future. Sometimes this view derives from pushing for initiatives that will deliver their own career ambitions, but claims on the future do also derive from a genuinely held consideration of what must be done to deliver greater profitability, shareholder value, or deliver the aspirations of a not-for-profit organisation. In making such claims managers usually have a clear mental picture of how, if the organisation responds to the claims, this will create long term gains, or avoid disasters that will have long term negative consequences.

Often the claims sound operational and immediate and can be dismissed by others as not relevant to the strategic future of an organisation. Nevertheless, when operational claims are attached to a high level of frustration they are often of strategic significance, and when the manager is encouraged to explicate their frustration, the strategic consequences emerge. Operations and strategy are not disconnected; they are integrated in delivering the future. In this book we go beyond a level of generality about what is to be done and examine strategy as something that is more obviously and clearly linked to operations, and, at the very least, strategy provides a framework within which everyday issues and problems are dealt with.[3]

This chapter encourages a *strategic* conversation about what managers believe to be important, and so recognises a very significant aspect of managerial life. The issue management forum encourages a conversation based on the intuitions, frustrations and claims a manager makes about what needs to be done to ensure success or avoid failure. Taking seriously the claims of experienced and multidisciplinary managers, understanding how the claims interact with one another, and understanding their 'portfolio' impact on the future form the basis for developing a good strategy.

The key assumptions we make relating to this chapter are:

- Managers' wisdom, intuition and experience are to be taken seriously.
- Managers have much of their lives occupied by strategic issues – potential disasters or missed opportunities.[4]
- Most managers see the strategic planning processes and their outcomes as largely irrelevant to their lives, but they are very much aware that they take actions which have important long term consequences.
- Thinking and acting strategically demands dealing with messy and complex situations where there is no 'right' answer.

The attraction of the issue management strategic conversation – a *strategy forum* – promoted in this chapter is that it recognises managers have a sense of urgency about some issues. These issues are expected to have a serious impact on creating a successful strategic future. Even though most managers appreciate that they should be able to take a 'blue skies' approach to thinking strategically, they cannot avoid the significance of dealing with urgent issues that, if not dealt with, leave both them and the organisation exposed. Unless managers are allowed to debate and argue about these issues, then they will not be engaged. Their issues will be addressed and resolved through other processes, and so a strategic future *will unfold* regardless of the outcomes of strategic planning meetings.

STRATEGIC VISION

A vision provides the motivation to do things but little help with how to decide and behave in relation to specific issues. An outcome of strategy making is to change the way in which decision makers make sense of their role and the things that are going on around them. A strategy will provide them with new ways of thinking about their world, new ways of doing things – a new 'recipe' or guidebook that can *link the vision to action*. In this sense the strategy provides a framework for 'acting thinkingly'[5] rather than simply 'muddling through'.[6] And so, strategy is expected to be an instrument of social control by directing managers to act coherently with a degree of alignment between their actions and the actions of others, and also in a manner more in line with the desires of those who have power.

> *The usefulness of a management team depends upon each member of a team having a different perspective on what is best for the organisation.*

Needless to say, a *strategy forum* based on the management of strategic issues will always be set within the context of organisations as political cauldrons. The politics of organisational life derive from aspects of human interest: pure self-interest, ambition and careerism, tangled together with a natural inclination to want to fight for what you believe is best for the organisation. While pure self-interest is an important consideration, it is the fight to get your views to be heard and to influence agreement and action that is, and should be, most significant in the strategy forum.

The usefulness of a management team depends upon each member of a team having a different perspective on what is best for the organisation. When those different perspectives collide organisational politics is inevitable. Rather than the common presumption that organisational politics are a bad thing, on the contrary, organisational politics will often be a sign of real debate – a fight for what is believed to be best for the organisation. Thus, organisational politics derives from the legitimate attempts of one person to persuade others to their own point of view.

The purpose of a carefully designed strategy forum is to facilitate the negotiation across multiple viewpoints, and to do so in such a way that the negotiation outcome is not a compromise but rather a creative combination of multiple perspectives.

Unless the design of strategy making recognises the difficulties in exploiting wisdom and expertise then the dominant and surface (and mostly trivial) views remain foremost.

Unless there are different perspectives[7] – different claims on the future – then there is something wrong with the team. A team should bring together different backgrounds, experience, wisdom and roles. 'When considering the working of teams in organisations it seems important and indeed commonsensical that such working involves the interaction and negotiation of shared *and* idiosyncratic understandings. A team is continually involved in some process of negotiating reality amongst its members. Much of this negotiation, however, is likely to remain implicit, as in most social interaction. Members of teams are rarely given the facility, explicitly or systematically, to explore different as well as similar perspectives. We see as critical to capitalising upon the intersubjective nature of issues, the provision of a *facility* for making the process of negotiating reality explicit ... issues belong to people; an issue is not the objective characteristic of some objective sequence of events to be discovered by a consultant and proffered by his superior expert judgement as the real issue. ... we find that it is best to conceive the world as being individually constructed, with each person's reality being separate and distinctive.[8]

Each member of the team should, therefore, bring to the table their own understanding of what might be a successful future and how that might be achieved. Making strategy must encompass different perspectives and use them creatively and as a whole to enable the development of a negotiated agreement about priorities. Strategic *management* is about *agreeing* where to *practically focus* energy, cash, effort and emotion.

A carefully designed strategy forum to address issue management will release deeper knowledge, beliefs and expertise. By doing so differences in beliefs can be exploited as a creative tension and the summation of deep knowledge as a systemic whole can be utilised rather than as individual isolated chunks of expertise. On the surface managers entertain apparently similar interpretations of situations. The lack of a design that will help surface deeper beliefs and knowledge, and an inherent lack of 'air time' for managers to express other than surface beliefs and knowledge, mean there can be little understanding of alternative perspectives or opportunity to reflect upon them. The political stance taken towards alternative perspectives is what then drives negotiation. Unless the design of strategy making recognises the difficulties in exploiting wisdom and expertise then the dominant and surface (and mostly trivial) views remain foremost in conversation and in thinking and in action. The issue management strategy forum seeks to address realities of behaviour in and around organisations, understandings of which should underpin any effective approach and method to deliberative strategy making.

If we cannot change which strategic issues are surfaced, the way in which issues are viewed, or the way in which they are dealt with, then it does not matter what a rational analysis of the environment reveals or what a rational analysis of stakeholders (such as competitors) suggests.

We expect managers to see issues and opportunities they would not have seen before, and no longer notice issues that are less significant for determining strategic success. Thus, strategy making is about forgetting and ignoring as well as about seeing new and different opportunities. Managers will not be surprised or disappointed by the actions of others, rather they will see them as obviously congruent with an intended *strategic direction*. In this way there will not be a separation of thinking from action or vice versa. There is also no presumption that all can be known – that implementation follows choices which have been made against certain and unambiguous data. Strategic action will be framed not constrained.

EMERGENT STRATEGISING

How issues are resolved and the impact of these resolutions on the strategic future of the organisation is what is called emergent strategising.[9] In other words, in all organisations, whether or not there is a deliberate strategy that is expected to guide decision making, there will be patterns of thinking and systems that will create a particular type of strategic future – an emergent strategy. Strategic futures arise from 'separate episodes of analysis … actions, whose controlled execution consolidates fragments of policy that are lying around, gives them direction, and closes off other possible arrangements'.[10]

In this chapter we recognise the significance of emergent strategising. We avoid pretending it does not exist, and so forcing managers to undertake what to many of them are abstract 'academic' analyses that presume a 'blank sheet' starting point. Changing the strategic direction of an organisation is always difficult, and unless we recognise the powerful constraints of emergent strategy we will not recognise the extent of what we need to change. So, we focus on building a strategy from a recognition that managers' concerns are based on sound experience and legitimate role perspectives.[11] We accept that the purpose of a management team is to exploit the importantly different perspectives of each team member – the differences in role expertise, ways of thinking and informational power.

Much emergent strategising will be influenced by the way in which some events are defined as potential disasters and others are not. Emergent patterns will reflect as much what managers wish to avoid as what they see as desirable. Thus, for example, it is our experience that managers at all levels are frequently driven by the perceived requirement to address urgent issues – reactivity not pro-activity. The process of dealing with *strategic* issues that arise from attempts to sustain relationships and adapt and/or react to the environment generates tensions among the management team. These tensions derive from the extent to which adaptations to the environment and to stakeholder's expectations require resource shifts, possible restructuring – down-sizing, up-sizing, right-sizing, etc., new products, new ways of working and so on. These shifts, in turn, inevitably mean there will be winners and losers in the organisation. No change can be made without, at the very least, perceptions of potential loss and gain. By anticipating such outcomes powerful managers in the organisation play up some issues,[12] play down others, and fight to retain their own power. Political negotiation, dependent upon the thinking, power and information provision, will be a central feature of attempts to be opportunistic and flexible and agree upon strategic action. Indeed the 'need for flexibility' will often be used as a part of the rhetoric for maintaining 'logical incrementalism'[13] or sequential issue management rather than explicit strategic agreements. In this way managers retain the right to fight again – the fortunes of those currently losing battles are not sealed. The outcomes of behaviours that play up some issues, and the political battles that might underlie them, will not be totally coherent or thought out as a pattern but rather may be implicit in the behaviour, language and action of the managers.[14]

Any manager will also, to some extent, copy the underlying 'recipes'[15] used by other managers (particularly those defined as successful), including those in other organisations. Similarly managers act out habits, routines and traditions of their group.[16] For example, as managers continually watch their competitors and react to them they will be seeking to maintain competitive positioning to adapt to the environment and exploit opportunities, which generate debate, argument and political negotiation, out of which strategies emerge to maintain competitive positioning. The 'logic' in logical incrementalism is the apparent logic of dealing with each strategic issue in turn.

Creating a strategic future relies on individual action and the idea promoted by Karl Weick[17] that the implementation of strategy ultimately depends upon the extent to which managers are able to 'act thinkingly' given the human being's limit to the amount of information they are able to process.[18] The challenge becomes that of creating a *mental framework* or schema for strategic action. That is, strategy is about creating a new mental framework that influences construal (the way in which a manager interprets the events around them), and so the way they take action to change things.

There is substantial research by social psychologists[19] that suggests that it is not easy for groups to accept different perspectives – the group coalesces around views that all the members agree about and that each of them would have expressed. In the strategy making forum presented in these issue management chapters we intend to surface *different* views, to exploit how views are rarely in total conflict but rather come together to produce a new, and more complete, view. This combined view is the basis for agreeing strategic priorities, and so creating a strategy that is realistic and has the commitment of most team members. In addition we expect to use designed processes that promote procedural justice[20] in order to encourage the surfacing of different perspectives.

Most significantly the above considerations suggest no separation between process design and content management in seeking to surface multiple perspectives. Without addressing process issues it is unlikely that multiple perspectives will be made explicit. Thus, in developing a group understanding of what everyone in the group believes is important to be done, attention must be paid to achieving both substantive *and* process outcomes – where process outcomes are an end in themselves but also significantly influence the extent to which substantive outcomes can be achieved.

The designed strategic conversations are the starting points for what is known as 'issue selling'[21] where each manager seeks to influence their colleagues' view of what is important. In crisis, managers fight harder for their views and the drive for action means they reveal – often implicitly – more of their embedded vision, surface more of their assumptions, and take one another more seriously than on 'special' occasions designated for strategy making (for example 'away-days'). However, the urgency involved in dealing with strategic crises can mean that while each manager surfaces more of their strategic assumptions, there is less time for other managers to check out their understanding of these assumptions. Consequently assumptions can be surfaced and missed, or can be severely misunderstood. These misunderstandings occur because the important stage of sharing meaning and making sense may have been bypassed, and each participant is forced to make untested assumptions about the implicit beliefs embedded in proposals for action coming from colleagues.

When a group surfaces issues they believe must be addressed and understands these as a system of interacting issues, then they can formulate a strategy by deciding where to focus attention in order to create the future they want[22] (see box 3.1 for a vignette about developing issue priorities). The process of developing a strategy through the management of priority issues acknowledges emergent strategising by allowing the management team to understand the way in which the organisation's strategic future is emerging, reflect on this, and adapt and change it. The process does not pretend that an organisation has no past ('path dependency')[23] or present.

Box 3.1   'Overwhelmed by Policies'

The Chief Executive of a Prison Service in Europe had been under governmental pressure for many years to implement a wide range of so-called 'policy initiatives'. The number of initiatives was growing every year and none seemed to disappear! He felt that he and his senior staff were 'initiative weary' and were unclear about where to devote their managerial energy. The managers each had their own view about which of these initiatives were now important, as well as their own ideas about new initiatives. In particular they each had strong views about potential disasters facing the organisation and that would have serious ramifications for the future of the prison service.

Alongside these circumstances the Chief Executive was under pressure to submit a strategy for the Prison Service. The strategy was to be set out in a predefined way and be constructed using a 'textbook' set of guidelines. The guidelines were seen as 'academic' and wholly irrelevant to the needs of the organisation. The organisation was caught between powerful stakeholders making the demand for a 'textbook' strategy, and senior managers being continually battered by the real demands of the strategic issues faced by the organisation. The Chief Executive could not ignore his senior colleagues, but could not see how the organisation could usefully address all the old initiatives let alone the new initiatives being demanded. His managers were patently not stupid – there were no grounds for ignoring their concerns. In any case, they would 'vote with their feet' and simply use their energy as they thought best and without consideration for how different strategic moves might interfere with each other.

The Chief Executive was attracted to the notion that strategy could be seen as agreeing issue priorities and so highlighting the significance of some against others. The process might enable him and his team to argue for dropping many initiatives, as well as enabling them to focus on those that really matter. He was attracted to developing what he regarded as a realistic strategy, which could subsequently be morphed into a document that would meet the demands of powerful stakeholders.

In this chapter we devise a strategy making forum that accepts that a strategy can be as simple as prioritising issues so that they become strategic initiatives. The process pays attention to where 'managers are at'. Managers will, regardless of the 'agenda', want to focus the attention of other managers on what they claim to be of most significance – issues they believe to be of great importance for the future of the organisation. There is no point in ignoring these issues, because they will be forced into the agenda. In effect, each manager will seek to claim a 'burning platform', a crisis,[24] which other managers should pay attention to.

THE *ISSUE MANAGEMENT* STRATEGY FORUM

The manager-client needs to feel comfortable.

An issue management forum is an unusual way of making strategy, and so the manager-client and sponsor must have a good understanding of what will unfold and why. The manager-client will be concerned with generic issues related to forum design, but also the manager-client will need to feel comfortable with the group creating its own 'burning platform' – something that the group decides they want to work on together. The group may create a 'picture' of the future that raises agendas that the manager-client regards as irrelevant or politically sensitive, and thus needs to be prepared for this possibility. If a group raises issues and they are dismissed then members can feel more disillusioned than if the issues had not been raised at all. Substantive issues, for group members, will often be thought of as short term and not strategic by the manager-client. There has to be a sympathy for, and appreciation of, these more operational issues being seen by others to have major strategic consequences and so they must be encouraged.

There are also other more straightforward, but nevertheless difficult, issues that will need to be resolved with the manager-client of the forum: the question that will be the focus for eliciting issues, deciding the time horizon for the strategy to deliver significant outcomes, overall design and timing of the forum, and group composition.

Getting Issues and Concerns 'Out on the Table'

Managers become aware of the bigger picture.

Meetings of almost any sort will allow for the surfacing of issues, however, the early claims usually close down avenues of thought and so increase the dangers of a limited search and no innovation (the 'quick fix') – a common failure in group decisions.[25] In many meetings, the typical situation is for the first person to argue for their view, which inevitably will require a 10–20 minute discussion based on this first issue. If this were to happen for all of the issues then this demands a considerable amount of time for the meeting. However, more typically not all the issues get raised as time gets short or participants give up trying to make their views heard. For example, typical meetings will raise the equivalent of 10 issues, where the issues raised come from a small number of participants.[26] An issue management forum however, is likely to raise 40–70 issues in a third of the time and from all of the participants. By seeing the different concerns and their context in one structured space participants are able to build on the views, adapt ideas and, as a group, craft possible new solutions.

The issue management forum can use an electronic support system such as Decision Explorer®, but also much can be achieved using sticky labels.[27] The role of the software support system is a crucial differentiator from 'normal' meetings because it creates a publicly viewable image that encourages continuous gathering and editing of issues, and movement of the issues around the publicly viewable screen to create clusters. As participants become involved in 'dumping' issues they gradually learn how to speak and 'write' issues in a manner that provides enough meaning to suggest strategy as action, as change – the phrasing becomes action-oriented through use of verbs. Figure 3.1 shows the early stages of eliciting issues.

As we suggested earlier, we must encourage the declaration of different perspectives, but be aware that surfacing disagreement can sometimes not be easy in a team. So, what stops people from disagreeing? A member of the team may believe that their view is 'out on a limb' from the rest of the group, and so feel they may be subject to ridicule for expressing an alternative view. It is possible, of course, that everyone in the group feels this way. There may be 'trading agreements' with others in the group, which would be broken if they expressed a view which opposes that of their trading partners – to do so would have consequences for support on other issues. To dissent from the view of the group may risk team cohesiveness – the camaraderie of being a team.[28] Surfacing issues so that they are visible to all other participants allows managers to 'get things off their chest', and this is an important side benefit that encourages participants to

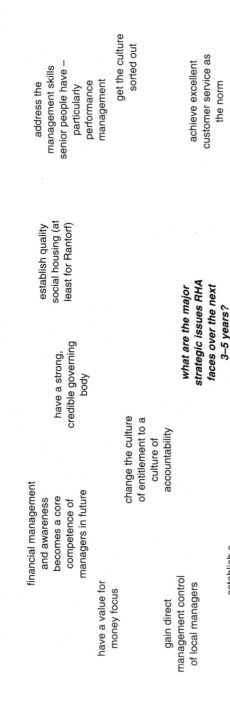

financial management
and awareness
becomes a core
competence of
managers in future

have a value for
money focus

change the culture
of entitlement to a
culture of
accountability

gain direct
management control
of local managers

establish a
positive, creative
and rigorous
performance
management ethos and
systems

have a strong,
credible governing
body

develop an
understanding of
effective customer
outcomes/our purpose

establish quality
social housing (at
least for Rantorf)

*what are the major
strategic issues RHA
faces over the next
3–5 years?*

revisit our
operating model and
AT THE SAME TIME
address staff and
managers' attitudes
and behaviours

address the
management skills
senior people have –
particularly
performance
management

get the culture
sorted out

achieve excellent
customer service as
the norm

Figure 3.1 Starting the Process of 'Dumping' Issues

'move on' and listen, learn, understand and negotiate. The designed process for surfacing different perspectives must acknowledge these characteristics of group behaviour.

The speech act, and its realisation through being listened to (others seeking to understand), is a part of the dynamic of each of us changing our position – our thinking – and so our actions. Furthermore, the words we use express a part of our thinking, just as our thinking is influenced by the language and scripts we have available to use as speech acts.[29] In focusing on the individual team member as an instrument for change we do not dismiss the arguments that change requires top management commitment, ownership, shift in culture and changes in the balance of power – as each of these factors is important. Rather we suggest that each of these is dependent upon the politics of the 'management of meanings' within an organisation.[30]

Surfacing issues so that they are visible to all other participants allows managers to get views about what will contribute to a successful strategic future out 'on the table' (typically 70–90 issues will be surfaced in 30–45 minutes). Additionally managers become aware of the bigger picture as the forum provides the means for surfacing not just the issues facing one manager but the issues they believe are facing other managers, the department or organisation commissioning the forum. In this way a more holistic perspective is gained.

Inevitably, if we have succeeded in opening up the strategy debate, the big picture is messy. Building and roughly labelling clusters of related issues into themes helps manage the complexity of the unfolding material as well as prompt more issues. Clustering the issues ('chunking' into themes) with respect to their content can help start the structuring process and help the group manage the initial complexity of the material. So, for example, in a commercial organisation we might use the well-established thematic headings of finance, operations, human resource management, etc., and allocate each issue statement to one of these headings. However, using these 'standard' thematic headings usually fails to realise the natural themes that emerge from the actual data.

Becoming aware of the bigger picture involves facilitating divergence and comprehensiveness within a short time (typically up to 45 minutes). Everyone should be heard and so ownership, not agreement, of the developing picture of individual issue statements and thematic clusters can be assured. Indeed, if there is agreement about the entire picture then we have likely failed to surface fully the differences in perspective!

This introductory issue surfacing aims not only to address the social process issues, discussed in chapter 2, but also to acknowledge productivity benefits: involving everyone, getting at different perspectives and expertise, and doing so in a short time.

This first stage may be usefully supplemented by shifting the issue gathering from the perspective of each participant and considering issues as they would be stated by other stakeholders. Thinking about what other stakeholders might regard as issues that must be addressed can open up the potential for developing a broader view of how to think about creating an effective strategic future.

The Interaction Between 'Strategic' Issues: Issues as a Network

Strategic issues are not independent, they impact one another.

Strategic issues are not independent, they impact one another. The process of linking issues adds value to the forum in three ways. The first benefit is that through the linking process participants can begin to understand in more detail how the surfaced issues relate to one another. Significantly the process moves away from thematic clusters to action clusters where many of the links identified go across the thematic clusters as well as within them. This causal map[31] is action-oriented because it captures a means-ends structure where each linking arrow represents a 'means' statement and an 'ends' statement at the head of the arrow. The causal links reveal the mechanisms for strategic change. This process of revealing a network helps to build a shared understanding of the issues facing the group. Secondly, linking also enables a better understanding of the relative importance or significance of the issues. Clues to the significance of issues derive from understanding how issues relate to each other. Thus managers are able to look at the issue picture in a more systemic, holistic and revealing manner. Finally, the process prompts participants to articulate more deeply held views – unrehearsed, almost tacit, knowledge – allowing this to be captured and thus giving rise to a more complete and subtle picture of the issues.

Organisations in the same industry do not face the same strategic issues.

By building up the network of issues – a causal map – a clearer picture of the uniqueness of the organisation's issues will be revealed. Contrary to assertions in much of the strategic planning literature, organisations in the same industry do not face the same strategic issues, let alone the way they relate to each other. A unique set of issues based upon the history, skills and focus of the organisation will be revealed.[32] A key purpose of strategy making is to identify and exploit differences and distinctiveness. If the issues surfaced are the same, in content *and* links – and have the same meaning as those that a competitor might surface, then it is likely they are at too high a level of abstractness.

The process of detecting how issues impact upon one another is found by most managers to be an activity that they can easily relate to – this is because we all use causality in order to make sense of our world.[33] Group causal mapping aims to release deep knowledge and wisdom to get beyond the apparently similar descriptions of situations and into the subtle, but important, differences of what has to be done and why. The process raises alternative formulations and therefore opens up new options and new understandings.

Causal maps provide a device for exploring meaning – through illustrating not just what the facts/issues are but how they fit together. The map ensures, through its qualitative fuzziness and imprecision, a sufficient degree of equivocality to encourage negotiation.[34]

However, it is important to note that, while we are hoping to get a feel for emergent strategising, the picture created will be a crude but, nonetheless, relatively effective attempt. Figure 3.2 shows an extract from a causal map being developed using Decision Explorer®. The statements surfaced rarely fully or accurately describe the patterns of behaviour and decision making in the organisation. That is to say, we should be aware of the difference between 'theories in use' (how people actually think and act) and 'espoused theories' (how people account for how they think and act).[35] Clearly official (espoused) statements are an important source used to justify action, and develop stories that influence the culture of the organisation. However, there is no substitute for capturing 'theories in use' employed by managers as they deal with strategic issues 'on the run'.

Causal mapping provides a structure to the merging of perspectives and is our best chance at avoiding the danger of reducing the complexity of the 'real-world' by focusing on only a small number of considerations. Group maps comprising in excess of 60 issues (claims) can represent effectively a merging of the views of many people.

By seeing the different concerns and their context in one structured space participants are able to build on the views, adapt ideas and as a group craft possible new solutions. This opening up of the situation facilitates *creativity*. In essence the group is 'piggy backing' off one another.[36]

Move from a set of divergent perspectives to a more shared understanding.

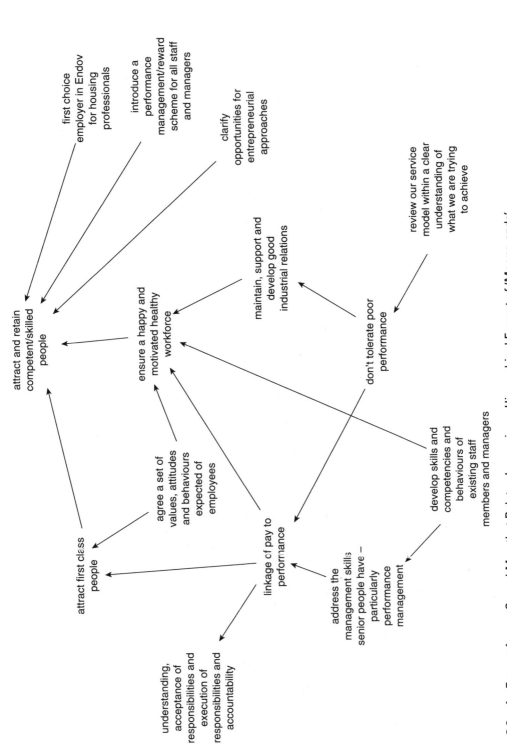

Figure 3.2 An Extract from a Causal Map that Relates Issues in an Hierarchical Format of 'Means-ends'

The process of explicating the causal relationships allows the group to move from a set of divergent perspectives to a more shared understanding. The process of not just surfacing the issue but also capturing the consequences of the issue and some of its explanatory issue statements enables both added value in terms of managing the complexity and additional insight and learning.

As new linked clusters emerge from the network it will become clear that the initial unlinked content clusters are likely to be misleading – partly as there will be different understandings of the issues surfaced and partly as the linking process will mean that the final clusters will be *based on an action focus* rather than content analysis. Collecting the issues into thematic headings ignores the action orientation implied by the way in which people make statements in order to persuade others to act in particular ways. There is no *a priori* reason why the links between claims and proposed actions should be thematic. Indeed, there is a reasonable expectation that strategy making involves consideration of implications that are across many themes. Linking the issues together enables the participants to begin considering how to manage each issue while recognising implications for other issues. The linking shows visually that some issues drive and reinforce others. The group map helps counter the problem of buying 'into a claim without understanding its motivating concerns, [and so] misdirect effort'.[37]

> *Complexity can be debilitating for the group.*

Paying attention to multiple perspectives is expected to increase an awareness of the complexity of the situation. This complexity can be debilitating for the group – the need to take account of 'intersubjectivity'[38] is overwhelmingly challenging.

> Most particularly an awareness of complexity can sap the desire or felt capacity to act. The world is complicated enough, it may be argued, without seeking to make even more of the complexity explicit and, thus, even more of the difficulties of acting effectively in the world apparent … Encouraging members of a team to listen both caringly and analytically to each other is inevitably consuming of both time and energy.[39]

Increasing complexity, if encouraged, must be *managed*, not reduced. If it can be managed then it will more likely be recognised as an important aspect of the challenge of good strategy making. In the next section we address ways of managing, rather than reducing, complexity: through analysis of the structure of the causal map, including generating powerful overviews without losing richness, as well as through categorisation of the map content.

As a first step, structuring the resultant issues into an hierarchical structure provides an initial overview – patterning – of how one issue might support, or be supported by another, and most significantly, visually reveals issues that are central to the organisation's future. Creating a 'tidy' map in a hierarchical two-dimensional form is immensely revealing – it becomes advisable to move central issues to the centre of the picture, otherwise the map will be unnecessarily complex because of too many crossing arrows.[40] And what finishes up in the centre tends to be central to the organisation's future.

In the next section we suggest that the structure of the network will reveal, at least, important emergent properties that provide candidate strategic priorities.

Prioritising Issues: Agreeing Strategies

When issues are evaluated singly they may appear not to be the most significant to the organisation's strategic future. However, once the issues have been linked together and a network structure formed, it is easier to see which issues are central or potent to the overall structure. These issues become potential priorities. Using a designed analytical process for prioritisation seeks to avoid the trap of 'pressure goad[ing] you into selecting among competing claims instead of finding concerns suggesting a claim all could agree to'.[41] However, the role of judgement in relation to the network of issues will be an important part of establishing priorities – the analysis of the structure only provides useful guidance.

The network of linked statements will have structural properties – for example, clusters, where statements are tightly linked to each other and yet relatively isolated from other tightly linked statements. In the extreme these clusters may be 'islands', implying that within the situation there are a series of independent strategic arenas. In such an extreme case each strategy arena can be dealt with independently, having no implications for one another. However, this is not a typical situation – at the very least, attention to multiple perspectives will have generated intersubjectivity and so interdependence. Nevertheless, in order to help manage complexity and the potentially debilitating nature of it, identifying interacting clusters is likely to be helpful to the group. It is difficult to attend to the requirement that 'best practice calls for a comparison of competing ideas to select the one that comes closest to providing the hoped for results'[42] without seeking to manage complexity.

Identifying clusters is, in itself, problematic because there are many ways of doing so. Using a simple, and visually attractive, method, rather than a more statistically 'accurate' but opaque method, can avoid arguments within the group about what the clusters should be rather than addressing the substantive situation.

The process of a group identifying and labelling clusters is an important part of participants listening to one another. By asking the group to suggest clusters, each participant will listen to others through the process of reading statements other than those contributed by them.

'Headline Issues' – Draft Organisational Goals?

Identifying and understanding the structure of the issues network can make a significant contribution to managing complexity and so developing an effective strategy. Those statements at the top of the hierarchy of the network (with no out-arrows – 'heads') provide the best indication of the desired or undesirable outcomes that result from the issues subordinate in the hierarchy. Some of these statements may be goals – desirable ends in their own right or at least represent 'headline' issues for the subordinate statements.

The Significance of Vicious, Virtuous and Self-correcting Cycles

Recognising the interdependence of strategy themes leads to the possibility of their being connected so that they feed off each other. Looking at the network's structure will reveal whether there are self-sustaining feedback cycles where potentially vicious or virtuous cycles create dynamic behaviour – continuous changes over time might be a significant aspect of the future. The complexity of a situation is typically increased considerably when there are dynamic behaviours, and, while these might not be understood, they are intuitively felt.

Research on managerial judgement suggests that the need human beings have for imposing order on data, through seeking causality in order to make sense of their world, will make it less likely that they can entertain alternative problem formulations.[43] In addition there is evidence that, without specific encouragement within designed processes, managers are unable to pay adequate attention to 'feedback properties' in evaluating the dynamic behaviour of their own organisation.[44] The sum of beliefs of each individual manager is rarely deliberately related to the beliefs of others. Each manager has a bounded view of the organisational world, both internal and external. It is only when these views are linked to each other that it becomes possible to identify how one set of beliefs impacts another set which impacts yet another set and so creates a feedback effect (a closed loop) which may encourage self-sustaining virtuous circles or unhelpful vicious circles of organisational behaviour. It is often the case that situations created by the policies and internal processes of the organisation will be incorrectly attributed to the behaviour of the external world (and vice versa), be it the marketplace or other environmental variables. In this way the strategic opportunities for using internal policies are missed because they are seen as environmentally determined. Similarly the interaction of beliefs across several individuals can indicate negative feedback where undesirable, or desirable, feedback control is created – self-correcting dynamic behaviour. Here strategic change is inhibited by the forces of stability which may be easy to change if only they are appreciated. Strategy making must address possible *dynamic* futures, and so feedback dynamics need to be identified, understood and reflected upon. Feedback is of significance because it represents the potential for changes over time without any further active management interventions.

The feedback loop shown in figure 3.3 demonstrates how a group gradually built up links and noticed feedback showing that the danger of acquisition was continually increasing over time – through two vicious cycles. Once these feedback loops had been identified they seemed blatantly obvious to the team, but they had not up to this time realised the dynamic! On this particular occasion the issue surfacing forum came to a complete standstill and participants diverted all of their attention to thinking about how to stop the feedback dynamic working in this negative fashion. They considered each link in turn to see whether they could devise ways of breaking the loops. They ultimately agreed to focus considerable energy on both tackling the link between the danger of acquisition and staff leaving, and secondly a major initiative to address product quality and so switch the dynamic from vicious cycles to virtuous cycles.

In complicated messy situations the identification and realisation of feedback often can be difficult. Even though a causal map, as opposed to other representations, will be more likely to capture feedback, a feedback loop may not be identified. As we have seen, the causal map which represents multiple perspectives is likely to be complex. Identifying feedback through visual inspection is often impossible. However, the software (Decision Explorer®) ensures that feedback loops in the causal map will always be identified through the use of a simple analysis command. It is common for a group to see the discovery of feedback as a significant step in effective strategic thinking, even though later it seems obvious (this was the case for the example shown in figure 3.3). Vicious cycles can destroy the desired impact of strategies, and virtuous cycles can ensure their success – their identification is a crucial part of any strategic conversation and so is fundamental in the prioritising of strategic issues so that they become strategies.

Finding 'Hot Buttons'

As groups gradually develop and accept a shared definition of the situation, they tend to naturally identify with the parts of the causal map where individual statements have most links with other statements. In effect they see those issues that are 'central' or 'busy' gain significance in terms of their importance as there are numerous relationships either linking into or out of them. Paying attention to these central statements (the 'hot buttons') and related points is likely to be important in resolving at least one major strategic issue.

The structure of a hierarchy can reveal other potentially important hot buttons. The resolution of some issues within the hierarchy will resolve more headline issues than others. In other words, there are multiple paths of consequences that each lead to different final outcomes (heads). Some of the consequence paths may lead to good outcomes and others to bad outcomes and so suggest a dilemma with respect to acting on the issue. Nevertheless, each of these multiple

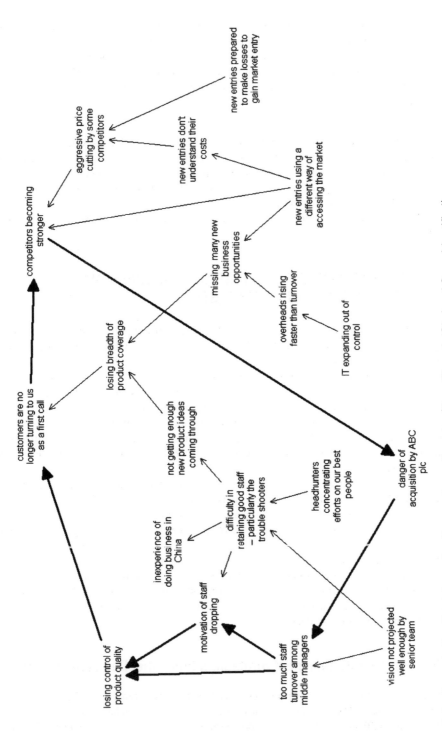

Figure 3.3 Example Feedback Loop that Emerged as a Surprise (Even Though 'Obvious' Once Identified)

consequence issues is 'potent' in its impact and so must be worth evaluating as potential strategic priorities. When the potency is positive in all consequences, then unless the impact on outcomes is extremely weak, the issue must be regarded as a candidate strategic priority.

Eliciting at least one hot button in each of the strategic themes (or clusters of material) is an appropriate way to start using judgement for the evaluation of priorities.

Agreeing Priorities

The properties of the network help establish strategic priorities through a re-evaluation of issues as a result of seeing them (listening to them) in the context of other issues. In addition the different analyses that can be undertaken through visual inspection or through using analysis techniques embedded in the causal mapping software (Decision Explorer®) provide powerful assistance in informing good judgement about priorities.

The priorities represent a strategy – a negotiated agreement about where to focus energy, cash, effort, emotion.

THE ISSUE MANAGEMENT FORUM STRATEGY DELIVERABLE: A STATEMENT OF STRATEGIC INTENT (SSI)

The delivery of a statement of strategic intent (SSI) as a brief but pointed deliverable from a strategy forum is an important symbol of closure and also a more public document than ever a causal map can be. A one-page statement will be more familiar to staff in an organisation – causal maps, although containing a tighter and more precise statement, are nevertheless often difficult to relate to. However, the main purpose of constructing a statement of strategic intent is that it will be written as a strategy, albeit a crude and incomplete one.

The statement of strategic intent represents strategic priorities and their context – the relationship between each priority – where some priorities will resolve others and other priorities will be resolved. The statement will also be able to recognise what attention to them will achieve – a sense of purpose.

A good test of an effective strategy is that it should be distinctive and so reflect the particular nature of the organisation – the strategic priorities for this particular point in time. Even when some priorities seem very similar across organisations, as statements, the network of strategic issues within which the priority is set will be different. For example, many organisations may have a strategic priority to 'increase the motivation of their production operatives', but each organisation would have different purposes in doing so (out arrows), and different ways of making it happen (in arrows). For example, an organisation may be focused on improving product quality as a result of increasing motivation, whereas another may be focused on lowering absenteeism. It is these differences in meaning that locate distinctiveness. These differences of meaning must be encompassed in the statement of strategic intent.

The Strategy as a Statement of Strategic Intent – the 'Dementia' Example

Figure 3.4 shows a summary of the priorities agreed by the multi-organisational group working on a dementia strategy. The strategic priorities were developed during a half morning forum with participation from 30 staff from a range of organisations. The map has been 'collapsed' so that it can show all the summary links between each priority – thus, in some cases, a single arrow represents a chain of links.

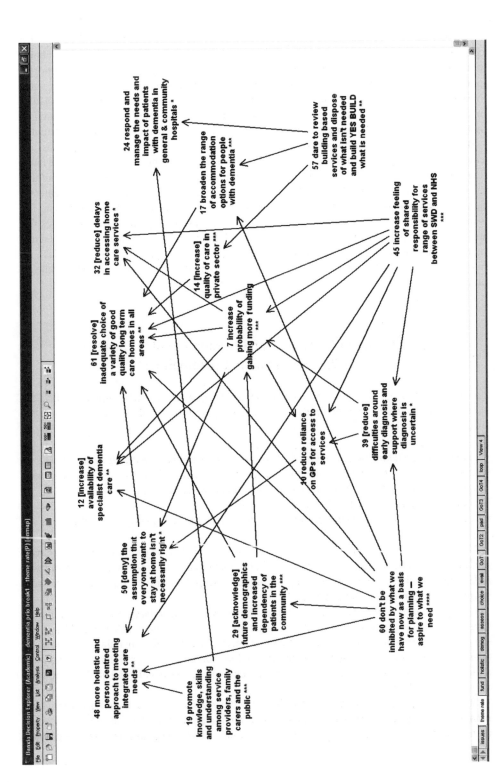

Figure 3.4 Summary of Issue Priorities Developed by a Multi-organisation Group

Priorities are typically agreed on the basis of three levels of priority (in figure 3.4 a three-star scale has been used). In the above example, it is notable that one top priority that was initially awarded three stars with a very high degree of consensus, became re-graded as a four-star priority because it was agreed that it was of outstanding priority. In this case it is of note that all three-star priorities were agreed with a high degree of consensus, with less consensus about the relative importance of the lower rated priorities. (This is a phenomenon that occurs often where there is a lot of agreement about what is most important and less agreement about what is less important.)

Box 3.2 shows the result of converting the priorities map into a statement encompassing sentences and paragraphs. In box 3.2 the text in bold is an exact replica of the text in the map. There are many ways this can be achieved, but in all instances it is important that it is a faithful translation of the map. In this example, because of its agreed significance, the first sentence focuses on the four-star priority – the 'bottom' of the map, or action point – rather than, for example, the outcomes or statements that are closest to representing goals. In other cases the first sentence might have focused on 'increasing availability of specialist dementia care' (statement 12) and then discussed statements 48 and 61 (as two-star goal-oriented priorities). In this example the goal-oriented statements have been inserted as commentary in the middle of the document.

Box 3.2   Initial Statement of Strategic Intent for Strategy to Manage Dementia (Example)

Our primary strategic focus will be to **not be inhibited by what we have now as a basis for planning – and rather aspire to what we need**. We expect this attitude to be a key driver for developing our ability to:

- *acknowledge future demographics and increased dependency of patients in the community*
- **broaden the range of accommodation options for people with dementia** and [resolve] inadequate choice of a variety of good quality long term care homes in all areas
- **increase availability of specialist dementia care**
- provide a **more holistic and person centred approach to meeting integrated care needs**

Alongside **aspiring to what we need** there will be a parallel focus on creating an *increased feeling of shared responsibility for range of services between Social Work Department and NHS*. Together these priorities will help us **reduce difficulties around early diagnosis and support where diagnosis is uncertain.**

Taking a *shared responsibility* will *increase the probability of gaining more funding*, which is central to helping resolve most of our strategic priorities. In addition it will help us attack our key goals of: **increasing availability of specialist dementia care, reducing delays in accessing home care services, providing a more holistic and person centred approach to meeting integrated care needs, and resolving the inadequate choice of a variety of good quality long term care homes in all areas**.

Significant strategic priorities will be to *increase the quality of care in the private sector* and *broaden the range of accommodation options for people with dementia*. Delivery of these priorities will be supported by our **daring to review building based services and dispose of what**

(Continued)

(Continued)

isn't needed and build **YES BUILD what is needed**, which will help us **respond and manage the needs and impact of patients with dementia in general and community hospitals**.

However, more importantly success will help us to **resolve inadequate choice of a variety of good quality long term care homes in all areas**.

Our last key strategic focus is to *promote knowledge, skills and understanding among service providers, family carers and the public*, in order to help us **provide a more holistic and person centred approach to meeting integrated care needs and also respond and manage the needs and impact of patients with dementia in general and community hospitals**.

WHAT MIGHT BE WRONG WITH MAKING STRATEGY THROUGH ISSUE MANAGEMENT?

The Judgement Criteria Are Too Implicit?

The priorities are established without much explicit discussion of the outcome criteria – the goals, success criteria or objectives of the organisation. The process does not use explicit criteria against which the strategy priorities are judged. Therefore priorities are judged against one another and *implicit goals*. The implicit criteria that inform the judgement made by the group may derive too much from the structure of the issue network. However, this is not a risk as long as the structure of the map is used to identify *candidate* priorities and then subsequently managerial judgement is used.

Some goals are identified at the top of the network hierarchy – the heads. Heads are as close to goal outcomes as can be identified through considering the network of claims/issues. Implicit goals could be made explicit by continuously extending the hierarchy by asking what the head is expected to achieve – either by helping avoid disasters, or seeking to support aspirations.

This process of asking why the resolution of the issues is important is one contribution to *developing strategy through determining purpose* (see chapters 5 and 6 on strategy as purpose). By considering issue priorities as the basis for exploring purpose we discover emergent goals – the goals that are actually driving the organisation, not necessarily those we want, or those that are espoused by senior managers, or published in strategy documents.

Too Inward Facing?

Inevitably a focus on issues may be regarded as too inward facing. Although issues encompass the range of strengths, weaknesses, opportunities and threats (SWOT) according to what each participant sees as an issue, in practice there is a tendency to be alert to things that are worrying *within* the organisation. Building strategy from issue management is designed to recognise that managers use emotional energy on wanting to put right things that signal a potential for strategic disaster. These can often be dominated by problems of making an organisation work better – the culture, ways of doing things, ways of relating, gaining appropriate levels of resources, etc. Clearly there is nothing wrong with such a focus, but it might not encompass those aspects of strategy making that are typically regarded as important for creating a good strategy – 'blue sky thinking', customer orientation, the five forces of supplier power, barriers to entry, threat of substitutes, buyer power and degree of rivalry.[45] This is possibly a danger, but only if analyses such as Porter's five forces are regarded as preferential to open-ended judgement that can then be informed by such analyses, rather than the other way around.

An analysis of over 200 of our own interventions suggests that there is indeed an emphasis on internal issues that have strategic consequences and that these consequences are indeed of strategic importance. But, in addition to the internal focus, external opportunities and threats *are* addressed, *and* other strategic considerations are also raised.

However, it is likely that a coverage that is wider than just an internal focus relies, to some extent, on prompts from facilitators. Thus, the facilitator continuously monitors categories of issues in such a way that they are able to suggest that 'there is a focus on threats, but little on opportunities – is this an accurate picture?' or 'are there issues of supplier power that could seriously affect the future?' and so on. This prompting, or questioning, is done in a low key manner in order not to destroy the ownership and cathartic outcome that comes from managers working with the issues as they see them. To a great extent managers' judgement and wisdom is not at fault – they raise issues without necessarily having seen them within the categories proposed by management gurus. Rather the issues of managers are categorised with respect to why they matter – the consequences (or 'out-links').

Primarily approaching strategy from an issue management perspective acknowledges, and works with, the energy and natural inclinations of the managers.

Unreliable and Imprecise?

The issue statements made by participants are mostly under researched and not evidence-based, thus raising questions about the validity they have for making a good strategy. This unreliability and imprecision is often a matter of great concern to all participants and particularly facilitators. The forum's process is fast, statements are unrefined and each is not carefully evaluated, and causality is estimated and may be a reflection of an urban myth.

As a group works together with the network of issues, most, if not all, participants change their mind about the relative importance of the issues they see before them. Some of the claims they make are seen, by them, to be less significant than originally supposed and others become more central as they are seen within the context of other issues. There is never enough time to evaluate carefully each issue, or even a majority of the issues. Thus, an important aspect of strategy making is to focus evaluation and the need for evidence on what is a strategic priority. Not only is strategy about focus, but also strategy *making* is about focus – focusing energy and time on what is most important. Strategy is about the future – there will not always be reliable evidence about the future – thus, we must make *judgements* about how things will work when there can be no evidence.

As a group progresses with the forum their issue management map gradually focuses and becomes tighter. The language of the important issue statements is continuously in transition and causal links are validated (even if only through careful evaluation rather than empirical research). The emergent properties of the map suggest where to focus attention and the detailed analysis suggests areas for discussion and evaluation. Thus, the rough and ready initial maps are continuously refined. Undoubtedly they could be refined ad nauseam but a 'Pareto' approach is appropriate – get 80 per cent of it right in 20 per cent of the time!

As others[46] have noted, the symbolic use of analysis to deflect attention away from issues gives the impression of action. Adopting the symbolic analysis route may be the result of a group being unable to manage their social relationships and so failing to find ways of opening up the real issues.[47]

NEXT STEPS – EXTENDING THE SCOPE OF THE STRATEGY: LINKING TO OTHER STRATEGY MAKING FORUMS

Working with issues as the starting point for strategy making is designed to avoid taking an unrealistic and idealised view of the organisation and what it can achieve. Major strategic issues engage managers; their time is largely devoted to seeking to avoid possible future disasters, managing their own ambitions, protecting their own reputations, and ensuring projects are kept on track. Some issues are urgent, some are interesting, some are less or more strategic, and some are tedious but require immediate attention. If strategy making does not at least pay some attention to these dominant drivers of the organisation then the forum will be seen by the managers as not connecting with the real world. Strategic planning becomes something of no practical import – it is an idealised notion.

The issue management forum implicitly respects the history of the organisation. The forum reflects the organisation's ways of thinking and acting in practice. This process contrasts with statements espoused through written documents or well-rehearsed organisational goals and objectives. Dealing with live strategic issues is what drives the strategic future of the organisation. Issue surfacing gets closer than any other equivalent approach to understanding the organisation's embedded strategic future (emergent strategy).

It is usual for an issue management forum to generate considerable interest in further strategy exploration. The interest arises as much from participants as the manager-client, with participants interested in knowing what would usually be done next. This provides an opportunity to raise several possibilities, each of which can be undertaken in a half-day strategy forum.

Although we present several ring-fenced strategy making forums throughout this book, with a suggestion that each of them can be undertaken on their own or in any order, this first forum dealing with priority issues is typically the first step. Starting with what are regarded as major strategic issues is importantly cathartic and so releases energy that can be used where greater creativity, wisdom and general expertise is required.

The discussion with the manager-client about next steps can follow several avenues:

1   Developing a sense of direction and purpose – *goals system* exploration: developing strategy through issue management has assumed implicit business goals in prioritising the issues. It would make sense to have a clearer view about goals – as criteria through which issues can be re-prioritised. Reference to current organisational goals might be a first step in re-evaluating priorities. But, typically in seeking to translate a currently published set of goals into a coherent system of criteria, many legitimate queries are raised. Conflicting goals, missing goals and a missing logic of the system of goals (means to ends) are discovered.

    However, having a clear understanding about the nature of strategic goals and how they fit together is a worthwhile task in its own right. Thus, the next forum may be focused on exploring the nature of the existing goals system, and on understanding the goals implied by the priorities established in the issue management forum (each priority is then seen as implicitly avoiding attacking a goal or implicitly supporting a goal). The outcome of a goals system exploration establishes a revised goals system that fully attends to the need for a coherent goals system that emphasises an appropriate set of aspirations for a successful strategic future. Issues will almost undoubtedly be reprioritised to reflect better the goals.

    See chapters 5 and 6.

2   Strategy making through managing *competitive advantage* and seeking out new business: inevitably the issue management forum will have focused some attention on the problems of organising to

realise a successful strategic future. This internal focus is likely to have avoided addressing fully the ways in which the organisation has and uses distinctiveness that can deliver what the customer values in a manner that provides competitive advantage – even in the not-for-profit sector.

The internal focus is not likely to have explored fully the capabilities (individually or in combination) available to realise the successful strategic future. These capabilities or resources may be distinctive – offering clear customer value – or maybe simply be necessary in order to exist. Regardless it is important to be clear about what they are and how they support one another in order to be able to leverage competitive advantage.

A competitive advantage forum seeks to establish whether the resolution of the priority issues helps maintain and develop competitive advantage and discover the subtle and connected capabilities of the organisation. Issues will almost undoubtedly be reprioritised to reflect better the needs of competitive advantage. The forum is also likely to introduce new ideas about how to seek out new business that exploits distinctiveness.

See chapters 7 and 8.

3 Increasing the success of issue management through *careful stakeholder management*: many who have a stake in the strategic future of the organisation – stakeholders – will have been mentioned in the issue statements – both internal and external stakeholders. Some of these stakeholders will have a high degree of interest in how priority issues are to be addressed and some stakeholders will have significant power to shape the extent to which issues are resolved. Thus, the mention of a specific trade union shop steward implies an internal stakeholder with an interest in the possible outcomes of an issue's resolution. But the mention of a shop steward also implies the possible interest of the trade union itself. Moreover, the union is, as a stakeholder, likely to have immense power to influence how the issue is addressed. Similarly, another priority issue may mention a key competitor who is interested in tracking what the organisation is doing to strategically manage itself. The competitor may have resources and connections that make it able to respond powerfully to actions taken to resolve the priority issue. A stakeholder forum focuses usefully upon the bases of interest and power of key stakeholders, and so determines strategies for the better management of these stakeholders to increase the probability of the successful resolution of priority issues.

See chapters 9 and 10.

Each of these forums makes sense as a next step, and so a manager-client is able to choose to continue a strategy making process on an incremental basis without the need to plan a full scale approach.

NOTES

1 Raimond and Eden introduced this description (Raimond and Eden, 1990).
2 Paul Nutt in his book *Why Decisions Fail* refers to the way in which managers make 'claims' on the future by arguing for particular courses of action to be prioritised. Opening up the issue means the group can address problems of limiting the search (Nutt, 2002: 43). The complexity from conflicting claims means there will need to be a process to manage issue reconciliation. Failure to reconcile claims – negotiation – leads to poor ownership and poor implementation (see Nutt, 2002: 24–5).
3 Discovering issues, claims or dilemmas as core to strategy development is widely described in the literature about strategy and strategic decisions. Pettigrew (1977) argues that contextual backgrounds form dilemmas or issues which receive organisational attention and,

out of their partial resolution, evolves strategy. Claims define the 'arena of action' which should be explored, going beyond the initial claim and being reconciled in order to come to good strategic decisions (Nutt, 2002). Nutt and Backoff (1992) additionally argue that strategic responses are sought according to issues raised.

4   Consider for example Henry Mintzberg's 1975 article in the Harvard Business Review – 'The Manager's Job: Folklore and Fact' (Mintzberg, 1975). Also, there is a relationship between issues and action that relates to strategy delivery (Dutton and Duncan, 1987).

5   Weick (1979).

6   Lindblom (1959).

7   'The theoretical and conceptual commitment to the notion of intersubjectivity of knowl-edge, which guides our work with teams is conceptually derived from phenomenology (see for example Bittner, 1973), the sociality of defining situations, and the work of cog-nitive psychologists such as Kelly (1955) and Neisser (1976). Here man is seen as con-structing his individual reality according to the psychological frameworks he has evolved to make sense of and act in his world, rather than perceiving some objective reality. In particular we find helpful the succinct aphorism of Thomas and Thomas (1928) where if "men define situations as real they are real in their consequences". As Ball (1972) has said "what Thomas is basically arguing here … is that … in order to understand social conduct we must look … to the meanings of situations and the situated meanings within them as they are phenomenologically experienced by the actors located within them" … but this is not to suggest that meanings and realities are not shared. We see a dialectic between the individuality of reality and reality as a "social construction" (see particularly Berger and Luckmann, 1966) in which meanings are socially sustained and experienced as social facts (Silverman, 1970) and it is this dialectic which gives rise to the complicated notion of intersubjectivity' (Eden, Jones, Sims and Smithin, 1981).

8   See Eden, Jones, Sims and Smithin (1981).

9   Most organisations demonstrate patterns of decision making, thinking and action, often 'taken-for-granted' ways of working and problem solving coming from the habits, history and 'hand-me-downs' of the organisation's culture. Whether the organisation members are aware of this *or not*, even if they define themselves as 'muddling through' rather than acting strategically, such enacted patterns inevitably take the organisation in one strate-gic direction rather than another. Organisations do not act randomly, without purpose. It is this process of going in one strategic direction rather than another that we call 'emergent strategising'.

Any organisation, big or small, *will* be acting strategically whether the emergent strat-egising is quite unselfconscious, or rather more deliberate, as, for example, when there is a knowing reinforcement of the existing ways of working by key members of the organisation in pursuit of particular outcomes or purpose. In either case the emergent strategic direc-tion (Mintzberg, 1987), and its implicit or explicit goals and purpose, are detectable and, to a greater or lesser degree, amenable to change. For some organisations we can envisage this implicit or 'emergent' strategy to be best *for that particular organisation*. Emergent strategis-ing is a key concept.

We thus relate the notion of strategy, and so strategic management, to a number of important statements about organisations:

Policy making is typically a never ending process of successive steps in which continual nibbling is a substitute for a good bite. (Lindblom, 1980)

> Emergent strategy means, literally, *unintended order*. Strategy [is] *pattern in action*. (Mintzberg (1990) our emphases)

It follows that we see effective strategy as *a coherent set of individual discrete actions in support of a system of goals, and which are supported as a portfolio by a self-sustaining critical mass, or momentum, of opinion in the organisation.*

For many organisations the nature of strategy will be most contingently influenced by the chief executive – their personality, skills and personal aspirations. Indeed, some organisations are driven by the single-minded entrepreneurial capability of this one person. While the chief executive may be described as a 'man (or a woman) of vision', the vision often will not be articulated, but rather will be detected through their style and the pattern of entrepreneurial steps taken. In some ways this is the epitome of an emergent strategy. Patterns can be detected, but only just, opportunism rules, and 'muddling through with success' could be an appropriate description of the organisation. To insist that such an organisation should have a well-defined strategy may kill strategic success – as long as the chief executive remains in post. Similarly a charismatic manager-client may drive an organisation by creating entrepreneurial energies in others. This energy is channelled by following the merest of hints at strategic direction that emit from the manager-client as he or she stamps their personality on the organisation. The chief executive also often has the power simply to say there will be no strategic management.

Pure emergent strategising – that is, a process of letting the future emerge without appreciating that this is what is happening – is not strategy making. However, when a management team appreciates that embedded ways of working are determinants of a strategic future, and the organisation *deliberately chooses not to understand and reflect upon these patterns*, then the strategy of the organisation is a *deliberate emergent strategy*.

10 Weick (1983).
11 Regner's (Regner, 2008) view of inductive strategy making at the periphery of organisations (as opposed to deductive central approaches) resonates with this point – that relevant experiential knowledge from implementation/managing in practice can be an important source of strategic opportunity identification.
12 For a discussion of the notion of issue selling, see Dutton and Ashford (1993).
13 Logical incrementalism in this context derives from Quinn (1980) and 'muddling through' from Lindblom (1959).
14 See Dutton, Ashford, O'Neill and Lawrence (2001).
15 The notion of a recipe has been used particularly to introduce the idea of an industry having an entrenched and emergent way of working – similar costing systems, ways of thinking, etc. (Spender, 1989). Here we use the term in a similar way to suggest that organisations coalesce around a particular recipe for successful operations.
16 See chapter 2 in our discussion about groups in organisations.
17 Weick (1995).
18 Reflecting the notion of 'bounded rationality' – that 'people act intentionally rational, but only limitedly so' (Simon, 1957: xxiv).
19 See 'hidden profiles' research in Stasser and Titus (1987).
20 We discuss in detail the powerful notion of procedural justice in the chapter on groups (chapter 2). The significance of procedural justice to an issue management strategy forum is that we need to promote circumstances in which fairness facilitates the surfacing of genuinely held different perspectives.
21 See Dutton and Ashford (1993) for the notion of issue selling. However, in their paper, despite a more general initial overture, issue selling is more directed at managing up. In

part issue selling relates to 'sensegiving' (e.g. Gioia and Chittipeddi, 1991) – the process of attempting to influence the sensemaking and meaning construction of others towards a preferred redefinition of organisational reality.

22   As Gallimore (2010) has argued: 'There are different perspectives on how strategic issues should be incorporated into a strategy process (Dutton and Duncan, 1987) including formal planning processes (King, 1982), subsystems to address specific strategic issues (Quinn, 1978) and managing agendas of strategic issues (Ansoff, 1980; Stacey, 1993; Langley, Mintzberg et al., 1995). However, although their importance is acknowledged, it is difficult to identify strategic issues, being variously described as controversial, ambiguous, uncertain, incomplete, equivocal, ill defined and conflicting (King, 1982; Dutton, Fahey and Narayanan, 1983; Dutton, 1986; Dutton and Ottensmeyer, 1987; Dutton, Walton and Abrahamson, 1989; Bansal, 2003). They are also usually found in combination with and interconnected to other issues (Thomas, Shankster and Mathieu, 1994) and simple linear models provide a poor description of how issues are addressed (Bansal, 2003). Appreciating an issue combination containing a large number of issues is difficult since individuals can only pay attention to a limited number of issues (Miller, 1956) and their information processing capacity is limited (Dutton, Walton and Abrahamson, 1989).' This view is fundamental to the basis of this chapter on developing strategy from the management of priority issues.

23   Teece, Pisano and Shuen (1997) suggest that the notion of path dependency is that history matters and that bygones are rarely bygones. Thus a firm's previous investments and its repertoire of routines (history) constrain its future behaviour. See also Ambrosini, Bowman and Collier (2009).

24   For more on the role of crisis in strategic change see Kotter (1995).

25   One of the characteristics Paul Nutt identified in his research (2002: 33).

26   Research on distribution of issues raised across a group, for example, Shaw (1961).

27   Using 'oval mapping' to develop causal maps can be effective, even though they are poor as a 'transitional object' because sticky labels are rarely rewritten and links are too difficult to change regularly. However, see Ackermann and Eden (2001b); Ackermann and Eden (2010b); Bryson, Ackermann, Eden and Finn (1995: Resource B); Bryson, Ackermann, Eden and Finn (2004); Eden and Ackermann (2001a).

28   Group-think and the need for social identity explains this phenomenon. See Janis (1972).

29   Mangham and Overington (1987); Winograd and Flores (1986).

30   Pettigrew (1977).

31   Causal maps are expressions of belief about how the world can be changed. As long as the causal arrows express properly means-ends relationships then the map constructed will be amenable to analysis (Eden, 2004) that can reveal central issues, potent actions, high-level outcomes, etc.

32   See Eisenhardt and Martin (2000) who refer to commonality of factors in an industry but idiosyncrasy of detail in firm-specific strategic challenges and organisational processes.

33   The psychology of personal constructs (Kelly, 1955) emphasises that we are all actively seeking to 'make sense' of our worlds. Karl Weick in particular focuses on sense making in organisations (Weick, 1995).

34   Equivocality in negotiation oils the process allowing face saving and a shift in views without seeing it as a shift.

35   Argyris and Schon (1974) introduced this distinction between what we say and how we act.

36   See Shaw, Ackermann and Eden (2003).

37   Nutt (2002: 62).

38   Intersubjectivity refers to accepting that there are different perspectives that overlap.

39 Eden, Jones, Sims and Smithin (1981: 43).
40 Complexity and the ability to address it, rather than pretend it does not exist, is an important component of strategy making. But, what do we mean by complex situations? Strategic issues that are complex are made up of many problems. Some have referred to these situations as 'wicked problems' (Rittel and Webber, 1973) and 'messy' problems (Ackoff, 1981), and others call them a problematique (Ozbekhan, 1974). Wicked problems are a network of interacting and interconnected decision areas (Friend and Hickling, 1987). The network of strategic issues is a network of interacting strategy arenas.
41 Nutt (2002: 76).
42 Nutt (2002: 58).
43 Hogarth (1987).
44 See Richardson (1991) for a treatise on 'feedback thought', and Forrester (1961) for the original writing on translating the concept of feedback control in engineering to the management domain, and Sterman (2000) for a more recent well-established reference work to the field of system dynamics, and Warren (2002) that sets dynamics within the context of strategic management. Peter Senge's (Senge, 1990) popular book – *The Fifth Discipline* – also sets out the significance of feedback in thinking about organisations. Eden, Jones and Sims (1983) consider the exploration of feedback loops within the context of problem construction.
45 Porter (1980).
46 Brewer (1981) and Feldman and March (1981).
47 Whittington, Molloy, Mayer and Smith (2006).

Further Reading

Ackoff, R. L. 1981. The Art and Science of Mess Management. *Interfaces*, 11: 20–26.
Nutt, P. C. 2002. *Why Decisions Fail: Avoiding the Blunders and Traps that Lead to Debacles*. San Francisco: Berrett-Koehler Inc.
Pettigrew, A. 1977. Strategy Formulation as a Political Process. *International Studies of Management and Organization*, 7: 78–87.
Rosenhead, J. and Mingers, J. (eds). 2001. *Rational Analysis in a Problematic World Revisited*. Chichester: Wiley.

4

THE ISSUE MANAGEMENT FORUM

Fran Ackermann and Colin Eden

WHAT DOES AN ISSUE MANAGEMENT STRATEGY FORUM LOOK AND FEEL LIKE?

What Does it Look Like to a Participant When You Walk in the Room?

We were seated in a semicircle facing a large projector screen and the facilitator was at the front to the right.

The facilitator was using a laptop computer that was connected to a projector displaying a blank white screen.

What Happened?

We were asked for our own views about what needed to be done to make us successful in the long term. It was nice for me to be presented with an opportunity to express fully my views. Each of us, in turn, was given a chance to have our say, and also listen to the views of others made easier by seeing all the views captured on the screen. Following this, we looked at the interactions between the views surfaced – how each of the views related to one another (using arrows) – and I was surprised that my views impacted the views of others in more ways than I had realised. I was also pleased to see that many of my concerns were similar but, in a number of cases, importantly different to those of others.

To help structure all the different views, the facilitator was pretty good at moving the individual views around the screen so that we could see that some of the views were more tightly integrated than others. One of the interesting insights was that a number of the more operationally oriented views turned out to have important long term impacts – something we had not considered fully before (or at least not as a group).

Gradually after using the different bundles of interacting views to guide our debate, we seemed to agree, as a group, about what was most important for us to do something about and we reached better agreement than usual about what things we needed to focus on. This agreement was not really a strategy of the sort I'm accustomed to, but certainly a basis for taking key actions forward that would deliver what we wanted to achieve in the long term, so I suppose it was more of a practical strategy.

We finished up with a written statement which explained why we were doing particular strategic activities and the rationale for their being a focus for our energy. It was useful to have this concise version take-away that reflected the work we had done.

What Did it Feel Like?

At first, I found it a bit odd – having the opportunity to talk about and then *see my views on a screen where everyone else could read them*. I got the feeling that as a result of them being captured and publicly displayed others took more notice of what I said – perhaps because they had to read them to consider where to put links between their contributions and mine (see box 4.1).

Box 4.1   A Participant's View (from a Small Start-up Company with Seven Participants Attending)

At first we were sceptical about undertaking such an activity. Key members of the business were required to attend the event and if there was no tangible benefit at the end it would have wasted time. However, the company found the process extremely rewarding.

It was also interesting to see how the 'pictures' of the statements and links seemed to fall into different 'bundles' of material. Significantly most of the bundles included actions that had implications across all of our different functional areas. I felt that this 'bundling' helped manage the mass of information that was unfolding in front of us. We could begin to explore the big picture without feeling too overwhelmed. That said, I would have to say that it was all more complex than any of us had originally supposed – probably the result of us not taking such a parochial view of what should be done as is often the case.

I was surprised, though, how none of the agreements we made about where to focus our energy involved just one of us in its delivery – it made me realise how much of a team effort this was going to be. It showed just how much some of the actions I needed to take to address the priorities were impacted by those of my colleagues and vice versa. If you like, the picture was giving powerful clues as to how to conduct the project management of implementing actions that have long term consequences.

What Did I Go Away With?

We were all given copies of the pictures showing what we'd agreed to do and why. I could see how important it was to have a clear view of exactly what outcomes we expected from agreed strategies. In a couple of hours' work we'd looked at all of the views, explored how they impacted one another, discussed where to focus our energy and started getting agreements about who'd take responsibility for what. We did need another meeting to tidy this up though and give ourselves time to feel confident about what we'd agreed.

However, it did seem to me that the pictures, showing the statements and arrows linking them, would not mean much to anyone who was not there, as they could be opaque and would look too complex to others. I think you need to be there, listen to the conversations, and get familiar with the process of building a network of interacting views, to fully appreciate the value of the resultant pictures. To help manage the cryptic nature of the pictures, we produced a draft statement of what we had agreed, written in normal sentences and paragraphs. The next step will be to write it again more carefully so that others understand fully what it means without losing the richness.

Was it Worthwhile?

I was surprised at how much we got through in a short time, and that we got a deliverable at the end – a product that was, in effect, the 'minutes' of the meeting written by us all in real time. The session was much more productive than our usual meetings and certainly had us more involved in working together. The product certainly gave us a sense of focus, and that is what we'd hoped for. It was obviously only part of a draft strategy and we needed to do some more work as a team, but it is something we can use in practice, and my impression is that we all bought into it!

RESOURCES

- 1–2 hour meeting of facilitator and manager-client (to agree the design of the forum); this time is still necessary when the facilitator and manager-client are the same person as the design is still required.
- 1 hour setup by the facilitator.
- 2–3 hours of group work – it is usual to complete this forum in half a day but it can be done in as little as 2 hours.
- Decision Explorer® (the software that captures the views and links) loaded onto a laptop, and a small table positioned so that the facilitator can see the public screen and the group.
- 1280×1024 pixel data projector (this resolution works best, as it permits more material to be explored at one time).
- Large public screen.
- Room with chairs (preferably on castors) – one for each participant.

MAPPING OUT STRATEGIC SUCCESS: STRATEGY AS PRIORITISATION

Designing the Forum

Script for: The manager-client needs to feel comfortable

Tasks:

1 Craft the 'starter question' (focal point) to be addressed to start the forum: 15–20 minutes
2 Agree whether to focus on a specific time horizon and, if so, what the time horizon is to be: 10–15 minutes
3 Agree participant composition: 20–25 minutes

Deliverable: starter question and participant list
Script timing: minimum 45 minutes, expected 60 minutes

Task 1: Craft the 'Starter Question' (Focal Point) to be Addressed to Start the Forum

Although managers typically have little difficulty in being able to talk about their views on organisational issues/concerns, having some clarity about the scope (boundaries) of the task assists the group by reducing the amount of uncertainty felt by participants regarding what type of issue should and should not be surfaced. The starter question helps do this and also provides clarity about who the strategy is for (that is, is it focused on the department, division or whole organisation?). Additionally, crafting the starter question carefully usually helps the manager-client refine their own thinking about the purpose of the forum (see box 4.2).

Box 4.2   Designing a Starter Question

When working with a not-for-profit organisation that had been formed from the merger of two existing organisations (one dealing with counselling and the other family mediation), and wanting to develop a strategy to manage the many strategic issues facing the newly created body, the below question was presented.

'What are the opportunities and strategic issues facing our new organisation in seeking to achieve our given mandate over the next 4–5 years?'

The starter question is key to providing clarity regarding the objective and content of the forum, getting it right is paramount, and so:

- **Avoid questions that elicit a 'yes' or 'no' response**. For example the question, 'should we move into China?' will limit the number and range of issues surfaced. Instead, try wording the question so that it opens up the potential for a range of perspectives, for example 'what are the issues and opportunities we face if we move into China?' or 'how do we move into China successfully?'
- **Consider whether to explicitly include both positive and negative elements within the question**. The word 'issue' has, for many, a negative connotation and therefore by deliberately designing the question to encourage a more optimistic stance, those involved are encouraged to think more broadly about the topic. The example in box 4.2 provides an illustration of this by including the word 'opportunities' within the question.
- **Ensure that the wording is not inappropriately jargon-full**. Avoid using terms that might not be understood by all attending. This is particularly the case when working across departments, divisions or organisations – as one person's jargon is another person's everyday language. Also, do not use inappropriate 'business school' jargon – even the word strategy may be jargon in some settings.
- **Don't worry about taking time to get the question right**. It typically takes longer than expected.

Task 2: Agree Whether to Focus on a Specific Time Horizon and, if so, What the Time Horizon Is to Be

Determine Whether to Include a Time Horizon   Including a time horizon within the starter question may assist in identifying a realistic scope for the forum (see box 4.2). However, when discussing with the manager-client whether to impose a time horizon, determine if it is necessary or desirable to have one. In some situations, for example where strategy is being made under crisis conditions, the natural inclination of managers is to focus on a relatively short time horizon and so ignore the long term ramifications of short term actions. Encouraging a longer term perspective may ensure that creating a sustainable direction is considered. In any event, it is highly likely that long and short term issues will be surfaced in relation to whatever time horizon is set. Thus, giving a time horizon of four to five years will elicit issues that appear to have two year consequences, and also elicit issues with eight year consequences. As the issues are linked later in the forum short term issues may become or contribute towards long term issues and so long term issues are the consequences of short term issues!

The nature of the environment within which the organisation is operating will also influence the decision to include a time horizon or not. For example, in fast moving environments, such as computing or telecommunications, it may be best to focus the scope of strategy making to just two to three years in order to make it realistic to those involved in the forum. In contrast, many of those working in not-for-profit organisations might consider longer time horizons (for example three to five years).

Finally, the tenure of many managers is an important consideration when making the decision. Working beyond a five year horizon means that, for many, they will have left the organisation, or been promoted, before the end of the designated time horizon. This means that it may be problematic for the facilitator to pay attention to the notion that strategy demands very long term considerations as compared to the reality of the time horizon over which the managers are expected to deliver successful strategic changes.

Task 3: Agree Participant Composition

Decide Who Should Attend the Issue Management Forum   Ensuring the inclusion of participants with differing perspectives will help ensure that key issues are not missed; therefore, consider involving participants with relevant expertise and information as well as those responsible for the delivery of strategy. In drawing out a range of different expert views, consider those who are in different discipline groups, and those who are familiar with external as well as internal issues. An additional benefit from involvement in the forum is an opportunity to learn about the department or organisation as a whole (through the focus on interacting issues). Thus the involvement of new managers and fast-track personnel may be appropriate as it will assist them in getting up to speed (see box 4.3).

Box 4.3   Developing a Level of Comfort for Both Facilitator and Manager-Client

AIM to have the leader say: 'I feel more comfortable about letting this forum happen and handing control over to you'.

'Now I understand why looking at strategic issues is a good first step in *getting the team involved in developing a strategy*'.

AIM for the facilitator to think: 'I have a good feel of some of the issues that might be difficult to manage because of the group dynamics'.

One of the 'invisible' benefits of an issue management forum is that it will result in participants gaining some emotional relief (a cathartic experience) from sharing their concerns in a structured and supportive environment. This benefit may have specific implications for who should be involved. Where there are agitated, angry and powerful potential participants their case for being included may be stronger than traditional logic would imply.

Given the specific needs for encompassing multiple perspectives, it is tempting to continually increase the number of participants attending the issue management forum. However, research on effective group size consistently suggests five to seven participants is best. While there will be occasions when very much larger groups will be necessary, for example in some multinational organisations the top team can be 150 presidents/vice-presidents, and it may be essential to include all of them, this is not ideal. In these circumstances the use of carefully designed sub-groups may be necessary (for example, 30 sub-groups of five people, organised by expertise). However, because the forum's purpose is to open up and discuss issues, in practice this will mean that a typical forum includes 8 to 16 participants. For a first time facilitator, starting with around five participants increases the likelihood of managing a successful forum.

See also chapter 11 *Facilitating Groups in Strategy Making.*

Deliverable: starter question with possible timeline and participant composition
Timing from forum start: 45 minutes minimum, expected 60 minutes

---

Getting Issues and Concerns Out On the Table

Script for: Managers become aware of the bigger picture

Tasks:

1 Setup for the forum: 5 minutes
2 Introduce the issue management forum process and carry out the first phase of issue surfacing: 15–25 minutes
3 Review material and conduct another round of issue surfacing: 10–25 minutes
4 Develop and review thematic clusters: 15–20 minutes
5 Consider issues from different stakeholder positions (optional): 10–20 minutes

Deliverable: a printout of issues surfaced and the emergent strategic themes
Script timing: minimum 55 minutes, expected 95 minutes

Task 1: Setup for the Forum

Display the Starter Question   Either **write up the starter question** on a flip-chart sheet and/or place it in a central position on a Decision Explorer® view to be projected onto the public screen.

If using Decision Explorer® it is also useful to **set up some different styles** in advance so that they can be selected easily when necessary. Styles comprise different fonts and colours allowing categorisation of the contributed views (for example, identifying candidate priorities or emergent goals).

See Appendix: Using Causal Mapping Software: Decision Explorer®, 2.4 Creating and Using Styles

Task 2: Introduce the Issue Management Forum Process and Carry Out the First Phase of Issue Surfacing

Set the Scene   The primary objective of the introduction is to **put the group at ease** with the forum setting and **provide a review of agenda, purpose and process**. In addition, it is important to **provide an introduction to the initial issue management tasks** – the 'rules of the game' and the starter question – both of which provide participants with a clear set of guidelines for behaviour:

- **Encourage participants to use their judgement to surface their experience and wisdom as well as hard evidence**. Remind the group that the aim of the session is to **elicit issues that are perceived to have a strategic or long term impact on success**. Encourage all to contribute, and be open, as this is important for ensuring the robustness of the strategy as well as ownership.
- **Initially consider, in a non-judgemental manner, all points of view** (see box 4.4). As is often the case in meetings, considerable amounts of time can be spent debating different possible meanings of particular statements, sometimes apparently unproductively. The issue surfacing process is designed to **allow for diversity and inclusivity** by encouraging many meanings to be captured rather than, at this stage, expending time trying to resolve which the 'right' one is. These subtle differences in opinion may trigger further issue statements and may turn out to be more different than first thought. Evaluation comes later in the forum, where the discussion is focused upon those aspects that begin to emerge as really mattering for developing strategy. Making it clear that this *modus operandi* is to be applied to all participants helps ensure more equal participation. Remember, strategy is about focus, but also making strategy is about focusing valuable time on what emerges as really mattering.

Box 4.4   Example of an Opening Script

All of you believe there are important strategic issues facing the organisation. We want to allow all of you to have the fullest possible opportunity to (a) speak out, (b) listen to others, (c) think about what you want to say, (d) react to others, (e) build off what others say, and to do this in a short time.

- **Explain to participants that the aim is to become aware of the bigger picture**.

Introduce the Starter Question   Once these 'rules of the game' are established, **introduce the starter question** to the group. If the question has been written on a flip-chart sheet, it can be attached to the wall and kept in clear view throughout the forum. If using Decision Explorer®, reveal the question during the introduction rather than having it showing when participants arrive, and have a clearly differentiated style (colour and font) for the question as this helps retain its prominence as other material is developed on the screen.

See Appendix: Using Causal Mapping Software: Decision Explorer®, 2.1 Using Views

It is important at this stage to **check whether all the participants are clear in their understanding of the starter question** *and* why it is an appropriate question to start the forum. However, refrain from extensive arguments about the exact requirements that follow from the starter question – discussion about what is exactly meant by, for example, 'long term' is unhelpful, rather accept vagueness.

Provide a Brief Description of What an Issue Might Be   A question often raised during the early stages of issue surfacing is 'What is an issue?' Issues may be seen as past, present or anticipated events or circumstances, internal or external, which cause some concern for the future (either as problems or potentially missed opportunities). As such issues are evaluative in nature – for example *something is performing badly, processes are not working properly, opportunities are being missed* (see box 4.5). Moreover, as can be seen from these examples, many issues are negatively construed – they are identified because they are 'attacking' implicitly or explicitly some desired outcome, or expected to result in a disaster.

Box 4.5   Examples of Issue Statements

Falling sales of iron ore in the China market; marketing is losing too many of its good staff; losing benefit of developments in new production processes.

Encourage participants, where possible, to **use around 6 to 15** words per contribution. More than 15 words will usually encompass two issues, less than six words might make the issue cryptic to others and often miss out expressing the evaluative aspect of the issue, for example, stating an issue as 'HR', where there is no indication of what the issue is about. The issue may be 'HR too slow in dealing with applications for jobs', or 'HR do not help us recruit the best staff', etc. Added value from the issue surfacing task arises from providing sufficient detail to the wording (rather than contributing a headline of one to two words). Single words or very short statements may result in alternative contributions not being made. This is because a summary issue statement made by one of the participants is seen by another participant to be the same as a statement they might have proffered. In these circumstances two different views are missed because they are presumed to be the same.

Stress the need to **focus on surfacing strategic issues and concerns** – those activities or events that are potentially attacking or supporting organisational aspirations. The aim is to surface wisdom and experience rather than off-the-wall ideas. The process is not about brainstorming or lateral thinking.

Carry out the First Issue Surfacing Phase, Making Sure That all Participants Contribute Going around the group asking each participant for a view (a 'round robin') ensures all participants feel the process is fair (see box 4.6).

Box 4.6   Example Instructions

What I am going to do is ask each of you in turn to come up with one significant issue. I will try to record this as best I can. Let me know if I get it wrong.

When prompting for contributions, **encourage participants to contribute in a 'yes and' mode** rather than a 'yes but' mode. This will increase the likelihood of surfacing a more comprehensive range of issues as participants feel less evaluated, and so open up due to the more collaborative atmosphere. This can be furthered by asking participants to **avoid suggesting that issues be removed** stressing that this part of the forum aims to be as divergent as possible.

Watch for too much group conformity (what is referred to as group think – see chapter 2) where, in order to sustain group cohesion, all the issues being surfaced appear to be around the same area(s) or similar in nature/disposition and false agreement arises as members of the group are protected from significant disagreements. If this appears to be the case, challenge the group to consider team cohesion as related to exploiting the benefits of different perspectives.

As each of the issue statements is made, **capture the issues on the Decision Explorer®️ screen** so that all participants are able to continuously keep it in mind. **Keep as much as possible to the language of the participant** as this will ensure ownership and will ensure that the contribution reflects their views, not your own (that is, not those of the facilitator). The screen acts as a continuously changing organisational memory.

Don't worry if most of the issues are expressed negatively – this tends to reflect the demands on managers where their life is dominated with the felt need to deal with problems and potential disasters. Once the immediate flurry of contributions has slowed, encourage participants to think of more positively oriented issues.

Task 3: Review Material and Conduct Second Phase of Issue Surfacing

Review the Issues   While it is important to avoid overwhelming participants with too many different demands, once participants have become familiar with the surfacing process, **spend a little time returning to the coding guidelines** to ensure effective wording of statements. Using examples from the first tranche of issues can help to ensure clarity, comprehension and most importantly the action orientation that derives from including the evaluative phrase.

Below are some guidelines that have been found to be useful when prompting participants to elaborate the issue statements:

- Remind participants to **stick to one issue statement for each contribution**. This will help when the forum moves to linking the issues (where the group will recognise that issues often impact upon one another). It will also help make clearer what the specific issue is about. Where issue statements have the words 'to' or 'through' or 'because' within the text separate them into two – the connector word implies causal links between the two parts of the statement. For example, the issue statement noting that 'the department is experiencing falling sales because distributors are going out of business' implies two issues that are causally linked in a means-end manner – 'distributors going out of business' is believed to cause 'falling sales'. It is important to keep the separated statements adjacent on the screen.
- Aim to **reword issues so that they are more actionable**. This in essence means taking the issue, for example 'poor understanding of the customer' and converting it to 'avoid poor understanding of the customer'. Include a verb in the statement. An action orientation focuses the group on strategy as change, as action. It is important to note that the insertion of a verb does not imply agreement to act, but rather implies possible action. However, recognise that in some instances the issue statement reflects a statement of history or fact and so cannot easily be modified with a verb.

- As much as possible **avoid prescriptive words** such as 'should', 'ought', 'need' as these can inhibit negotiation and openness and add little in the way of additional meaning. They will also have an adverse effect when trying to connect the issues together (as carried out later on in the forum).

These guidelines are not rules for their own sake but rather to encourage an action orientation to strategy. Participants quickly 'get the hang' of the rules because they prove to be helpful. While there will be cases where the statements don't always meet the rules, typically even these statements will be edited naturally to conform to the rules as the forum unfolds.

See examples in figures 4.1a and 4.1b – part of an initial exploration – showing an example of before and after the review (task 3). Note the changes to the language, for example, statement 10 has had the word 'must' removed and statement 8 has been provided with an action orientation. Also note that statement 7 has been revised to highlight (written in upper case) a particular aspect to make the emphasis clear.

A significant benefit from the early review of the contributions – particularly their wording – is that participants will **become familiar with the material already captured** and begin to see whether and how their issues compare and relate to the views of others.

Surface Deeper Issues   The review of the issue statements consequently stimulates further thoughts that tend to lead to the surfacing of deeper considerations and **go beyond the everyday scripts** that have been presented many times before (see boxes 4.6 and 4.7).

Box 4.7   Example of Surfacing Deeper Considerations

An issue regarding *too many customer complaints about projects being completed late* might give rise to further issues regarding other forms of customer complaint as well as further issues relating to the project being late etc.

Conducting the second, and following, round robins also captures responses to the material shown on the screen by allowing participants to view and elaborate or express alternative views, but without simply stating that they agree or disagree. Therefore **encourage clarification (not evaluation) of issue wording** so that further material can be surfaced.

Use the extended issue surfacing phase to continue to **encourage contributions from all participants**. It also stimulates a wider coverage of views across the emerging themes, and therefore greater ownership. This begins the process of negotiation as better understanding of the issues unfolds and all are expected to feel the process is fair.

The second and subsequent phases of surfacing issues also provide a useful time to **ensure that both internal and external perspectives** have been taken. A cursory analysis of the data emerging might suggest that there has been a concentration of attention to threats, ignoring opportunities, or a focus on weaknesses and ignoring strengths (**SWOT**). This analysis is informal and should not imply that there must be coverage of all of the elements of SWOT. Similarly, a cursory analysis with respect to **Porter's Five Forces** can prompt the facilitator to ask gently whether the group might have missed important perspectives on their strategic future (see box 4.8 on page 77). It is imperative that jargon terms are not used with the group, but rather the concepts and techniques help the facilitator to encourage the group in a useful

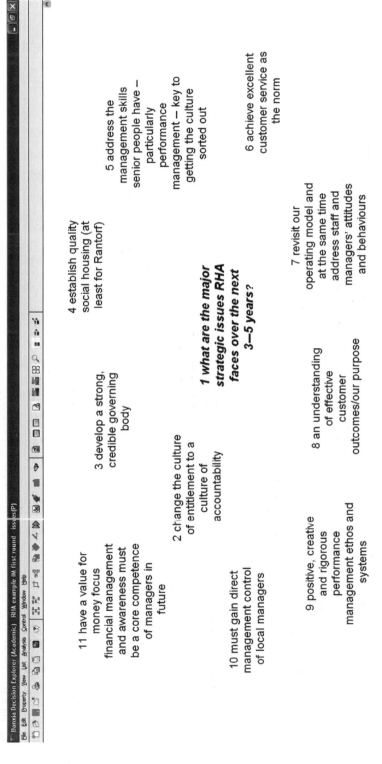

Figure 4.1a   First Part of an Initial Dump Before Wording Changes

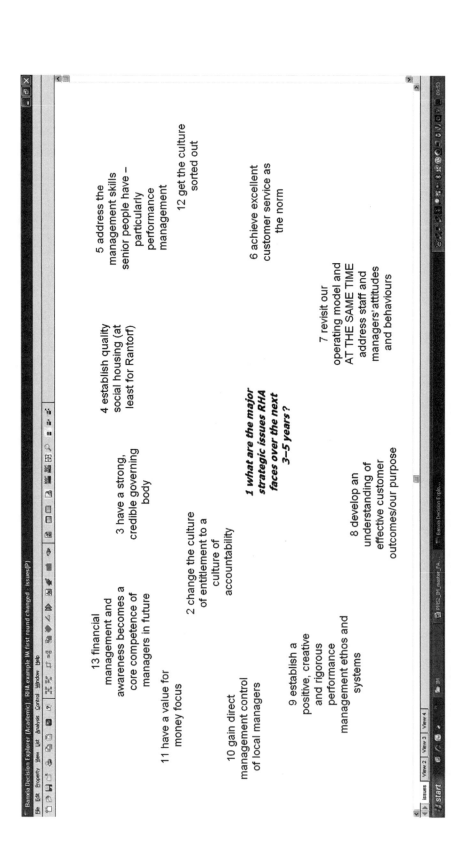

Figure 4.1b First Part of an Initial Dump After Wording Changes

way. Typically by this stage, with a group of around 5 to 6 participants, around 15 to 20 issues will have been surfaced.

Box 4.8   Example of Checking for Missing Issues

A recently formed public sector organisation was considering its strategic direction and had just completed surfacing their issues when one of its members commented, 'we haven't considered any of the issues concerning patients – shouldn't we do so?' This stimulated others to note that they also hadn't thought about other key constituencies and that it would be worth adding their views of the pertinent issues to the picture. A flurry of further issues suddenly emerged.

Task 4: Develop and Review Thematic Clusters

Either during, or once the initial flood of issues has significantly slowed, the facilitator begins to **move the issue statements into thematic clusters** (with space between the different clusters). This activity helps the group begin to make sense of the growing body of material and not feel overwhelmed, and it will encourage further contributions to be made (too much unstructured material can be off putting). By moving the issues into clusters it is also possible to avoid participants' tendency to stop contributing material when they feel the space on the screen has been 'filled up'. The clustered material also reveals further areas for contributions as the process of clustering helps reveal to participants potential missing themes. Additionally, by introducing to the group the possible thematic clusters the facilitator is able to provide the means for each participant to further listen to the views of others.

Participants tend to read the statements in each cluster in order to comment on the 'validity' of the clusters formed by the facilitator.

Building and roughly labelling clusters into themes helps manage the complexity of the unfolding material as well as elicit more issues. Some guidelines for helping with this clustering process are:

- **Don't worry if, initially, you can't see any clusters forming** as the material is surfaced. This is why waiting until the initial flood has slowed is usually best – having enough material to work with helps – it usually takes a little time to see the patterns emerging.
- **Be prepared to change the clusters** if alternative and better clusters emerge. This might mean breaking down a big cluster into two or three sub-clusters (see box 4.9).

Box 4.9   Example of Breaking Down Clusters

When working with a Passenger Transport System team, there emerged a very large cluster on communications. While having a cluster on communications wasn't unusual in this organisation (or indeed most!), the size of it was. However, as more material was surfaced and participants explained some of the content, it became clear that there were in reality three different forms of communication. There was firstly communication within the organisation itself. This was separate

(Continued)

(Continued)

from communication between the Transport System and other transport providers e.g. bus companies. Finally there was also a theme about communication between the Transport System and the general public. By making three clusters, participants commented that for the first time they began to get a handle on the strategic implications of different communications arenas.

- **Put those issues that don't seem to fit obviously into an existing cluster into a 'query' cluster**. The contents of this cluster usually sort themselves out during the latter stage of the clustering process as the process of examining each cluster in more depth reveals the 'location' of these issues.
- **Keep an open mind** – don't get too fixated on early clusters.
- **Don't get too concerned with the clusters being 'absolutely right'**, try to get them into rough bundles of related material. Encourage participants to suggest alternative clusters. When moving to the linking stage, the clusters will change. The purpose of the initial clustering is to provide a summary of progress so far.
- **Structure the clusters so that they can be visualised as 'tear drop' shaped** (see figure 4.2) with those more detailed statements at the bottom of the cluster and the broader outcome-oriented issues at the top. Rearrange the issue statements so that the very broad-based outcomes are at the top of the cluster. Then place those more detailed issues further down (but again don't worry about getting this absolutely right, when working through them the group will provide help). Placing statements into tear drop clusters will also facilitate the next stage of linking issues.
- **Provide a quick overview of the clusters or themes** as this is a good way of giving participants a means of making sense of what has surfaced (see box 4.10 and box 4.11). Clustering helps participants and the facilitator begin to manage the complexity of so much material and provides them with a clear summary for this part of the forum. Clustering can either be carried out during a break or refined in the break.

Box 4.10   Example of Reviewing Material

A possible commentary from the facilitator on reviewing this map is: 'in that short time we have managed to capture around 80 issues which seem to me to form seven to nine clusters (one or two of the clusters are quite closely related). Can we quickly go through each of these to explore the clusters' contents and to check that I have put the issues into the right clusters? It will also help us to see what others have contributed'.

Box 4.11   Vignette: How it Unfolds – Understanding the Impact of the Economic Climate on Construction

As part of a strategy-making intervention, a group of senior managers from a large construction company got together for a half day to consider a strategy for dealing with the various issues facing the industry as a whole and in particular their business. They also wanted to capture all of the issues in one place – to get a good overview of what faced them.

(Continued)

(Continued)

On arrival they noticed that there was a large public screen with chairs positioned in a semi-circle in front of the screen. This was a little unusual. However, after the facilitator had explained why the room was set up the way it was – that the intention of the screen was to ensure all could see the issues easily – and the purpose of the session, the managers felt better. They also felt that they had a clear idea of what was expected of them – after all, they were quite looking forward to surfacing all the issues, some of which were really troubling them.

They got going quickly. It was easy to generate issues and it was helpful to have the starter question there to keep them focused. As is typically the case the process started with a flurry of issues as everyone there was raising those concerns that were of immediate concern to them, and had usually been raised many times before. The facilitator was hard pressed to keep up with the material. By going around the participants in turn everyone was able to have their say but some were not so disciplined to stick to generating just one when their turn came – the facilitator had to be quite strict. Within 20 to 25 minutes there were about 40 to 50 issues on the public screen (which is pretty representative when working with groups of around seven to nine participants). The managers were really amazed and delighted – as well as being a little overwhelmed by the enormity of the situation.

Once this flurry had slowed down, the facilitator managing the process, knowing that it is worth prompting for further issues to ensure the surfacing goes beyond 'obvious' and often repeated concerns asked them to review the screen – what was missing? She also asked the managers to consider the issues already generated in the context of other parts of the organisation and external environment as this often gave rise to further important material. It was interesting to see managers getting really engaged with the issues, being surprised by some (which they hadn't realised were issues).

Quote: 'It was a bit like opening Pandora's Box. I knew that there were a lot of issues to be considered but frankly was afraid to raise them because by looking at them all at once I knew I would feel overwhelmed. It was far easier to just nibble at one issue at a time – but I never knew which one I should be dealing with first'.

Task 5 (optional): Consider Issues from Different Stakeholder Positions

Ask participants to identify who might be some of the **significant stakeholders** for the particular department/division/organisation (depending on the focus taken for the forum). Alternatively, use a break, if available, to **test out the manager-client's view on whether to consider stakeholders and their views of which issues the organisation should be addressing**.

Once the stakeholders are identified and depending on time, select a few of the most important stakeholders and **ask what might be the issues each of these stakeholders see facing the organisation?** This allows for a wider consideration of issues that might be significant in the development of a robust strategy. Capture these issues on the Decision Explorer® view (possibly using a different style so as to easily distinguish them from the earlier material).

Another way of surfacing different stakeholder issues and appreciating different view points comes from **using 'role-think' with subgroups**. Ask the subgroups to imagine themselves as one of the stakeholder/stakeholder bodies – what would be the issues they feel the focal unit should be focusing upon. This allows for a more detailed and in-depth consideration as well as enabling all participants to be fully involved.

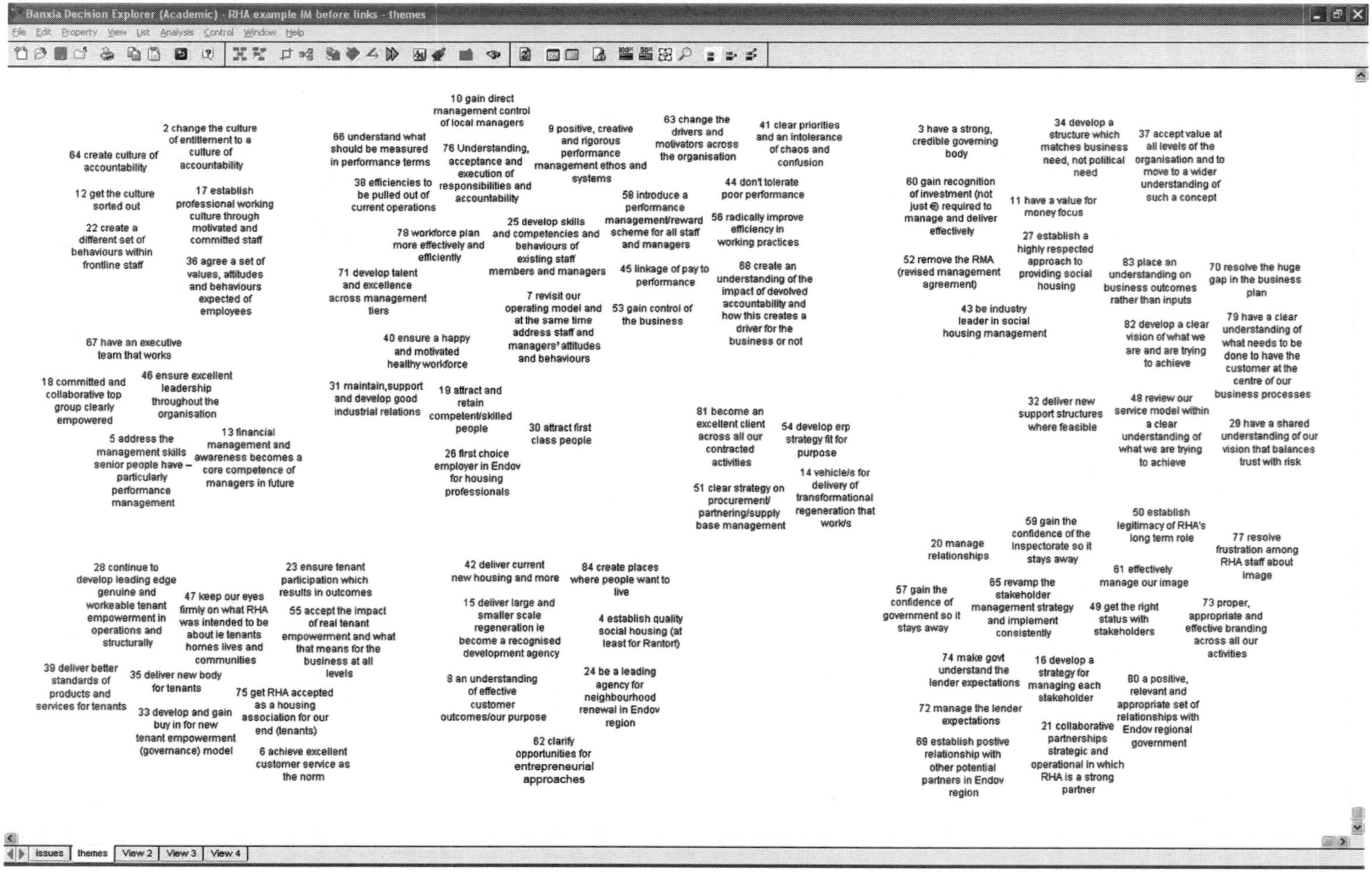

Banxia Decision Explorer (Academic) - RHA example IM before links - themes
File Edit Property View List Analysis Control Window Help
64 create culture of accountability
2 change the culture of entitlement to a culture of accountability
12 get the culture sorted out
17 establish professional working culture through motivated and committed staff
22 create a different set of behaviours within frontline staff
36 agree a set of values, attitudes and behaviours expected of employees
67 have an executive team that works
18 committed and collaborative top group clearly empowered
46 ensure excellent leadership throughout the organisation
5 address the management skills senior people have – particularly performance management
13 financial management and awareness becomes a core competence of managers in future
10 gain direct management control of local managers
66 understand what should be measured in performance terms
76 Understanding, acceptance and execution of responsibilities and accountability
38 efficiencies to be pulled out of current operations
78 workforce plan more effectively and efficiently
71 develop talent and excellence across management tiers
40 ensure a happy and motivated healthy workforce
31 maintain,support and develop good industrial relations
19 attract and retain competent/skilled people
30 attract first class people
26 first choice employer in Endov for housing professionals
9 positive, creative and rigorous performance management ethos and systems
25 develop skills and competencies and behaviours of existing staff members and managers
7 revisit our operating model and at the same time address staff and managers' attitudes and behaviours
63 change the drivers and motivators across the organisation
58 introduce a performance management/reward scheme for all staff and managers
45 linkage of pay to performance
53 gain control of the business
41 clear priorities and an intolerance of chaos and confusion
44 don't tolerate poor performance
56 radically improve efficiency in working practices
68 create an understanding of the impact of devolved accountability and how this creates a driver for the business or not
81 become an excellent client across all our contracted activities
54 develop erp strategy fit for purpose
51 clear strategy on procurement/ partnering/supply base management
14 vehicle/s for delivery of transformational regeneration that work/s
3 have a strong, credible governing body
60 gain recognition of investment (not just €) required to manage and deliver effectively
52 remove the RMA (revised management agreement)
43 be industry leader in social housing management
34 develop a structure which matches business need, not political need
11 have a value for money focus
27 establish a highly respected approach to providing social housing
37 accept value at all levels of the organisation and to move to a wider understanding of such a concept
83 place an understanding on business outcomes rather than inputs
70 resolve the huge gap in the business plan
82 develop a clear vision of what we are and are trying to achieve
79 have a clear understanding of what needs to be done to have the customer at the centre of our business processes
32 deliver new support structures where feasible
48 review our service model within a clear understanding of what we are trying to achieve
29 have a shared understanding of our vision that balances trust with risk
28 continue to develop leading edge genuine and workeable tenant empowerment in operations and structurally
47 keep our eyes firmly on what RHA was intended to be about ie tenants homes lives and communities
23 ensure tenant participation which results in outcomes
55 accept the impact of real tenant empowerment and what that means for the business at all levels
39 deliver better standards of products and services for tenants
35 deliver new body for tenants
33 develop and gain buy in for new tenant empowerment (governance) model
75 get RHA accepted as a housing association for our end (tenants)
6 achieve excellent customer service as the norm
42 deliver current new housing and more
84 create places where people want to live
15 deliver large and smaller scale regeneration ie become a recognised development agency
4 establish quality social housing (at least for Rantorl)
8 an understanding of effective customer outcomes/our purpose
24 be a leading agency for neighbourhood renewal in Endov region
62 clarify opportunities for entrepreneurial approaches
20 manage relationships
59 gain the confidence of the inspectorate so it stays away
50 establish legitimacy of RHA's long term role
77 resolve frustration among RHA staff about image
57 gain the confidence of government so it stays away
65 revamp the stakeholder management strategy and implement consistently
61 effectively manage our image
49 get the right status with stakeholders
73 proper, appropriate and effective branding across all our activities
74 make govt understand the lender expectations
16 develop a strategy for managing each stakeholder
80 a positive, relevant and appropriate set of relationships with Endov regional government
72 manage the lender expectations
21 collaborative partnerships strategic and operational in which RHA is a strong partner
69 establish postive relationship with other potential partners in Endov region
issues
themes
View 2
View 3
View 4

Figure 4.2 Issue Map with Content Related Clusters

Deliverable: a printout of issues surfaced, clustered into emergent strategic themes
Timing from forum start: 100 minutes minimum, expected 155 minutes

The Interaction Between Strategic Issues: Issues as a Network

Script for: Strategic issues are not independent, they impact on another

Tasks:

1 Explain the causal linking process to participants: 5 minutes
2 Carry out initial linking and capturing of argumentation: 20–30 minutes

Deliverable: a messy, partially structured issue map

3 Tidy the messy map: 10–15 minutes

Deliverable: a printout of the refined linked map of the issues
Script timing: minimum 35 minutes, expected 50 minutes

Task 1: Explain the Causal Linking Process to Participants

What Are Links?   Linking issues is an effective way of managing the unfolding complexity as it shows the interdependencies between issues. It is an obvious next step for participants, and follows from noting that the issues are not independent of each other, and so it makes sense to establish the network of interrelationships. However, it is important to **provide participants with a clear idea of exactly what the links represent** thus ensuring that the links captured have a single meaning (rather than being open to multiple interpretations and thus increasing the complexity). Explaining the linking guidelines to the participants is therefore an important start to this script.

In issue management (as opposed to Mind Maps, influence diagrams or other diagramming techniques) the links represent causality. Therefore they can be interpreted as 'x' *may lead to* 'y'. Thus one issue may lead to, that is 'have an impact upon', another. The link may also be described as 'x' is a *means to the end* 'y'. In each of these cases the link implies causality (see box 4.12).

Box 4.12   Example of Linking

Increasing loss of good salespeople *may lead to* (be linked to) diminishing understanding of what the customer wants. An explanation of loss of salespeople might be 'poor working conditions'. Thus a chain of argument is expressed.

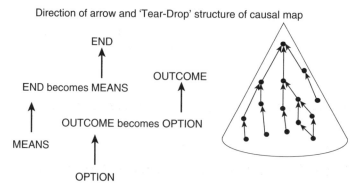

Direction of arrow and 'Tear-Drop' structure of causal map

Figure 4.3   Direction of Arrow and 'Tear-drop' Structure of Causal Map.

How Do Links Work?   Mapping out the causal network (causal mapping) gives meaning to each statement by setting it within a context of action: why it matters (consequences – 'out arrows'), and what needs to be done to change it (explanations – 'in arrows'). Instead of interpreting a statement by reference to a dictionary, meaning is determined through action and purpose – strategic management. The focus, therefore, is one of encouraging participants to avoid arguing over the precision of the words and concentrate instead on the action context of a statement as this helps with the development of a shared understanding and sees meaning through action with purpose. It also provides some clarity in terms of next steps – answering the 'so what?' question and further elaborating the map. A way of helping participants decide the hierarchy of links is to **provide a diagram** depicting an explanation about how the links work (see figure 4.3).

Use an explanation in support of a view already made by a participant to illustrate a causal link. For example, a participant while arguing why a particular issue should appear in one of the clusters (tear drops) notes that it contributes to one of the issues in the designated cluster – use this explanation to illustrate a link.

Task 2: Carry Out Initial Linking and Capture of Explanatory Argumentation

Start with One of the Thematic Clusters (Tear Drops)   Usually it is best to start with a cluster that is not too contentious and appears to be relatively easily understood. **Ask participants how the different issue statements in the cluster relate to each other**. This usually results in a range of different links (showing how significant causality is in determining meaning). For example, one participant might argue that 'issue statement A leads to issue statement B'. To explain the reasoning she uses a chain of argument to defend her case. **Ensure the extra explanatory material is captured** on the screen with the links showing her line of argumentation. This contribution might stimulate another participant to argue that 'statement A leads to statement D' (an alternative explanation which links to material in another cluster). To explain this assertion he presents his rationale. Capture this new material with the links. From this process a shared understanding is developed and the map elaborated both in terms of contributions and relationships. It may be helpful to **use a round robin process to establish links** by asking each participant, in turn, to propose a link.

Watch for issue statements containing more than one phrase as the different outcomes or actions might have different explanations or consequences. This makes linking difficult, as the relationship is only applicable to one of the phrases embedded in the issue statement. Separate the two phrases into individual issue statements and capture the link(s). A clear indicator of multiple issue statements are those with 'linking' words embedded in them. For example: 'and', 'due to', 'because', 'through', 'in order to'. In each of these occurrences examine the statement to identify the two statements embedded together and separate as the connecting words can be interpreted as links between these two parts of the statement (see box 4.13).

Box 4.13   Example of Statements With More Than One Issue

A participant might suggest as an issue *increase and improve services*. There may be issues that relate to increasing services that are nothing to do with improve services and vice versa. Separate the two so that one issue reads *improve services* and the other *increase services*. This might also prompt further elaboration to the wording of the issue statement, increasing its comprehensibility.

Example of 'due to': *fall in visitors to the restaurant due to economic recession* becomes *economic recession* links (causes) to *fall in visitors*, that is a link from *economic recession* to *fall in visitors*.

Example of 'because': *because staff are badly trained we're unable to get productivity gains* becomes *staff are badly trained* links to (causes) *unable to get productivity gains*.

Encourage **participants to call out the links** using the numerical tags automatically supplied by Decision Explorer® when entering statements. For example, a participant might say '32 to 33', and so the facilitator types 32+33 and a link will be displayed from 32 to 33. In this way the process can be completed quickly.

Recognise that participants may see the directionality of the link differently. For example 'turning things around means we have to win every battle in the next five years' may be coded with 'winning every battle' as the desired outcome from 'turning things around'. However, an alternative linking would see 'winning every battle' being required in order to 'turn things around', depending on the desired ends of the group. **Check that participants have a basic understanding (not necessarily agreement) of the chains of argument**.

When working through cluster by cluster, **don't worry if the first cluster takes longer than expected**. Once participants get the hang of the process, the remaining clusters will go more quickly. It is usually also a good idea to **reassure participants** that this is the case.

The linked clusters will usually be significantly different from thematic clusters. Linked clusters are derived from an action perspective – they deal with thinking about the means for changing the world. **Look for further links across clusters**.

Review the Structure   See if there are any 'orphans' – issues that are not currently linked to any others. Where these exist explore whether, with the addition of further explanatory material, they could be incorporated into the network. Alternatively are they isolated issues that have no strategic impact elsewhere?

Don't worry about the same issue being linked to more than one thematic cluster – those that appear in a range of thematic clusters are often more potent as they impact a number of strategic themes. **Be prepared for the map to 'grow'**. It is not untypical to see the statements on the picture increase by nearly a third as a result of the linking argumentation generating further material.

Sometimes there are situations where an issue impacts 'negatively' on another. For example an issue of 'falling student numbers' leads to NOT 'overlarge class sizes'. The link itself is not negative (a matter of concern) but rather relates to the fact that one issue impacts the 'opposite or contrasting aspect' of another issue. **Capture these negative links by using the minus symbol rather than the plus symbol** (for example, type 32–33). It is not crucial to get these absolutely correct at this stage as participants will usually presume the negative link because that is what would make sense (see box 4.14).

Box 4.14   Example of a Dilemma

Allowing both types of links can also reveal dilemmas where one chain of argument links 'positively' to the outcomes but a second has a counteracting impact. For example, an issue relating to the need to 'lay off staff' may lead to 'reduce head count' which in turn contributes to 'cut costs'. However, an alternative line of argument might be that the necessity to 'lay off staff' results in 'having to re-engage staff later as expensive consultants' and thus has the consequences of having a negative impact on 'cut costs'.

Deliverable: a printout of the messy partially structured issue map (see figure 4.4)

Provide participants with a printout at this stage (see figure 4.4) as this gives them a record of the raw network of issues and represents a product of the group. They will often find this messy issue map to be a useful reference 'picture' of something they created themselves and so act as a summary picture of progress – a record of achievement. Although the map is messy, participants are able to work with it because they created it incrementally. In addition, this product helps reinforce the emotional high most participants feel at this stage (see box 4.15).

Box 4.15   Aim for the Relief from Getting Things Out on the Table

At the coffee break (after issue surfacing and structuring):

'There is a real buzz – folks are on a high – comments like "this is amazing" and "great set up" are being made. They liked the equality of voices, that everyone is able to input so we captured all the different points of views. They really liked the fact that there were no ice breakers'.

(A multi-organisation strategy workshop: 30 participants)

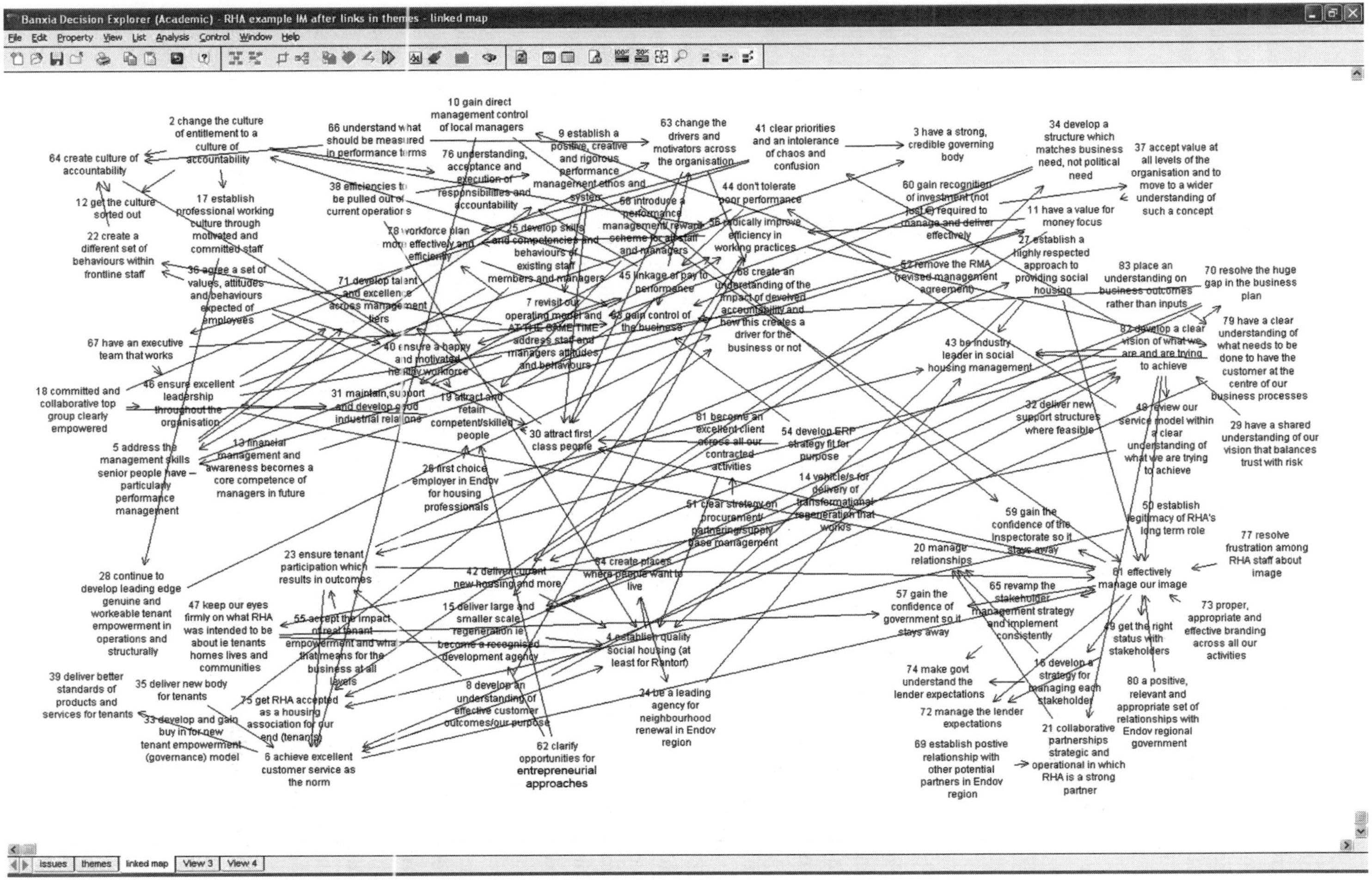

Figure 4.4 Example of a Linked Issue Map

Task 3: Tidy the Messy Map

Create a Rough Hierarchical Picture   Use a new view (tab) in Decision Explorer® for creating the 'tidied' picture as it enables the group to see both the original messy picture and the revised and tidy one. An easy way to do this is to use the 'bring layout from' facility in Decision Explorer® (right click on a tab). Converting the mess into a hierarchy will **allow the structure of the network of views to emerge** – and the structure will communicate important properties. Creating the hierarchy can be done by:

- Moving those statements with no out-arrows to the top.
- Reducing crossing arrows (shifting statements either left or right).
- Moving those statements with no in-arrows to the bottom of the map.

See Appendix: Using Causal Mapping Software: Decision Explorer®, 2.1 Using Views

Review the Tidied Picture   As the group reviews the picture new insights will emerge. For example, **issues that are central will tend to appear in the middle of the hierarchy**, and potentially **powerful actions points will appear at the bottom** with many arrows out of them. At times causal clusters will emerge that are likely to be quite different from the content-oriented clusters (see figure 4.5a and 4.5b below). This comparison will provide new insights to participants, for example, new action-oriented themes each of which represents a different strategic arena.

Sometimes it is difficult to tidy the messy map because the map is highly linked. If this is the case then there is a clear message for the group to reflect upon: their strategic situation is difficult to unravel into sub-strategies or discrete strategic arenas. This will have significant implications for the implementation of any strategy agreed – it is likely to be cross-disciplinary and more difficult to project manage. Another explanation leads to the need to **reduce 'over-linking'**. Over-linking may occur as redundant links are captured, so masking the emergent patterns. It is very easy for participants to add 'summary links' during the process of linking. For example, the chain A>B>C>D which includes also A>C, B>D and A>D may suggest redundant links as the latter three do not add anything new to the understanding and simply act as summary links. Each link must express a different chain of causality. If it does not, then remove the link. If it does, try to capture the differences in chains of argument by adding new material.

When there are over 35 statements it may be helpful to **tidy the messy map in a group work intermission** as the amount of moving around can be distracting to the participants. Figure 4.5 shows a complex map tidied during a break in the forum of 15 minutes. In the example below there are over 40 statements.

See Appendix: Using Causal Mapping Software: Decision Explorer®, 2.2 Managing the Map

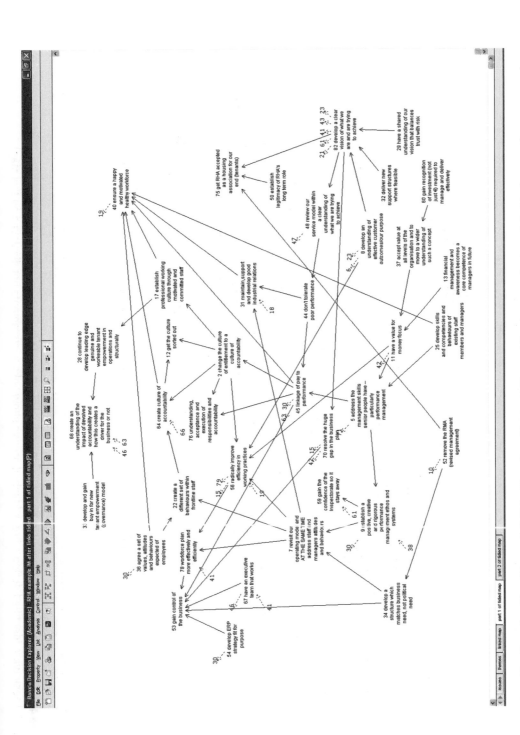

Figure 4.5a The Complex Map (Figure 4.4) Tidied into Two Clusters. Figure 4.5a shows a cluster related to 'pay, performance, and motivating the workforce'. These were identified during a break (dashed arrows show links to statements not displayed on this map)

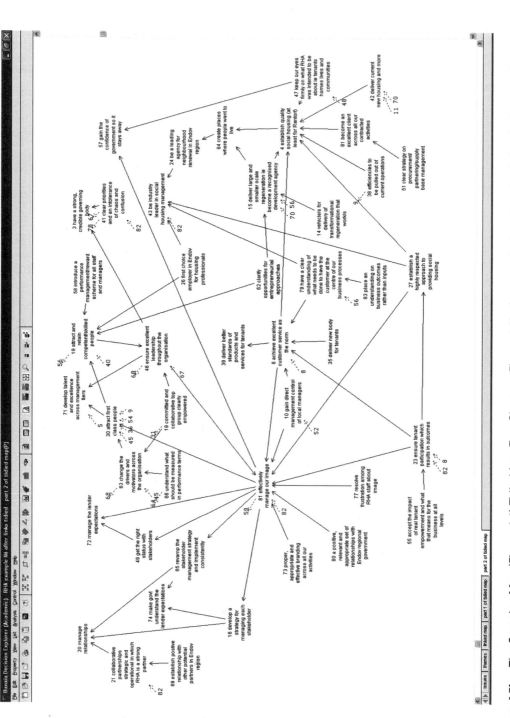

Figure 4.5b The Complex Map (Figure 4.4) Tidied into Two Clusters. Figure 4.5b shows a cluster related to 'effectively managing image'. These were identified during a break (dashed arrows show links to statements not displayed on this map)

Box 4.16   Vignette: How it Unfolds – Constructing the Picture!

The group broke for coffee on a high – they had managed to surface all of the issues (that they could think of at this particular time) and while being somewhat concerned about the number they felt that at least they had captured them all in one place. It had also been interesting to see the differences in the issues surfaced by the different parts of the organisation – there had been some surprises. The review of the thematic clusters had been helpful – partly because it helped manage the amount of material but also because it highlighted areas that had been missed. However, there were still a few issues they weren't completely clear about … hopefully it would be made clear after the coffee break.

After coffee break the facilitator explained that the next step was to consider how the different issues impacted upon one another. This step was easy to understand as frequently, in raising and explaining the issues, interactions between the issues had been commented upon. Moreover the step was relatively painless. All participants had to do was call out the links (each issue statement had a number tag and so requesting that the facilitator linked statement 4 to statement 54 was trivial). Sometimes there was discussion regarding the direction of the link. Initially this was due to getting their heads around the linking guidelines, that is, the directionality of links – but this soon dissipated. Another reason for discussion was that there were some very different understandings of the issue statements. More issues emerged as the rationale for the different linking combinations made the extra material explicit.

At the end of this part of the forum, not only did the managers comment that they got a sense of beginning to understand in detail how others saw the situation (which in some cases was significantly different) and thus build a common understanding, but it also helped them begin to structure the material in a manner that meant that they began to feel they could do something (rather than feeling as though they were 'drowning in issues'). And it had 'only taken us a couple of hours!' They had endured several day-long meetings discussing their situation and 'never felt this much in control'.

Deliverable: a printout of the refined linked map of the strategic issues
Timing from forum start: 135 minutes minimum, expected 205 minutes

---

Prioritising Issues and Agreeing Strategies (Issues)

Script for: Strategic thinking demands understanding the character of the network of interacting and interconnected strategy arenas

Tasks:

1   Carry out analyses of the issue network and refine the map: 20–30 minutes
2   Agree priority strategies: 20–30 minutes

Deliverable: a printout of the summary map of priorities
Script timing: minimum 40 minutes, expected 60 minutes

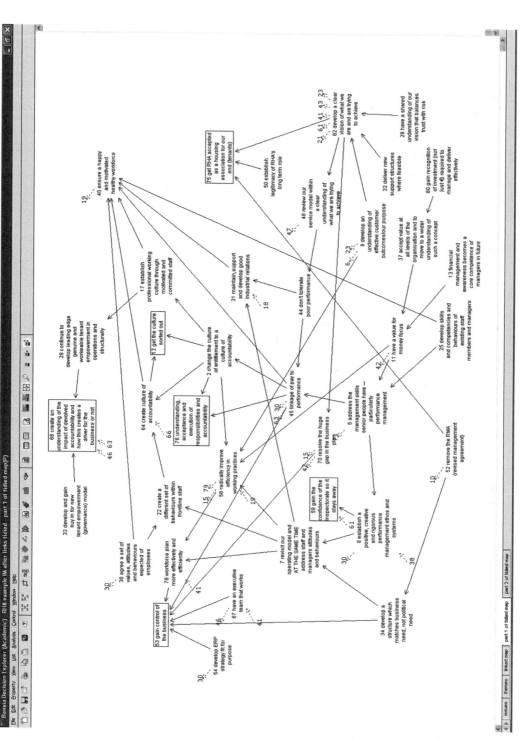

Figure 4.6 RHA Map with Head Statements Highlighted from First Part of Tidied Map (Figure 4.5a)

Task 1: Carry Out Analyses of the Issue Network and Refine the Map

Identify Goals or Headline Issues   This is achieved by looking for those issue statements that do not impact, that is link into, other issue statements (they are at the 'head' of chain(s) of argument) (see figure 4.6). These are the most superordinate statements in the hierarchy. In some instances they give some clues regarding *possible goals*, and if not goals, do provide headline descriptors of the body of issues impacting them and are as close to expressions of goals that have been proffered.

> See Appendix: Using Causal Mapping Software: Decision Explorer®, 3.1 Listing Heads

Identify If There Are Any *Feedback Loops* in the Map   Feedback loops indicate either self-reinforcing behaviour – vicious or virtuous cycles or alternatively a self-balancing loop where action taken results in a move back to the status quo.

Sometimes feedback loops are the result of incorrect links where a reversal of a link to correct it removes the loop. **Check the links** by looking at the loops with the group to **ensure that the loops are valid**.

Explore the nature of the feedback loop(s). This is a crucial aspect of strategy making because loops show change over time – change that may be worth retaining or change that must be stopped. Loops may depend on the belief systems of those contributing to the issue map. For example in figure 4.7, the relationship between 'expanding the range of courses' and 'business experience' can result in either a feedback loop or a hierarchy depending on whose point of view is taken.

When genuine loops appear it is useful to establish the nature of the feedback. When the loop contains an odd number of negative links (assuming the negative links are accurate!), the loop is depicting self-control. That is, any change in the state of the issues in the loop will result in stabilising dynamics. Alternatively, an even number of negative (or all positive) links suggests regenerative or degenerative dynamics where changes result in exponential growth (virtuous cycle) or decline (vicious cycle). It is worth ensuring that there is time to **direct the attention of the group to exploitation of virtuous cycles or removal of vicious cycles**. It is important to note that all statements in a feedback loop must be capable of being viewed as variables – try putting increase/decrease in front of the wording. A feedback loop implies that there will be continuous change – a dynamic is present (see box 4.17).

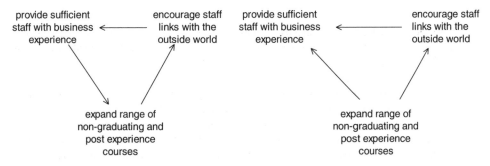

Figure 4.7   Two Ways of Expressing Beliefs – One Leading to a Virtuous Cycle and the Other a Hierarchy

See Appendix: Using Causal Mapping Software: Decision Explorer®, 3.2 Identifying Feedback Loops

---

Box 4.17   Example of Identifying Feedback Loops

In the example shown in figure 4.8, on the discovery of a nested feedback loop the group became excited by its significance for them. It seemed obvious to them once they had appreciated it, but had not been obvious until this point in their causal mapping! Indeed the loop itself had not been noticed visually, it was found by Decision Explorer® being used to undertake a loop analysis. The example shows a simple nested loop where dropping motivation of staff as well as too much staff turnover are an explanation for losing product quality.

Help the group to consider the means for intervening to exploit or minimise/manage the impact of feedback. There are three obvious ways of intervening in the loops.

- **(1) Exploit or (2) minimise the behaviour of a positive feedback loop**. When it is a virtuous loop, look for possible options for reinforcing one or more of the issues by exploring influences on each of the variables (issues) in turn. Where it is a vicious cycle (see box 4.18) 'rub out' one of the arrows by a change in policy or change the nature of one of the causalities: (a) make the loop into a controlling loop (negative) by changing the direction of causation, or (b) destroy the causation or (c) find a number of influences on nodes that can shift the direction of behaviour so that a vicious circle becomes a virtuous circle.

Box 4.18   Example: A Senior Police Officer Notes a Feedback Loop

'this vicious circle is so obvious – now we've seen it. But it is so significant – sorting out what to do about it must be our top priority for the year otherwise our long term future is going to be hell!'.

(Police Top Management Team: 10 participants)

- **(3) Manage the behaviour of a negative feedback loop** if the degree of control is undesirable. If possible, break the loop by a change in policy. Alternatively change the direction of causation so that the loop behaves as a virtuous circle.

Try to **avoid double-headed arrows** as these are cryptic representations of a feedback loop and do not provide much help to the group in either understanding or managing the feedback phenomenon. However, often double-headed arrows show a genuine difference of opinion about what is the means or option and what is the end or outcome. Try to get those proposing the links to elaborate how A might lead to B and vice versa and capture this expanded reasoning. In fleshing out the relationships, participants are able to get a better handle on the apparent loop. This might reveal that the implied feedback loop is not accurate – it is a case of faulty logic.

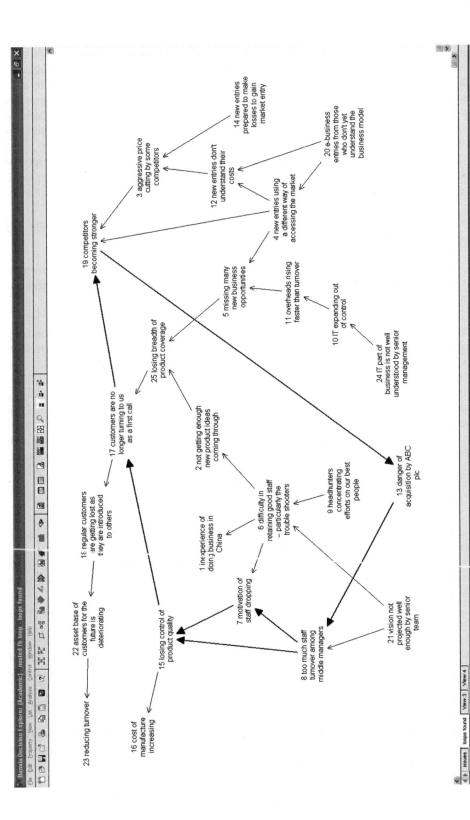

Figure 4.8 The Discovery of Two Significant Nested Feedback Loops

Identify *Structurally Potential Key Issues*   These are the issues that have a lot of links around them – they are fundamental to the network's structure. One simple way of considering the position of an issue in the network is to **examine the relative number of links directly connected to each issue statement**. Examining the immediate domain of an issue sometimes can be done visually, as the eye is able to detect those that are very busy (see figure 4.9). Decision Explorer® will undertake a more precise analysis and will often reveal busy statements not noticed by an informal scrutiny.

A more sophisticated analysis allows the group to use the software to **look at a wider level of issue connectedness** by considering links encompassing several levels (rather than the immediate domain). This form of analysis is called 'central' and requires the help of Decision Explorer®.

See Appendix: Using Causal Mapping Software: Decision Explorer®, 3.3 Finding Busy and Central Statements

For those statements that are well connected, **consider using a different style in Decision Explorer® to clearly indicate their key status**. These statements are likely to be important because they act as candidate priorities.

Examine the Possible Key Issues   Produce a map of those key issues that are extensively interconnected within the network by using, on a new 'tab', the 'explore' command in Decision Explorer®. This command will produce a map (figure 4.10a) showing the focal issue in the centre of the screen with issues that are either linked one level in or one level out. The software additionally can show the other links (to currently 'hidden' statements) and these statements may give some clues about areas that maybe worth displaying. For example, if one particular statement on the map is shown with five or so 'hidden arrows' this might suggest that 'bringing' on this material to elaborate the map would further participants' understanding. **Use different views for each of the explorations** rather than over-write views already developed that may need to be retained.

See Appendix: Using Causal Mapping Software: Decision Explorer®, 2.2 Managing the Map and 2.3 Managing the Material Captured

In figure 4.10a two of the statements are busy (statements 30 and 82) and so will be explored, each in their own right. However, statement 8 is noted to influence three statements (82, 23 and 6) and so might be added to the map; similarly statements 20 and 74 are consequences of both 16 and 65 and so are also worth adding to the context of the central statement (61). Figure 4.10b shows these additions.

As analyses are undertaken and maps of specific aspects are **created the group naturally checks out, discusses and changes links**.

In figure 4.10b the group noted that not only were there redundant links, but also some links were incorrect. The small cluster about managing relationships (20) prompted a helpful discussion about the relationship between image and stakeholder management. The links were changed to reflect the discussion. Figure 4.10c shows these changes. (Arrow from 77 to 61 reversed; arrows from 61 to 65 and from 16 to 65 deleted; arrow from 16 to 65 added; arrow from 16 to 20 deleted.)

Reviewing links may be aided by asking participants to **consider *causal clusters* rather than the entire network**. Decision Explorer® provides a number of ways of focusing in on parts of the whole (see below). There are two different methods for 'slicing' the map into 'bite sized' chunks. These are (a) cluster analysis and (b) hierarchical set analysis.

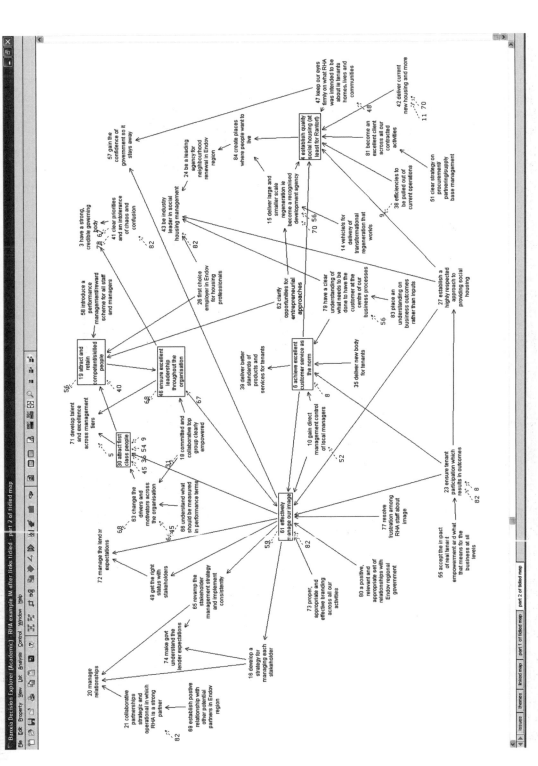

Figure 4.9 Structurally Key Statements Highlighted (Shown in Boxes) from Figure 4.5b

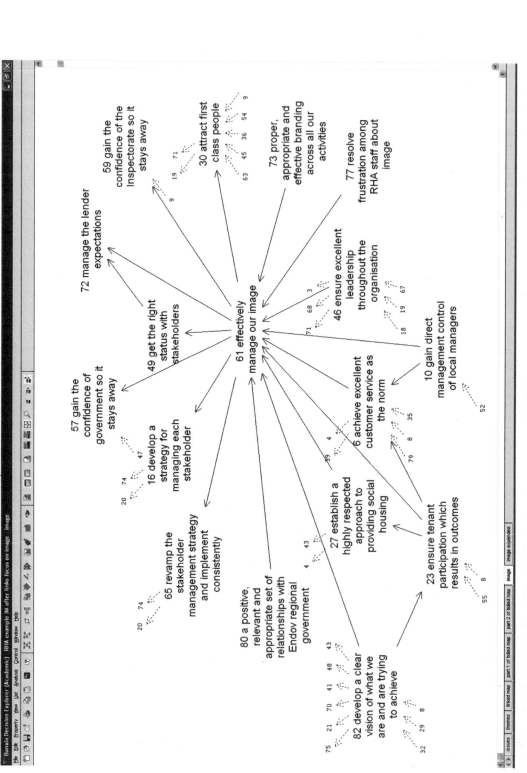

Figure 4.10a Exploring a Key Issue

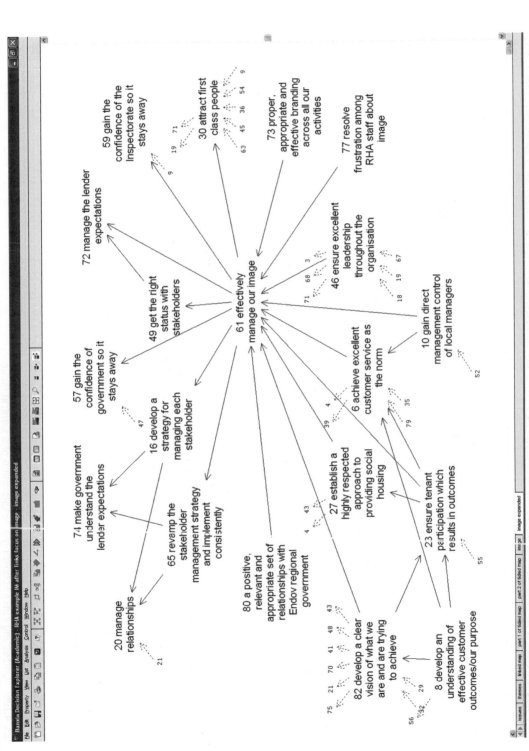

Figure 4.10b Expanding an Exploration

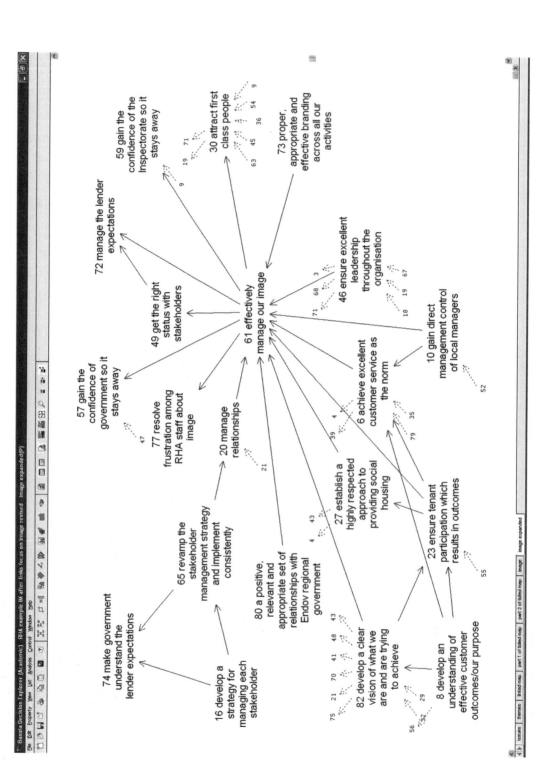

Figure 4.10c Correcting Links Following an Exploration of a Central Issue

Carry Out a Cluster Analysis   The cluster analysis considers the relative similarity of the meaning (the statements linked in and out) of one issue statement relative to another in the map. Where statements have a relatively high degree of similarity then the two statements are placed within the same cluster. Where there is little, if any, similarity between the two statements then a new cluster is started. The intention of the analysis is to create mutually exclusive clusters (islands) with a small number of cross links (bridges) between them.

Examine each cluster in turn, in a new 'tab' within Decision Explorer®, as each is likely to contain at least one key issue. If there isn't a key issue within the cluster then examination of the cluster might identify further candidate key issues.

See Appendix: Using Causal Mapping Software: Decision Explorer®, 3.4 Slicing the Model into Chunks

This analysis, more than any other, relies on good coding of the map – particularly the need to avoid redundant links. The analysis is also affected by any feedback loops as these loops tend to result in large clusters as everything that is captured in the loop is placed into a single cluster. It is difficult to undertake this analysis without the software. However, the principle of causally related clusters (as opposed to topic based clusters) is an important one, and it is possible to undertake rough cluster analyses based on structure. Note that although the analysis is based on structure, the structure was based on content, and so clusters are content analyses.

Carry Out a Hierarchical Cluster/Set ('Hieset') Analysis   Hierarchical clusters (sets), as their name suggests, take each member of a 'seed' set (that is a set of statements that provides the starting point for the analysis) – in this case the key issues – and drills down all the chains of argument impacting the seed statement. Each of the statements linking into the seed (see figure 4.11), along with all of the material that links into them, is captured essentially producing a tear drop shaped set.

As with clustering, where the resultant hierarchical set (called 'hieset' in the software) is very large (over 40 statements) consideration should be given to whether a further key issue exists within the set and therefore whether to include an additional seed statement (and redoing the analysis).

See Appendix: Using Causal Mapping Software: Decision Explorer®, 3.4 Slicing the Model into Chunks

Examine each hierarchical set. As with the cluster analysis, these sets are also useful for providing structured bundles of material to participants as they reveal each key issue with its entire attendant supporting material (they are therefore *not* mutually exclusive, as are cluster sets). Undertaking this analysis with the software is quick and easy. However, as with cluster analysis, the principle of hierarchical clusters/sets is an important one because it seeks to show all of the options that can influence a chosen outcome – the seed statement (key issue or goal).

Identify 'Potent' Issues   These are issues that if dealt with will resolve, or contribute to the resolution of many other 'headline' or seed issues. These potent issues can be identified by a visual inspection of the total network (in essence looking for those statements that supported – directly or indirectly – the key issues); however this can be unreliable and certainly can miss some at the bottom of the hierarchy whose impact spreads across the network – therefore using the analyses in Decision Explorer® can assist.

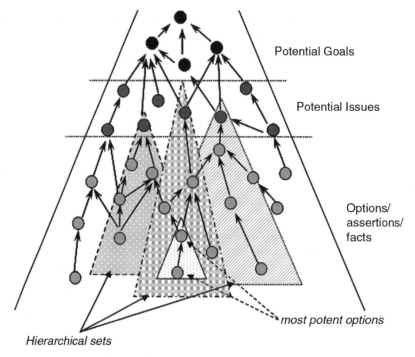

Figure 4.11 Illustrating Hierarchical Sets

Significantly the analysis can also reveal the extent of dilemmas that are a common consequence of the recognition of multiple ramifications of issues. Each potent node may have both positive and negative consequences, indicating the recognition of a dilemma (see box 4.19).

Box 4.19   Example of a Dilemma

When looking at reducing overheads one possible option open to management might be to *make some staff redundant* as *reducing the headcount* will help *decrease the overheads* and thus *make cost savings*. Consequently there is a positive link between *make staff redundant* and *reduce operating costs*. However, a second, longer term consequence might be that as a result of making staff redundant, managers find that they now need to *buy in knowledge and skills* and have to do this through *employing consultants*. This, however, adds to the costs and therefore illustrates a negative route between *make staff redundant* and *make cost savings*.

Decision Explorer® has a range of analyses including a method for identifying potent issues.

See Appendix: Using Causal Mapping Software: Decision Explorer®, 3.5 Identifying Potency of Statements

Identify *Potential Priority Issues*   All of the analyses above provide only *indicators* of possible priority issues that might be reworded to become agreed strategies. As the analyses are conducted and possible candidate priority issues identified, **categorise candidate priorities with a new 'style'**.

A common trap at this stage is to identify candidate priorities at too high a level. For example, the group can easily agree that a possible focus of energy should be to 'be industry leader in social housing management' (one of the statements appearing at the top of the RHA map hierarchy – see figure 4.12 below). This type of statement can be seen by the group as an obvious priority, but the statement does not describe a potentially actionable strategy. This type of overarching statement is more likely to finish up potentially describing a goal or objective or aim and might usefully be tagged using a newly created 'goal' style. Thus, it is important to **encourage the group to consider candidate priorities at an actionable level**.

The analyses identify only *candidate* priorities. Ask the group to **use judgement to refine the candidate list and possibly add to it**. One reason for a review is that some of the candidate priorities may be thematically similar in meaning to one another and so only one of these issues is necessary and thus tagged as a potential priority. The review also allows participants to add further candidate statements to the candidate priority list – and reflect on why they have not been revealed through the analyses. Often this is because they were not well elaborated in terms of impact, possibly because some participants took for granted their impact even though their impact is not obvious to others in the group.

Figures 4.12a and 4.12b show the final candidate priorities agreed from the analysis and judgement with respect to the maps shown in figures 4.5a and 4.5b. Note that some of the links and statements have been changed as a consequence of discussing the results of analyses. The maps in figures 4.12a and 4.12b show candidate goals identified and feedback links highlighted. In the example shown by figure 4.12a, statement 82 – 'develop a clear vision of what we are and are trying to achieve', is a problematic statement. The statement should be regarded as redundant because it describes the overall purpose of a making strategy forum. However, in this instance group discussion led to it being retained because the specific outcomes and actions (out-arrows and in-arrows) were of particular importance for this organisation.

Consider whether it is necessary to carry out some or all of the analyses with the group or during a break with the results ready to show the group. This is because some of the analyses take a little while to run. Furthermore, beware that throughout the forum discussions in the group result in changes to the map. **Periodically re-run the analyses** as different results may emerge. Finally the use of different views in Decision Explorer®, one for each analysis result, enables a group to cycle attention from one result to another. The results of analyses are also often worth retaining for future reference (so, **label the views**).

See Appendix Using Causal Mapping Software: Decision Explorer®, 2.1 Using Views

Task 2: Mark Up Priority Issues and Create a Summary Overview

Review List of Candidate Priorities to Ensure None Are Missing   Start with those issues that have been identified using each of the analysis methods: loop, domain, central and potent analyses. A further means of doing this is to **check whether each hierarchical cluster and/or thematic cluster of material has at least one priority issue highlighted**. Where this is not the case, examine the cluster to ensure that a key issue has not been missed.

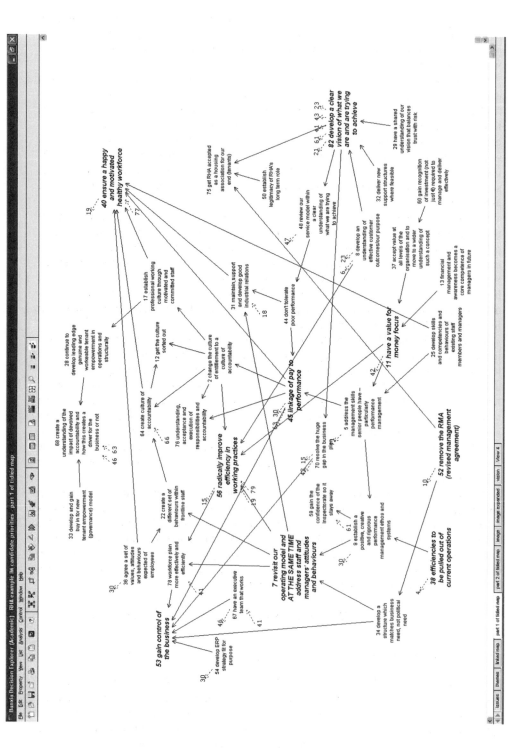

Figure 4.12a   Candidate Priority Themes Identified from the Issue Network Shown in Figure 4.5a

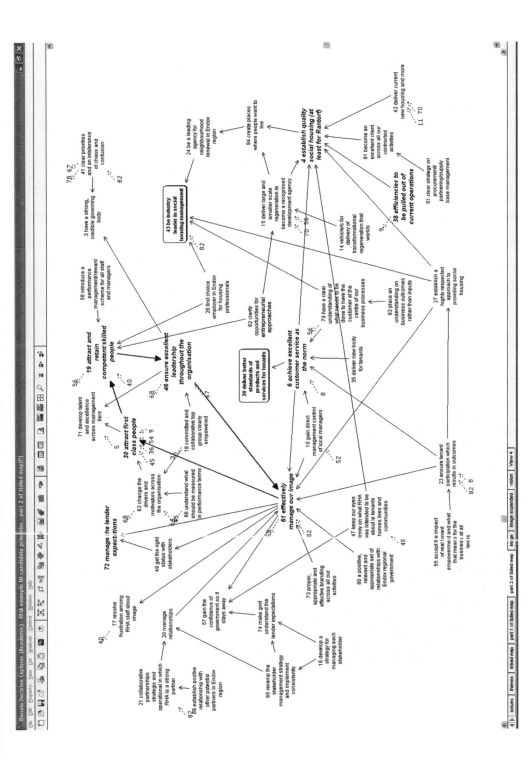

Figure 4.12b   Candidate Priority Themes Identified from the Issue Network Shown in Figure 4.5b

In addition, **consider as candidate key issues possible interventions to manage the feed-back loops** identified by the group. This is because feedback loops tend to be very significant to good strategic thinking.

Mark those issues that are agreed as candidate priorities – consider using a different Decision Explorer® style.

As the list is likely to be quite long (perhaps as many as 25 to 30 issue statements) **prioritise the key issues**. To do this, **ensure a high degree of consensus about priorities**. One option for doing this is to **ask each participant to individually rank their own view of the relative priorities** as this will allow for an evaluation of the degree of consensus. This can be simply done through using a three-step ranking scale with *** depicting the most important, and ** and * being less important. Where there is little consensus about the priority of some candidate key issues this might suggest a focused discussion, a modification of the map, and another round of ranking. Typically disagreements are the result of different understandings of outcomes and actions required. As the map is elaborated more subtle understandings develop and the likelihood of greater consensus increases.

A final check on priorities must consider judgement/'gut feel' in addition to those statements identified as significant through analyses. **Do not ignore the role of judgement**; *the mapping process is designed to inform judgement*. Where there are discrepancies between the results of analyses and judgement, this acts as a useful prompt for focused discussion.

The process of prioritising can take much less time than expected. At this stage the group have developed a good sense of the whole map as a result of the process of working on it. The analyses have focused the group's strategic conversation, led to changes and developments in the map, and so increased their awareness of the potential key 'hit-points' which become prioritised strategies.

Produce an Overview Map   Typically it is useful, as a means of reducing the complexity, to produce a summary map focusing just upon those issues identified as priorities. This is achieved by producing a map that comprises the priority issues and displays both direct and summary links between them (see box 4.20). To do this, create a new view and then bring onto the view the prioritised issues.

Box 4.20   Illustrating the Concept of an Overview Map

This overview or 'road map' is similar in concept to a road atlas, which on the front cover depicts the country along with the major cities/towns and their apparent associated road connections. However, this picture typically suggests direct routes between the major cities (for example a direct route between Glasgow and Edinburgh) which when examined in further depth proves not to be the case (the Glasgow Edinburgh route actually travels through Linlithgow, Falkirk, etc.). The same process is possible using the analysis, resulting in a 'collapsed' picture of the prioritised issues (cities and towns) with the various chains of argument (routes) between them (both those that are direct as well as those that traverse additional argumentation).

Given the significance of feedback loops, it may be helpful to add some further detail of their content into this summary map. Likewise adding the 'headlines' or goals to the map may also add richness but beware that this can result in an overly complex summary map.

Often a summary map of this type will be produced to help review the prioritisation. In these instances, the group will often flip between the detailed (micro) maps and the summary overview.

> See Appendix: Using Causal Mapping Software: Decision Explorer®, 3.6 Producing an Overview of the Model's Content – Collapsing the Model

Figure 4.13 shows a summary map that followed from identifying the candidate priorities shown in figures 4.12a and 4.12b. Often these summary maps, which show all possible paths of linkage between the candidates, can be complex (as in this case). However, as the summary map is tidied it will tend to reveal important summary characteristics of the network of issues – for example, centrality is reinforced, in this case the significance of statement 82 (a possible title for whole map, as discussed above) stands out, as does the significance of statement 61.

Although the forum 'script' suggests that priorities are agreed on a three-star scale, it is notable that in the RHA case presented in the figures, one priority, agreed with a very high degree of consensus, deserved to be identified as a four-star priority because it was rated much higher than all others. In this case it is of note that all three-star priorities were agreed with a high degree of consensus, with less consensus about the relative priority of the lower rated priorities. This is a phenomenon that occurs often – agreement about what is most important and less agreement about what is less important. See also chapter 3.

Deliverable: a printout of the summary map of priorities (and possibly other sub-maps showing the detail of priorities and analyses) (see figure 4.13)
Timing from forum start: 175 minutes minimum, expected 265 minutes

---

Creating the Strategy Deliverable

Script for: Writing up the statement of strategic intent

Tasks:

1 Create a first draft of the statement of strategic intent: 10–20 minutes
2 Review and refine the SSI with the group: 10–20 minutes

Deliverable: an agreed statement of the strategic intent
Script timing: minimum 20 minutes, expected 40 minutes

Task 1: Write the Statement of Strategic Intent

It is important that the statement of strategic intent (SSI) is produced soon after the forum (preferably the same day) and distributed to all participants. As the forum may take place during a morning the SSI can be written during lunch, reviewed by the manager-client, and distributed immediately after lunch. If the group is able to reconvene for a short while after lunch the SSI

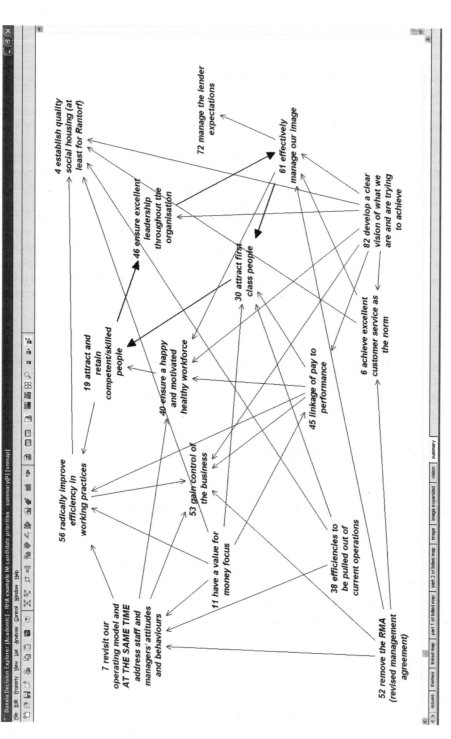

Figure 4.13 Example of Summary Map Depicting the Overview Interaction Between Potential Priorities Depicting the Impact of Some Key Feedback Loop Variables

can be validated by the whole group and then be a genuine take-away that gives a nice sense of closure to the forum.

Focus on the Top Priorities   To start the process of writing the statement, **identify the top priorities**, particularly if they stand out from the crowd as having a high degree of consensus among participants. **Take one of these and note the prioritised issues linking out of it**. Next formulate the text so that the prioritised issue appears after some introductory text, for example 'our major strategic priority is " x"'. This sets out a punchy beginning. Follow this with what will be achieved through this focus, for example, 'this will allow us to manage [specific prioritised issues immediately linking out from the focal issue]'. Try to **use the minimum of connecting phrases**, so as to focus on the map's content.

Depending on the hierarchical position of the top priorities, either take the next issue (if they are similarly positioned in the map) and repeat the process. Alternatively, when laddering up through the map, reinforce the significance of the issue. For example, 'this will help us achieve the prioritised issues' which are seen as critical to our strategic success. Similarly it is worth commenting specifically when dealing with feedback loops reflecting their importance to the overall strategic direction.

Stay Faithful to the Issues Map   As much as is possible, try to **keep the language of the issue statements** and ensure that the linking text **reflects the causality** thus staying truthful to the overall structure and meaning of the map.

Consider Style and Presentation   To facilitate the process, **copy and paste bundles of statements from Decision Explorer® in a word processor**. They will appear in numerical order, rather than any chosen order, but can be re-sorted quickly. **Use bold and italic formatting for emphasis**. This helps with navigation around the text and highlights the key points.

> See Appendix: Using Causal Mapping Software: Decision Explorer®, 4.2 Copy and Paste Map Material into a Word Processing Document, or PowerPoint

Try to **keep the text on one page** as this ensures that the statement is both concise and easily read.

Box 3.2 in chapter 3 shows the result of converting the priorities map into a statement of strategic intent encompassing sentences and paragraphs. In this example the first sentence focuses on the four-star priority – the bottom of the map, or action point – rather than, for example, the outcomes or statements that are closest to representing goals. In many cases the first sentence might have focused on 'increasing availability of specialist dementia care' (statement 12) and then discussed statements 48 and 61 (as two-star goal-oriented priorities). In this example the goal-oriented statements have been inserted as commentary in the middle of the document.

Task 2: Validation with the Manager-Client and Group

Validate the SSI   It is crucially important to **ensure both the manager-client and group 'sign off' the SSI document**. Although, if written well, it will be a direct translation of an agreed priorities map, the translation into sentences and paragraphs may indicate a different emphasis and meaning to participants.

Ensure the Language and Emotion Reflect the Issue Map   Where possible meet with the group (perhaps after a break in the forum) and review the draft document. **Check with the**

group that the language is easily understood by all those in the department or organisation and not just by the group. In addition make sure that the statement is not just a good reflection of what has been agreed in a simple easy to understand text format but that it also **gets at the emotion – the hearts and minds – of the intended audience.**

Deliverable: a statement of strategic intent
Timing from forum start: 195 minutes minimum, expected 305 minutes

---

5

STRATEGY AS PURPOSE: AGREEING GOALS AND ASPIRATIONS FOR THE ORGANISATION

Colin Eden, Fran Ackermann and
Kevin Gallimore[1]

The strategic direction of individuals or organisations can be derived only from clarity of purpose, even if the defined purpose is necessarily chosen to be flexible or vague. Organisations are collections of individuals and one way of viewing an organisation is as a bundle of individuals acting as if they had some common purpose, even if this has not been agreed, declared or published. Determining both how agreement about purpose is to be achieved, and what makes a good expression of purpose, is problematic.

Over the last two decades, managers have been bombarded with vision statements and mission statements, many of which are regarded as a joke by them and others in the organisation. In the public sector the use of these business-oriented terms sometimes causes resentment because they trivialise public service, and so ensure that strategy statements are ignored.

> *Vision or mission statements (statements of purpose) are either regarded as obvious ... or unrealistic.*

However, very few organisations in the western world believe that they can get away without a statement that starts 'our mission is ...'. But, at the same time, a document entitled 'the mission statement' has become disreputable in many organisations, and organisational cynics about strategy use mission statements as an example of strategy nonsense. Their case is that the mission statement is meaningless, unrealistic, not related to what the organisation is really doing, has no impact on the behaviour of senior management, and so on. They are often absolutely right. Many such vision or mission statements (statements of purpose) are either regarded as obvious – because they are 'motherhood' statements that apply to all organisations in their sector, or unrealistic because they state aspirations that cannot possibly be achieved with current resources and within a reasonable time frame. In addition, a careful analysis of many statements of purpose demonstrates incoherency – emanating from unrecognised conflict and incompatibility of goals. The process of *reverse engineering* an existing statement of purpose into a hierarchy or network of causally linked goals (discussed later in this chapter and in Chapter 6) can be very revealing – highlighting the inadequacies of existing goal statements and making the activity an uncomfortable process.

ORGANISATIONAL PURPOSE

There is often confusion about what the difference is between a vision statement, mission statement, statement of values, statement of goals, statement of strategic objectives, and so on. While the academic community has taken great trouble in defining each of these terms (and disagreeing about the definitions), managers simply want a way of expressing a sense of direction and purpose – a statement of strategic intent and a framework for action. To make things worse, when examining organisations' published strategic intent there are frequent examples of double messages where the statement of intent/purpose that is made public is not taken seriously by the management team (as evidenced by their behaviour). Sometimes there is confusion on the part of all in the organisation, senior managers and other staff, about the role of a mission statement. It has been published in order to manage powerful players outside the organisation such as financial analysts and customers and yet, at the same time, create internal strategic change. In this book we are not concerned about whether mission or vision statements are appropriate descriptors of purpose but rather focus on the process of agreeing organisational purpose and what the statement of purpose is.

Humans are purposeful and employ choice in attempting to realise their goals.

The requirement for a statement of purpose finds clear expression in the strategic planning literature.[2] Strategic planning is argued to be fundamentally related to organisational purpose[3] and is concerned with the objectives and aims of the organisation, and how these will be achieved.[4] One aspect of strategic planning therefore is the coordination of diverse elements of the organisation.[5] Adopting a planning approach to strategy requires identifying a series of steps leading to the achievement of goals.[6] Within the planning process a goal hierarchy is established *in advance of* taking action, with the achievement of more clearly defined specific goals leading to the achievement of less clearly defined, broader goals.[7] The persistence of goals as a central theme in the literature is not surprising since the majority of the strategy literature assumes humans are purposeful and employ choice in attempting to realise their goals.[8]

A statement of purpose can also be seen as playing a role in encouraging managers to feel that they are able to contribute to the organisation beyond just ensuring continuing production or service provision at the operational level. Managers usually like to feel that their contributions link with the attainment of the purpose – a vision of the future – and that they have the power and ability to play their part in creating that future. Demonstrating the linking of strategic programmes and lower level responsibilities to grander organisational goals, linking changes in operations to strategic outcomes, and linking rewards for managerial thinking and action to the delivery of strategy is of course difficult. Yet it is only when this can be done that the individual manager can feel more than a 'cog in the wheel'.

The goals system that emerges will always be a result of managing the constraints and political processes between organisational actors.

We see effective strategy as a coherent set of discrete actions by managers and others in the organisation in support of a system of goals, where these actions are supported by a self-sustaining critical mass, or momentum, of opinion in the organisation. Organisations are collectives in which individuals are instrumental in goal delivery and also goal formation,[9] and disagreement about goals, and the means of achieving these goals, can be a source of conflict.[10] Strategy, from an organisational purpose perspective, is about attempting to achieve goals in interaction with or against other members of the organisation.[11] Consequently, the goals system that emerges will always be a result of managing the constraints and political processes between organisational actors.[12] Attempts to describe organisational goals as being unitary either in terms of reflecting a single individual or a group consensus is likely to be misguided, presenting an unrealistic description of goals and goal formation in organisations.[13] Political processes are significant factors that often prevent organisational actors from establishing a consensus about comprehensive long term outcomes[14] and the group processes we present in this chapter and the next seek to attend to this situation.

While tensions over conflicting goals are typical of public sector and not-for-profit organisations,[15] as more organisations work collaboratively, or change their internal arrangements and/or their relationships to external structures, organisations must increasingly accommodate conflicting goals.[16] Also, conflicting goals may occur in relation to time horizon considerations, where some goals aim for short term benefits which potentially cause long term damage but might be required for survival.

Some research suggests that goal diversity, rather than consensus, promotes higher economic performance.[17] Thus, in some circumstances, attempts at developing goal consensus may be counterproductive for organisational performance. However, assumptions of goal consensus with the senior management team and the organisation as a whole persist.[18] And, for the most part, and for most organisations, a high degree of goals consensus is important. Even where a diversity of goals from a range of organisational perspectives is acknowledged, for example in developing a 'balanced score card',[19] it is assumed that these goals can be integrated coherently. A balanced score card perspective has a goal hierarchy of organisational, departmental and individual goals forming an 'integrated set of objectives ... agreed upon by all senior executives' with any lack of agreement resolved by non-political processes of discussion and communication.[20] The 'strategy as purpose' forum starts with a similar *objective* – that of seeking consensus about organisational goals – not only with respect to the broad statements at the top of a goals hierarchy, but also for their relationship with departmental and even personal goals. The creation of a statement of purpose in this way also seeks to acknowledge, as a matter of importance, that operations and strategy are integrally linked.

Goals and Effective Strategic Thinking

Effective strategic thinking involves an appreciation of a goals system, that is, a pattern of goals consisting of multiple and interlinked goals.

People in organisations act with intentionality, some more strategically than others, even if this action is regarded by others as misguided. Research on the nature of effective strategic thinking suggests some characteristics of thinking are particularly important, and the first of these is an appreciation of a *system* of goals.[21] Effective strategic thinking involves an appreciation of a goals system, that is, a pattern of goals consisting of *multiple and interlinked goals* rather than a single goal or a simple sequence of goals. This system of goals includes an appreciation of goals relating to different entities, for example, supra-organisational, organisational, departmental and personal goals. Goals are expected to be in conflict as well as alignment, for example, inevitably many attempts to manage costs will be in conflict with the requirements to generate revenue. An appreciation is also required of *negative goals* (for example 'staff burn out'), which are ends to be avoided (ramifications) but which may be more tangible and drive action more strongly than more easily expressed positive goals. Risk is associated with these negative goals, and actions may be required in terms of damage limitation from inevitable downside outcomes. Furthermore, an appreciation of a goals system involves seeing consequences beyond the immediate, including not just a temporal interpretation but also a causal one.

Emergent Purpose

Patterns of habitual action can form despite managerial intentions, but which reflect the intentions of some organisational actors.

In practice, action occurs in both a routine, habitual and unreflective way and also in a more considered, reflective way[22] and strategy is developed via both emergent and planned actions.[23] This emergent strategising[24] is probably the most realistic description of the delivery of strategy. Emergent strategising is a combination of muddling through in a manner that reflects the culture of the organisation – the habits of thinking and behaviours. In the 'issue management' chapter (chapter 4) we sought to understand how this emergent strategising revealed itself through the nature of the issues, identified by managers, whose resolution was crucial to deliver a successful strategic future. In this chapter we shall consider, as one approach to developing a goals system, how to reveal the emergent purpose of the organisation by seeking to understand the implications of issue prioritising as the basis for determining strategic focus: the strategic goals of the organisation.

A strategy may also, however, emerge through mindless coping, through actions arising from habituated tendencies and internalised dispositions rather than from deliberate, purposeful, goal-setting initiatives.[25] The primary mode of strategy may be a purposive mode which becomes more prominent when there is a dislocation of expectations, and this may cause a switch from automatic processing to more conscious engagement.[26] Even though it is reasonable to presume that much human action takes place in a form of *mindless coping*, the mindless coping is purposive, but not necessarily with an overall grander goal in mind. Similarly, although some authors emphasise the random and emergent nature of action in organisations, the use of phrases such as 'discovering preferences' and 'trial and error' suggests a degree of purposefulness in action.[27] Thus, patterns of habitual action can form despite managerial intentions, but which reflect the intentions of some organisational actors.[28]

Thus, at one extreme actions are seen as deliberate, methodical and sequential as in a linear, planned approach to delivering strategic goals.[29] At the other extreme, organisational systems and procedures are seen to generate action in an automatic and unreflective way, with the benefits of those actions poorly articulated, understood or even considered.[30] In this and the next chapter we therefore consider the role of the 'strategy as purpose forum' as:

1 Developing a clear understanding of the published goals of the organisation – as a *system* of goals – by reverse engineering a published document into a network of causalities (a causal map) that shows the systemic patterning, or not, of the goals.
2 Creating a goals system from scratch with a management team.
3 Understanding and developing the emergent goals system, prompted through an issues management forum, into an appropriate articulated goals system.

In developing and agreeing a goals system there is a tension between the presentation of certainty to gain a degree of commitment and legitimacy and yet the need for recognition that uncertainty is inevitable and flexibility and opportunism are usually required.[31]

UNDERSTANDING GOALS

What Is a Goals System?

The relationship between goals is usually one way in which the goals of one organisation are distinctive from that of another.

What do we mean by a 'goal'? For us, a goal is something that is 'good in its own right', in other words it is something that the group or an individual want to achieve even if other goals were not met. For example, in the academic world a goal might be 'carry out good research'. For an organisation working with social and economic regeneration, it might be 'improve the living and working environment of the area'. Other examples of a goal might be 'build the strongest digital brand' or 'grow the business through diversification'. However, 'develop more links with local companies' is probably not a goal, as it is currently worded in a manner that suggests it is a means to an end rather than an end in its own right.

It is normally the case that an organisation aspires, emergently or deliberately, towards more than one goal and these goals are interconnected – each goal is supported by others, and in turn each goal supports other goals – the goals make up a *system of goals*. For the academic world – the goal regarding research might contribute to a superordinate goal relating to 'sustain an excellent reputation', whereas for the regeneration group they might 'work to regenerate the local economy' to support the goal of 'improving the environment'. This is how we get a system of goals. The relationship between goals is usually one way in which the goals of one organisation are distinctive from that of another. For example, many organisations would state 'better motivation of staff' as one of their goals; however, the distinctiveness of this goal derives from the particular goals supported by 'better motivation', and the particular goals that support the attainment of 'better motivation' (see figure 5.1 where two extracts from goals systems show different meanings of the motivation goal). Usually we expect any organisation to display distinctiveness through its goals system, as well as distinctiveness in the ways in which it achieves its goals (the business model that represents the causal links between distinctive competencies and the aspirations – goals system – of the organisation – see chapter 8). The goals system expresses the unique purpose of the organisation.

Goals in a goals system may be quite broad and general or more narrow and specific. Goals can be positive, in terms of something to achieve, or negative, in terms of something to avoid. Goals are always multiple, and usually reflect the interests of a number of stakeholders. Hence, sometimes goals may be consensual or conflicting. Consensual goals may lead to support from other stakeholders while conflicting goals may lead to resistance. Goals may differ in the extent to which they are predetermined or emergent as a result of constraints and political processes between managers.

Generic Goals and Business Goals

Generic goals do not distinguish one organisation from another organisation in the same sector.

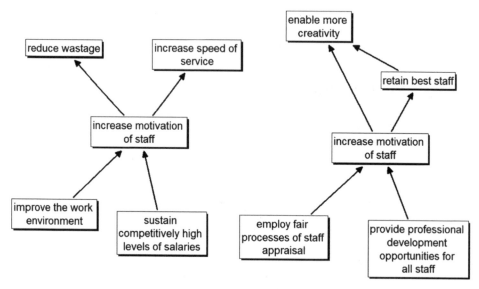

Figure 5.1 Two Different Meanings for the Goal of Staff Motivation in Two Organisations (the arrows represent support by, and support of, other goals)

Usually a system of goals portrays broad based and fairly generic goals at the top of a hierarchy.[32] In the for-profit sector these generic goals will be statements such as 'increase revenue', 'better control of costs', 'increase motivation of all staff', 'higher sales turnover'. And, of course, the ultimate top of the hierarchy is likely to be 'increase profitability', 'increase profit', or 'increase shareholder value' – each of which are generic goals. In the not-for-profit organisations, the superordinate goal is often the mandate from government, its funder or, in the case of a charity, the raison d'être for the creation of the organisation. These generic goals do not distinguish one organisation from another organisation in the same sector (for example, 'holding securely those committed to our charge' is likely to be a goal common to all prisons).

Moving further down the hierarchy there will be goals that are more specific to the nature of the business. These specific business goals differentiate 'the business we're in' and these will service or support the generic goals. These business goals will be focused on both (1) delivering products or services that are of value to the customer, and so deliver revenue, and (2) delivering managed costs. Of course, many business goals increase costs with the expectation of generating revenue, for example a goal of creating more effective advertising is expected to deliver customers, costs money, and does not deliver customer value. Although note that advertising may not be seen by some organisations as a good outcome in its own right but rather only as a means to an end, and so would not usually be a goal. However, other organisations may see effective advertising as an important symbol of a successful organisation, in which case it might be legitimately regarded as a goal. The dual structure of costs and 'revenue' is represented by figures 5.2a (for-profit) and 5.2b (not-for-profit). Thus, for example, the structure (hierarchy) and categorisation (business and generic) helps conceptualise a goals system for a for-profit enterprise into those goals that manage costs, those that deliver customer value, and those that are focused on revenue generation without adding value for the customer. Business goals will primarily satisfy one of these routes.

Figure 5.2a   The Structure of a Goals System Delivered Through Strategic Priorities for a For-profit Organisation

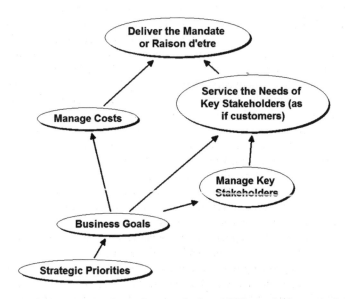

Figure 5.2b   The Structure of a Goals System Delivered Through Strategic Priorities for a Not-for-profit Organisation

It is important to remember that the nature of any specific goals system will be contingent on the nature of the organisation, the nature of the environment, and the competences of the organisation that provide it with competitive advantage. For not-for-profit organisations the notion of a customer is complex and the structure of the goals system will not match that of a for-profit organisation (see figures 5.2a and 5.2b). 'Customers' will not usually pay for the product or service and so will not be the strongest determinant of the nature of the product or service, rather the mandate or raison d'être defines the nature of the product or service. For most charities a number of goals will be associated with managing powerful stakeholders who have no interest in the mandate or raison d'être of the organisation but can determine the success of the organisation. Thus, for example, Amnesty International has 'customers' who receive the service of protecting them from torture through the work undertaken by Amnesty in managing both stakeholders with a direct interest in sabotaging that work, or in supporting it. Also Amnesty are likely to have a set of goals that are about managing other actors who have no direct interest in torture but indirectly encourage it.

> *Organisations are often slow to change in the face of environmental factors and environmental selection processes might better explain organisational change than goal directedness.*

In constructing a goals system, broad goal statements may be more useful than specifically articulated goals in accommodating fast environmental changes.[33] For example, 'deliver higher quality products' – without specifying the nature of quality – may be the only sensible goal that can frame action. Organisations are often slow to change in the face of environmental factors and environmental selection processes might better explain organisational change than goal directedness.[34] The value of broader goals also finds expression in the notion of stating strategic intent in which longer term organisational obsessions, which cannot be defined precisely, are designed to inspire employees to personal effort and commitment in the pursuit of highly ambitious goals.[35] Thus, for example, an organisation may have what they see as the ambitious goal of being 'recognised as one of the very best in Europe' but precisely specifying the definition of 'best' at this time might be unhelpful. In addition, sometimes the competitive advantage of the organisation depends upon its ability to exploit opportunism[36] and in these circumstances a *rough* and equivocal framework for action may be advantageous.

Business goals provide distinctiveness. Moreover, it is likely that the goals that deliver customer value are more specifically distinctive while those that manage costs tend to be relatively more generic because the ways of managing costs are more likely to be common across any sector. However, although each goal statement supporting managing costs will also be generic, often there will be a very specific *particular goal focus* (even though other goals would still be valid) for the business given its circumstances. Thus, for example, 'reducing waste' is likely to support the managing cost goal for most organisations, and one that may not even need to be explicitly stated. However, for a specific organisation there may need to be a strategic focus on this goal for many years in order to correct disastrous levels of waste – in which case it would be explicitly stated and a differentiation goal. In addition the uniqueness of a goals system will often derive from the specific structure of the network of goals: several organisations may, as noted above, have a goal statement about increasing the motivation of all of their staff, but in each case the manner in which they will do this (the supporting goals and strategies), and the outcomes they expect to achieve, will be specific to the organisation and so differentiate this goal (see figure 5.3). Thus, to recap, it is the *network* that shows differentiation of purpose as well as the statements themselves.

Goals as Multiple Criteria: Ways of Helping Make Judgements About Strategic Priorities?

When evaluating possible strategies it would seem sensible to consider them in relation to their contribution to delivering each of the goals in a goals system. The goals system thus

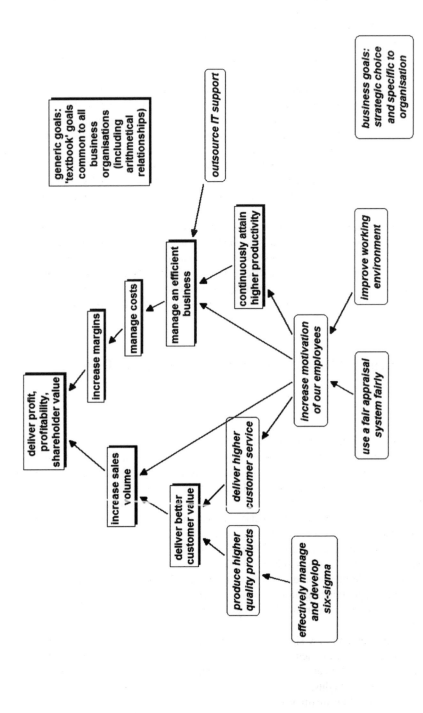

Figure 5.3 An Example of a Goals System Where the Goals Have Been Split Between Generic and Business Goals. For a goals system, statement of purpose, to be useful it must go beyond generic (textbook) goals and express the strategic focus of the particular organisation. (Italics indicate business goals and non-italic shows generic goals)

makes a hierarchy of criteria and each goal can be weighted differently to reflect its overall importance. A technique known as multiple criteria decision analysis can be used for the evaluation.[37] The use of the technique depends upon having a tidy tree structure where each goal has a series of subgoals and those subgoals service only one higher-order goal. In practice, real goals systems present a more complicated structure where each goal serves more than one superordinate goal.

However, the principle of exploring potential strategic priorities by considering the relative leverage of a strategy on multiple goals is helpful in making judgements about the potency of strategy. A strategy that helps deliver many goals might be considered a higher priority than one that addresses fewer goals. Similarly, such considerations may also help in judgements about the extent of resource to be applied to the delivery of a particular strategy.

Thinking about a goals system as multiple criteria has some conceptual similarity to producing a balanced scorecard from strategy maps.[38] Not only does the balanced scorecard place emphasis on building consensus around strategic objectives (goals) but, in addition, encourages participants to consider explicitly how each of the means for measurement are linked both across the four perspectives and across objectives. Furthermore, the use of the four perspectives (customers, financial, processes and new business) in the process of identifying objectives helps encourage a wider set of objectives – a process not dissimilar to using the prompts noted above relating to considering business versus generic goal categorisation, and/or using consideration of both wider and organisational goals. Nevertheless, a restriction to the suggested four perspectives does not encourage the 'free-form' outcomes that can arise from the approaches taken in this book.

Real Goals Versus Published Goals: The Role of Negative Goals

Negative goals tend to give as strong a clue about the emergent strategic direction of the organisation as do positive goals.

Managers act to avoid negative outcomes, with no clear conception of a positive future organisational state.[39] Many priority strategic issues are resolved in order to avoid disastrous outcomes. These disastrous outcomes are negative goals – that is 'aspirations to avoid'. As we suggested above, negative goals tend to give as strong a clue about the emergent strategic direction of the organisation as do positive goals. For negative goals, (1) the contrasting circumstance would not be expressed as a goal, but the outcome (disaster) is of the same status as a goal (but is negative) and must be avoided, or (2) the negative goal may be incorporated into the goals system by negating it. For example, a governmental organisation such as a school may identify a major issue related to drug taking in schools; this may be seen as the consequences of their own actions or those of others. While they would never have adopted a goal related to drug taking in the normal course of strategic thinking, now they have to deal with the negative goal (disaster) of drugs and so they may revise their own goals system to include the goal of 'keep drug taking under control'.

One way of understanding how significant negative goals can be is to consider them at the personal level. We gain a clearer sense of ourselves by reflecting upon what we seek to avoid and what causes a feeling of great anxiety as we anticipate the future – understanding the thinking that produces sleepless nights.

Apparent patterns of action are often attempts to work within a set of organisational constraints which are, in effect, goals.[40] However, if managers were to be asked what their goals were then they would be unlikely to talk about the way in which their behaviour is framed by the avoidance of negative outcomes or managing within constraints. It is somehow only legitimate to talk of positive goals. And yet, this focus on avoiding disastrous outcomes is a perfectly legitimate activity. This perceived requirement to talk only about positive goals is reinforced when considering some of the well-known approaches to dealing with messy organisational problems. These approaches start with an assumption that managers know what their objectives are, or that problems are to be formulated against an idealised conception of where the organisation wants to be.[41] Thus, managers are used to the idea that unless they know what their goals are and can clearly articulate them then they are lousy managers. This requirement reinforces a view that goals not only should be known but also should be positive – managers rarely regard a discussion about negative goals as being legitimate.

Espoused goals (published and spoken) can be ignored when deciding how to act. The beliefs and aspirations that surface as managers act, either directly or indirectly, are the basis for understanding the real – emergent – goals. Confusion between real goals and espoused goals can be further exacerbated when senior managers, who believe they are acting consistently within a world of complex multiple goals, are perceived to be acting inconsistently by others who are more singularly focused on their tasks. Double messages can abound, particularly where senior managers demands one thing from their subordinates but appear to pay little attention to it themselves by doing the opposite.

Thus, in understanding purpose we, (1) do not presume that we know what goals drive the behaviour of the organisation, because we may not know what they are, and it can be dangerous to presume that they are those published, and (2) accept that goals can be negative.

'Umbrella' or Meta-goals

Meta-goals are particularly rife for public and not-for-profit organisations.

Often strategy making is not undertaken for the whole organisation, but rather for a department, strategic business unit or division of a large organisation. In these cases it is important to recognise that the goals system of a department is expected to relate to the goals of the organisation as a whole. The goals of the organisation as a whole are an umbrella that encompasses the goals of the department – the goals of the organisation do not belong directly to the department but are hierarchically superordinate to them. Goals of the department may only be strategies for the organisation as a whole.

Similarly, meta-goals are goals that no one part of the organisation could attain on their own, or in the case of alliances or collaboration they could not be attained without all of the organisations working together.[42] Only when meta-goals can be identified is it possible to conceive of the means for supplying a potential *collaborative advantage*[43] for the members of the collaborative. The trick for the 'sponsor' of the collaborative is to anticipate the potential for collaborative advantage and to manipulate a sharing of perspectives in such a way as to enable the collaborators to see meta-goals that will coincide with the strategic intent of the sponsor.

Meta-goals are particularly rife for public and not-for-profit organisations and most particularly among multi-organisation collaborations.[44] Thus the goal is a goal of the collaborative – addressing a public problem that requires one's own actions and those of others. The meta-goal is deliberately created by the collaboration.

'Not-our-goal' Goals

An organisation may also actively support the goal throughout the collaboration but not adopt it as its own goal because it is not prepared to be held accountable for it.

Identifying umbrella goals, and so the boundary between the goals of a part of the organisation and those of the wider organisation and stakeholders, will define what can usefully be called 'not-our-goals'. This type of goal is a not-our-goal because it is not a goal that the organisation can adopt without the help of others in its achievement and not necessarily explicitly agreed across several organisations. With collaboration it *may* become a goal for the organisation. An organisation may also actively support the goal throughout the collaboration but not adopt it as its own goal because it is not prepared to be held accountable for it – this is not-our-goal. Not-our-goals 'do not belong to us', they will include the goals of powerful and interested other parties (stakeholders). These others have such powers that the goals act as constraints to the actions of the organisation. Thus, instead of being at the bottom of a strategy map as constraints, they represent outcomes 'we must drive towards, because they are the goals of stakeholders in our future (not necessarily supportive stakeholders)'. Sometimes this means that not-our-goals are goals that 'we are not prepared to be accountable for the achievement of *but must support*'. They may also be goals that are higher up the goals hierarchy and to which 'we wish to contribute to, but could not achieve on our own'.

This category of goal is particularly useful in working out purpose for a not-for-profit or public sector organisation. For example, the chief executive of a prison service saw it as very important to acknowledge a goal of 'keeping prisoners safely housed' but would only acknowledge that he contributed to 'reducing recidivism (re-offending)' – reducing recidivism was a not-our-goal for his organisation, but one worth expressing at a hierarchically superordinate level because it signalled that he expected his organisation to make a contribution. Thus the prison service was pleased to collaborate with other social support agencies in helping reduce recidivism but was not prepared to be held accountable for this goal. However, the chief executive was particularly keen to ensure that all his staff were wholly committed to seeking to reduce recidivism but his management team wanted to be clear that this was not-our-goal and they did not wish to be judged against it. Achieving their own goals – and the larger public goal of reducing recidivism – involves supporting the actions of others in the collaboration, where the not-our-goal relates to the larger public issue. A not-our-goal would arise when there were significant positive externalities. It is, however, possible that this circumstance amounts to implicit collaboration, because it is appreciated only by one organisation. In this case the goals of the organisation are seen as paramount and the larger public goal is a by-product.

SMART Goals Versus Vague Goals

Some management, and particularly project management, books argue that unless goals are SMART[45] – specific, measurable, attainable, realistic and timely – then they serve no useful purpose and will not drive behaviour. In some instances this is a reasonable stance to take, however, in other situations opportunism is a perfectly rational response to uncertain and rapidly changing ('high velocity')[46] environments. Opportunism and flexibility within a framework of purpose is thus appropriate.[47] The rate of change of events and the unpredictability of opportunities and problems means that it is sensible for goals and processes not to be elaborately developed – it may be much better to have a plan that is loose and easily adapted. Thus, in articulating purpose it is not always necessary that goals be SMART goals.

Sometimes designed ambiguity in strategy, and in particular in mission statements, is important. The mission provides no more than a rough framework for strategic action.

Cyclical Goals

It is important to recognise that sometimes the impact of one goal upon another can generate self-sustaining goal-oriented outcomes. Recognising that some goals can feed off one another derives from considering goals as a system. Success breeding success is the most common form of positive feedback relating to a goals system. Thus higher profitability facilitates increased investment in delivering detailed actions which deliver strategies that service business goals which in turn feeds profitability. However, in strategy making it is frequently unhelpful to be explicit about this generic form of feedback: in other words, explicitly recognising such feedback makes it more difficult to identify important feedback *within the structure of the goals system* itself.

Illustrating the Nature and Characteristics of a Goals System

The example in figure 5.4, showing the goals system of Strathclyde Poverty Alliance, illustrates many of the characteristics and issues related to developing and agreeing a goals system.

The goals system shows two (possibly three?) superordinate goals that express the raison d'être for the creation of the organisation: *influence decision makers* and *empower people*. The third superordinate goal of *survival* was queried by the group because they were emotionally committed to the notion of doing themselves out of a job (not surviving), but realised that getting rid of poverty was unrealistic even over the very long term, and so survival was a crucial goal. However, ultimately they saw the goal as the equivalent of the generic way in which business creates profit in order to invest: the cycle of investing to create profit to invest.

The goals system was developed by exploring the strategic issues that were regarded as high priority and seeking to understand why the management team had made that judgement. In doing so the team produced a 'ladder' of causality that encompassed many outcomes that were on the boundary of strategies versus goals. For example, the team had a useful discussion about the significance of 'communicate the work we do and the ethos behind it' – was it really a goal or just a strategy for delivering goals. The statement sounds operational not aspirational, it was not regarded as a difficult or particularly complex task, but it was regarded as difficult to get right. What swayed the debate was their sense that it was a good outcome *in its own right*, in other words they would celebrate success in its achievement and reckon that communication, in the right way, was a key purpose of their organisation (in this discussion the word 'ethos' was of great significance in capturing a part of the essence of the 'right way').

The team were particularly interested in the significance of the goals *system* – the pattern of goals. They had never before seen the split in their purpose between (1) addressing those in poverty and (2) managing the public agenda. They realised, with some considerable force, the significance of this for the skills base of their management team – those with the skills to operate within the community of those in poverty required very different skills from those needing to influence policy makers. As with so much of strategy making, the realisation seemed obvious once they had discovered it! In this example we see a clear sense of business goals that are focused on managing stakeholders (collaboration with partners), but also in managing actors who may have no interest in the 'customer' (the public, and decision makers). Because the customers are themselves powerless, they cannot act as normal customers, indeed the stream of goals on the left of figure 5.4 is about seeking to make them more like customers. Notably we see no goals associated with managing costs – a possible weakness of the goals system. However, a goals system is designed to focus attention on the strategic priorities over the time period relevant to the strategy making, and so it may be that managing costs is regarded as under control over that period and therefore not a strategic focus for managing the future.

The Mission or Vision Statement

We have, earlier in this chapter, presented concerns about mission/vision statements. Although these concerns matter, a mission statement can act as an important 'call to arms' or 'battalion flag' that can be a motivator for strategic change. A mission statement, or vision statement, can be a summary of a goals system. At one extreme, the statement can be a short and pithy statement (a couple of sentences) which differentiates the organisational aspirations from those of other organisations and is used for external consumption. At the other extreme, it can be a full page of contentful material that clearly sets out the full nature of the goals system as a realistic statement of strategic intent and which is designed for internal consumption.

Fortunately there is good research material indicating how an effective mission statement should be constructed[48] – and noting that purpose, values, strategy, and standards and behaviour must be linked together. In this chapter we are considering only purpose. But, expressing the statement of purpose is a necessary condition for a mission or vision statement, even though it will be desirable also to include statements about organisational values and standards of behaviour.

At the end of this chapter we consider how to convert a goals system into a statement of strategic intent (SSI). The SSI will, of course, only focus on purpose and will not include material that expresses values, strategy, or standards and behaviour. If the purpose SSI is linked to the SSI produced from an issues management forum then it becomes more complete, but significantly will still miss the important aspects of values and standards and behaviour.

THE STRATEGY AS PURPOSE FORUM

We stated earlier that the role of the strategy as purpose forum is to: (1) develop a clear understanding of the published goals of the organisation – as a system of goals, by reverse engineering a published document into a causal map that shows the systemic patterning, or not, of the goals; (2) create a goals system from scratch with a management team; and (3) understand and develop the emergent goals system emanating from an examination of a set of priority issues (possibly created through an issue management forum) into an appropriate articulated goals system – see box 5.1 for an example of a possible setting for exploring goals. In this section we present a brief overview of each of these possible forums. The purpose of this section is to provide some illustration of the concepts discussed above and how they are important for establishing purpose.

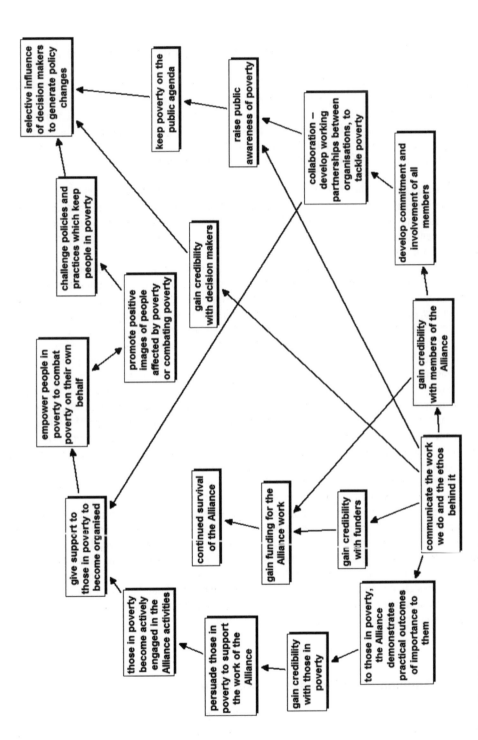

Figure 5.4 The Goals System for Strathclyde Poverty Alliance

Box 5.1 Vignette: 'Mission Statement Having No Real Impact'

The vice-president responsible for a large IT support division in a multinational company was disappointed that there seemed to be little real impact of the mission statement she had written a year ago. She was pleased with the statement, and it had followed some careful consultation with her managers in each of the country units around the world! But the division seemed to be continuing with 'business as usual'. She thought it might be a good idea to get all of her 23 top managers together off-site and revisit the statement and if necessary relaunch it across all of her staff.

She was attracted to the idea of 'starting from scratch'. Over half of her managers had moved on, and she accepted that a mission statement needed 'buy-in' if it was to change behaviours and deliver goals that would effectively service the rest of the organisation – her customers. The division seemed to be doing just a 'standard IT support job' and not seeking to help make the business more competitive.

Discussion, with the facilitator, about umbrella goals in the corporate goals statement, such as 'make the business more competitive', led to an exploration of how the current mission statement expressed the links between the work of the IT support division and the requirements of the business. As the discussion progressed, the facilitator crudely began to map on to a Decision Explorer® view what she was saying – building up the hierarchy of goals. It became clear to the facilitator that the map was revealing a very different structure of means-ends to the impression the facilitator had gained from reading the published mission statement. Although the purpose was to move forward from the existing statement, the facilitator suggested 'reverse engineering' the current mission statement into a means-end map of organisational purpose. This was suggested for two reasons: (1) to explore why there appeared to be a difference between the existing mission statement and the VP's verbal statements, and (2) unravel the logic of the mission statement. Each of these reasons was felt to be a useful preface to designing a group forum. The reverse engineering process was completed 'live' with the VP in her office and took about one hour. It was revealing – statements of purpose seemed to be disconnected (four 'intermediate' goal statements did not express any purposeful consequences), there was a mixture of language from obvious aspirations to non-aspirational statements of what is (such as 'we are a highly skilled IT group'). What was perhaps of most importance was the revelation that the published mission statement did not express what the VP had intended. The original statement she had drafted had been 'tidied up' by the HQ communications staff and had clearly got lost in translation. In addition she realised how she had emphasised outcome and not the causal links, thus missing an expression about 'why one thing led to another'. She could now understand how it might be possible that this was at least one reason why her staff had 'not got the message'.

She was now more convinced that a goals forum might help to develop some clarity about the means-ends relationships as well as develop ownership.

Reverse Engineering a Published Goals System

Most existing organisations have some published expression of purpose lying around. Sometimes these expressions of purpose have been written for consumption by the marketplace and customers, sometimes they have been published to be read by financial analysts, and sometimes they have been broadcast with the intention of influencing the behaviour of members of the organisation. On many occasions the final published document has been polished by public relations experts and so may be more focused on style than content. Nevertheless, it is a document that should not be ignored when considering strategy as an expression of purpose as it is one expression of purpose that may influence the strategic future of the organisation. These published expressions of purpose very often display a lack of clarity about causality, show too little aspiration, and confuse.

In our first example we consider the published goals of Glasgow airport (box 5.2). It is expressed as a vision, but we treat it as a statement of strategic intent. The first steps are to separate each of the different goals in the text (see the underlined material in box 5.3). The process of identifying each goal usually raises questions about what is meant. Thus, for example, statement 7 might have been separated into two parts: (1) social, and (2) economic prosperity; however, the judgement call was to imply that for BAA they saw the coupling of both parts as important. Also the goal of 'serve Scotland well in the future' has been treated as an overall heading for the text rather than taken out as a separate goal, or alternatively is taken to be the same as 'supporting Scotland'. Each of the judgements could be mistaken, but the lack of clarity is often of importance in seeking to unravel a goals statement and rewrite it.

Box 5.2   The Vision Statement for Glasgow Airport

The vision for **Glasgow Airport** is simple: through sustained and sensible investment in the airport's infrastructure and through the continuing development of a strong and lasting route network, Scotland's busiest airport will become Europe's most successful regional airport, supporting Glasgow, supporting Scotland, and promoting social and economic prosperity. In doing this, BAA Scotland willingly accepts its responsibility to local communities and we restate our commitment to long-term engagement with all airport neighbours, to ensure we remain a responsible and trusted partner in Glasgow and Renfrewshire's future.

If Glasgow Airport is to serve Scotland well in the future, it must continue to provide first-class facilities, and this Master Plan represents a blueprint for the airport of the future. (As published on BAA Glasgow website March 2010)

Box 5.3   Separating Each Goal in the Vision Statement for Glasgow Airport

BAA's vision for Glasgow Airport is simple: through (1) sustained and (2) sensible investment in the airport's infrastructure and through the (3) continuing development of a strong and lasting route network, Scotland's busiest airport will (4) become Europe's most successful regional airport, (5) supporting Glasgow, (6) supporting Scotland, and (7) promoting social and economic prosperity. In doing this, (8) BAA Scotland willingly accepts its responsibility to local communities and we restate our (9) commitment to long-term engagement with all airport neighbours, to (10) ensure we remain a responsible and trusted partner in Glasgow and Renfrewshire's future. If Glasgow Airport is to serve Scotland well in the future, it must (11) continue to provide first-class facilities, and this Master Plan represents a blueprint for the airport of the future.

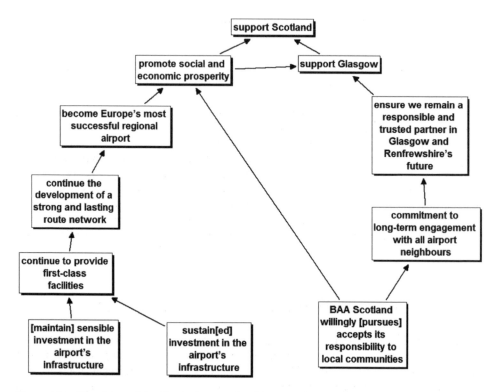

Figure 5.5 The Map of the Goals System for Glasgow Airport

The next step is to map out the causal links between each of the goals statements. Again, often significant judgement is required and sometimes it becomes impossible to determine with any surety when links exist. It is sometimes necessary to leave some statements with no links because it is not at all clear what other goals support or what other goals are expected to be the outcome. In building the goals *system* some words are changed in order to express the goal as an aspiration or to make the goal a variable (for example, adding maintain to the phrase 'sensible investment in the airport's infrastructure'). In doing so another judgement has been made by adding 'maintain' rather than, for example, 'grow' or 'create'.

Figure 5.5 shows the map of the goals system. The structure suggests two sets of goals – the left-hand side shows business goals and the right-hand side goals that are likely to be related to stakeholder management by showing the contribution of the airport to local communities, neighbours, the geographical setting, the local city (Glasgow) and to the country (Scotland). Similarly the top goals of supporting Scotland and promoting social and economic prosperity are not related to the business of running an airport, and cynically we might suggest play little part in managing the strategic future of the organisation. The goals on the left-hand side of the goals system do little to differentiate the airport from any other regional airport.

Our second example shows the translation of a very simple statement of 71 words of strategic intent into a goals system. IKEA sets out its vision (?) or goals (?) as a concept statement – see box 5.4.

Box 5.4   The IKEA Concept

The IKEA Concept is based on offering a wide range of well designed, functional home furnish-ing products at prices so low that as many people as possible will be able to afford them. Rather than selling expensive home furnishings that only a few can buy, the IKEA Concept makes it possible to serve the many by providing low-priced products that contribute to helping more people live a better life at home. (From the IKEA website October 2010)

Box 5.5 shows the first step of separating the goals. It is interesting that in this example we see several contrasts expressed – thus, 'as many people as possible will be able to afford them' is contrasted with 'only a few can buy'. The process of explicating contrasting circumstances often provides important richness of meaning. In unravelling the separate statements it is often helpful to identify the key parts of each phrase – in this case these have been shown using italics. Being clear about the key parts of a phrase helps the next step of identifying causality. Thus, it is a matter of debate as to whether 'well designed' and 'functional' represent two distinct goals. In this instance we are assuming that, for IKEA, the coupling of the two outcomes together is important, and both parts are taken in a single goal.

Box 5.5   Separating Goal Statements

The IKEA Concept is based on (1) offering a wide range of *well designed, functional* home fur-nishing products (2) at *prices so low* that (3) as *many people as possible* will be able to afford them. (2) Rather than selling expensive home furnishings that (3) only a few can buy, the IKEA Concept makes it possible to (4) serve the *many* by (2) providing low-priced products that con-tribute to (5) helping *more* people live a better life at home.

Figure 5.6 shows the goals system as reverse engineered from the IKEA Concept statement. It is a clear expression of a mission (or vision?) statement. There are no detailed business goals, which is not surprising for a 'concept statement'. However, it does differentiate the business and offer goals against which performance indicators could be developed with relative ease.

Creating a Goals System: Starting from Scratch

It is often unhelpful to take too much account of published goals, rather it is better to ensure that a purpose forum is not tightly framed by the past. Inevitably participants will have been influenced by existing published goals, but we might wish this to have the least possible impact upon considering appropriate goals for the future. Thus, instead of reverse engineering a vision/ mission/purpose statement it might be appropriate to 'start from scratch'.

In this forum we ask a very simple question: 'what should be the purpose of the organisation for the next *x* years?'. The significant payoff from this forum is (1) the construction of a goals *system* – a pattern of interacting goals set out as a network, and (2) the crafting of appropriate

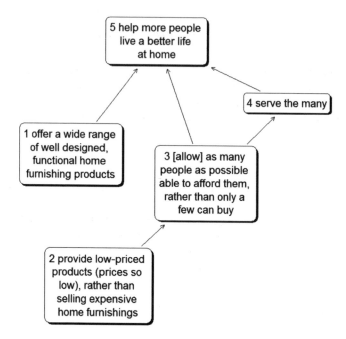

Figure 5.6   The Map of the IKEA Concept Statement

aspirational wording that enables the system to make sense – that is, ensuring that the meaning of any one goal satisfactorily relates to the other goals that helped deliver it, and the other goals that it helps deliver. In addition, there is likely to be significant organisational learning that derives from building a goals system together so that members of a management team *show themselves* how different parts of the organisation fit together and are systemically dependent on each other.

In answering this question about purpose the terms used to prompt appropriate answers will acknowledge the nature, culture and language of the organisation. In some organisations it will be appropriate to prompt the elicitation of purpose by asking for objectives, in others for aims or success factors. Often answers encompass operational actions and strategies as well as more obvious goals. As we have argued above, the boundary between goals and strategies is fuzzy. Drawing the boundary between goals and strategies across the material surfaced usually prompts a helpful conversation where the discussion forces the team to separate optional strategies from non-optional outcomes. Making this separation will be a pragmatic as well as conceptual consideration – there is a temptation to be too inclusive because each member of the team views some optional strategies as non-optional, that is they are fixed in their own views about what must be done to achieve important goals outcomes. However, there will be a limit to the complexity that the management team accept as a statement of purpose – in practice a goals system that goes much beyond 25 goals is likely to be overly complex.

As with discovering a goals system through reverse engineering a public statement, in this forum we are unlikely to surface negative goals, and this is an important weakness – a weakness that is less likely when following an emergent strategising forum that works off priority strategic issues.

Box 5.6   30 Suggested Goals for the Institute Science Grouping

9 increase income from non-public funded research visitors
10 exchange of staff
11 research collaborations
12 enhance our profile
13 enhanced reputation of the science grouping within the Institute
14 make us more recognised around the world
15 increase revenue
16 raise more income from collaborative opportunities
19 enhance reputation in the world
21 create community of scholars drawn from UK and abroad
22 increase profile of work done at the Institute
23 flexible and reliable source of income
24 knowledge exchange opportunities
25 research papers with overseas partners
27 enhance experience of our staff
28 gain a more international outlook
30 research staff exchange possibilities
31 create strategic alliances
32 become more competitive
33 tap into capacities (hardware)/themes that we have not thought of
35 enhance the research exchange possibilities
36 lose best research staff to linked institutes
37 learn from other institutions
53 gain joint funding with o/s partners
54 identify our research strengths
55 attract and recruit more international research staff
56 identify research needs
57 horizon scanning of funding opportunities
58 wider range of topics with o/s partners
63 build upon existing international links

Consider a team of scientists reviewing their goals for internationalisation, where each member of the team has, in turn, suggested distinctive outcomes that are 'good outcomes in their own right'. The suggestions are made by going around the team in turn until each participant runs out of contributions. Box 5.6 shows an example of the output from this task (note that the reference numbering from Decision Explorer® implies that some suggested goals were merged with others and some deleted).

Some of these goals were regarded as synonyms and so were easily merged (although sometimes phrases considered very similar by the facilitator are very different for the participants who proffered them – see the discussion on motivation above and figure 5.1). One of these statements is a negative goal that might be converted into a positive negative goal: '36 lose best research staff to linked institutions' becomes '36 AVOID losing best research staff to linked institutions'. Many were quickly identified as strategies rather than goals. The statements were reduced to candidate goals reasonably quickly (see box 5.7), even though there were still some that were taken to be on the border line and needed further discussion.

Box 5.7   Twenty-two Candidate Goals

9 increase income from non-public funded research visitors
10 exchange of staff
11 generate more research collaborations
12 enhance our profile
13 enhanced reputation of the science grouping within the Institute
14 enhance reputation in the world and make us more recognised around the world
15 increase revenue
16 raise more income from collaborative opportunities
21 create community of scholars drawn from UK and abroad
22 increase profile of work done at the Institute
23 deliver a more flexible and reliable source of income
24 create knowledge exchange opportunities
25 publish research papers with overseas partners
27 enhance experience of our staff
28 gain a more international outlook
31 create strategic alliances
32 become more competitive
33 tap into capacities (hardware)/themes that we have not thought of
35 enhance the research exchange possibilities
36 AVOID losing best research staff to linked institutes
37 learn from other institutions
55 attract and recruit more international research staff

The next step was to ask the group to consider important causal links between the candidate goals. In this step it is not unusual for participants to use 'upside-down' links where the means-ends relationship is incorrect. Also after the group have offered links then it is likely that summary links are entered as well as direct links. This task will encourage participants to revisit the boundary between strategies/actions and goals.

The first attempt at linking produced the goals system shown in figure 5.7. The map is complex and shows an examples of summary links (for example, 35 enhance the research exchange possibilities may lead to 24 create knowledge exchange opportunities, which can lead to 25 publish research papers with overseas partners; but also 35 enhance the research exchange possibilities may lead directly to 25 publish research papers with overseas partners: is the summary link of 35>25 necessary? Does it say anything different from the indirect link?). In the example given the group believed that the direct link was in addition to the indirect link.

The group also noticed a feedback loop implying that 12 enhance our profile may lead to 14 enhance reputation in the world which can lead to 9 increase income from non-public funded research visitors which can lead to 23 deliver a more flexible and reliable source of income, which reinforces 12 enhance our profile. While the group believed that the feedback was legitimate, for the purposes of expressing their goals they felt that it was more important to identify

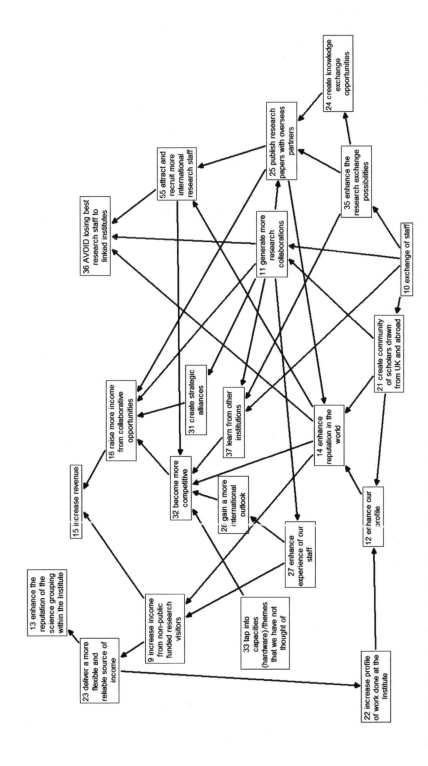

Figure 5.7 Mapping Out the First View of Candidate Goals

the hierarchy of importance, and so they opted for displaying statement 23 as the most hierarchical goal. The implications of such a feedback loop, in this case, are similar to the generic feedback loop often displayed in for-profit strategy statements where increases in profit leads to increased investment in strategic programmes which in turn delivers more profit.

Figure 5.8 shows the first draft of the final goals system. It was significant for the group that the key drivers that would follow from the delivery of an internationalisation strategy were now seen to be 14 enhance reputation in the world and 25 publish research papers with overseas partners. At this stage they were keen to include explicitly the negative goal.

This forum can often be a one-to-one forum where a facilitator works with the manager-client to unfold their view of the goals of the organisation. However, such a forum has significantly reduced benefits when compared to those identified above.

Emergent Strategising – Understanding Purpose Through Issue Management

Whether strategies are deliberate or emergent, some degree of intentionality by organisational actors appears to be present in all organisations,[49] although this intentionality might not be that of the senior management team.[50] It is this intentionality that we aim to capture in this forum.

One of the most significant complaints about strategy is that it is abstract, too high level, and so not practical. This is because often strategy is only a focus on outcomes and purpose without any clear expression about the link between action/operations and goals. Operations and strategy must be seen as integral to each other. Often a small operational decision is undertaken to drive out major strategic consequences, and often the actions are taken to resolve a short term problem without the long term strategic consequences for goals being considered. It is the link between priority strategic issues, which may be operationally focused, and goals that this forum seeks to unfold.

As attempts are made to decide how to resolve issues there often develops an understanding of the relationship between the issues and the purpose of their resolution. Ends (goals) and means (actions) are interactive components of strategy[51] – they are the causality that drives action and so purpose. Figure 5.2a, above, shows the link between issues and goals. The rationale for identifying the goals system derives from the assertion that problems or issues can only be seen as such, by an individual or an organisation, if a situation described by the issue statement attacks a desirable outcome, or creates an undesirable outcome (a negative goal). These envisaged outcomes are seen as seriously good or seriously bad.

However priority issues are determined, be it through an issues management forum (see chapter 4) or simply through the agreement of strategic priorities in a normal meeting, these priorities say something about the emergent goals of the organisation.

In principle the most hierarchical set of superordinate statements are assumed to be potential goals. Priority issues are a low level 'sort-of' goal and we need to elicit, in this forum, the positive or negative goals that might suggest or explain why the issues have been seen as priorities. This process of beginning to identify and structure the goals system that is emerging from an exploration of strategic issues helps in clarifying what the strategic direction of the organisation will be *if no deliberate actions are taken to change it*.

The process of trying to understand the implicit, unconscious or tacit sense of purpose implied by strategic priorities is a process of laddering up to goals and negative goals through the detail of business goals upward to generic goals. The forum follows a process of taking the

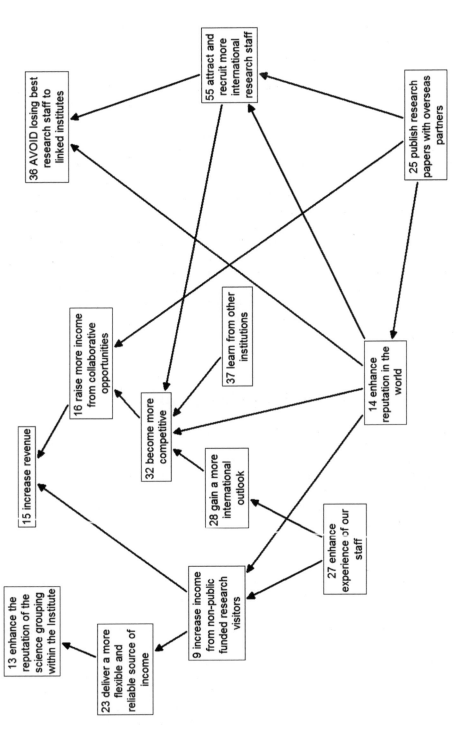

Figure 5.8 First Draft of a Goals System

highest priority issue and asking: 'what might happen, that's undesirable, if we don't address it?' or alternatively, 'what will we achieve if we were to find an effective way of addressing the issue?'. And then asking the same question of that answer, and so on, until the answer given is a goal or negative goal (an obviously bad outcome or good outcome *in its own right* for the organisation). This elicits the lowest level of business goal – a goal that is distinctive for the organisation and will be related to either revenue generation or cost management for a for-profit organisation (see figure 5.2a).

Box 5.8 shows the strategic priorities for a central marketing department of a large corporation. The aim was to use these judgements about (operational) strategic priorities as a way of understanding the emergent goals of the department. The top priority, as agreed by the group, was 'mktg dept find out more of what competition is doing' and so this was the first to be addressed as a basis for laddering up to goals. For the group this was easy – their answers were 'better management of the competition', what for? – 'to show the potential and value for money of the marketing dept', what for? – they argued that this was the most significant 'top' goal for the department. The group were directed back to 'mktg dept find out more of what competition is doing' and asked for any other purposes – 'marketing find the gaps in the market', what for? – 'better management of the competition'. They pondered whether there were other purposes (other than value for money) that followed from managing the competition – 'increase market share', although they did not take this as a goal that they saw themselves as wholly responsible for delivering. Figure 5.9 shows the ladder created through this conversation.

Box 5.8   Priority Strategic (?) Issues

mktg dept find out more of what competition is doing
stop a reactive frame of thinking
create opportunities to use mktg execs' time more efficiently
conduct more crude, quick and dirty research rather than throw money at it
create slack in mktg dept to cope with launches
mktg help develop new products rather than just concentrate on successful products
better sharing of information between execs

The conversation in the forum switched to the next highest priority strategy – 'create slack in mktg dept to cope with launches'. The first response to 'what for?' was to help deliver another strategy: 'mktg help develop new products rather than concentrate on successful products'. Both were thought to support the purpose of 'better and more successful launches', which was agreed to be a goal for the marketing department.

Figure 5.10 shows the first draft of the emergent goals system, based on the priority strategies (goals are those in a box, and others are issues). The figure shows the gradual development of the goals system where the reference numbers illustrate the order in which the statements were developed. Following the first draft the group refined the wording and links to ensure that the laddered up goals were goals for the department. They subsequently checked the goals system to see whether the emergent goals mapped on to their intuitive view of what they thought the goals system should look like – what was missing, what was unrealistic, what was not aspirational enough, whether the positive negative goal of 'stop the decrease in morale'

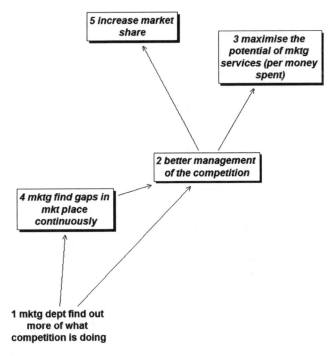

Figure 5.9 Initial Laddering Up from the Top Priority (reference numbers show the order the goals were elicited, goals are shown in boxes)

would be best expressed as 'increase morale' or whether it was better left because it would then be more realistic.

THE STRATEGY DELIVERABLE: A *STATEMENT* OF STRATEGIC INTENT (SSI)

The last task of a strategy making forum is that of converting the causal map of the goals system into the more usual recording principles of sentences and paragraphs – thus creating a statement of strategic intent. The causal maps have been used to facilitate a structured strategic conversation rather than be an outcome in their own right. A statement of strategic intent is designed to set out in a persuasive manner the purpose of the organisation as an aspirational, and yet realistic, intention that will guide behaviour and decision making as the organisation seeks to create a sustainable, successful future. A brief written statement of organisational purpose will be more familiar to staff in an organisation – a goals system expressed as a causal map, although showing means-ends relationships clearly, is often cryptic to anyone other than the group creating the map.

Production of the SSI

This task follows directly from a strategy as purpose forum, or from a meeting with the manager-client following adaptation and improvement of a reverse engineered goals statement.

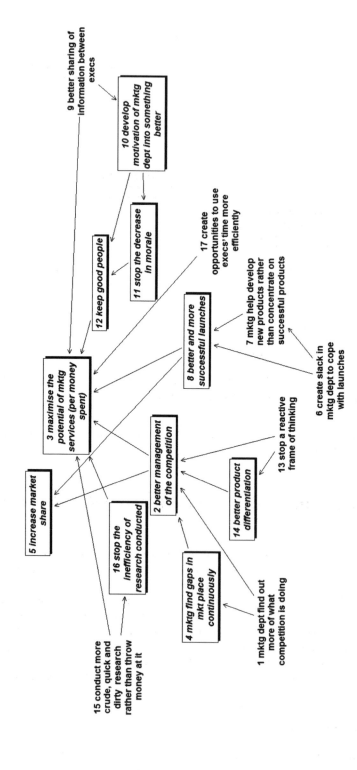

Figure 5.10 The First Draft of an Emergent Goals System (reference numbers show the order the goals were elicited, goals are shown in boxes)

It is important that the SSI is produced soon after the forum or meeting (preferably the same day and distributed to all participants). If the forum takes place during a morning then the SSI can be written during lunch, reviewed by the manager-client, and distributed immediately after lunch. If the group is able to reconvene for a short while after lunch the SSI can be validated by the whole group and then be a genuine take-away.

As we have discussed earlier, a good test of an effective goals system is that it should be distinctive and so reflect the particular nature of the organisation. This will show very clearly in a map, but it is important that the distinctiveness of the goals system is also translated into the SSI.

Developing a Statement of Strategic Intent – The Telecoms Example

Figure 5.11 shows the goals system agreed in a forum where the group sought to establish a realistic goals statement that was also aspirational. The goals had been developed through a combination of uncovering emergent goals from priority issues and paying attention to their own sense of what should be in the goals system. The goals network was developed during a morning forum with participation from 11 staff. In this case the group did not wish to prioritise the goals, but rather saw the network *as a whole* communicating a holistic picture of their strategic aims.

The most hierarchical goal reflects their desire for realism. The particular wording – increasingly profitable (rather than declining business) – indicates a clear wish to reverse a poor current situation and gradually to raise profitability. There are no 'bullish' targets that would set expectations too high, and yet there is an expression of the need to continually improve – the top goal can never be achieved.

Statement 9 – attract, develop and retain the best telecoms engineering talent – lies at the bottom of the hierarchy, but is very potent because it hits almost every other goal. However, the statement itself is almost textbook like – a general statement about any organisation. Therefore, does it serve any useful purpose in offering distinctiveness of purpose?

In this organisation the goal of retaining the best engineering staff is expected to deliver very specific outcomes/goals:

- Become an international innovation centre for telecoms solutions (statement 21).
- Create a differentiated customer support experience (not hardware): reliability, help, development (statement 26).
- Be at the forefront of on-line electronics digital marketing (statement 7).
- Productivity improvement across customer facing services (statement 16).
- Achieve better cost efficient and effective solution (statement 8).

This sense of purpose is specific to this particular organisation and makes it clear what sort of engineers need to be retained and recruited – innovative, and yet particularly focused on cost efficiency and effectiveness through being at the forefront of digital marketing, customer support focus, and delivering productivity improvements. Thus, for this particular organisation the aim is to deliver key goals through engineers – retaining the best and recruit the best to deliver very specific ends.

In this way we are beginning to use the structure of the map to write the statement of strategic intent. The result is shown in box 5.9.

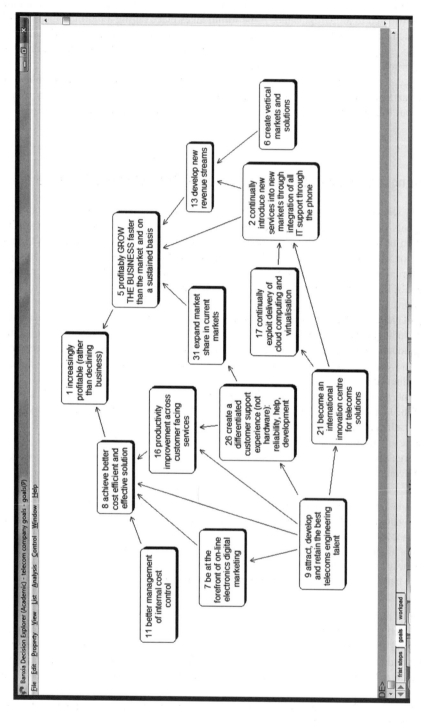

Figure 5.11 The Goals System Agreed in a Forum Where the Group Sought to Establish a Realistic Goals Statement that Was Also Aspirational

**Box 5.9   A Goals Map Converted to a
Statement of Strategic Intent**

Initial Statement of Strategic Intent – Expressing Organisational Purpose for a Telecoms Company [EXAMPLE].

Our key goal is to become **increasingly profitable** (rather than a declining business). Significant in the ultimate delivery of this aim is our goal to **attract, develop and retain the best telecoms engineering talent**. This talent will seek to **achieve better cost efficient and effective solutions** including enabling **productivity improvement across customer facing services** by using our engineering talent to **create a differentiated customer support experience (not hardware): reliability, help and development**. In addition our engineers will achieve better cost efficient and effective solutions because they will **be at the forefront of on-line electronics digital marketing**.

Our telecoms engineers will also enable us to **become an international innovation centre for telecoms solutions** which will **continually exploit delivery of cloud computing and virtualisation** and so **continually introduce new services into new markets through integration of all IT support through the telephone**.

As well as managing costs we will **profitably GROW THE BUSINESS faster than the market and on a sustained basis** by aiming to **develop new revenue streams** through our target to **continually introduce new services into new markets through integration of all IT support through the telephone** including focusing resources to **create vertical markets and solutions**.

Through our focus on creating a differentiated customer support experience – reliability, help, development – we aim to **expand market share in current markets**.

Our wish to achieve better cost efficient and effective solutions is not only dependent on the talent of our engineers but also importantly on **better management of internal cost control** by all of us.

Needless to say, it is crucially important to gain the 'sign off' of the SSI document from both the manager-client and the group who created the goals system map. Although, if written well, it will be a direct translation of an agreed goals network, the translation into sentences and paragraphs may indicate a different emphasis and meaning to participants. Note that the distinctiveness of this statement of purpose lies very much in the expression of the particular means-ends links.

As can be seen in the SSI created, the final statement will be regarded by many as the equivalent of a mission statement. Whether it should be labelled as a mission statement will be a matter for the management team rather than a matter of definition. In the case of the telecoms company, for which the map was developed, they were of the view that their mission statement needed to encompass more than was included in their SSI. For them the SSI represented a clear strategic focus for the organisation – an internal document that focused energy for the next three to five years. They thought of a mission statement as something that would be published for external stakeholders as well as their own staff and would be long lasting and so broader.

WHAT MIGHT BE WRONG WITH MAKING STRATEGY THROUGH AGREEING PURPOSE?

The Goals Will Not Be SMART

That is, they will not be specific enough and not measurable quantitatively, although they should be attainable, realistic and timely. There is, of course, some double counting in this acronym – specific (S) and measurable (M) are similar, and attainable (A) and realistic (R) are the same.

We commented earlier that it is sometimes appropriate for goals to provide only a framework for purpose and direction. In this case it will be important that they are appropriately fuzzy but nevertheless provide a distinctive framework for action.

Nevertheless, it is more often the case that goals do need to be specific – that is, the wording needs to ensure that managers cannot fudge every decision they make by being able to claim that their chosen strategies fit the purpose, whatever they are! There is a risk that, in the early stages of developing a goals system, the wording of goal statements will tend to be sloppy. Specificity can also be seen as the same thing as measurable, and measurable can imply both quantitative and qualitative measures. Indeed, it is rare for quantitative measures to be the only appropriate type of performance indicators that might be embedded in a goal statement. The age old saying that 'what gets measured gets done' applies,[52] and so often too much quantitative measurement pushes the delivery of goals in an unintended direction. This sentiment was put more admirably by Albert Einstein: 'Everything that can be counted does not necessarily count; everything that counts cannot necessarily be counted'. So, in developing and agreeing goals we need to balance the need for SMARTness with the need for promoting behaviours in a particular direction.

This is not to imply that developing key performance indicators (KPIs), as measures, with respect to each goal is not helpful. In most cases KPIs help by giving managers a clue to how they will know when they are making progress towards a goal. However, such KPIs need not always be measured quantitatively adding qualitative measures avoids losing the essence of a goal.

A Statement of Purpose Is Not a Strategy

Purpose is rarely enough to specify strategy, but sometimes it can be: when purpose is designed to provide a framework for action that also allows for opportunism. Most importantly a statement of purpose is a requirement for any strategy. What is a matter for debate is whether strategies pre-empt goals or goals pre-empt strategies, or is it an important interaction between the processes of thinking about purpose in the context of strategies, and vice versa. In general we prefer to start strategy making with attention to emergent strategising – find out what we're up to and decide what change is needed. Thus, we would incline towards an issue management forum as a start, rather than a purpose forum. It is rarely possible for an organisation to start from a blank page, rather the really big challenge is managing strategic change, which will get an organisation from its emergent strategy to one that it wants.

The Statement of Purpose as a Goals System Is Too Complicated

Strategy is about change, change is about causality – stating what actions are expected to achieve. Causality complicates statements of purpose by requiring statements of means-ends with respect to each goal. Undoubtedly it is almost always impossible to create a flowing piece of text when trying to express the nature of a network of goals – repetitive statements are required. However, repetition can be minimised through clever and careful writing. In our telecoms company SSI there is some repeated text that can be less irritating when the statement is refined.

Often a network of goals is overly complicated because everything leads to everything else – which it sometimes does! However, what is important is to capture the key drivers (strong arrows) and those that will be primarily used to deliver the future – focus on high leverage, pragmatism, least expensive, quickest to attain, and so on. Each of these characteristics of causality embedded in the goals system requires sound managerial judgement, and it is the job of the purpose forum to utilise fully good judgement within a management team.

Attention to Emergent Goals Risks Repeating the Past

When developing a goals system by exploring the reasons for prioritising strategic issues an emergent goals system is created. To the extent that judgements about strategic priorities are made with too much attention to the past then, there is a risk that the future of the organisation, as expressed by the emergent goals system, will be driven by the past. However, such a concern is founded on judgements about priorities being inappropriate. A good management team will be paying attention to the past but also seeking to adapt the organisation to anticipated futures.

If the priority strategies have been derived from an issue management forum then the risk of the past driving the future might be greater. In an issue management forum there is a danger of managers paying too much attention to current concerns and issues, simply because these are inevitably at the forefront of their thinking. In addition there is some risk that issues will be too inward facing (see 'what's wrong' in chapter 3), and a goals system needs to be both inward and outward facing. However, as we argue in chapter 3, in the issue management forum external opportunities and threats are addressed, and other strategic considerations are also raised.

Alongside these considerations there lies a more fundamental consideration about the nature of realistic strategic change. Attention to strategic priorities as the basis for developing a goals system will recognise incremental change as realistic. Paying attention to the past as well as the future will lead to realistic change programmes which recognise that stopping attention to emergent goals is not easy – simply writing them out of the goals system does not stop management attention to them. But, it may be argued that a goals system which is based on emergent goals is likely to be less challenging, more conservative, than might be achievable.

Finally, the strongest case for working from priority issues to the development of the goals system is the requirement not to miss negative goals. Recognising negative goals – goals that express the need to avoid outcomes – are a very important part of a good strategy. As we argued earlier in this chapter, negative goals are rarely considered unless they are understood through asking why some strategies (resolution of strategic issues) are a priority.

Too Little Attention to Vision and Mission

Although we have argued earlier that mission and vision statements can be dysfunctional, they are, nevertheless, an important part of strategy making for many organisations.[53] As we have seen through the examples throughout this chapter, it is relatively easy for a goals system to be the same as a vision or mission statement. However, research suggests that a successful mission statement must encompass more than strategic goals and strategies – it must also include a values statement and a statement about expected standards and behaviour from all staff. The values statement will present what the organisation believes in and enables the relating of personal values to the values of the organisation – why you should work here. The statement of behaviours addresses the politics and behaviour patterns that guide how the organisation operates. As we suggested earlier, these two aspects of a mission statement are missing from each of the three approaches to developing a statement of purpose that have been outlined in this chapter.

NEXT STEPS – EXTENDING THE SCOPE OF THE STRATEGY: LINKING TO OTHER STRATEGY MAKING FORUMS

Working with organisational purpose – goals – as the starting point for strategy making is most suitable for groups that are inclined to want to express objectives clearly before deciding how to act. Some organisational cultures, and personalities of leaders, tend towards a need to sort out objectives before discussing action, and others vice versa. On other occasions powerful external stakeholders demand a clearer statement of purpose. However, a statement of purpose is unlikely to be enough to create strategic change, even though it can provide a framework for change – providing it expresses clearly a means-ends structure. The need to go further by developing strategies to support the goals and action programmes to support the strategies provides the basis for further strategy exploration.

The interest in a further strategy forum arises as much from the participants as the manager-client, with participants interested in knowing what would usually be done next. This provides an opportunity to raise several possibilities, each of which can be undertaken in a half-day strategy forum.

A discussion with the manager-client about next steps can follow several avenues:

1   Developing strategies to support each of the goals is the most obvious next step. The forum to do so can follow closely the issue management forum. Except that, in this case, rather than a free-form invitation to raise all important issues that must be dealt with to assure a successful strategic future, the focus is on dealing with issues that will block or sustain goals. Thus, for each goal the forum would explore what needs to be done to deliver the goal – bearing in mind its full meaning: what goals support it, and what goals it supports.

    Through the process of resolving issues with respect to goals it is usual for each goal to gain a relative priority for strategic focus. Here, the priorities will indicate focus not importance in a general sense. Thus, the forum is likely to focus attention on those goals that are difficult to deliver.

2   Strategy making through managing *competitive advantage* and seeking out new business. It is unusual for a goals system to be created without some attention to the marketplace and competitors. In our example above, the telecoms company set out a goal to 'expand market share' and 'profitably grow the business'. Such aims require deliberation about the basis of competitive advantage.

    Discussion of organisational purpose will rarely explore the capabilities (individually or in combination) available to realise market growth goals, but this is a key element. These capabilities or resources will be most useful when they are distinctive – offering clear customer value. It is important to be clear about what they are and how they support one another in order to be able to leverage competitive advantage and so deliver market-oriented goals.

    A competitive advantage forum seeks to discover the subtle and connected capabilities of the organisation. The realism of market-oriented goals will be tested severely. However, it is also not unusual for the forum to introduce new ideas about how to seek out new business that exploits distinctiveness and so introduce either new or more aspirational goals.

3   Increasing the success of issue management through *careful stakeholder management.* Many who have a stake in the strategic future of the organisation – stakeholders – will be keen to understand a clear statement of organisational purpose, even though it may have been designed for internal stakeholders only. Some of these stakeholders will have a high degree of interest in how the goals are to be delivered. Some stakeholders will have significant power to influence the degree of their attainment. In particular competitors will seek to respond to some market-oriented goals. The competitor may have resources and connections that make it able to respond powerfully to actions taken to deliver goals. A stakeholder forum focuses usefully upon the bases of interest and power of key stakeholders, and so determines strategies for the better management of these stakeholders to increase the probability of the successful delivery of goals.

Each of these forums makes sense as a next step, and so a manager-client is able to choose to continue a strategy making process on an incremental basis without the need to plan a full scale approach.

NOTES

1   Dr Kevin Gallimore is principal lecturer at Manchester Metropolitan University in the UK.
2   Although strategic planning has been somewhat discredited since its heyday it remains an important activity in at least some organisations. See Whittington and Cailluet (2008).
3   Mintzberg (1978) identifies strategic planning as one of three modes of strategy, all of which make reference to organisational purpose, goals or vision.
4   However, the relationship between planning and the achievement of organisational objectives is difficult to demonstrate clearly, in part due to methodological inconsistencies. See Knight, Pearce, Smith, Olian, Sims, Smith and Flood (1999) and Miller and Cardinal (1994).
5   Anderson (1982) suggests that this requires appreciating conflicts and competition for scarce resources between functional areas.
6   Mintzberg (1994) suggests an interesting contrast between strategic planning as primarily analytical and strategic thinking as primarily synthetic.
7   Quinn (1978) describes a normative formal planning approach but also recognises the power and behavioural aspects of strategy. These different approaches are reconciled in his suggestion of logical incrementalism.
8   Child (1997) provides a useful overview of the development of the concept of strategic choice and a balance between the extremes of determinism and voluntarism.
9   Daft and Weick (1984) draw attention to the important role of individual interpretation and the development of shared conceptual schemes among the senior management team in giving meaning to data.
10   Conflict about goals and how to achieve them may not be necessarily detrimental if it leads to better strategic decisions through, for example, dialectical enquiry or devil's advocacy. See Schwenk (1995) for a discussion of central themes in strategic decision making.
11   Child (1997) notes that even a dominant organisational group may have to respect the interests of other organisational actors because of the mutual dependence between different groups or elements of the organisation.
12   Constraints and political processes may be encapsulated in what Child (1997) calls the 'Rules of the Game'.

13 See Cyert and March (1992).

14 Stacey (1995) suggests that other difficulties in establishing long term outcomes arise from complex, non-linear feedback processes in which cause–effect relationships are essentially unknowable.

15 See Denis, Langley and Rouleau (2007) for an example from the healthcare sector.

16 The argument is that pluralistic organisational contexts are becoming more common as organisations increasingly have multiple divergent goals, diffuse power structures and knowledge-based work processes. See Denis, Lamothe and Langley (2001) and Jarzabkowski and Fenton (2006).

17 In a study of 20 firms Bourgeois (1985) concluded that goal diversity rather than consensus was related to performance, irrespective of environmental volatility. In a study of 19 firms Dess (1987) concluded that consensus on *either* goals or competitive methods were positively related to performance and speculated that attempts at achieving goal consensus might lead to dysfunctional conflict.

18 This is known as the 'adaptive' (Mintzberg, 1978) or dialectic perspective (Garud and van de Ven, 2002; van de Ven, 1992) and acknowledges the conflicting goals of organisational actors (Mintzberg, 1978), the multiple goal structures of organisations (Quinn, 1978), and the multiple aspirations of organisational actors (Stacey, 1993).

19 See Kaplan and Norton (1992), Kaplan and Norton (1993) Kaplan and Norton (1996a) and Kaplan and Norton (2000). Strictly speaking the balanced scorecard is a performance measurement system but a performance measurement system must reflect organisational goals.

20 See Kaplan and Norton (1996b: 76).

21 Gallimore (2008).

22 Ocasio (1997) suggests that these two modes are influenced by which issues the individual pays attention to and whether the associated data are processed in an automatic or controlled fashion.

23 That strategy is multifaceted and involves different types of process is well established, see for example Chaffee (1985) and Mintzberg and McHugh (1985). The key consideration is the relative importance of those different processes, from either a normative or descriptive stance.

24 Any organisation, big or small, will be acting strategically whether the emergent strategising is quite unselfconscious, or rather more deliberate, as, for example, when there is a knowing reinforcement of the existing ways of working by key members of the organisation in pursuit of particular outcomes or purpose. In either case the emergent strategic direction (Mintzberg, 1987), and its implicit or explicit goals and purpose, are detectable and, to a greater or lesser degree, amenable to change. For some organisations we can envisage this implicit or 'emergent' strategy to be best *for that particular organisation*. As we have noted, emergent strategising is a key concept in this book.

25 Chia and MacKay (2007), reflecting on the emerging strategy-as-practice field, argue that its focus should be the historical, cultural and social settings that lead to these habituated tendencies and internal dispositions that themselves produce patterns and consistencies in the flow of actions.

26 Chia and Holt (2006) draw a distinction between habituated purposive action directed at overcoming an immediate impediment and more conscious purposeful action directed at achieving a longer term predetermined goal. The change between these two modes of engagement in strategy making may relate to what Louis and Sutton (1991) call 'switching cognitive gears'. See Ocasio (1997) for a discussion of factors that influence how the attention of organisational decision makers is directed.

27 See Cohen, March and Olsen (1972) who suggests that organisational action arises from the interaction of streams of problems, solutions, participants and choice opportunities.

28 Mintzberg and McHugh (1985) go as far as to suggest that patterns of actions that are significant for strategy can develop despite or even in opposition to managerial intentions. In this respect see also Whittington's (Whittington, 2001) account of the first synthesis of polythene at ICI. The effectiveness of corporate goals as encapsulated in strategic plans versus managerial autonomy is discussed by Andersen (2000).

29 For example the linear process described by Chaffee (1985) or the strategic planning process described by Andersen (2000).

30 For example the Garbage Can Model (Cohen, March and Olsen, 1972) or Starbuck's (Starbuck, 1983) contention that an action-generating mode is a better description of organisational behaviour than a problem-solving mode.

31 Isenberg (1987) suggests some ways that managers deal with this tension, including experimentation, avoiding being too detailed and specific, and turning a blind eye to certain issues.

32 See Eden and Ackermann (2001b) for a discussion of strategy hierarchy.

33 Mintzberg (1994) suggests that only when the organisational environment is known to be stable and internal activities need tight coordination is the loss of flexibility warranted.

34 See Hannan and Freeman (1989) whose work shifts the focus from individual organisations to populations of organisations.

35 With the notion of strategic intent Hamel and Prahalad (1989) argue for a more dynamic approach to competition driven by organisational aspirations that appear substantially beyond current organisational resources and capabilities.

36 Isenberg (1987).

37 See Belton and Stewart (2002) for an overview of multiple criteria decision analysis. See Belton, Ackermann and Shepherd (1997) for an example.

38 Kaplan and Norton (2004).

39 See Morgan (1983) for a cybernetic perspective on strategy in which the organisation arrives at its present state through the elimination of alternative, less desirable states rather than the purposive design of a preferred state.

40 See Simon (1964) for a discussion of how multiple organisational constraints interact to constrain managerial latitude for action and hence influence the construction of goals.

41 Ackoff (1974); Checkland (1981); Kepner and Tregoe (1965); Ozbekhan (1974) imply idealised goals.

42 The notion of a meta-goal is important for collaborations and is the expression of the potential for 'collaborative advantage' Eden and Huxham (2001). See also Ackermann, Franco, Gallupe and Parent (2005); Bryson (1995: 377–378).

43 The term 'collaborative advantage' was captured by Huxham and discussed in Huxham (1996).

44 Ackermann and Eden (2010a) discuss the issues of negotiating collaboration goals between a nuclear power company and the government regulator – the agreement to meta-goals.

45 See Doran (1981).

46 Eisenhardt (1989).

47 Such features of management behaviour lend some support to the ideas of Isenberg (1987).

48 See Campbell and Tawadey (1990).

49 See Wensley (2003).

50 See Mintzberg and Waters (1985).

51 For example Bourgeois (1980) and Dess (1987) talk about corporate goals and competitive methods to achieve those goals. Mintzberg and Waters (1985) talk about leadership intentions and what organisations actually do.

52 Kerr (1995).

53 See O'Brien and Meadows (1998) on visioning.

Further Reading

Ackermann, F. and Eden, C. 2010a. The Role of Group Support Systems: Negotiating Safe Energy. In Kilgour, D. M. and Eden, C. (eds), *Handbook of Group Decision and Negotiation*. Dordrecht: Springer: 285–299.

Mintzberg, H. and Waters, J. A. 1985. Of Strategies, Deliberate and Emergent. *Strategic Management Journal*, 6: 257–272.

Simon, H. A. 1964. On the Concept of Organizational Goal. *Administrative Science Quarterly*, 9: 1–22.

Wensley, R. 2003. Strategy as Intention and Anticipation. In Cummings, S. and Wilson, D. (eds), *Images of Strategy*. Oxford: Blackwell.

6

THE STRATEGY AS PURPOSE FORUM

Fran Ackermann and Colin Eden

WHAT DOES A STRATEGY AS PURPOSE FORUM LOOK AND FEEL LIKE?

What Does it Look Like to a Participant When You Walk in the Room?

We were seated in a semi-circle facing a large blank projector screen and the facilitator was at the front to the right.

The facilitator was using a laptop computer that was connected to the projector.

What Happened?

We started with a brief introduction to the forum by the facilitator which included an explanation of the purpose of the workshop, and some of the terminology that was to be used, before moving on to explaining how the forum would unfold. The facilitator noted that there were three different ways of getting started: (1) reverse engineering our current strategy document to try and under-stand its structure as a set of interacting goals, (2) starting from scratch and creating what we thought the goals system should look like, and (3) building on from our issue management forum that had agreed our strategic priorities. Because there was little credibility given to our existing strategy document – the previous chief executive had put it together – and it was relatively out of date, the facilitator noted that the new chief executive thought it might be worthwhile to see what emerged if we started from scratch.

Consequently, each of us was asked what we saw as the goals for our organisation, taking into account both the organisation as a whole and also our particular part. We then looked at what all of us had said and considered the interactions between these goals. Where there were relationships we captured these using arrows to show what supported what. This generated quite a bit of debate and gave me a new sense of what my fellow managers thought our purpose was. It also provided a structure that could ensure our efforts were more focused.

As part of helping manage all the different views and the relationships, the facilitator moved the contributions around the screen positioning them in locations which minimised crossing arrows and ensured all the arrows pointed upwards. It was amazing how much clarity this added to the picture. It was also interesting to note that there were a number of themes. For example, one theme focused totally on managing our costs and another on improving our services.

Gradually after editing both the statements and the links and adding some more material that reflected other stakeholder perspectives, it felt as though, as a group, we had arrived at an understanding about where the organisation should focus its efforts. We could see how energy spent achieving one goal would have knock on effects on other goals. This was remarkably enlightening.

We finished up with a written statement which explained how the goals affected one another – making it clear that the organisation had to work in concert. It was useful to have this concise version as a take-away that reflected the work we had done and which we could show to others on our staff.

What Did it Feel Like?

Having been to a number of strategy workshops, I was a little uncertain of what might unfold and sceptical whether anything would come out of it – it seemed to me that our purpose was pretty clear and obvious. However, from the beginning I felt better about us using time to do this. The facilitator's clear explanation, not just to the process but the rationale behind it was helpful.

Although we had been given some help regarding the type of statements to contribute, I wasn't too sure whether my suggestions were 'in the right ball park' and it was reassuring to see some of my colleagues struggle too. Once we got going, it was really interesting to hear how others viewed the direction of the organisation – sometimes I found myself initially disagreeing and then, having listened to their explanation, and seeing how important their links to other goals were, I became convinced that at least we should consider them seriously. The positive and informal atmosphere of the forum promoted this. I also enjoyed having the time to explain my own views and be listened to!

I liked the linking process – once I got used to it – because it seemed to reflect more naturally the fact that goals affect on another – they did not work in isolation. Our last mission statement had just been a list of separate goals.

The final take-away showed just how much some of the actions I needed to take to address the priorities were impacted by those of my colleagues and vice versa. If you like, the picture was giving powerful clues to the project management of implementing our strategy.

What Did I Go Away With?

We were all given copies of the pictures showing the tidied goals network. In a couple of hours work we had captured a wide range of goals, explored how they impacted one another, discussed where to focus our energy and started getting agreements about who'd take responsibility for what. We also did need to write this in normal text form as I can't see that the pictures of the statements and arrows would mean much to anyone not present for the session. I think you need to be there, listen to the conversations, and get familiar with the linking process, to appreciate fully the value of the resultant pictures. However, the written version we produced at the end resolved this problem as it managed to retain the richness of the connections between goals while being in a more 'traditional' format.

Was it Worthwhile?

I was surprised at how much we got through, and that we got a clear deliverable at the end – a product that was, in effect, the 'minutes' of the meeting written by us all in real time. The product gave us all the same sense of purpose and focus, and that is what we'd hoped for. It was obviously only part of an overall strategy, but it is something we can use in practice, and we all bought into it!

RESOURCES

- 1–2 hour meeting of facilitator and manager-client (to agree the design of the forum); this time is still necessary when the facilitator and manager-client are the same person as thinking through the design is still required.
- 1 hour setup by the facilitator.
- 1–3 hours of group work – it is usual to complete this forum in half a day but it can be done in as little as 2 hours.
- Decision Explorer® (the software that captures the views and links) loaded onto a laptop, and a small table positioned so that the facilitator can see the public screen and the group.
- 1280x1024 data projector (this resolution works best, as it permits more material to be explored at one time).
- Large public screen.
- Room with chairs (preferably on castors) – one for each participant.

MAPPING OUT STRATEGIC SUCCESS: STRATEGY AS PURPOSE

Strategy as Purpose Forum: Surfacing Goals

There are three different ways of starting a strategy as purpose forum depending on whether (1) there is an existing strategy document that must be taken into account, (2) it is important for the group to start from scratch in order to increase the chance of opening up new ideas about the purpose of the organisation, or (3) to start with an exploration of agreed high priority strategic issues (perhaps following on naturally from an issue management forum). Each of these can then be refined using the same script.

Surfacing Goals through 'Reverse Engineering' the Published Goals System

---

Script for: Reverse engineering the published goals system

Tasks:

1 Determine which of the strategy document(s) available will be used for the exercise: 5–10 minutes (off-line with the manager-client)
2 Examine the strategy document to capture potential goals: 20–30 minutes

(Continued)

(Continued)

3 Examine the strategy document to capture potential relationships: 10–20 minutes
4 Check wording and relationships with the group: 5–10 minutes

Deliverable: first draft of the goals system
Script timing: minimum 40 minutes, expected 70 minutes

Task 1: Determine Which of the Strategy Documents Available Will Be Used for the Exercise

With the manager-client (rather than with the group) **decide which of the various strategy documents to focus upon** as it is likely that in many instances there will be a number of strategy documents available for this re-engineering task. **Consider the various options carefully.** Candidates may include mission statements, strategy documents, policy papers etc. During the selection process **consider when the documents were produced** (that is, are they out of date, or very recent) and if possible **identify who were the authors** (so as to pay attention to stakeholder management issues). **Keep a note of this consideration** so that it can be explained to the group at a later stage.

Task 2: Examine the Strategy Document to Capture Potential Goals

Identify Candidate Goals   Read through the chosen strategy document and **highlight specific statements that are candidate goals.** This might be carried out initially with a highlighter.

Capture the Candidate Goals in Decision Explorer®   Once the candidate goals have been identified **capture the goal candidates in Decision Explorer®**. As you enter each one into the system, **make a note on the original text of the numerical tag allocated by Decision Explorer®**. This will ensure that it is easy to identify each statement in the text (see box 6.1)

See Appendix: Using Causal Mapping Software: Decision Explorer®, 1.2 Capturing Statements

As with task 1, this task is typically carried out with the manager-client (rather than the group). However, there may also be circumstances where at least a first draft is completed off line by the facilitator.

Box 6.1   Example: The Mission Statement for the Royal University for Women (Bahrain)

'Offer students a rewarding [1] and challenging multi-cultural learning environment [2] that cultivates strong well rounded personalities [3], encourages leadership [4], and builds character [5], social consciousness and community [6].'

Note: there are six statements identified in figure 6.1.

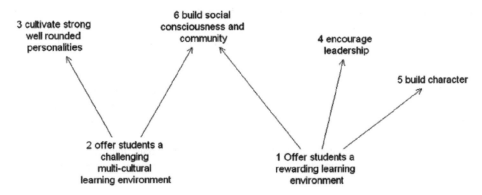

Figure 6.1   Map of Statements Developed from the Mission Statement in Box 6.1

Task 3: Examine the Strategy Document to Capture Potential Relationships

Examine the Text for Relationships (Links) Between the Goals   Some of these might be easily identified through the language used. For example, the phrases 'because' or 'due to' might be used.

Capture these Relationships in Decision Explorer®   See box 6.2 and figure 6.2. As with the candidate statements, **note on the text the link**. Don't worry if there are statements that are not linked at all, that might appear to be under-connected or where there appear to be contradictions. These can be reviewed with the group and resolved in task 4.

See Appendix: Using Causal Mapping Software: Decision Explorer®, 1.5 Linking Statements

Ensure the Statements are Captured Accurately   Once you have captured all of the statements and links in Decision Explorer®, **check the text to ensure statements are captured accurately** and that none has been missed.

This task of the script may take place outside of the strategy forum itself – particularly if (1) the document is quite lengthy (it may be tedious for the group to slowly work through each page) or (2) the document has been constructed by someone in the group.

Task 4: Check the Wording and Relationships with the Group

Review the Text Alongside the Map   If the process of mapping the document has been undertaken with the group, then there already will be a high degree of understanding of the relationship between the document and the attendant map. However, where the initial mapping has taken place 'off line', then it is important to devote about 30 minutes with the group to **review the text alongside the map**. This will allow them to appreciate the map's construction and feel reassured that it is a reasonable picture of what the text stated.

Develop a First Draft of the Goals System   As many strategy documents contain a large number of inconsistencies, conflicts and uncertainties (as noted in chapter 5) it is worth working with the participants to **develop a first draft of the goals system they feel comfortable with** rather then spending a lot of time concentrating on minor editing considerations. Reviewing the wording to ensure that the meaning is clear to all is a good first step. This might then be followed with reviewing the links. By focusing attention on those potential goals that are under (or not at all) linked it is sometimes possible to identify weaknesses in the document where either links are implicit or completely missing in the document. Where there are apparent contradictions, check the source of confusion, as it may be that the candidate goal is seen to achieve more than one superordinate candidate goal hence the different understandings of the consequences.

Note that in this forum we are unlikely to surface negative goals (dangerous outcomes to be avoided), and this is an important weakness of building a new goals system following this script only.

Box 6.2   Example: McKinsey – September 2009: What We Do and How We Do It (see www.mckinsey.com/aboutus/whatwed/ accessed January 2010)

Our clients call us when they have [1] **something pressing on their minds – whether it is a major strategic or operational need or an organizational challenge**. They look to us for [2] **honest, objective, thoughtful, and experienced advice**.

Our [3] **clients talk to us** when they find themselves [4] **under pressure to deliver results**. They call us in [5] **uncertain times**. They talk to us when [6] **information is difficult to get and insights are scarce**. They call us when they [7] **need to make decisions that will have major consequences for their people, their organizations, and the countries in which they operate**. They call us when they want a [8] **truly global perspective**.

With our [9] **broad reach across industries, functions, and geographies**, we [10] **speak our clients' language**. We [11] **live where they live**. We [12] **understand their business**.

We [13] **help people and companies explore extraordinary opportunities**, [14] **manage and sustain growth**, and [15] **maximize revenue**.

We do this using these core principles:

[16] *Follow the top management approach*
We [17] **find and solve the most critical and challenging problems**. We [18] **take an overall, independent, and fact-based view of a client's performance**. We [19] **rely on facts** because they [20] **provide clarity and align people**. [21] **Facts are the global management language**. We work with facts to [22] **provide credible recommendations**. We [23] **work directly with leaders** who can [24] **partner with us to develop and accept recommendations** and have the [25] **ability to implement them**.

[26] *Use our global network to deliver the best of the firm to all clients*
[27] **No one at McKinsey 'owns' a client relationship**. We [28] **rely on multiple people, not a single consultant or a single office**, to [29] **provide leadership and our high standard of client service in each situation**. We [30] **draw on our global network of internal or external expertise** to [31] **bring together the right minds for the right solutions**.

(Continued)

(Continued)

[32] *Bring innovations in management practice to clients*
Our **[33] clients need new insight**. We ask our people to **[34] bring their best thinking to our clients**. We **[35] invest significant resources in building knowledge**. We see it as our mission to **[36] bring this knowledge to our clients** and we **[37] publish it** *for the* **benefit of business and government leaders worldwide** and to force ourselves to think about what is next.

[38] *Build client capabilities to sustain improvement*
We **[39] work with our clients as we do with our colleagues**. We **[40] build their capabilities and leadership skills at every level and every opportunity**. *We do this to* **[41] help build internal support, get to real issues, and reach practical recommendations**. We **[42] bring out the capabilities of clients to fully participate in the process and lead the work after we have left**.

[43] *Build enduring relationships based on trust*
We **[44] earn our clients' trust**. *We do this through our* **[45] consistently superior service**, our **[46] professional conduct**, and our **[47] complete commitment**. **[48] Each one of us is responsible for earning and keeping our clients' trust** *with our* **[49] individual behavior** and the **[50] quality of our work**. We **[51] care for our clients as people and organizations, even when we are not serving them**.

An Example   The task of reverse engineering publicly stated goals-oriented text is never easy because the interpretation of many statements may demand local knowledge – judgements always have to made. Thus, the results of the reverse engineering of the McKinsey web statement is likely to be different for each of several competent people seeking to code the text.

In reverse engineering the McKinsey text many of the statements were not phrased as goals (non-optional, or actions to deliver the goals) that appear to be good outcomes 'in their own right'. The reverse engineering process revealed that although some of the text sounded like a goal – for example, although 'honest, objective, thoughtful, and experienced advice' sounds like it might be a goal for McKinsey, it is not stated as such – rather it is describing what the client expects. Perhaps this client expectation ('they look to us for …' is an expression of a customer value) should have been more clearly stated as a goal for McKinsey? Other material is contextual. From a possible 51 statements, 17 goals were identified for the map shown in box 6.3. It is interesting to note that only some of the 'core principles' can be easily made a part of the goals system. In this case it became helpful to separate client goals from the goals that indicated how McKinsey would help the client deliver these goals.

The map is revealing because of the significance of the elaborated tear drop of goals supporting 'help people and companies explore extraordinary opportunities'. The structure of the goals system suggests three main themes (tear drops): help people and companies explore extraordinary opportunities; deliver results under pressure; and build client capabilities to sustain improvement.

After converting text in box 6.2 into the causal map displayed in figure 6.2, the map was converted back into a statement of strategic intent following the procedures outlined in chapter 5 (and later in this chapter). Boxes 6.3 and 6.4 show the two step rewritten purpose of McKinsey. The process highlights duplication of some statements (for example, 22 and 25). In the process of rewriting the goals system the wording had to be modified in order to make it more goal-like and yet keep to the original wording as much as possible. The most difficult part in writing about multiple causal links is that of finding ways of not repeating too often those statements with many links in or out of them.

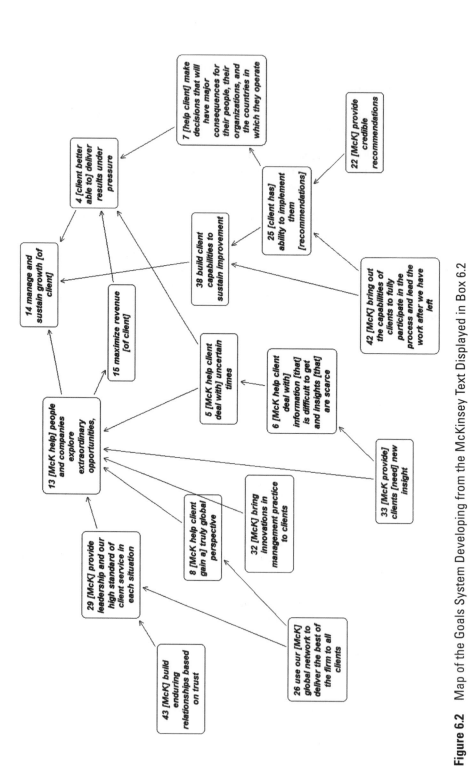

Figure 6.2 Map of the Goals System Developing from the McKinsey Text Displayed in Box 6.2

A last step would be required in order to produce a statement that is more engaging rather than literal – adding style and drama to the statement.

Box 6.3   The First Step of the Two Step Progression of Rewriting the Statement of Strategic Intent from the Reverse Engineering Goals System Causal Map

We aim to help 14 **manage and sustain growth [of client]** by 13 **[McK help] people and companies explore extraordinary opportunities** to 15 **maximize revenue [of client]**, and also by 4 **[client better able to] deliver results under pressure** and by 38 **build client capabilities to sustain improvement**.

We will **[McK help] people and companies explore extraordinary opportunities** by 29 **[McK] provide leadership and our high standard of client service in each situation**, 8 **[McK help client gain a] truly global perspective**, 5 **[McK help client deal with] uncertain times**, 32 **[McK] bring innovations in management practice to clients**, and 33 **[McK provide] clients [need] new insight**.

We will 5 **[McK help client deal with] uncertain times** by 6 **[McK help client deal with] information [that] is difficult to get and insights [that] are scarce** which will be supported by 33 **[McK provide] clients [need] new insight**.

We will achieve 4 **[client better able to] deliver results under pressure** from 7 **[help client] make decisions that will have major consequences for their people, their organizations, and the countries in which they operate**, which will be facilitated by 25 **[client has] ability to implement them [recommendations]** from our 22 **[McK] provide credible recommendations**, and 42 **[McK] bring out the capabilities of clients to fully participate in the process and lead the work after we have left**.

Our aim to 38 **build client capabilities to sustain improvement** is also supported by our **[client has] ability to implement them [recommendations]** and 42 **[McK] bring out the capabilities of clients to fully participate in the process and lead the work after we have left**.

It is important that we 26 **use our [McK] global network to deliver the best of the firm to all clients** and 43 **[McK] build enduring relationships based on trust** in order to 29 **[McK] provide leadership and our high standard of client service in each situation**.

Box 6.4   The Second Step of the Two Step Progression of Rewriting the Statement of Strategic Intent from the Reverse Engineering Goals System Causal Map

We aim to help our clients **manage and sustain growth** by helping **people and companies explore extraordinary opportunities** in order to **maximize our clients' revenue**, and also by our **clients being better able to deliver results under pressure** and by **building our clients' capabilities to sustain improvement**.

We expect to **help people and companies explore extraordinary opportunities** through **providing leadership and a high standard of client service in each situation; helping clients gain**

(Continued)

(Continued)

a truly global perspective; helping clients deal with uncertain times; bringing innovations in management practice to clients; and providing clients with new insights.

We will **help clients deal with uncertain times** by **helping our clients deal with information that is difficult to get and insights that are scarce.**

We will enable our **clients to be better able to deliver results under pressure** by **helping them make decisions that will have major consequences for their people, their organizations, and the countries in which they operate.** This will be facilitated by enabling the **client to implement our credible recommendations,** and **bringing out the capabilities of clients to fully participate in the process and lead the work after we have left.**

Our aim to **build client capabilities to sustain improvement** is also supported by our providing the **client with the ability to implement our recommendations.**

It is important that we **use our global network to deliver the best of the firm to all clients** and seek to **build enduring relationships based on trust** in order to **provide leadership and our high standard of client service in each situation.**

Deliverable: first draft of the goals system
Timing from forum start: 40 minutes minimum, expected 70 minutes

---

Surfacing Goals: *Starting from Scratch*

Script for: Starting from scratch

Tasks:

1 Provide a clear description of the purpose of the forum and what is a goal: 5 minutes
2 Encourage participants to surface candidate goals: 10–20 minutes
3 Capture links between goals: 10–20 minutes
4 Check wording and relationships with the group: 10–15 minutes

Deliverable: first draft of the goals system
Script timing: minimum 35 minutes, expected 60 minutes

Task 1: Provide a Clear Description of the Purpose of the Forum and What Is a Goal

Explain the Purpose of the Forum   Alongside ensuring that the participants are clear about the ground rules of the forum and general logistics, spend some time explaining **the specific focus of the forum**. In answering this question about the purpose of the forum – the development of a goals system – it is important to recognise that the terms used to prompt appropriate contributions will acknowledge the nature, culture and language of the organisation. In some organisations it will be appropriate to **prompt the elicitation of purpose by asking for goals**, in other settings, **for objectives, aims or success factors**. Often answers encompass operational targets and strategies.

Having a clear question as a starting point can ensure participants appreciate the focus of the forum. For example, the focal question/starting point for the forum might be expressed as 'what should the purpose be for the organisation over the next z–y years'. **Ensure that a rough time horizon for the expression of organisational purpose is provided to participants**.

Explain What Types of Statements Constitute a Goal
The definition used in this forum (and process of strategy making) is to consider a goal as something that is **'good in its own right'**, in other words it is something that the group or an individual wants to achieve even if other goals were not met. Therefore a goal might be 'significantly reduce accidents on site', 'build the strongest digital brand' or 'grow the business'. However, 'develop more links with local companies' is probably not a goal because it appears, as it is currently worded, to be a means to an end – for example a way of meeting the goal of 'ensure that our activity meets the needs of the individuals/businesses/whole community'.

Task 2: Encourage Participants to Surface Candidate Goals

Surface Candidate Goals
Once participants are relatively clear regarding the nature of the statements required, **encourage contribution of candidate goals**. **Use a round robin approach** to ensure that contributions are captured from each participant. At this stage **don't get too fussed about getting the wording precisely correct** as it is important to ensure that participants feel able to contribute their 'raw' thoughts. **Don't worry either if some of the initial contributions don't appear to be goal like** – it is better to be comprehensive at this stage. Later on in the forum there will be an opportunity to review the status.

Capture Each of the Statements in Decision Explorer®
Check with the proponent to ensure the wording roughly matches their intent. Seek to **reduce the possibility of participants presenting views derived from attendance at management courses**.

Task 3: Capture the Interrelationships Between Goals

Although it is possible that some differentiation between the focal organisation and others in the same industry will emerge through the generation of goals, it is this task of showing causal links in the strategy as purpose forum that gives rise to further potential differentiation and thus possible competitive advantage as the interrelationships will suggest different meanings for similar goals stated by competitors. Thus a pattern of interacting goals set out as a network enables the system to make sense – that is, ensuring that the meaning of any one goal satisfactorily relates to the other goals that helped deliver it, and the other goals that it helps deliver.

Identify Relationship Between Goals
Ask participants to **consider whether there are any relationships between the candidate goals**. For example, among many suggested goals, it might be that there is a goal of 'make the organisation the first point of call' and one of the participants feels that this would help in achieving 'sustainable growth'. Another participant,

however, might feel that 'decrease customer churn' also helps with 'ensure sustainable growth', with 'gain client satisfaction (both projects and services)' supporting the decrease of churn. These relationships can be illustrated through causal links where the statement at the tail end of the arrow is seen to support the statement at the head of the arrow. These links can be entered easily into Decision Explorer®. See figure 6.3 for a first draft of the linked goals system that encompasses the outcome of this discussion.

See Appendix: Using Causal Mapping Software: Decision Explorer®, 1.5 Linking Statements

Task 4: Check the Wording and Links with the Group

Once a couple of rounds have been made and about 15 to 20 goals elicited have a look at the contributions. Is each goal clear in meaning to other participants? If not, **edit the goal so that its meaning is more explicit**. Check also whether each statement appears to meet the goal definition – is it an outcome that is taken to be non-optional and would be celebrated if achieved. **Check to see if the group believe that any goals appear to be missing**. Box 6.5 describes a small part of a case, with figure 6.4 illustrating the final goals system.

Box 6.5   Building a Goals System from Scratch

Vignette. A group of individuals in a small town were keen to develop an historic site into a resource that all of the community could share and get value from. They believed that the development would have a number of benefits – not just economically but also socially and many believed it would ensure that the town retained its spirit and character rather than becoming just another feeder town to an adjacent big city. However, in the process of developing an application to gain public monies they began to realise that while they all felt that they had these common goals – the development of the historic site, retain the spirit and character of the town, all the community share and get value from the site – in practice they were a group of individuals with quite different views about the development and the route to achievement (the 'business goals'). Therefore if they were to gain the public funding necessary to make the change they would have to present a unified and coherent view.

   As one of the key requirements of the funding proposal format was to clarify objectives of the development, they agreed that spending a couple of hours clarifying their goals would be worth the time (a big step given that there was precious little funds available). They therefore agreed to invite in an external facilitator (rather than use one of their own, potentially biased, members as 'facilitator') to support their decision making process. This process was assisted by the fact that one of the individuals knew of someone who was expert with this type of requirement and could brief her with the background and the situation. He also knew what resources would be needed. A date and time was agreed – with the majority of the group wondering what was going to unfold and slightly nervous whether it would be worth the time and cost.

   After a brief introduction, which seemed to make perfect sense to all those attending, the facilitator asked each individual to contribute what they saw as the goals of the initiative. Over the course of 20 minutes the group came up with 10 goals – some dealing with education, some with culture and others taking a much more economic point of view. This was the easy part but

(Continued)

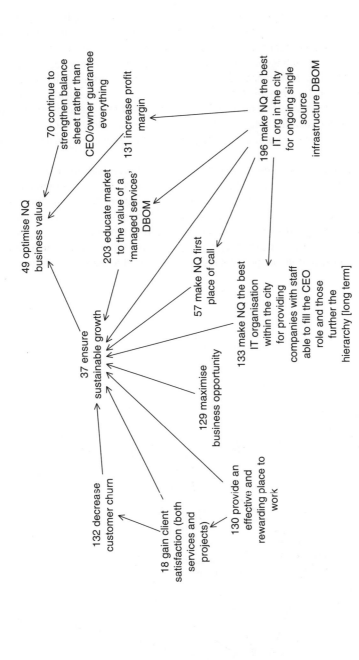

Figure 6.3 First Draft of a Goals System Developed from Scratch

Note: the organisation's name has been changed to NQ for confidentiality purposes. DBOM is the abbreviation for Design, Build, Operate and Maintain

(Continued)

it did help them feel that they were making progress and they began to see the diversity! The next part of the forum – getting the group to consider how the goals linked together to form a structure (necessary for coherence) proved to be a bit more challenging. However, with the facilitator's assistance they began to consider which goal(s) supported other goals and began to build the network. This was fascinating as it revealed all sorts of different ways of thinking. As a result it took some time to agree that the most superordinate goal – the goal all were striving towards – focused on regenerating community spirit. They felt that the structure certainly would help them build the case for funding – it clearly showed how the different objectives could support one another, gave coherence and tapped into the current public policy of building communities.

But in the process of developing the system they realised that in fact the resultant goals system showed a system that was self-sustaining – there were a number of feedback loops. If they could make this dynamic unfold then it would ensure the continued healthiness and viability of the proposed development and could provide a further point in their favour when arguing the case for funding – the funding would 'kick-start' a long term positive outcome that would get better as each year passed. The group were delighted – they had an agreed structure, one that clearly met public policy aims, and illustrated a sustainable future.

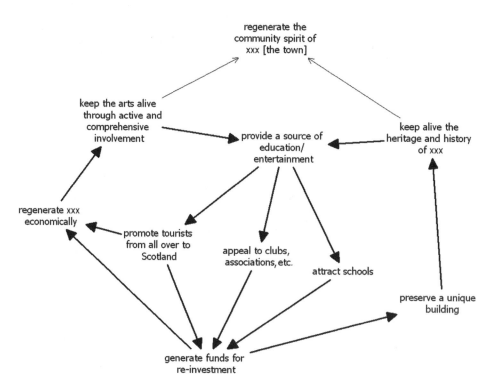

Figure 6.4   The Goals Map Developed from the Vignette Noted in Box 6.5

Deliverable: first draft of the goals system
Timing from forum start: 35 minutes minimum, expected 60 minutes

Understanding Purpose through Issue Management

Script for: Understanding purpose through issue management

Tasks:

1   Identify and prioritise key issues: 15–30 minutes
2   Ladder up from key issues to candidate goals and negative goals: 20–40 minutes
3   Review negative goals: 10–20 minutes
4   Check wording and links and ensure all goals are captured: 5–10 minutes

Deliverable: first draft of the goals system
Script timing: minimum 50 minutes, expected 100 minutes

Task 1: Identify and Prioritise Key Issues

This task is redundant if an issue management forum has taken place or if the organisation has already identified a set of strategic priorities.

Identify Issues   **Ask the group to identify those issues they perceive to be 'key' when considering the organisation's future.** Typically it is useful to **suggest that participants express the issue in a manner that reflects the concern** rather than very brief descriptors. For example, rather than capturing an issue stating 'IT services', explore why IT services presents an issue – thus possibly surfacing 'sort out our slow and unhelpful IT services'. A good way to ensure this fuller account is to **encourage participants to use between 6 and 14 words. Ensure that all participants have a chance to contribute**, perhaps by using a round robin and **capture these on a Decision Explorer® screen.**

See Appendix: Using Causal Mapping Software: Decision Explorer®, 1.2 Capturing Statements

Identify Links Between Issues   Once participants have exhausted those issues that immediately come to mind, begin to **explore how the issues might link together**. This helps to structure the material and add greater clarity. For example, if one of the issues concerns 'poor HR systems' and another issue notes 'losing good job applicants' a link from the first to the second can be made. **Capture the links between issues as participants note them**. While capturing these links, **be open to further issues being surfaced** as participants often provide these when presenting the rationale for links. Capture these new issues.

Identify Issue Priorities   Finally ask the group to **identify the relative priorities of each of the bundles of issues**. In order to arrive at a reasonable consensus ask each participant to identify their own list of relative priorities – perhaps on a 1 to 10 scale with their top priority scored at 10 and their lowest at 1. Aggregate the scores and consider the degree of consensus among the top level of priorities (less consensus among the lower priorities is less important). Where there is substantial disagreement for top priorities invite discussion followed by a new allocation of priorities based on the discussion – usually this process will gradually lead to an acceptable level of consensus. (See also guidelines for the issue management forum, p. 89.)

Task 2: Ladder Up from the Top Priority Strategic Issues to Candidate Goals and Negative Goals

Identify Prioritised Issues and Emergent Goals   If following on from an issue management forum, review the issue management key issues map (see chapter 4) and **identify the relative priorities** that emerged (both from the analysis of the issues and the group's judgement). In addition, **identify the emergent goals** that may have also emerged during the issue management forum. **Bring these onto a new view in Decision Explorer®.** If there are not more than 15 consider bringing on to this new view the 'heads' as all these provide useful material for considering the emergent goals system.

> See Appendix: Using Causal Mapping Software: Decision Explorer®, 2.1 Using Views and 3.1 Listing Heads

Identify Consequences for Each Prioritised Issue   **Start by selecting one of the issues that has been allocated as a top priority.** Examine whether any consequences (out arrows) have already been identified for this prioritised issue. Where there are consequences **bring these consequences onto the Decision Explorer® view.** Where there are no consequences **ask the group to consider what would happen should the priority strategic issue not be resolved,** i.e. what are the consequences? Capture this new material on the view. Encourage group members to be as encompassing as possible thus getting an extensive representation of the possible outcomes, both positive and negative. Typically groups might identify three or four different consequences for each issue. If the group views a particular statement as a goal but it is currently worded in a manner that suggests it might be an issue or option, **reword the statement to enable it to reflect purpose.**

Consider Supporting Statements   Where the head (top) statements are considered to be candidate goals, **look at the material supporting that statement**, that is, what are the statements linking into the proposed goal? For example, 'provide integrated family and relationship support as a right not a privilege', which earlier was identified as a possible goal and is a head, might have 'support increased availability and range of services to a wider diversity of clients' supporting it. Check whether this supporting statement is also a goal (albeit a supporting goal).

Capture Further Consequences   Once the consequences have been identified, **repeat the exercise by asking 'what are the consequences of these consequences'.** A useful way of expressing this is to ask the group 'why do these consequences matter'. **Don't worry if some of the consequences are detrimental to the organisation,** e.g. losing market share. These 'negative issues or goals' are important to surface, as at this stage of the process it is important to gain an appreciation of the situation as it currently stands. As with the first iteration of this activity, **make sure that multiple consequences are captured.** In addition, **watch out that the**

group doesn't ladder up to solutions (which is likely to happen if the causality of the links is replaced by chronology).

See Appendix: Using Causal Mapping Software: Decision Explorer®, 2.2 Managing the Map (Bring Statements)

For example, in figure 6.5, the issue 'customers are no longer turning to us as a 1st call' has four consequences. However, the figure shows that 5 'regular customers are getting lost as they are introduced to others' and 9 'competitors are getting stronger' illustrate negative or detrimental consequences.

Identify Positive and Negative Goals   Those statements that are worded negatively and which, if resolved, could be reworded as goals are distinguished by labelling them negative goals. **Explain to the group that these will be reviewed later to determine how to resolve them.** In addition it can be helpful to **allocate a style to negative goals as with (positive) goals** to make them easily distinguishable. Red can be a powerful colour for illustrating negative goals as it suggests a warning and black with a larger typeface might help highlight goals.

Again review the consequences and ask the group what are the consequences, if any, for these? In figure 6.5, considering the consequences of 5 gives rise to first statement 10 and then 6. **Continue to ladder up until either the group is unable to surface more material or the contributions appear to be goal like.**

The definition used in this forum (and process of strategy making) is to consider a goal as something that is **'good in its own right'**, in other words it is something that the group or an

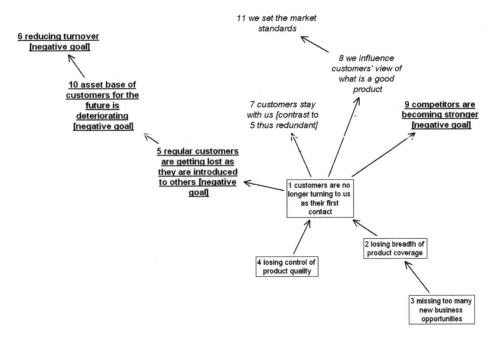

Figure 6.5   Laddering Up from an Issue (1) with Goals (italics) and Negative Goals (underlined and bold) Shown Along with Related Issues (boxed)

individual want to achieve even if other goals were not met. Therefore a goal might be 'significantly reduce accidents on site', 'build the strongest digital brand' or 'grow the business'. However, 'develop more links with local companies' is probably not a goal because it appears, as it is currently worded, to be a means to an end – for example a way of meeting the goal of 'ensure that our activity meets the needs of the individuals/businesses/whole community'.

In addition to attending to the effects of the issue should nothing be done, also **consider if the issue could be resolved, what might be the consequences**. Here more positively worded potential goals can be detected. For example, in figure 6.5, if we can resolve 1 'customers are no longer turning to us as a 1st call' then it is possible that a consequence is 8 'we influence their view of what is a good product'. **Encourage participants to consider both the positive and negative ramifications**.

Note, however, that it is important to **avoid duplication**, that is where the positive goal is a reworking of the negative – for example in figure 6.5, 7 is the reverse or opposite of 5 and therefore should not be captured separately. However, it might add clarity and ownership if the statement is edited to capture the positive wording as the contrast of 5 for later consideration. Where an issue, if resolved, leads to a positive goal, **use a negative link to reflect this requirement**. For example, taking figure 6.5 as an illustration, the statement 'customers are no longer turning to us as a 1st call' may lead to [NOT] 8 'we influence their view of what is a good product'.

The focal issue should now have a number of chains of argument laddering out of it, with those statements at the top of each line of argument representing either goals or negative goals. Be more inclusive at this stage of the process – it is worth building up an elaborated picture (see figure 6.6).

See Appendix: Using Causal Mapping Software: Decision Explorer®, 2.4 Creating and Using Styles

Repeat the Laddering Up Process   Once the laddering up focused on one issue has been exhausted, **select another prioritised issue and repeat the exercise**. To avoid the view becoming too busy, it might be worth carrying out this activity on another view. However, **watch that any new material generated doesn't replicate material already identified** through laddering up from previously worked on issues. For example, should the second or third prioritised issue lead to an existing issue, goal or negative goal link the issue (or its consequences) to this material rather than generate a duplicate. This can either be carried out by bringing on the required issue, goal or negative goal or through creating the link so that the argumentation is captured. A quick way of doing this is to use the command line (for example, xx + yy). **Stress to the group that as the issues are elaborated, each will take less time as they connect with existing material**, as this will reassure them.

Consider the consequences of loops carefully as these may be the result of incorrect causal links. Watch also for loops being generated as negative goals link back to issues producing dynamic and vicious cycles (see box 6.6 and figure 6.6).

The resultant structure typically provides a pyramid or tear drop shaped map with all of the issues laddering up towards a small number of superordinate goals or negative goals. One of the important consequences is recognising that new issues will emerge. Reviewing the priorities of the issues in the light of these newly surfaced issues might give rise to new insights.

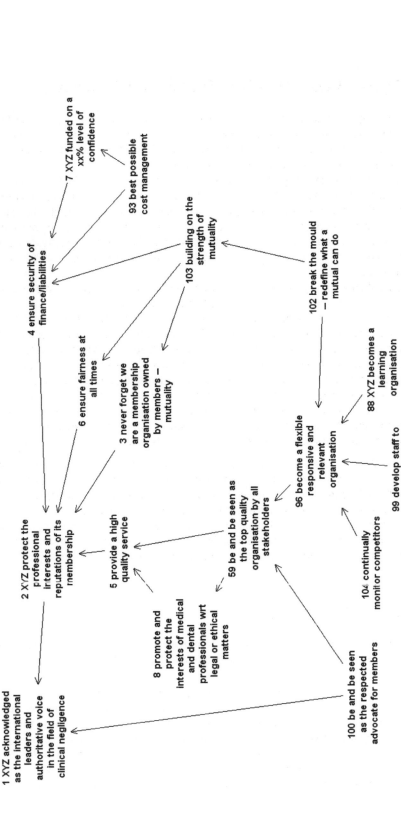

Figure 6.6 Example of a Goals System Created by Laddering Up from Issues

Box 6.6   Developing a Goals System from Priority Issues

Vignette: An organisation that had a well established reputation and had been in business for a long period of time was both interested in growing its business but also responding to external pressures. They were conscious of the changing economic climate, the shifts in technology and the different demands and requirements of their customers.

Each of the top management team also sensed that they needed to gain some clarity of where to go next – growth to date had been organic and opportunistic. It seemed a perfect time to take stock of the current situation surrounding the organisation, consider the issues and most importantly determine the goals of the organisation. A combined issue management and strategy as purpose forum would provide them with this. However, as they were a busy team, the maximum time that they would have available was a morning – from 0800 to 1230. They needed to work fast.

The first part of the morning focused on the surfacing of issues, structuring and prioritising them. By coffee they felt that they had made excellent progress and all had learnt a lot (it was amazing how different some of their concerns were). However, they now needed to determine what these issues meant for their future. After coffee they therefore started with one of their priority issues and began the process of laddering up. This lead to further issues which they hadn't initially considered and was a bit depressing but they continued to work at it and as a result began to surface candidate goals. The process also revealed some interesting insights – namely the difficulty they had in providing a consistent service! One of the issues had been to *cope with a changing and increasing remit*. However, on exploring the consequences they realised that this meant that it would *increase the span of work*, which negatively affected *consistency of decision making and follow through internally*. They had some work to do.

The above vignette describes, in summary, the process and outcome from a 'understanding purpose through issue management' forum. The feedback loop (statements 67, 23, 73) illustrates a vicious feedback loop recognising that the changing remit (continuously growing) caused the span of work to increase which in turn made it hard to ensure consistency and thus imposed a negative effect on coping with the changing remit. This cycle meant that providing a quality service and attracting staff was difficult. Something that had been recognised by the management team but until this discussion it had only been at a fairly subconscious level.

Task 3: Review the Negative Goals

As the aim of the strategy as purpose forum is to provide a positive future/direction for the organisation, reviewing the negative goals is an important step.

Reword Negative Goals   As noted earlier, it is important that each goal is worded in 'goal like' language – that is being aspirational. When working with negative goals, however, **stress to the group that a balance has to be taken between rewording the statement so that it is positive but paying attention to the issues that generated it**. For example, if the negative goal is *continuing loss of market share* then question whether the wording might be *stem the loss of market share*, or can the goal be more positively worded, for example, *slowly increase market share*. It may help as a starting point to simply put either the words 'avoid', 'stop' or 'not' in front of the negative goal.

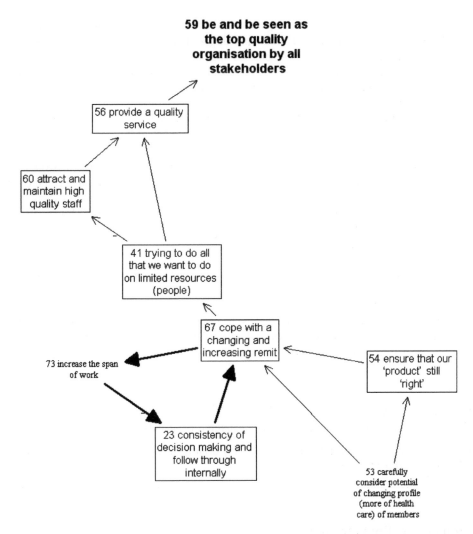

Figure 6.7   Laddering Up from an Issue Based Feedback Loop to Determine the Goals

Check the Links   As the language of the goals is refined, continue to **check the links to ensure that they are still valid** – particularly when converting a negative goal into a positive one.

Task 4: Check Wording and Links and Ensure All Goals Are Captured

The process of laddering up from priority issues can mean that links are missed between the goals and negative goals. This is because each priority issue has been examined individually, typically on a separate view, resulting in appropriate 'within issue' goal linking but little 'cross issue' goal/negative goal linking (although where an issue relates to a goal, negative goal, or further issue created on another view, the avoidance of duplication does help in weaving together the different issue to goal/negative goal representations).

Create a Single Goals Map   **Create a new view (possibly titled 'goal map') and bring all of the goals and negative goals onto this single view**. Having a composite view helps participants identify any missing links. Some tidying up (moving statements around to produce a tidier map) of this view might be required so **consider doing this tidying activity in a coffee break**. **Encourage participants to look for missing links**.

Producing a single goals/negative goals map also helps the group to **resolve any duplication of goals or negative goals** that might have emerged. In addition, it provides the means by which the facilitator can **enable the group to get a single holistic view of the system**.

Analyse Goals, Particularly Links and Loops   The goals map provides a network ame- nable to analysis. For example it becomes possible to determine which goals are central (from having many goals linking in and out of them), which are triggers or potent goals (where there are lots of arrows linking out, or multiple paths up to higher order goals, etc.) It may also be worth looking to see whether there are any loops in the structure (see box 6.6). This analysis can be useful later on when prioritising goals.

> See Appendix: Using Causal Mapping Software: Decision Explorer®, 3.2 Identifying Feedback Loops

By looking at the representation and the results of the analysis the group is able to compare their judgement with the map's structure and where there are differences explore whether the structure is an accurate representation.

Deliverable: first draft of the goals system
Timing from forum start: 50 minutes minimum, expected 100 minutes

Note: the following scripts are appropriate to any draft goals system created using the three different scripts noted above.

Refining the Goals System

Script for: Refining the goals system

Tasks:

1 Consider wider organisational goals: 10–20 minutes
2 Categorise goals into generic and business goals: 5–15 minutes
3 Review the goals map in the light of stakeholders: 10–20 minutes

Script timing: minimum 25 minutes, expected 55 minutes
Deliverable: revised goals system

Task 1: Consider Wider Organisational Goals

Unless the group is the top management team of the whole of the organisation, consider whether the goals are shared by the entire group or whether some of the goals are either individual or relate only to a particular division/department. This process can help test out how shared they might be and therefore the level of organisational support and thus ensure both political but also resource feasibility (see box 6.7).

Box 6.7   Strategies and Goals

The management team of an IT department were considering their goals system. When they came to examining it alongside the organisation's strategic direction, they realised that a number of their goals appeared to either replicate or be very similar to the strategies presented for achieving the organisation's goals! They realised that this direct connection would help them argue better for retaining the resources they had – rather than have to lose staff due to financial constraints.

Encourage the Group to Consider Wider Organisational Goals

For example, if working for the top team of an operating company, consider the parent, umbrella or corporate goals. Alternatively if working for a division or department, consider including into the system the corporate goals. This will provide the group with two benefits. Firstly it will ensure that there is congruence with the rest of the organisation (or if not this is clearly seen and implications considered). The second benefit is that it will increase political feasibility – as it will allow the participants to show how their area of the organisation contributes to the wider whole. One means of doing this is to **ask participants how the goals system might be viewed by those more senior members of the organisation**.

Where the goals are individually focused **consider whether the wording can be amended to make the goal more widely held**. It is typically the case that those goals towards the bottom of the goals map are less widely held than those overarching goals at the top of the hierarchy.

Capture These Goals and Link Them into the Goals System

If it seems helpful, consider either giving them a different style or highlighting their different status through, for example, placing CG for corporate goal at the end of each. Get the group to next see what impact this might make to the structure. Does their addition bring some goals to the fore as they relate extensively to the corporate goals?

Task 2: Categorise Goals into Generic and Business Goals

Review the goals system to determine which of the goals are generic, i.e. those that any organisation in the same sector might state and which are more specific to the particular organisation. This activity can help in ensuring that a good range of goals are identified and that the organisation is clear about how it differentiates itself from its competitors. **Make sure that there is a balance of both.**

Examine the Superordinate Goals   A good place to start is to **look at the top of the hierarchy** as these superordinate goals typically constitute the generic goals. For example, they might encompass statements about profit, profitability, shareholder value if working with a private organisation, or represent the organisation's mandate where the organisation is a not-for-profit (see box 6.8). Those goals further down the hierarchy tend to be more business oriented.

Box 6.8   Considering the Most Hierarchical Goal

An organisation dedicated to the welfare of the natural environment on reviewing their goals system put as their most superordinate goal *'achieve statutory responsibilities of conserving and enhancing, fostering understanding and facilitating enjoyment and sustainable use and management of the Natural Heritage'*. This was supported by a number of other goals – some customer focused and others concentrating upon clarifying the type of organisation in terms of culture.

As noted in chapter 5, in many organisations there are two routes to the generic superordinate goals – one focusing on revenue and delivering customer value and the other concentrating on costs and their management. **Check whether both these routes have been considered**.

Examine the Business Goals   Finally **consider which of the goals relate to the business itself**. That is examining the specific values and or objectives of the organisation which differentiate it from others in the same industry/area. Encourage the group to review the map to ensure that there is distinctiveness of the business goals. If the goals system has been developed from the issues identified in an issue management forum, then the chain of argument might be similar in nature to that presented in figure 6.8 below showing priority issues, business goals and generic goals.

If it helps, **use a different style to highlight generic goals from business goals**.

Figure 6.8   Illustration of the Goals System

Task 3: Review the Goals Map in the Light of Stakeholders (optional)

In addition to considering how those further up the organisation might view the goals system, it might also be worth understanding how external stakeholders (or other internal stakeholders, e.g. unions) might view the system.

Identify Key Stakeholders   **Determine a number of key stakeholders who would be interested in what the organisation was doing** (and any goals system that might be published). Depending on how much time, and the range of stakeholders surfaced, **select between three and five key stakeholders, being careful to consider different perspectives** (for example, take a mix of governmental bodies, competitors, regulators, customers, etc.).

Consider Key Stakeholders' Response to the Goals System   For each of the stakeholders, get participants to **imagine how they (the stakeholder) would respond to the goals system** (see box 6.9). If positive, would they support it, could the goal be made more ambitious? If the stakeholder was to have a perceived negative response, what editing might be done to make the goal more acceptable? In addition to increasing the likelihood of success this activity also helps participants to **ensure that the language of the goals is unambiguous**.

Box 6.9   Considering Stakeholder Responses

A not-for-profit organisation had developed its goals system and was reviewing it in the light of external stakeholders. First the participants discussed which of their many stakeholders (not-for-profit organisations typically have a vast array) they would concentrate their review upon. After considering the possible list against both their power (to affect the success of the intended direction) and interest (in the direction) they narrowed their view down to four key stakeholders. The participants then reviewed the goals map imagining how members from these four stakeholder bodies might interpret the intentions and respond. Two insights became apparent. The first centred on the language of the goals – while those involved felt that the language was appropriate, they realised that others – particularly external stakeholders – might not see it this way – there was room for misunderstanding. Some of the goals were not clear enough with regards to the customers; others did not clearly support government objectives. Some revisions to the wording were required. The second insight pin-pointed the fact that there appeared to be a possible omission. There was no clear goal attending to an associated body's mandate (the organisation had to work in tandem with this organisation). Reviewing the structure encouraged the group to add a new goal. They then had to look at how the issues they had been reviewing impacted this new goal.

Where changes are suggested, if an issue management forum has been carried out, consider what the implications of these changes are for the issues supporting/contributing to the goals.

Deliverable: revised goals system
Timing from forum start: 60 minutes minimum, expected 115–155 minutes (recognising three different options for initial development of the goals system)

Prioritising Goals

Script for: Prioritising goals (optional)

Tasks:

1 Prioritise goals: 10–20 minutes

Deliverable: prioritised goals system
Script timing: minimum 10 minutes, expected 20 minutes

Task 1: Prioritise Goals

Where the goals system is large (encompassing between 20 to 30 goals) the group may find it beneficial to **prioritise goals so the resources available can be concentrated upon these goals. Stress to the group that while a select bundle will be concentrated upon, the map structure allows for the other goals to be supported**. For example, by keeping the goals in context (the map structure) synergies may be able to be achieved through effort being focused on one goal being channelled in a way that increases the likelihood of other goals being achieved. Viewing the goals as a map or network also ensures staff members are clear about how the prioritised goals fit into the organisational direction as a whole.

Prioritise Goals by Analysing the Structure   Prioritisation of goals can be based on both analysis and judgement. Focusing on the map's structure may provide insights into those goals that are significant in terms of the network. One means of doing this is to **determine whether there are any natural clusters of goals**. Where this is the case, this might suggest that selection of priorities should draw from all clusters to ensure representativeness.

A second means of assessing priorities is to **examine the structure of the map looking for those goals which either are very busy** (lots of goals linking in and out of them) **or support a lot of other goals** (lots of goals linking out). In both cases, focusing on these goals will increase the likelihood that greatest leverage of resources can be achieved as these goals are pivotal in terms of the overall direction. In the example noted in box 6.10 and illustrated in figure 6.9, the goal about 'confidence' was clearly central to ensuring that the police force were able to meet their mandate (top most goal). This is different from focusing upon a decision tree comprising criteria. Likewise those that appear to attend to external bodies may be selected.

Box 6.10   Reviewing the Goals System

A police force was reviewing their goals map. What struck them was the centrality of the goal concerning 'ensure communities have the CONFIDENCE in the ability of the police' as this was a main conduit through which they would be able to meeting their mandate regarding 'safer communities'. The other insight the system revealed, and one which was reassuring to them (as it was something that many of them felt was key to their strategic success) was the potency of 'continue to develop stronger community PARTNERSHIP WORKING'. If they could put in place strategies to support this, it would have a significant effect on their mandate.

The team also found it useful to highlight the significant aspects of each of the goals by capitalising key words.

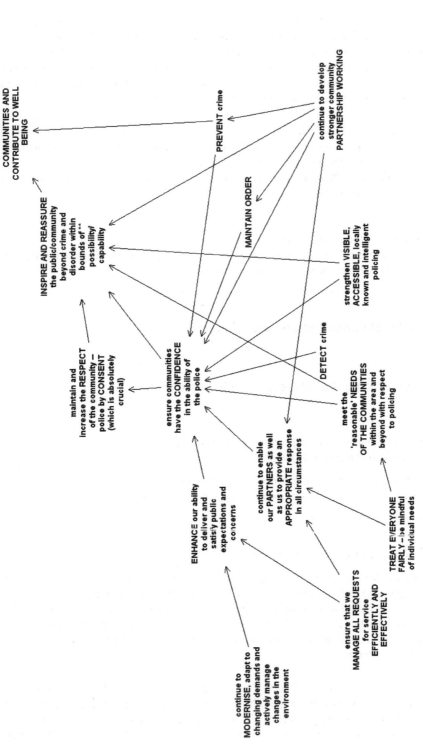

Figure 6.9 Goals System Map Representing the Example Shown in Box 6.10

(note the use of uppercase wording to highlight the keywords)

Prioritise Goals Using Judgement   Alongside using the structure of the goals system to determine priorities, **ask participants which, in their view, are the most important**. Incorporating judgement into the process is important. One particular reason for considering judgement is to pay attention to external factors – for example, stakeholder considerations. Another reason is that participants may want to focus on those goals which help ensure the organisation's distinctiveness. This will help in building competitive advantage.

Devise a System to Highlight Prioritised Goals   Once a set of goals has been identified as possible priorities, **use a simple system to easily distinguish them**. An example might be to use a 3*, 2*, 1* classification process to highlight the prioritised goals.

   Consider this prioritisation process as being cyclical where both the analysis and the judgement inform one another.

Deliverable: prioritised goals system
Timing from forum start: 70 minutes minimum, expected 135–175 minutes (recognising three different options for initial development of the goals system)

Writing the Statement of Strategic Intent

Script for: Writing the statement of strategic intent

Tasks:

1   Write the statement of strategic intent: 20–40 minutes
2   Validate SSI with group: 5–10 minutes

Deliverable: easily shareable text form of the goals system
Script timing: minimum 25 minutes, expected 50 minutes

Task 1: Write the Statement of Strategic Intent

It is important that the statement of strategic intent is produced soon after the forum (preferably the same day) and distributed to all participants. As the forum may take place during a morning the SSI can be written during lunch, reviewed by the manager-client, and distributed immediately after lunch. If the group is able to reconvene for a short while after lunch the SSI can be validated by the whole group and then be a genuine take-away that gives a sense of closure to the forum.

Focus on the Most Superordinate Goals   To start the process of writing the statement, **identify the most superordinate goal. Note the prioritised goals linking into it**. Next formulate the text so that the goal appears after some introductory text, e.g. 'our overarching objective is x'. This sets out a punchy beginning. Follow this with how it will be achieved, for example, 'this will be carried out by (specific prioritised goal immediately linking into the focal goal)' and if there is another goal directly linking into the focal goal, 'as well as the other immediately supporting goal'. Try to **use the minimum of connecting phrases**, so as to focus on the map's content.

Ladder Down to Cover All Goals

Once the most superordinate goal has been addressed as well as those linking into it, focus on one of these supporting goals and how the subordinate goal will be achieved. Continue this process laddering down the structure until all the goals have been covered. Where prioritised goals appear, it may be worth wording the text to **reinforce the significance of the prioritised goal**. For example, 'this 'goal' is particularly critical to our strategic success'. Similarly it is worth commenting specifically when dealing with feedback loops reflecting their importance to the overall strategic direction.

Stay Faithful to the Goals Map

As much as is possible, try to **keep the language of the goal statements** and ensure that the linking text **reflects the causality** thus staying truthful to the overall structure and meaning of the map.

Consider Style and Presentation

To facilitate the process, **copy and paste bundles of statements from Decision Explorer® in a word processor**. The goals will appear in numerical order, rather than any chosen order, but can be re-sorted quickly. **Use bold and italic formatting for emphasis**. This helps with navigation around the text and highlights the key points.

> See Appendix: Using Causal Mapping Software: Decision Explorer®, 4.2 Copy and Paste Map Material into a Word Processing Document, or PowerPoint

Try to **keep the text on one page** as this ensures that the statement is both concise and easily read.

Box 5.9 in chapter 5 shows the result of converting the goals system into a statement encompassing sentences and paragraphs.

Task 2: Validation with the Manager-client and Group

Validate the SSI It is crucially important to **ensure both the manager-client and group sign off the SSI document**. Although, if written well, it will be a direct translation of the goals system map, the translation into sentences and paragraphs may indicate a different emphasis and meaning to participants.

Ensure the Language and Emotion Reflect the Goals System

Where possible meet with the group (perhaps after a break in the forum) and review the draft document. **Check with the group that the language is easily understood by all those in the department or organisation** and not just by those in the group. In addition make sure that the statement is not just a good reflection of what has been agreed in a simple, easy to understand text format but also that it **gets at the emotion – the hearts and minds – of the intended audience**. Unfortunately, too often the copywriters lose the carefully embedded logic of the goals system and attend only to the good turn of phrase. This is not to underestimate the use of drama and rhetoric and good graphic design in publishing a goals statement. On the contrary, these are necessary but nowhere near sufficient requirements. The style and presentation of the statements are, in themselves, a statement about the organisation and so must be suited for the purpose.

Deliverable: easily shared text form of the goals system
Timing from forum start: 95 minutes minimum, expected 185–225 minutes (recognising three different options for initial development of the goals system)

7

STRATEGY AS COMPETITIVE ADVANTAGE

Colin Eden and Fran Ackermann

If any organisation has only core competences then they do not have competitive advantage.

Gaining and sustaining competitive advantage is a natural focus of all for-profit organisations. Differentiating products or services from those of others, in a way that is of interest to customers (new as well as existing), is an obvious challenge in protecting the strategic future of an organisation. This challenge also applies when the strategy making unit is a department or division, but in this case the customers will be other parts of the wider organisation. The more difficult it is to replicate or replace differentiation that is, or can be, desired by the customer, then the greater the possibility of long term profit.

Competitive advantage is often seen through a perspective of total protection such as patents or location. And yet, most competitive advantage lies in subtle differences in the way an organisation works. Very often these differences have developed by accident and luck over long periods of time. Thus, competitive advantage is the *potential* to do better than most competitors in any particular endeavour through a focus on customer value[1] as expressed through organisational purpose (see chapter 5). Of course some organisations are unable to discover significant competitive advantage and so their strategic future is always at risk from competitors. Nevertheless it is our experience that attention to distinctiveness in the manner presented in this chapter (and using the process discussed in chapter 8) will usually reveal some important aspects of competitiveness that need to be better exploited.

Attention to *distinctive* competences and core competences[2] is significant in explaining, and so managing, the success of an organisation.[3] Organisations with strategies based on core versus non-core competences are expected to survive recession better than others and emerge stronger as economic recovery develops.[4]

Competitive advantage is also increasingly a strategic consideration for public sector organisations.[5] Finding alternative and cost effective ways of delivering public services is now a matter of interest to most governments, and so a complacent public organisation may find itself under threat from investigations into the use of alternative providers or complete closure. Indeed, the process of exploring competitive advantage in the not-for-profit sectors usually provides the organisation with powerful insights into their own working and will provide the management team with increased confidence in their ability to manage their own future.

Knowing what your core competences are has become a requirement for any manager – they are expected to know what their core competences are and expected to use the jargon. And yet when discussing core competences few managers actually talk about competences, instead they proffer assets or broad unmanageable outcomes. Neither do managers know what core competences are at the core of. Indeed it could be argued that if any organisation has only core competences then they do not have competitive advantage – they have no competences that are distinctive. What we need to know, if possible, is what the core *distinctive* competences of an organisation are, and we need to know that they are at the *core* of the future success of the organisation. Of course, if we have no distinctive competences, and so no competitive advantage, then we would need to know what competences are at the core of the business – the core competences – and ensure we manage these as effectively as possible.

Discovering distinctiveness is very difficult. Rarely are individual competences distinctive.

Our own work with organisations on the practicalities of understanding and exploiting competitive advantage started over 20 years ago. Over this time we have worked with, and studied the nature of, competitive advantage and distinctive competences in over 100 organisations. Perhaps the most significant learning from these experiences has been that discovering distinctiveness is very difficult. Rarely are individual competences distinctive – most often it is patterns, bundles or portfolios of *relatively* distinctive competences that can be distinctive and provide competitive advantage. In addition, it is most often the case that distinctive competences are such that they would never be noticed by a customer, and often not understood by a competitor. This means that competences based on culture – 'world-taken-for-granted' ways we do thing around here – will be significant aspects of distinctiveness that can be exploited.

As noted above, applying the concepts of distinctive competences and core competences in organisational settings is difficult in practice. Identifying 'core competence has too often become a "feel good" exercise that no one fails'[6] and 'true core competences are hard to define precisely and are often discovered retrospectively. That is, as you experiment, you define your competences by simply describing your successes and failures'.[7] Other experts also have had difficulty: 'We talked to [core competence experts] and asked them to help us identify our core competences. But after having them work with our senior management, leading them through some group exercises, we really had a mess on our hands. We could not define what was core as opposed to non-core, and what was a competence as opposed to some process or offering we just did well'.[8]

Consequently, this forum, when done well, can be one of the most rewarding for a management team. The pay-off can be very significant as most organisations have never attempted to get to the bottom of where competitive distinctiveness lies or even consider what competences they have. They will usually have worked with lists of things that are not competences, things that are not capable of being strategically managed, and with no recognition of the need to understand the systemicity of competences[9] – that is interconnected networks of individual competences – in order to reveal current and potential distinctiveness. In this chapter we suggest that (1) the most likely form of resource distinctiveness arises through the identification of a unique *pattern of competences*, and (2) that core competences arise by analysing the *network of relationships* between competences and the distinctive business goals or purpose of the organisation. Thus core competences are central to (or at the core of) the network of relationships between competences and organisational purpose (see chapter 5).

The forum is also likely to introduce new ideas about how to seek out new business that exploits distinctiveness.

DISTINCTIVE *COMPETENCES* AND COMPETENCE *OUTCOMES*

Lack of clarity between ... the outcomes from competences and the competences themselves.

There are two specific difficulties in working with the concepts of distinctive competences and competence outcomes: what is a competence, and what is meant by distinctive? A further confusion is the lack of clarity between distinctive competence outcomes (that is the outcomes from the competences) and the competences themselves. Many examples used in the literature tend to focus on distinctive competence outcomes (for example 'reputation') rather than on the distinctive competences that create or sustain them. Alternatively, sometimes the focus is directly on the saleable commodity, as if it were the competence – for example, Bang and Olufsen equipment where the customer sees good design but the competences for delivering good design over a long period are embedded in the organisation. All are important and support one another. For example, both competences and outcomes are acknowledged and valued in an example presented by Collins and Porras.[10] They report that when David Packard (co-founder of Hewlett-Packard) was asked which product decisions he was most proud of, he answered entirely in terms of *organisational* achievements (competences and competence outcomes). Packard argued that developing an engineering team culture, designing a pay-as-you-go policy to encourage fiscal discipline, creating a profit-sharing scheme that stimulated co-operation, and constructing the 'HP Way' philosophy of management were the achievements. Cooperation and 'developing an engineering team culture' are competence outcomes. They are outcomes not competences because it would be difficult for others to easily identify the competences required to create these outcomes. The ability to create a profit sharing scheme that *will stimulate* cooperation within HP is a competence, and one that is possibly distinctive. This example also reveals aspects of systemicity, as causality is implied in statements such as 'creating a profit-sharing scheme *that stimulates* cooperation'. Similarly, as Hall commented: 'Jaguar cars enjoys the differentiation achieved by the reputation of the Jaguar name; the distinctive competence which the company enjoys, however, is the ability to build a special type, a quality car. This ability is founded on the skill and experience, or know-how, of the employees'.[11] This is an example of a product (the car) as the outcome of competences (design and build), where the competences that deliver the outcome are expressed in a way that enables them to be protected, and sustained, or exploited. Strategic *management* involves identifying what can be managed, and so it is most important that distinctive competences not outcomes are explored.

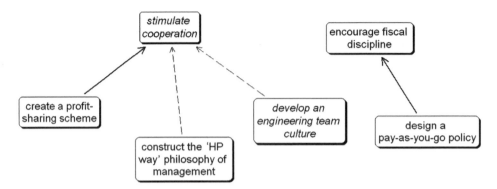

Figure 7.1 David Packard's View: An Illustration of the Hierarchy of Competences and Competence Outcomes

Outcomes or Competences or Assets?

Members of a management team find it difficult to identify *distinctive* competences, but easier to identify distinctive competence outcomes and distinctive assets. Typically when managers discuss distinctive competences they start by reporting the outcomes of competences. A distinguishing characteristic of a distinctive competence outcome is that it *cannot be managed directly*; rather it is the competences that deliver the outcomes that can be managed. For example, 'reputation for on-time delivery' is a competence outcome not a competence. It is the particular portfolio of competences (distinctive or otherwise) that enable the reputation to be gained so that it can be managed strategically. Similarly, low cost production is often argued to be a competence, whereas it is a competence outcome that (a) cannot be easily managed and (b) may not be distinctive unless it can be sustained through the continued exploitation of distinctive competences.

A distinctive competence, as a strategically useful resource, is: (1) amenable to being strategically managed in a relatively unambiguous way; and (2) an ability to do something, and so the phrase 'ability to' can be inserted at the beginning of the stated competence. Whereas, (3) distinctive competence outcomes more directly support a goal (for example, 'significantly low levels of waste'), or something the customer values ('consistent quality') – an outcome the customer appreciates directly. Competence outcomes are more externally focused. Finally, (4) a distinctive asset is typically an obvious resource, most often history, that can be exploited by competences (for example, 'extensive, and better, knowledge of customers'). Thus, the conceptual separation of distinctive competence outcome and distinctive competence implies a hierarchy that shows chains of assumed causality from manageable competences to the competence outcome (see figure 7.1 illustrating the possible mini-hierarchy identified by David Packard). The hierarchy illustrates that competences become increasingly manageable the further down the chain of causality they are from directly impacting the goals and customer values – thus it becomes clearer what the activity is and who is doing it.

Starting with *distinctive competence outcomes* allows a management team to naturally move on to discussing how these outcomes are realised. Rare and valuable assets are *distinctive assets* that can be exploited, and *distinctive competences* are those that exploit the assets, and support distinctive competence outcomes. Distinctive competences are properties of an organisation which can be managed. Distinctive competence outcomes are not competences but the outcomes of the management of competences.

Distinctiveness?

Distinctiveness is a relative concept,[12] and it is also dependent upon the time scale over which a competence is expected to remain distinctive. Creating a sustainable strategic future over a five year period makes different demands to that for 20 years. It is rare to find a situation where a management team is able to identify any *individual* competences that meet absolutely the characteristics of distinctiveness. The team are able to identify those competences that are more distinctive in relation to each other and the competition, and subsequently rate all the candidates on a scale of relative distinctiveness. Indeed, the process of developing a detailed picture of distinctiveness through debating whether (1) they are competence outcomes or not, and (2) they are distinctive or not, leads to the meaning and therefore wording of the competence or competence outcome being tightened and made more specific. This part of the forum is a significant part of the strategic conversation. The meaning of any one competence is generally uniquely defined by the supporting competences and supported outcomes.

DISTINCTIVE COMPETENCES AS A DISTINCTIVE PATTERN OF COMPETENCES

Position the organisation so that it is able to build, integrate and reconfigure organisational resources and competences.

Embedded in a network of competences may be causal patterns comprising unique bundles of competences. On some occasions a cycle of causal links arises revealing reinforcing feedback cycles where competences are self-sustaining.[13] The patterns indicate how it might be possible to position the organisation so that it is able to build, integrate and reconfigure organisational resources and competences.

The notion of seeking out unique bundles has been suggested by many academic writers, but the implications and means of doing so have been under-explored. Day, for example, suggests that 'capabilities are the *complex bundles* of skills and accumulated knowledge, exercised through organisational processes that enable firms to coordinate activities and make use of their assets'.[14] 'Strategic advantage for firms is often based on bundles of related resources'.[15] A competitor will find it difficult to overcome distinctiveness that arises from a complex *pattern* of internal coordination and learning – suggesting elements of causal ambiguity.[16] 'One explanation may be that the strength of some resources is dependent upon *interactions or combinations with other resources* and therefore no single resource – intangible or otherwise – becomes the most important to firm performance'.[17]

It is the way in which one competence supports or sustains another, and that, in turn, supports another, that may be distinctive. The process of causally linking competences and distinctive competences as an emerging network or pattern develops a 'causal map' of competences. By capturing this *network of competences*, as a causal map, portfolios of competences can be revealed which in themselves give rise to distinctiveness. For example, where each of the individual competences is believed to be held by another organisation, but the whole – the 'complex bundle' of competences working together as a system – is unique and therefore distinctive.

It is invariably the case that a portfolio of competences and a portfolio of relationships between them represent significant distinctiveness. This does not mean that feedback always occurs but when it does, it is a significant and sustainable form of distinctiveness. Specifically the pattern of relationships that represent the dynamic of continuing sustenance of the competences may be a powerful form of distinctiveness.

A reinforcing feedback loop of competences often makes the feedback loop, as a whole, a distinctive competence rather than the competences themselves.

As patterns are made explicit and displayed through a visual representation of the claims and causal links (a causal map) some hitherto unforeseen powerful potential distinctive competences – unique patterns – emerge. Moreover, a reinforcing feedback *loop of competences* often makes the feedback loop, as a whole, a distinctive competence rather than the competences themselves. It is the pattern that is unique. Similarly, a feedback *loop with at least one distinctive competence* in it is important because the self-sustaining loop sustains the distinctive competence. This is because *loops showing the ability to continuously build the distinctive competences* make the distinctive competences more powerful. A design (for strategy) may elicit 'not only static capabilities; it launche[s] "virtuous circles" that turn asymmetries into *ever-growing* capabilities'.[18] Feedback loops comprising linked distinctive competences are particularly important because they reveal the dynamic of self-sustaining all of the distinctive competences that make up the loop – the virtuous cycle is itself a dynamic capability. In this circumstance the distinctiveness of each element of the loop remains but the competences are reinforced by each growing more powerful as a result of another. Thus, a distinctive competence that is likely to be significant incorporates the sustaining *relationships* as well as the distinctive competence itself. Finally, a *patterning of competences*, for example as a *portfolio*, is often important. As noted above, the *pattern* is the distinctive competence because nobody else could achieve the pattern even if they had the competences. The identification not only of virtuous cycles but also *potential* virtuous and distinctive cycles is a crucial part of understanding the role of bundles in seeking out competitive advantage.

However, often the process of seeking out feedback loops of competences reveals a feedback loop that looks legitimate but includes within it a distinctive asset, for example 'history'. If the asset is history then it cannot be a variable because history cannot be changed. If a statement is part of a virtuous cycle – a feedback loop – then it must be a variable because the feedback loop reveals dynamic behaviour where the state of each variable changes over time. Thus, formally, the identified virtuous cycle is illegitimate. However, as with so much of the process of exploring competitive advantage, the conversation that ensues from seeking not to lose the potential of a powerful pattern can be extremely fruitful. It may be possible to convert the historical asset into a future variable, thus, for example, an asset of 'huge knowledge base of customers' becomes 'continue to grow the huge knowledge base of customers'. Furthermore, the rewording of the asset to make it into a competence will be revealing in terms of managing the resource more effectively. In some cases it is simply impossible to convert an historical asset into a future competence, but very often history can be continued into the future. In effect, the asset has become of major potential significance to the future success of the organisation.

Causal Ambiguity

Distinctive competences often go 'unnoticed because they are buried within an organisation and are therefore *subtle and causally ambiguous*'.[19] The process of elicitation, causal linking and categorisation (as competence or outcome) enables the codification of some 'uncodified' knowledge. This codification process partly resolves difficulties a management team experience in discovering distinctive competences. For example, it may help overcome situations where managers themselves do not know why their capabilities are successful.[20] Reducing the causal ambiguity for those within the organisation allows for more effective strategic management without reducing the causal ambiguity for competitors. However, unraveling causal ambiguity can facilitate a competitor getting to know how it works and so potentially copy it. The dilemma that arises from seeking to understand and so strategically manage competitive advantage is that in order to do so the uncodified working of an organisation becomes codified and so more amenable to replication.

DISTINCTIVE COMPETENCES AND SUCCESS

Core Competences?

As noted above, the definition of a core competence depends upon answering the question: 'core to what?' If managers are asked to elaborate their notion of coreness then they refer to a loose and intuitive understanding of importance rather than a precise conceptual or analytical understanding. Setting the distinctive competences within the context of the purpose of the organisation is, conceptually and analytically, a way of addressing this issue and so determining core distinctive competences. The strategic future of an organisation, or division, or business unit, or department, whether private, public or third sector, depends upon its ability to *exploit competences in relation to its business goals*.

> Evaluating a company's competences is not the same as determining the right competences for the company's future competitive position. Similarly, building consensus on the firm's competences is important, but it does not guarantee that the firm's managers will correctly identify the competences that will be most important for the future.[21]

The security and stability of an organisation's future – achieving the business goals – depends in part upon the distinctiveness of the competences that deliver these goals and upon their sustainability. Thus distinctiveness can also be seen as being determined by the nature of the business goals *system*[22] – these goals provide the benchmark against which distinctiveness can be assessed. For example, an organisation with a goal of being number one in a domestic marketplace would be comparing itself to other players in that marketplace and therefore viewing distinctiveness according to those competitors. However, if the organisation wished to be a world player then the number of competitors increases making distinctiveness more challenging.

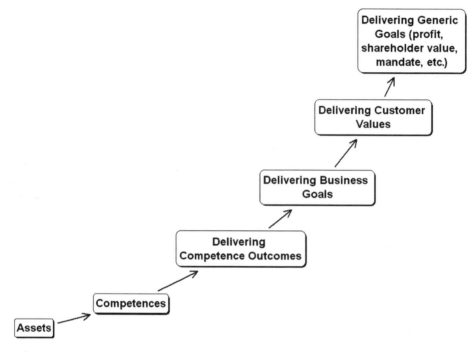

Figure 7.2a The Basic Structure of the Relationship Between Competences and Goals

To be clear, business goals are the specific and distinctive goals that deliver customer value in the context of not-for-profit, public or private organisations. These business goals, in turn, deliver the generic goals of profit, profitability, shareholder value or mandate, etc. Distinctive business goals are those that differentiate 'the business we are in' from the general requirements (goals) of conducting business (increase turnover, reduce costs, etc.). Thus, core competences are those that are core, are central, to achieving the system of business goals. Coreness is thus a feature or emergent property of the network which links competences to goals.[23] However, the other part of determining coreness relies upon a management team making judgements about the strength of the links as well as relative robustness. This elaborated conceptualisation is illustrated in figure 7.2a – where competences are shown to deliver competence outcomes, which in turn support business goals that deliver customer value and so realise generic goals.

Figure 7.2b shows the addition of distinctiveness and 'threshold' competences – those that 'provide the legitimacy to operate in the industry'.[24] Some call these zero level, operational or ordinary capabilities – those that permit the organisation to earn a living in the present.[25] The exploration of this structure enables the management team to identify the most critical resources controlled by the firm (see figure 7.2c), and thereby increase the likelihood that they will be used to gain and sustain strategic advantage. Core distinctive competences must be able to disproportionately contribute to the customer-perceived value[26] through the nature of their links to business goals (that is having a far greater number of supporting links to goals than other competences).

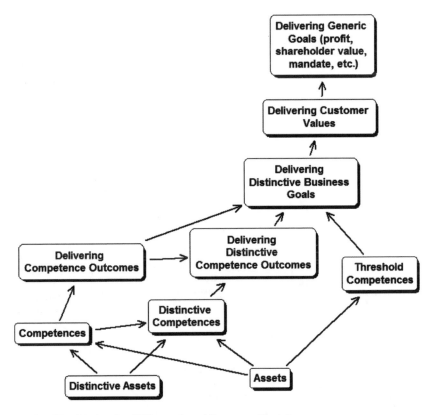

Figure 7.2b   The Distinctive/Differentiated Strategy Model

Discovery and Refinement of Coreness

Some competences that managers are proud of ... play no role.

The conceptualisation of core competences in relation to the business goals expressed, 'puts flesh on', the vague concept of coreness. As one CEO admitted: 'I always use the language of core competences, but really didn't understand what they really were; now I do'. Typically the exploration of the causal links between distinctive competences, competence outcomes and business goals leads to a realisation that some competences managers are proud of seem to be isolated from other competences, and play no role in the support of those which are now seen to be distinctive. This realisation forces a management team to consider the possibility that they are wasting energy protecting competences that no longer serve any useful purpose.

Sometimes distinctive patterns of competences, or individual distinctive competences, are disconnected from business goals. Consequently, either the business goals need to be changed so that the distinctive competences are exploited, or the energy that was going into sustaining these so called core competences becomes strategic slack available for use elsewhere. Similarly,

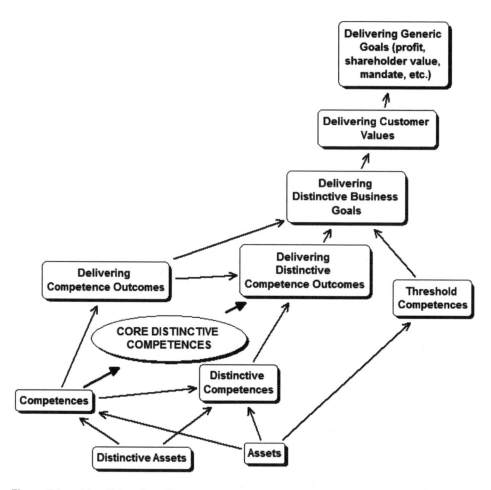

Figure 7.2c Identifying Core Competences

some business goals are shown to have no support from any distinctive competences, and so either new competences have to be developed (or existing competences refined to support the goals – thus creating new links) or the goals modified. *This cyclical process gradually reveals and refines those distinctive competences that are core and sharpens the goals system.* If there are no distinctive competences within the network then the competences that are most core to the network are *core competences* that are still worthy of identification, but do not provide significant competitive advantage, but must still be protected.

> *Often an organisation does not consider the exploitation of distinctiveness to claim new customers as a way of creating strategic growth.*

Exploring the linkage between competences (distinctive or not) and business goals enables a validation of: (1) the utility of the competences, (2) distinctiveness relative to specified goals, (3) the distinctiveness of *patterns* of competences and distinctive competences, and (4) the goals as being realistic. Invariably a management team identifies what they think are core competences and yet on inspection, these turn out to be of little importance in delivering business goals – they are often part of the legacy of the organisation. If the customer or the business does not currently value the consequences of any distinctive competences then there is no competitive advantage. But, if the customer can be persuaded to value the outcomes of a distinctive competence (through particular strategies) then it may create competitive advantage. Alternatively, the distinctiveness possibly can be exploited into new markets. Often an organisation does not consider the exploitation of distinctiveness to claim new customers as a way of creating strategic growth, rather they depend on acquisition as the obvious and quick way to grow.

It is important to note that if strategy is developed from customer values first, rather than from seeking to exploit distinctive competences, then it is possible that the exploitation of a distinctive competence might be missed. 'Firms should focus their analysis mainly on their "unique" skills and resources rather than on the competitive environment'.[27] The above notion of core competence varies from that suggested by others.[28]

'As If' *Core* Distinctive Competences

In this competitive advantage forum we are focusing attention on differentiation from others and its exploitation to good advantage. In doing so we discover patterns of competences that offer a chance for competitive advantage, regardless of whether current organisational purpose is or is not satisfied. In other words, regardless of the current 'business we're in' we might consider creating a 'new' business that exploits fully the discovery of differentiation and distinctiveness. In effect, the distinctiveness is so powerful that we should devise a goals system that makes the distinctive pattern the core of future business success. Thus, the distinctive competences pattern is going to be made into core distinctive competences by anticipating new or modified business goals that exploit them, even though the link between the distinctive pattern and business goals will not be explicated. The distinctiveness is to be exploited 'as if' it was core to the business model – if the business model was to be constructed then the distinctiveness is assumed to be at the core of it.

Thus, this forum does not need to go on to link distinctive competences to goals but rather anticipate the role of a distinctive pattern of competences with respect to future strategic success. Indeed, many new business ventures are created using the outcome of this forum as the basis for 'blue-skies' transformation of a business into new markets.

Sustaining Competitive Advantage

To argue that core distinctive competences must be sustained and maintained and so strategically managed is to state the obvious. Most capabilities become obsolete unless they are continually renewed and periodically reinvented. Some become core rigidities and need to be disposed of. Inimitability is at the heart of value creation because it limits competition. If the resource is inimitable, then any profit stream it generates is more likely to be sustainable. But, inimitability rarely, if ever, can last for ever. Competitors eventually will find ways to copy most valuable resources in a manner that can, at least, deliver a replicated distinctive competence *outcome*. Strategic management must, therefore, be expected to retain differentiation for as long as possible by building sustenance strategies around distinctive competences.

However, management teams rarely find that determining the best ways of sustaining core distinctive competences is easy. Often core distinctive competence sustenance depends on being able to release imprisoned and/or underleveraged competences and avoid unwittingly surrendering core competences through investment cuts or outsourcing.[29]

A core distinctive competence comprising only a few elements is much easier to understand and imitate than one that relies on a subtle network of competences working together in a distinctive fashion. Protecting distinctiveness as patterns is usually easier than protecting 'single' distinctive competences. 'Superior *combinations* of inputs can be more economically identified and formed from resources already used in the organisation than by obtaining new resources (and knowledge of them) from the outside'.[30] At the same time recognition of these competences' longevity is important – as it is to some extent dependent on their integration with the goals (and therefore sustenance) and the corporate direction and environmental conditions staying relatively stable. Therefore, core *distinctive* competences, by definition, cannot be purchased off the shelf but require strategic vision, development time and sustained investment.[31]

The only reasonable chance of *developing* (and even sustaining) distinctiveness is by putting strategies in place to create new links (patterns) between existing competences, in particular the creation of new self-sustaining feedback loops.

In some respects this can be seen as being related to 'dynamic capabilities'[32] – organisational and strategic routines by which firms integrate, build and reconfigure organisational assets to address swiftly changing environments or create advantageous market change. An organisation needs to build simple unharnessed competences into complex exploitable bundles – patterns of relationships – and to ensure that any virtuous cycles are identified and/or developed to nurture ever-growing capabilities. This is precisely what a management team can do once they have a picture of their own network of competences.

While there is always a danger of strategic inertia arising from protecting and developing core distinctive competences, it is the case that many management teams have not even got as far as understanding and reflecting upon their competence resources. Until they become better at understanding their own business there is little chance of them asking themselves about other considerations that must follow such understandings!

Outsourcing, Insourcing, Acquisition

Understanding the basis for competitive advantage provides an opportunity to review the potential for outsourcing, and by implication insourcing and acquisition. Often organisations consider outsourcing because that is what their competitors are doing – outsourcing particular elements of the business is becoming an industry recipe. And yet, following the crowd denies the potential for differentiation!

Figure 7.3 shows a table that facilitates the exploration of in-outsourcing and collaboration potential. The table considers the two dimensions of 'potential for competitive advantage', and distinctiveness as 'capability of delivery compared to competitors' – discovered from this forum.

There are occasions when an organisation will seek to acquire another organisation in order to merge two patterns of distinctive competences in order to gain greater competitive advantage. However, unfortunately in some instances the process fails because the acquiring organisation is too quick in imposing their own systems and structures after the acquisition. For example, an engineering organisation sought to enhance competitive advantage through the acquisition of another organisation who were seen to have a distinctive pattern of competences that enabled them to deliver fast and effective problem solving with respect to production issues arising following the commissioning of complex new products. This pattern, when merged with their own distinctive pattern of competences, was believed to provide significant competitive advantage that could be exploited to provide entry into new and desirable markets for growth. Their own competitive advantage lay in their ability to deliver a distinctive competence outcome of lower production costs through their pattern of competences relating to driving out a steeper learning

POTENTIAL FOR
COMPETITIVE
ADVANTAGE

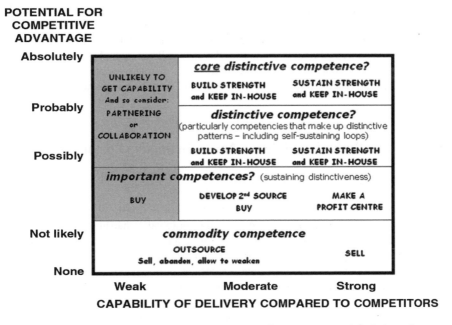

Figure 7.3   Considering the Potential for Insourcing, Outsourcing and Collaboration (based on Insinga, R. C. and Werle, M. J. (2000) Linking outsourcing to business strategy. *Academy of Management Executive*, 14(4): 58–70)

production curve than competitors – both accelerated corporate and personal learning curves. However, after the acquisition, the organisation immediately imposed their unique manufacturing system for lowering production costs on to the acquired organisation and in so doing killed the distinctive pattern that delivered the problem solving capability. They were keen to introduce their manufacturing system quickly in order to transfer some aspects of their own competitive advantage and also signal the change of ownership. But, the acquired organisation's problem solving capability resided in a culture – ways of working – that had grown over many years and the bureaucratic nature of the imposed manufacturing system significantly reduced flexibility of operations and also demotivated the workforce and so increased staff turnover.

Our experience suggests that due diligence during acquisitions usually pays far too much attention to financial aspects and too little attention to explicating distinctive patterns of competences let alone integrating the two sets together. The process of due diligence through its current application refocuses the acquisition away from competitive advantage and socially complex assets to financial issues and potential financial advantage. Indeed, many due diligence teams are trained in finance and economics rather than strategic analyses such as those demanded for an understanding of embedded and subtle patterns of competences.

THE *COMPETITIVE ADVANTAGE* STRATEGY FORUM

The key discussion topic, beyond generic issues in forum design, is that of encouraging the leader to see the forum as extremely important for the strategic future of the organisation – creating outcomes that are the essence of strategic *management*. It will be important for the leader to realise that most of the conversations that will have taken place about core competences will not have determined the subtleties that matter about how to strategically manage a system of competences nor addressed what is distinctive. Patience will be required as the group is encouraged to experiment with a variety of ideas about where distinctiveness might lie. The leader needs to understand that the forum may be a 'long-shot', but one where the payoff can be very significant if it works.

Surfacing and Gathering of Views About Distinctive Competences

Be expansive, non-evaluative and tentative.

The first, and obvious, step in surfacing distinctiveness is to ask 'What do or can we do exceptionally well that our customers perceive adds more value than alternative providers?'[33] An organisation stays alive by providing value to a stakeholder base. The stakeholders of interest are most often customers for private organisations, and for public organisations, some parts of the public sector who gain services as public goods as well as those stakeholders who directly fund or provide a mandate for the provision of the service (and other benefits such as attracting high quality staff). This value is derived from a combination of stakeholder demands and the distinctive competences of the supplying organisation in meeting the demands. Distinctiveness means some measure of difference, of being able to offer to the customers something that no other competitor can. For an organisation to be able to claim a position of sustainable profitability it has to be able to satisfy a customer market in a manner that resists easy emulation.[34] Thus, obvious types of competence distinctiveness may derive from:

- Difficulty of emulation – cannot be easily bought, or there is a very high cost of entry.

And this may derive from:

- It taking a very long time to attain the competence (for example the competences that deliver the distinctive competence outcomes of trust and loyalty of employees or customers).

Distinctiveness is most often about processes and culture rather than infrastructure. For example, the *complex harmonisation* of technology and production skills, the ability to *organise* work to deliver value, or even the ability to *exploit* competences effectively, could be considered.[35] Where the competence surrounds a particular piece of equipment (regardless of how expensive or new) there is always the danger that the distinctiveness could soon be eroded as competitors find ways of accessing this equipment.

Distinctiveness therefore is 'definitionally' related to uniqueness (where it is difficult to substitute), rare among a firm's competition, imperfectly inimitable, and valuable (through being able to exploit opportunities or neutralise threats). An example might be the distinctive asset of 'potent access to a *wide* variety of markets' possibly through a unique distribution network.

It is possible to encounter a type of distinctiveness that is seen to be important, but is extremely difficult to make explicit. Here it can be given a label but one that everyone is aware does not fully recognise the competence's subtlety:

- Competences that are uncodified are likely to be distinctive – you don't know how it works or how you developed it, thus others can't work out how it works either![36]

Some of the items often proudly presented as distinctive competences include large-scale production, high market share, successful diversification, or being the sole organisation in the marketplace. These are not distinctive competences but rather are usually the consequences or *outcomes* of the exploitation, either deliberate or emergent, of distinctive competences. Indeed they are most often the successful exploitation of a *system of interlocking* competences (only some of which might be distinctive). However, it is unhelpful to be too precise about what is required from the group – distinctive competence outcomes may not be manageable but they are a significant part of the story of competitiveness.

When carrying out the tasks embedded in this forum, it might also be worth considering the difference between competitive strategy at the level of a business and at the level of the entire company.[37] How can synergies be best exploited – the 2+2=5 objective (where the interaction between the two competences have more than an additive effect)? What often happens is that distinctions between strategic business units are seen only as sources of profit rather than as part of a coherent system and thus the potential to leverage further benefits is missed. This issue is even more significant when considering, for example, the business model of a corporate head office, where their contribution to corporate goals depends very much on bringing together competences that derive from the full range of strategic business units.[38]

This first step in the forum is most difficult because holding to the requirement of absolute distinctiveness discourages getting possibilities out on the table. The most helpful hint to a group is to concentrate on 'what we do, rather than what we are'. Thus, the first task in the forum is devoted to capturing any possible candidate aspects of distinctiveness. In practice this means surfacing, and displaying for all to see, ideas that will be competence outcomes, competences and assets, each of which might be distinctive (see figure 7.4). It is important that the group are encouraged to be non-evaluative.

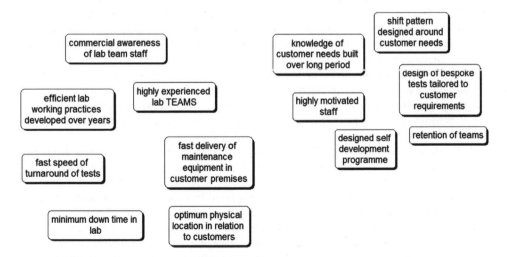

Figure 7.4   Initial Ideas About Distinctiveness

The requirement to be expansive, non-evaluative and tentative is critical to increasing the probability of finding distinctiveness. It depends wholly upon a group being expansive with respect to the question: what are your distinctive competences? Not only is it important to be non-evaluative about the extent of distinctiveness of suggestions made by other group members, but also to be non-evaluative about whether what is suggested is a competence. In other words, recognising that distinctiveness is hard to find will likely involve bundles of relative distinctiveness of competences, and requires getting at subtle attributes including refining the wording to reflect something deeply tacit.

Refrain from the temptation to link assertions about distinctiveness.

Although the aim of the forum is to explore the networks of relationships between competences (discovering distinctiveness from patterns), at this stage of the forum it is important to refrain from the temptation to link assertions about distinctiveness. It is important to avoid this temptation because it is problematic to link initial ideas into a network when it is likely that the proffered contributions will be poorly stated. In addition, there will be a mix of different sorts of distinctiveness, too few statements, and too few statements with enough subtle detail (making the detection of outcomes, assets and competences difficult).

Exploring Distinctive Competence Outcomes or Distinctive Competences or Distinctive Assets?

It is extremely difficult to identify distinctive competences, but easy to identify distinctive competence outcomes and distinctive assets.

Distinguishing competences from competence outcomes, and from distinctive assets, is important but difficult. It is important because it is competences that can be directly managed. If a manager was asked to manage competence outcomes they would struggle to know what the drivers are and how to manage them. Indeed if the competence outcome is distinctive then it is very likely that the drivers of the outcome are well hidden because they are subtle and combine to form a portfolio. In fact, a distinguishing characteristic of a distinctive competence outcome is that it *cannot be managed directly*; rather it is the competences that deliver the outcomes that can be managed. For example, 'reputation for on-time delivery' is a competence outcome, not a competence, as reputation is an elusive outcome to manage. It is a particular portfolio of competences that enable the reputation to be gained and it is these competences that can be managed strategically. Similarly, low cost production may be argued to be a competence; however, given its nature it is a competence outcome and one that may not be distinctive unless it can be sustained through the continued exploitation of distinctive competences.

It is extremely difficult to identify distinctive competences, but easy to identify distinctive competence outcomes and distinctive assets. It is helpful to see assets as being exploited by competences and distinctive competence outcomes[39] being supported by competences. Figure 7.5 shows the categorisation of the competences displayed in figure 7.4. In addition, figure 7.5 reflects the hierarchy with those that were regarded as competence outcomes being repositioned at the top, distinctive competences in the middle, and assets at the bottom of the picture.

The conceptual separation of distinctive competence outcomes and distinctive competences implies a hierarchy that shows chains of assumed causality from manageable competences to the competence outcome.

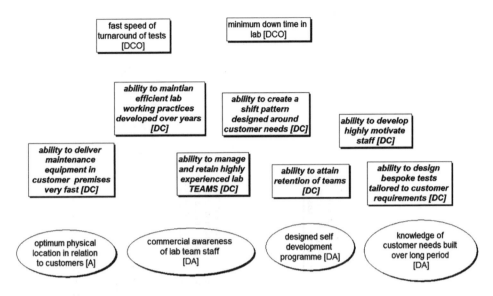

Figure 7.5   Initial Categorising of Some of the Initial Ideas (bold italic = distinctive competence, oval = distinctive asset, boxed = distinctive competence outcome)

By starting with distinctive competence outcomes it becomes possible for management teams to move on naturally to discussing how these are realised.

Developing the Network of Competences

The reason for delaying the linking of the three categories of statements is to increase the probability of new material emerging. A discussion about the categorisation of statements forces tighter thinking and so tighter wording. The discussion also prompts a need for proponents of particular views to offer explanation and in offering explanation new, and often important, material is surfaced. If development of the network is undertaken too early then it is likely that summary links arise that miss important subtleties which are often the real basis of managing competitive advantage. In figure 7.6 all of the linkages have implications for the top level distinctive competence outcome of 'fast speed of turnaround of tests', but in the process of linking, further material has been added to explain the 'ability to develop highly motivated staff' and the 'ability to create a shift pattern designed around customer needs'. Although this figure is an extract from a much larger network of competences it was, nevertheless, relatively independent of other patterns that had emerged and so could be explored as a separable cluster of competences. In developing this particular pattern, which is a tidy tear drop, the team began to ask themselves whether the pattern – taken as a whole – was distinctive. They had concluded that they were somewhat ambitious in their claims about the distinctiveness of individual items; each claim was just about distinct, but not significantly so. However, when they considered the pattern as a whole they felt more confidence in claiming something that might be better exploited as competitive advantage. Needless to say, as with all claims about distinctiveness, there will always be a requirement to seek out evidence of beliefs and judgements. If distinctiveness is embedded well within an organisation then it will always be difficult to make accurate

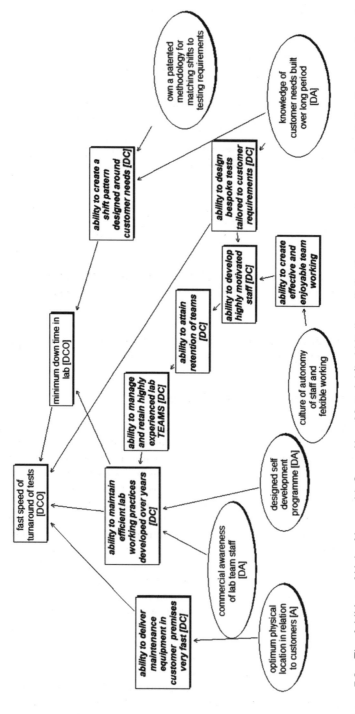

Figure 7.6 The Addition of Links Along with Some New Material (bold italic = distinctive competence, oval = distinctive asset, boxed = distinctive competence outcome)

judgements about the competences of competitors. However, once claims of distinctiveness become significant then they promote a research agenda where competitors become more thoroughly understood.

Distinctive Competences as a Distinctive *Pattern* of Competences

As a management team begin the process of seeking to identify possible distinctive patterns they may see a possible dynamic pattern showing a virtuous cycle. In figure 7.7 such a pattern looks like a self-sustaining feedback loop that may be the basis for competitive advantage (the figure shows only one small part of the emerging material, but looks interesting and worth exploring further).

The first stage of exploring this potential advantage lies in being clear about the status of the different statements: are they competences, competence outcomes, or assets, and are any of them relatively distinctive? Figure 7.8 shows this next stage in the thinking of the management team – here they have slightly edited the wording and categorised the claims. The team, at this stage of their exploration, are making significant claims about the distinctiveness of every statement. Often management teams are bullish about their distinctiveness during the early stages of exploration, but become more doubtful as discussion follows. However, the process of editing has encouraged a clearer identification of competences by adding the preface of 'an ability to', but doing so without changing the intention of the claim.

The identification of the feedback loop and refinement of the contents has revealed an issue about this loop being dynamic, because of the inclusion of an asset within the loop that is not expressed as a variable. The existence of a 'massive well structured database' was argued to be an asset that had been created in the past. The link from database (37) to statement 24 argues that the database can be used to aid the construction of simulation models, and the development of the database is argued to have derived from an ability to listen to customers (11). For the self-sustaining feedback loop to be a legitimate virtuous cycle the asset must change and continuously develop – and so be claimed as a competence (hopefully distinctive). Figure 7.9 shows this shift in the exploration of the pattern, where the team have now discovered the potential significance of ensuring that the continuous development of the asset, as a competence, is a crucial aspect of ensuring the sustenance of the feedback dynamic. It is the ability to make each of the three competences work together that makes the pattern promising for competitive advantage.

As the feedback loop began to look increasingly promising as one possible basis for competitive advantage it encouraged the team to ask themselves what else might support each of the claims in the loop (statement 66). The focus for the group became one of seeking validation of the level of relative distinctiveness of each individual statement and of the causal links. As they proceeded with this evaluation they became increasingly convinced that this feedback loop was a distinctive pattern. So, although listening to customers was a competence several of their key competitors would also claim, the ability to do this in such a way that a very particular database could be constructed that would facilitate an exploitation of simulation competences was exceptionally distinctive. In addition they were convinced that this process led to the potential customers declaring more about their operation than would otherwise be the case, and so enhancing in a unique way their structured database. They reckoned they had discovered competitive advantage, value creating potential, that was not being fully exploited – in other words, they concluded that this pattern of competences should be made into a core distinctive competence by adapting their business goals accordingly.

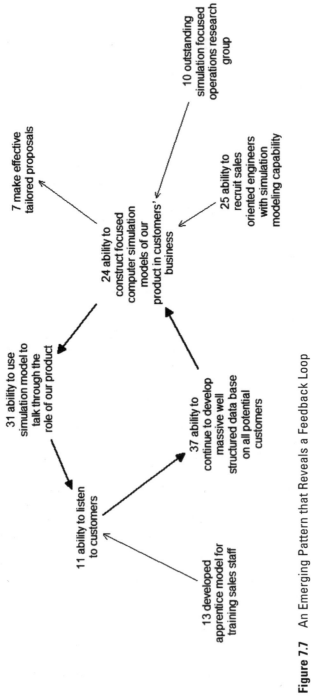

Figure 7.7 An Emerging Pattern that Reveals a Feedback Loop

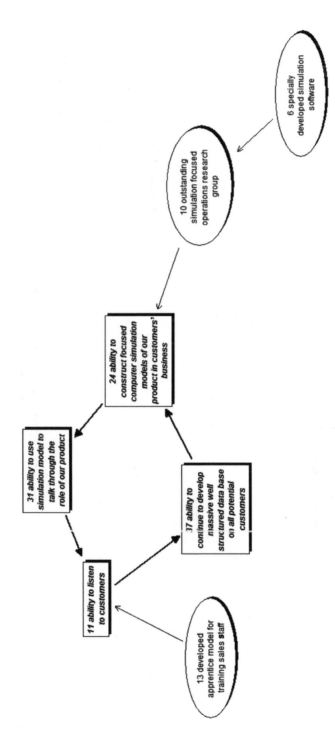

Figure 7.8 Beginning the Process of Editing Statements and Categorising Them (bold italic = distinctive competence, oval = distinctive asset)

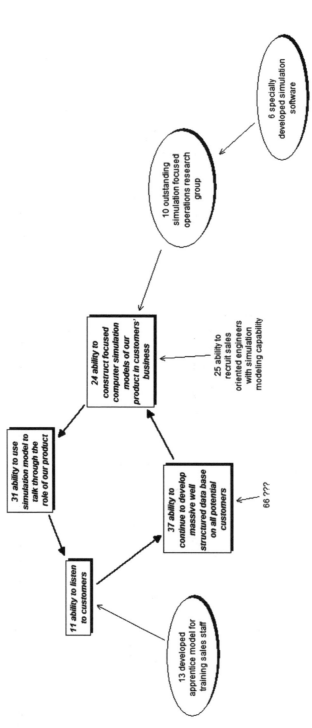

Figure 7.9 Exploring a Virtuous Cycle as the Basis for Competitive Advantage (bold italic = distinctive competence, oval = distinctive asset, boxed = distinctive competence outcome, other = explanations)

THE STRATEGY DELIVERABLE: A *STATEMENT* OF STRATEGIC INTENT (SSI)?

A one-page statement will be a more familiar means of delivering the strategic intent to staff in an organisation – causal maps, although more precise statements, are often cryptic to its audience. But, given that competitive advantage arises from patterns it is very important to capture in words and sentences the nature of a pattern, and so capturing the essential features of an often complex network is crucial.

The statement of strategic intent represents strategic priorities for the exploitation and sustenance of competitive advantage.

This is the last part of developing a strategy using a competitive advantage forum. As with all of the forums, it is important that the SSI is produced soon after the forum (preferably the same day and distributed to all participants). The forum may take place during a morning and so the SSI can be written during lunch, reviewed by the leader, and distributed immediately after lunch. If the group is able to reconvene for a short while after lunch the SSI can be validated by the whole group and then be a genuine take-away that gives a sense of closure to the forum.

Figure 7.10 shows a pattern of competences that were regarded as the core distinctive competences of a publisher's future business – and that the business goals had been modified to ensure

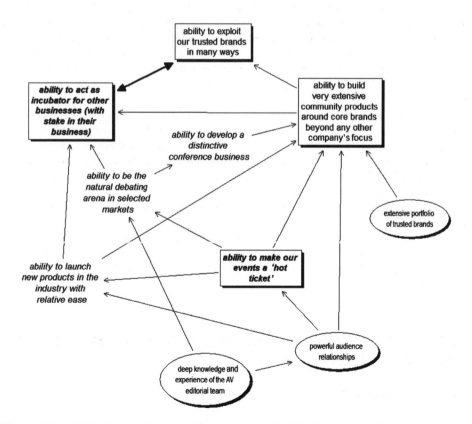

Figure 7.10   A Distinctive Pattern of Competences (bold italic = distinctive competence, oval = distinctive asset, boxed = distinctive competence outcome, no box = competence)

a better exploitation of this pattern. Although the pattern shows a feedback loop – a double headed arrow – this was not the crucial aspect of the pattern but rather, for the management team, a reminder of the extent to which the distinctive competence and distinctive competence outcome mutually reinforced each other.

At the centre of the pattern is the 'ability to make our events a "hot ticket"', and this is a driver of the outcomes but through other competences and with the support of assets. Box 7.1 shows the statement of strategic intent that represents a first draft designed to capture outcomes and the core distinctive competence. In addition the statement seeks to focus attention on the strategic needs for sustenance and development of the key assets that are to be exploited to facilitate crucial competences.

Box 7.1   A First Draft of the Statement of Strategic Intent that Derives from the Pattern of Competences in Figure 7.10.

Our future business success depends upon our ability to exploit a very powerful portfolio of competences, that when taken together, enable us to deliver to our customers products and services that are significantly better than our competitors.

Our strategic focus will be on the delivery of two linked outcomes that feed off each other and together will deliver future profit: our **ability to exploit our trusted brands in many ways** and our **ability to act as incubator for other businesses (with stake in the business)**. At the core of our competitive advantage lies our exceptional **ability to make our events a 'hot ticket'** and this is dependent upon **powerful audience relationships** and the **deep knowledge and experience of the AV editorial team.** We must protect and continuously develop these key assets.

Our ability to make our events a 'hot ticket' reinforces our ability to be the natural debating arena in selected markets and so enable us to develop a distinctive conference business. Alongside our extensive portfolio of trusted brands our **ability to make our events a 'hot ticket'** drives our exceptional **ability to build very extensive community products around core brands beyond any other company's focus,** which importantly contributes to our **ability to act as incubator for other businesses (with stake in their business).** Our **powerful audience relationships** gives us the **ability to launch new products in the industry with relative ease.**

At the core of our future business success lie our exceptional abilities to **act as incubator for other businesses (with stake in their business)** and **make our events a 'hot ticket',** and the entire portfolio of competences and assets that enable us to retain our competitive advantage.

WHAT MIGHT BE WRONG WITH MAKING STRATEGY THROUGH EXPLORING COMPETITIVE ADVANTAGE?

Rose-tinted Glasses?

Many senior management teams are disconnected from the realities of their own organisation and so make 'rose-tinted' claims about competences. As we suggested in the examples above, during the early stages in the exploration of distinctiveness it is important to encourage expansiveness and tentativeness. As long as it is patterns, portfolios and bundles of competences that are the likely basis of distinctiveness then many of the individual claims will inevitably be only relatively distinctive. Nevertheless, a pattern is, of course, more distinctive when it contains individual competences that are distinctive in their own right.

In cases where a management team has become aware of the dangers of 'seeing the world through rose-tinted glasses' then processes that might protect from this have been introduced. These processes are: bringing into the forum trusted outsiders, and repeating the forum with other cross-sections of participants. Engaging trusted outsiders such as customers, consultants and sub-contractors can be risky because of the confidentiality issues. However, trusted outsiders will often say 'but what about the way you do this – it's what makes you so competitive?', inviting consideration of an important taken-for-granted competence.

As with all aspects of good management, good judgement is crucial; however, in evaluating distinctiveness good judgement must be supported by evidence when possible. The use of a management team, with good and wide ranging experience, will ensure that different perspectives and appropriate analysis of the developing perspective will force testing of assumptions. But this will only happen through well-designed group processes that encourage openness, creativity and challenge (see chapter 2). Typically, when exploring distinctiveness, a team is necessarily self-congratulatory and subject to a rose-tinted view of their organisation. This is appropriate in the early stages. As the forum develops then the team will become more challenging of their assertions and conclusions, and a good facilitator will have earned the right to challenge. The challenges will very often lead to a substantial research agenda designed to question key assertions that are central to the most distinctive pattern of competences.

Ignores Weaknesses? Isn't a SWOT Analysis Better?

The purpose of this forum is to focus only on competitive advantage and not on disadvantage. The issue management forum (chapters 4 and 5) deals with a negative view of the world and identifying weaknesses. It is tempting to suggest that the identification of strengths and weaknesses through the use of a SWOT analysis will ensure that weaknesses are not missed. Strengths and distinctive competences (and so competitive advantage) are not the same. Discovering distinctiveness involves specific attention to 'what we do, not what we are' and seeks to address specifically that which can be strategically managed in terms of both exploitation and sustenance. As we have commented elsewhere in this book (chapter 5), SWOT analyses reflect four quadrants that are not easy to define operationally – too much time can be wasted arguing about which quadrant to place an assertion rather than making good use of the assertions themselves. In addition a SWOT analysis rarely captures the systemic relationships between all of the statements in the four boxes.

Needless to say, when a management team has undertaken both an issue management and competitive advantage forum then they will see weaknesses and strengths in the context of strategic action. In addition there will usually be apparent contradictions – where issues that need to be addressed as a result of deliberating on the network of issues imply that claims about distinctive competences cannot be valid. These are important discoveries that do not invalidate conclusions about competitive advantage but rather suggest that it is even more important to develop and sustain the distinctive competences and so realise competitive advantage at its highest level.

Ignores Threshold Competences?

Understanding the role of threshold competences – those competences that are essential for the business to work – is an important part of developing a sound strategy. But it is not the primary role of the competitive advantage forum. The competitive advantage forum will usually surface those threshold competences that are a part of the pattern of competences that determine competitive advantage and it will be important to recognise their particular role. Sometimes these threshold competences are so important that they must not be outsourced – to do so creates the risk that the leverage (causal links) from them as a part of making the pattern work, gets lost. In principle threshold competences can be an obvious candidate for outsourcing, providing the risks associated with the possibility of losing them are addressed. However, none of the competences associated with competitive advantage should be outsourced.

Unreliable and Imprecise?

The successful discovery of a pattern of distinctive competences involves creativity as well as a good and reliable understanding of them. The initial outcome of the mapping of a network of distinctive competences is expected to be 'rough and ready', and deliberately so, in order that subtle patterns might be discovered. As the forum progresses claims and assertions are gradually refined, but in a focused manner. As a promising pattern is discovered (see figures 7.7, 7.8 and 7.9) then the demands to verify both links and statements become stronger. Indeed, very often the most promising patterns become the specification for detailed research to test the veracity of the pattern. It is important that time and effort is not wasted testing the reliability of assertions and claims that are of little significance in discovering a potential core distinctive competence pattern.

What If I Have No Distinctive Competences?

Very many organisations have no competitive advantage. If there is no distinctive pattern of competences then the organisation faces an uncertain and more risky strategic future – and this is worth knowing! In any event developing an understanding of core competences (as opposed to core distinctive competences) is still an important exercise in strategic management – these will need to be sustained and protected and not outsourced. Core competences are those competences that do not provide competitive advantage, but are central/core to the delivery of business goals.

DISCUSSION WITH THE MANAGER-CLIENT ABOUT NEXT STEPS: LINKING TO THE OTHER STRATEGY MAKING FORUMS

As we discussed earlier in this chapter, competitive advantage arises with respect to the purpose of the organisation.

When a competitive advantage forum has provided a management team with a useful basis for creating a successful strategic future it will have been through an anticipation of the ability to deliver customer value and so revenue. The outcomes of exploitation of the distinctive pattern will rarely have been articulated. As with the example used above to show a statement of strategic intent (figures 7.10 and box 7.1), the team have made a judgement about the impact of their view about core distinctive competences on their business goals and changed both the competences and goals accordingly. However, an obvious next task, as a follow on from this specific forum, is to conduct a more formal process of linking the elements of the pattern to their declared goals system and so making changes in a considered and organised manner. If the team have already undertaken a strategy as purpose forum (chapters 5 and 6) then the process is about linking the core distinctive competences to the goals developed through that forum, and modifying both. On some occasions the competitive advantage forum will have identified the potential for adding substantially new business goals or being more ambitious as the organisation seeks to exploit the realised competitive advantage into new markets and so derive new revenue streams.

There are three obvious next steps that might be introduced to the manager-client.

1   We argued at the start of this chapter that the competitive advantage forum can be particularly rewarding for a management team, because they have rarely considered in any depth where their distinctive competences lie. The forum promotes an interest in other perspectives on strategy and leads naturally to the need to address issues of weaknesses rather than simply focusing on the good aspects of the organisation (see comments above on the use of SWOT). A query such as this introduces naturally the prospect of *an issue management forum* as the basis for focusing on those aspects of the future that will require priority strategic management. Inevitably the issue management approach to developing strategic focus locates thinking in areas of weakness, including possible lost opportunities. The issue management forum acts as a useful parallel strategic conversation to the thinking that is the focus of competitive advantage.

2   However, as we comment above, the prospect of exploring and building a complete *business model* [40] that encompasses the link between the distinctive pattern of competences (anticipated core distinctive competences) and business goals is attractive. Thus, there is a natural follow-on from a competitive advantage forum to the *strategy as purpose forum*. In this forum the goals *system* is explored, developed and constructed using the published goals, a 'blank sheet of paper', or through the use of material generated in the issue management forum. The goals will usually be split between generic goals (common to most organisations in the sector) and business goals which are less common and, when linked together as a system of goals, are distinctive to the particular organisation. The generic goals are superordinate to business goals, and it is the business goals that will be distinctively delivered through the exploitation of the core distinctive competence(s). The process of linking distinctiveness to goals usually implies a revision of goals or recognition that there is a mismatch between distinctive competences and purpose.

    However, having a clear understanding about the nature of strategic goals and how they fit together is a worthwhile task in its own right, as well as developing an understanding of the business model. The outcome of a goals system exploration establishes a revised goals system that fully attends to the need for a coherent goals system that emphasises an appropriate set of aspirations for a successful strategic future.

3   Careful *stakeholder management* is imperative in ensuring that distinctiveness can be exploited and sustained. Many who have a stake in the strategic future of the organisation – both internal and external stakeholders – will have an interest in destroying competitiveness or supporting it. The extent of their power to sabotage or support will be important for the delivery of a successful future. Similarly the interest and power of key stakeholders will need to be understood so that the most salient aspects of distinctiveness can be protected. Competitors may have resources and connections that make it able to respond powerfully to actions taken to both exploit and protect the distinctive pattern – often without doing so deliberately. A stakeholder management forum focuses usefully upon the bases of interest and power of key stakeholders, and so *determines strategies for the better management of these stakeholders to increase the probability of the successful delivery of competitive advantage.*

Each of these forums makes sense as a next step, and so a client is able to choose to continue a strategy making process on an incremental basis without the need to plan a full scale approach.

NOTES

1 This view of competitive advantage lies well with that provided by Jay Barne (Barney, 2002).
2 Selznik (1957) and Penrose (1959) were among the first to identify and label a distinctive competence as a particularly valuable resource for organisations. They believe that a key role for organisational leaders is to identify, invest in and protect such competences and the resources that underlie them. The resource-based view (RBV), and competence-based management (CBM) model of the firm (Barney, 1986; Barney, 1991b; Peteraf, 1993; Rumelt, 1984; Sanchez, 2002; Sanchez and Heene, 2004; Wernerfelt, 1984; Wernerfelt, 1989) focuses on the crucial importance of competences, assets and resources for organisational survival, growth and overall effectiveness. One of the key insights of the RBV is that 'scarce, valuable, and imperfectly imitable resources are the only factors capable of creating sustained performance differences among competing firms, and that these resources should figure prominently in strategy making' (Kraatz and Zajac, 2001: 632). Distinctive competences are regarded as one such resource. Thus, a necessary part of strategy making for any management team in any type of organisation – not-for-profit as well as for-profit – is to reflect upon organisational competences that are distinctive.
3 This view has been argued strongly by many, for example, Hamel (1994); Hamel and Heene (1994); Prahalad and Hamel (1990); Sanchez (2002); Schoemaker (1992); Selznik (1957).
4 See Bogner and Thomas (1994).
5 See Bryson, Ackermann and Eden (2007) for an example of exploring distinctiveness in a not-for-profit organisation.
6 Collis and Montgomery (1995: 123).
7 Dan Simpson, Director of Strategy and Planning. The Clorox Corporation, quoted in Coyne, Hall and Clifford (1997: 42).
8 Paula Cholmondeley, VP, Business Development and Global Sourcing, Owens-Corning Fiberglass.
9 See Eden and Ackermann (2000).
10 Collins and Porras (1995).
11 Hall (1992: 139).
12 Collis and Montgomery (1995).
13 See Collis (1994).
14 Day (1994: 38) emphasis added.
15 Barney (1991a: 107).
16 Prahalad and Hamel (1990).
17 Galbreath and Galvin (2008).
18 Miller (2003).
19 Miller (2003: 967).
20 Eisenhardt and Martin (2000: 1114).
21 King, Fowler and Zeithaml (2001: 102).
22 In chapter 5 we discuss the difference between business goals and generic goals – business goals are an expression of 'the business we're in' and will usually be unique to the specific business.

23 This view of core competence varies from that suggested by Prahalad and Hamel (1990) because it argues that (1) core *distinctive* competences provide competitive advantage, (2) core competences are *discovered* from an analysis of the relationship of competences to goals, and (3) the discovery of distinctive patterns suggests the exploitation of competences through the *modification or addition of goals*. Thus, the discovery of distinctiveness provides the basis for competitively growing the business in different directions through the exploitation of distinctiveness. In practice this is how many management teams establish a growth strategy that avoids growth by acquisition. If the question 'what are your core competences' can be answered at the outset of an exploration of distinctiveness then the organisation will be locked into an existing strategic future.

24 Johnson, Scholes and Whittington (2005: 119–120).

25 See, for example, Winter (2003).

26 Hamel (1994).

27 Dierickx and Cool (1989: 1504). This article has been one of the most influential and yet also of significance for strategic *management* (see Eden and Ackermann, 2007).

28 Notably this view differs from Prahalad and Hamel (1990) who were perhaps most influential in developing a managerial interest in core competences.

29 Prahalad and Hamel (1990: 88).

30 Priem and Butler (2001: 36), emphasis added.

31 See Amit and Schoemaker (1993).

32 Teece, Pisano and Shuen (1997: 537) define dynamic capabilities as the 'firm's ability to integrate, build, and reconfigure internal and external competences to address rapidly changing environments' (1997: 516). This definition should be adapted to include the word appropriately. See also, Ambrosini, Bowman and Collier (2009); Augier and Teece (2009); Eisenhardt and Martin (2000) and Teece, Pisano and Shuen (1997).

33 Van der Heijden (1996: 64–65) gives a number of examples of distinctive competences which he groups into five categories – institutional knowledge, embedded processes, reputation and trust, legal protection and activity-specific assets.

34 Johnson and Scholes (2002) consider how differentiation-based competitive advantage can be sustained by leveraging competences.

35 Stalk, Evans and Schulman (1992) discuss the four basic principles of capabilities-based competition in order to 'identify and develop the hard-to-imitate organizational capabilities that distinguish a company from its competitors in the eyes of customers'. They identify four basic principles in which processes play an important role.

36 Johnson and Scholes (2002: 177–179) discuss complexity and causal ambiguity in relation to competences.

37 Prahalad and Hamel (1990) discuss the issues surrounding core competences and SBUs.

38 van der Heijden (1996: 75–78) discusses the business idea in relation to SBUs, considering ways in which synergy between business units and corporate units can be exploited. He suggests that distinctive competences play a key role in this process.

39 It is not surprising that Priem and Butler (2001: 31) noted that, 'simply advising practitioners to obtain rare and valuable resources in order to achieve competitive advantage and, further, that those resources should be hard to imitate and non-substitutable for sustainable advantage, does not meet the operational validity criterion'.

40 The elaboration of a business model through the linking of competences to business goals is discussed in Eden and Ackermann (2010a). See also Eden and Ackermann (2010a).

Further Reading

Barney, J. B. 1991a. Firm Resources and Sustained Competitive Advantage. *Journal of Management,* 17: 99–120.

Peteraf, M. A. 1993. The Cornerstones of Competitive Advantage: A Resource-based View. *Strategic Management Journal,* 124: 179–191.

Sanchez, R. and Heene, A. 2004. *The New Strategic Management: Organizations, Competition and Competence.* London: Wiley.

Schoemaker, P. J. H. 1992. How to Link Strategic Vision to Core Capabilities. *Sloan Management Review,* 34: 67–81.

8

STRATEGY AS COMPETITIVE ADVANTAGE FORUM

Fran Ackermann and Colin Eden

WHAT DOES A STRATEGY AS COMPETITIVE ADVANTAGE FORUM LOOK AND FEEL LIKE?

What Does It Look Like to a Participant When You Walk in the Room?

We were seated around a semicircle of tables facing a large projector screen and the facilitator was at the front to the right.

The facilitator was using a laptop computer that was presenting a blank white screen.

What Happened?

We started by trying to identify those activities and processes we did well – those we felt made us different from the competition. To get things going, the facilitator encouraged us to be reasonably inclusive, and not get too fussed about how distinctive a particular activity was. This seemed like an easy task and I felt the output would not be particularly useful as we had done a similar exercise recently using a SWOT analysis. Once we had generated a few contributions we were able to use these as prompts for further ideas. After about 20 minutes we had 30 or so contributions, some of which looked to be distinctive to us and others less so.

We then reviewed these contributions and it was clear we had missed some of the 'things we do round here' that we probably took for granted – which prompted further material and some animated debate about how distinctive some contributions really were, prompting our facilitator to suggest that we avoid getting too concerned about the level of distinctiveness at this stage of the forum. In addition, the wording of some of the contributions weren't all that clear. We therefore worked on the language as we tried to explain our own views to others. It was interesting in that it took a bit of practice to get these worded right – sometimes it was just the addition of a single word that really captured the essence of the activity and its distinctiveness.

We then categorised the contributions into those that were competences, assets and outcomes, and began to get a feel for their relative distinctiveness. This part of the forum helped surface more material. It also began to give us a better sense of what we had and how we could manage these resources better. As we were working through the categorisation process it became clear we needed to look not just at the contributions but also how they impacted or supported one another. This insight helped us realise that the patterns, that is how the contributions were linked together, were probably more distinctive than the individual claims and were probably a better view of our organisation's competitive advantage.

We finished up with a pretty good grasp of what it was we had – as bundles of resources – and in a way that we could see the distinctiveness. The bundles communicated something very different from what had come out of the SWOT analysis. By the way, I hadn't realised how much of a contribution the particular way our HR department works makes to our competitiveness!

What Did it Feel Like?

Hard work at first – I simply couldn't think of very many things we did particularly distinctively. But with the facilitator's encouragement we persevered and gradually got at many aspects of the way we did things that would never be noticed by our customers, but nevertheless made a great contribution to the nature of our service. This helped lots as I found it easier to think in terms of activities and resources and suggest these. The process of looking at the material on the screen seemed to unlock my brain. I began to feel we were getting somewhere.

When it came to the review it was interesting to note that a number of the activities I hadn't thought were particularly distinctive actually were. But it wasn't until I heard the explanations that I thought 'yes, you are right, we do that really well!' By the end of the review I felt quite energised by what we had – it was a lot more than I thought it would be.

The categorisation process was particularly helpful. Thinking about whether a contribution was an outcome or a competence really helped us get at what we could actually manage – so much of what we were claiming did not get things in enough detail. Identifying distinctive assets was also rewarding as the group really got into thinking about what competences they could support and this part of the process helped us not only consider the contributions in their own right but also look at how they related to one another. As a result this part of the forum seemed to just flow to the next part – capturing the links. We ended up with a fairly messy network (which the facilitator was able to tidy up as we went along) which gave us another boost as it was clear that there were further sources of distinctiveness, namely the way the competences, assets and outcomes fitted together – with assets being exploited by our processes and then creating outcomes that, in many cases, would be seen by the customer.

I learnt a lot! It was harder work than I expected! But I felt much better about the organisation's competitive position at the end. How could we have been wasting so much of what we did by not appreciating its significance – also we must think about outsourcing some stuff – it has to be done, but not by us, and that will release some energy to make sure we keep doing the important things better.

What Did I Go Away With?

We were all given copies of the pictures reflecting how our competences fitted together and categorising them so that it was easier to know which to manage. In a couple of hours' work we'd captured a lot of material and really got an idea of where distinctiveness lay. It gave us a clear idea of where to focus our energy and started getting agreements about who'd take responsibility for what. We did need another meeting to tidy this up though.

However, I can't see that these pictures would mean much to anyone not at the forum as they are very cryptic! I think you need to be there, listen to the conversations, and get familiar with the linking process, to appreciate fully their value. But to help manage this, we produced a draft of a statement addressing what we had agreed in normal sentences and paragraphs. The next step is to write it again more carefully so that others understand fully what it means and we don't lose some of the value.

What Did it Cost?

There were seven of us in the forum in addition to the facilitator, so the time cost was about eighteen person-hours plus the costs of the facilitator.

Was it Worthwhile?

I was surprised at how much we got through, and that we got a product at the end – a product that was, in effect, the minutes of the meeting written by the group. The product gave us a sense of focus, and that is what we'd hoped for. It was obviously only a draft strategy, but it is something, it is helpful and we all bought into it!

RESOURCES

- 1–2 hour meeting of facilitator and client (to agree the design of the forum).
- 1 hour setup by the facilitator.
- 1–3 hours of group work – it is possible to complete this forum in half a day but it can be done in as little as 1 hour.
- Decision Explorer® (the software that captured the statements and links) on a laptop and a small table so that the facilitator can see the public screen and group and will be able to move easily from being behind the computer to being up front when necessary.
- 1280×1024 data projector (this quality works best as it allows all attending easily to see the material on the screen).
- Large screen.
- Room with chairs (preferably on castors) – one for each participant.

MAPPING OUT STRATEGY SUCCESS: STRATEGY AS COMPETITIVE ADVANTAGE

Surfacing and Gathering of Views About Distinctive Competences

Be expansive, non-evaluative and tentative.

Script for: Surfacing and gathering of views about distinctive competences

Tasks:

1 Surface distinctive competences: 10–15 minutes
2 Cluster emergent competences and check for missing competences: 5–10 minutes

Deliverable: a clustered set of draft competences
Script timing: minimum 15, expected 25 minutes

Task 1: Surface Distinctive Competences

Take a Broad View of Competences   After a brief introduction outlining purpose and agenda, start the competitive advantage forum by asking participants to **surface distinctive competences**. To get participants going **explain that there is a degree of similarity with surfacing strengths when undertaking a SWOT exercise**, but in this forum note they are not just looking for strengths but processes that differentiate the organisation from the competition and that this is more demanding than just strengths. Encourage participants to **generate as many contributions** as they can – be expansive and non-evaluative, the evaluation will come later. At this stage it is important to surface anything that might be distinctive – sometimes initial weak ideas become important good ideas as they are discussed and reworded to capture something that does seem distinctive. Furthermore, **reassure participants not to get too concerned about the level of distinctiveness**. Therefore recommend to a participant that if they aren't sure whether the competence they are considering is definitely distinctive then don't hold it back but rather **add it to the captured material. Take a broad view of distinctiveness** – as participants often will find it difficult to get started (see box 8.1 for an example).

Box 8.1   Difficulties in Surfacing *Distinctive* Competences

When considering distinctive competences, a group of oil company managers were struggling to make explicit what made them special. They had already noted that they were good at finding oil, that they had highly skilled international staff, and that they were able to make a matrix organisation work well. But this did not satisfy them. Then after much deliberating one of the managers commented 'it's our ability to work well with any government' – that is what is distinctive.

To help participants think about candidate competences, try using the following prompts:

- **Consider what the organisation does well that is *difficult to emulate*.** For example, it might be an 'ability to encourage creativity and innovation in staff' or an 'ability to work together collaboratively'.
- **Think about competences that *cannot be bought easily*.** Examples here might include 'an ability to understand the rules and procedures necessary when working with the European Parliament' or 'an ability to understand nuclear operations well enough to maintain and modify structures'. In

the first case the knowledge is more about human processes whereas the second is more technically focused. Both of these aspects are important and relevant.

- Ask participants what competences have a *high cost associated with their development/creation*. Examples here might include having an 'ability to tap a wide range of networks'.
- Similar to focusing on high costs, another prompt is to **ask participants to think about competences that take a *long time to attain*.** An example here might be the 'ability to generate high levels of trust from customers'.
- Typically owning equipment is not considered a distinctive competence (unless it is not available for any company to buy). However, it may be that one of the organisation's distinctive competences is its 'ability to harness the full power of the technology' rather than using it in a standard way, thus **look for distinctive processes.** For example, **consider whether the organisation has any special ways to harness technology and production skills**.
- Invariably it is cultural properties that are most distinctive and most difficult to emulate, so ask participants to **consider 'the way we do things around here'.** Often these aspects of differentiation are difficult to identify because they are very much taken for granted.
- Depending on what part of the organisation is being reviewed, if the forum is considering the organisation as a whole, it might be worth getting participants to **consider the difference between competitive strategy at the level of a business unit and at the level of the entire company** (see boxes 8.2 and 8.3 for examples). In many companies the underlying reward structure results in business units concentrating on their own particular remit sometimes at the expense of the organisation as a whole. However, where the company leverages the entirety of the organisation's competences then this 'ability to provide an extensive range of services' also provides competitive advantage.

Box 8.2   Combining Skill Sets Across the Business Units

A large multinational engineering organisation conscious of the challenges emanating from the economic climate wanted to make best use of its resources. Traditionally organised around a number of business units, for example, infrastructure and marine, there was a sense in the senior management team that the company wasn't leveraging their skills and assets as effectively as they could. Surely there were some synergies to be achieved. As such, they wanted to see if combining skill sets across the business units could enable them to offer more extensive services to clients and thus steal the march on their competitors. They considered using a competitive advantage forum.

Box 8.3   Exploring Central Services Distinctive Contribution

An HR department of a large private sector organisation was feeling very exposed. The company in responding to the depressed economic situation was looking hard at reducing its costs and felt that the natural place to start was with some of the central services (after all they weren't directly providing any goods or services to customers). The HR department, however, felt that they offered something special and rather than be outsourced or reduced decided to take time out and develop a clear picture of their competitive advantage to the company. At first they felt quite dispirited – it was hard to identify clearly distinctive competences – but once they got some captured more appeared and soon they were faced with a reassuring picture. This would be a good start to arguing their case!

- **Get participants to consider what their customers value particularly about their product or services, what the staff feel proud about, and what their competitors wish they had**.
- Finally, distinctiveness might also emerge from the **ability to uniquely organise work to deliver value** or an ability to be cognisant of, and fully exploit, the competences available within the organisation.

Reassure participants that the task is not easy and not to feel discouraged. As this forum is focused on leveraging the competitive advantage gained from resources in a way that is sustainable (i.e. it won't be immediately copied by someone else) it is likely that this advantage will be from subtle or tacit competences that are not easily identified (by either the competitor or company).

Capture the Competences in Decision Explorer®   As they are being surfaced capture the competences in a single view of Decision Explorer®. **Use a round robin approach** during the early stages to ensure all participants get the chance to contribute and so feel engaged. **Check you have captured the material correctly**, as with all forums important insights can arise from subtle phrasing. Try to **avoid single words** as this helps reveal the subtle details of distinctiveness. Therefore rather than 'HR' suggest contributions like 'ability to ensure that candidates fit the organisational requirements'.

Task 2: Cluster Emergent Competences and Check for Missing Competences

Arrange Competences into Clusters   As a means of helping participants manage the complexity, **try to position contributions into rough 'content-oriented' clusters** as much as possible. This management of the material often stimulates participants to add more. **Don't get too concerned about getting the clusters right** – participants will have time to review this material and confirm (or not) the character of a cluster (see figure 8.1).

Surface Further Competences   **Encourage participants to 'piggy back'** off one another's contributions. By carrying out a **review of the competence picture and clusters** participants can see what has already been captured and what might be missing. Encourage further conversation capturing both the new material and the changes to existing contributions. It is crucial **to surface at least 25 candidate distinctive competences** – distinctiveness will mostly arise from unique bundles, portfolios and patterns, and so more material is more likely to reveal distinctive bundles.

Review Cluster Content   **Look at the Decision Explorer® view and emergent clusters and consider their contents**. For example, see how many of the statements are about technology (which is relatively easy to imitate quickly and therefore will not be distinctive for long), how many are about products (which also have a short shelf life), whether the competency is linked to a specific individual (which might make the competence vulnerable). Where the material relates to either collective expertise or culture there is potential for sustainability as they are far harder to replicate. Get the participants to consider whether they have addressed these different aspects.

Deliverable: a clustered set of draft competences
Timing from forum start: 15 minutes minimum, expected 25 minutes

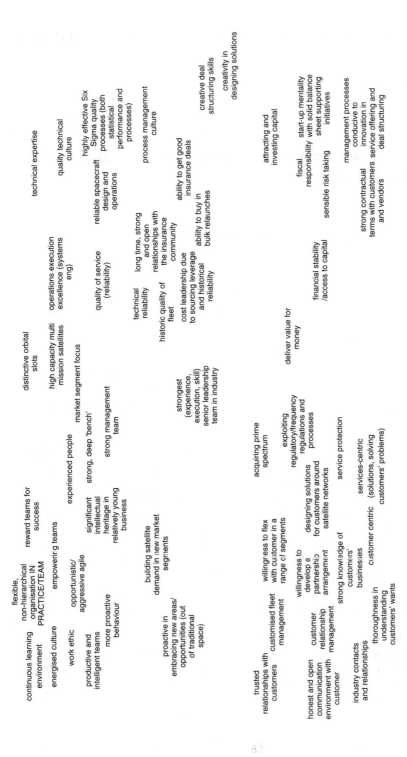

Figure 8.1 A First Pass at Surfacing Distinctive Competences

Note: as this is an early stage of the forum, the wording of some of the statements doesn't currently reflect a competence (this will be dealt with later). Also note that there are a number of emerging clusters.

Exploring Distinctive Competence Outcomes or Distinctive Competences or Distinctive Assets?

It is extremely difficult to identify distinctive competences, but easy to identify distinctive competence outcomes and distinctive assets.

Script for: Exploring distinctive competence outcomes or distinctive competences or distinctive assets

Tasks:

1 Categorise surfaced competency material: 25–35 minutes
2 Rate distinctiveness: 15–25 minutes

Deliverable: categorised and refined picture of competences
Script timing: minimum 40 minutes, expected 60 minutes

Task 1: Categorise Surfaced Competency Material

Once the material has been captured, it can be very helpful to **start to categorise it**. This will not only help in sharpening participants' understanding of the different contributions but will also (1) aid in the management of the competences and (2) stimulate further contributions.

Distinguish Between Distinctive Competences, Distinctive Competence Outcomes and Distinctive Assets
Typically when undertaking a forum of this nature, participants initially generate material that either tends to be of a 'distinctive competence outcome' (DCO) nature or surface 'distinctive assets' (DA) (as noted in figure 8.2). For example, for a police force, a distinctive asset might be that they are the largest police force in the nation. The asset is the staff, the size of the workforce providing distinctiveness. Alternatively, for a housing association, the asset might be their ownership of the largest housing stock in the city – which is again both an asset and distinctive. Assets therefore tend, in the most part, to be 'tangible' – number of people, size of stock (or cash), number of patents/IPR agreements, location of headquarters, etc. – they are what the organisation is made up of! A distinctive asset will most often have arisen over time and so be a part of the history of the organisation. The asset has often occurred without any deliberate intent.

Distinctive competence outcomes conversely tend to be very broad in nature and close to what customers value, or what drives cost management. For example, a distinctive competence outcome might be to 'have an excellent reputation' or 'provide service quality second to none'. These are, of course, also assets, but they are broad, most easily noticed by outsiders, and are the outcomes of competences. However, because they are so broad and therefore relatively intangible they are hard to manage strategically and so deliver.

Provide the Group with Definitions of Each Category
The following explanations can be helpful (though recognise that they are not precise).

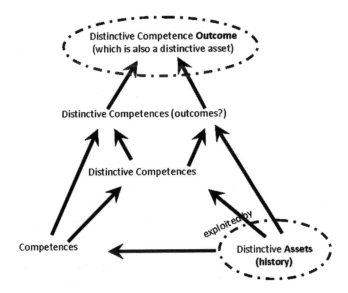

Figure 8.2   An Illustration of the Competency Hierarchy

Distinctive competences (and competences):

- Are **amenable to being strategically managed** in a relatively unambiguous way.
- Concern what the organisation does, that is its ability to do something. Thus **use the phrase 'ability to'** at the beginning of the statement to ensure that statements are competences.
- Aim to **deliver or support outcomes** (probably by driving a sequence of other statements (competences and outcomes) to the delivery of a DCO).
- Possibly are not seen by an outsider (customer) to the organisation. For example, 'ability to treat all staff with respect'.

Distinctive competence outcomes (and competency outcomes):

- More directly **support a goal** (for example, 'significantly low levels of waste'), or something the customer values ('consistent quality') – an outcome the customer appreciates directly.
- **Could become a goal** of the organisation if the business moved to a position of exploitation.
- Competence outcomes are potentially more externally focused.

Distinctive assets (and assets):

- Typically are an obvious resource (cash, staff), often part of the organisation's history (that is it may have arisen by serendipity) that can be exploited by competences (for example, 'extensive, and deep knowledge of customers').
- Look like they could/do deliver distinctive competences and competences.

In addition to these a further category that will arise is a *threshold competence*, which is:

- Not important for delivering distinctiveness, differentiation and so competitive advantage but essential to deliver basic aspects that the customer expects.

To help the categorisation process, **use different styles** to illustrate the different categories (see figure 8.3). For example, assets might be green whereas distinctive assets might be green but also bold and italic to highlight their uniqueness. Have the **styles already set up in advance** so there is no delay for participants.

See Appendix: Using Causal Mapping Software: Decision Explorer®, 2.4 Creating and Using Styles

Surface Further Competences Use this process to **tease out further nuances** in the language and **increase the picture** of competences. For example, it is possible that in the process of determining whether a contribution is an asset or competence the conversation might reveal that the contribution actually has two elements – one relating to the asset and the other to the competence it supports (see box 8.4). Alternatively in the process of explaining why a contribution is an outcome, the explanation might include a number of important and distinctive competences which can subsequently be captured. Continually **remind participants of the different categories** and how to interpret them. A good way of doing this is to have the categories written up on a flip-chart for easy reference. Make sure you are **alert to contributions containing more than one category**, for example, both asset and competence or competence and outcome. Remind participants that at this stage the **forum is not focusing on how distinctive** the contribution is and therefore to focus on surfacing rather than evaluating.

Box 8.4   Understanding Competences from Assets

One of the statements generated noted: *financial stability allowing the company to ensure that shareholders bought into their strategies.* On further reflection, however, the group realised that they had an asset: *financial stability and asset base of the company,* and a competence: *ability to get shareholders to buy into strategies.*

Why Categorise? Categorising is not undertaken for its own sake, but for encouraging three important outcomes for the group:

1 The process forces each participant to read all of the material as each item is categorised.
2 The process begins the development and identification of patterns by moving material to reflect a linked hierarchy – so moving distinctive competence outcomes to the top of the map, distinctive competences to the middle, and distinctive assets to the bottom.
3 The process encourages the development of more material and further work on getting the wording tighter (for example adding 'ability to' to competences and wording claims so that the claim is more distinctive without making it untrue!).

Task 2: Rate Distinctiveness

Typically there will be a lot of discussion when categorising the generated material into assets, competences and outcomes. This is particularly so when considering whether the statement is

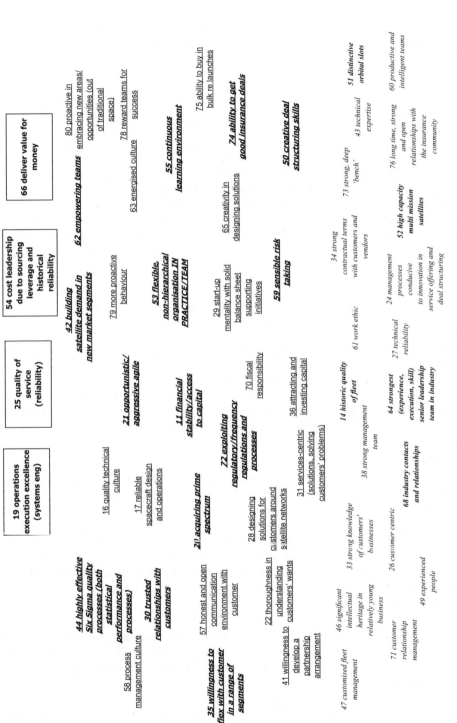

Figure 8.3 Showing Categorised Competency Picture. Those statements in boxes represent distinctive competency outcomes, those in italics and Times Roman font are *assets* with **distinctive assets** in larger font and bold. <u>Competences</u> are in Tahoma font and underlined, <u>**distinctive competences**</u> are bold and underlined

distinctive or not (distinctive asset or distinctive competence). Therefore it can be both interesting and informative to **get participants to rate relative distinctiveness** particularly in relation to the competences and competence outcomes.

Use a Rating Scale

A good starting point for this task is to **issue a printed copy of the competitive advantage material** to each participant for easy viewing. If time is available, having a printed sheet with each of the competence/competency outcomes down the left and a scale of 1 to 10 alongside each entry, can provide participants with a quick and easy means for recording their views. Otherwise ask participants to make notes directly onto the picture.

Ask each participant to note which of the competences/outcomes is the most distinctive and rate that at 10. Next **identify which competence/outcome is the least distinctive** and rate that at 1. This provides participants with a set of anchor points and a scale. Once these are chosen **ask the participants to rate the remainder of competences and competence outcomes in accordance with those that have been identified as the most and least distinctive**. Where there are two competence/outcomes that are similarly rated, **reassure participants that two can be given the same rating**.

Collate the Results

Depending on the group and their openness with each other, use one of the following two processes to collate the results.

- **Use a round robin to elicit the different results** and capture this information directly in the Decision Explorer® view. Ask each participant, in turn, to state the most distinctive competence, and then in the next round their next highest, and so on.
- As an alternative method for collating rating scores, **ask participants to write their scores on their picture** and collect the printouts once this has been completed. This will allow the responses to be anonymous and may ensure a more honest picture.

Consider Distinctiveness as a Relative Concept

As a means of helping participants when thinking about distinctive competences ask them to **consider distinctiveness with respect to the competition, rather than in terms of importance**. Distinctiveness is a relative notion and so the goals of the organisation will help rate distinctiveness. The goals will provide a benchmark against which to assess the competence. For example if the goal is to be number one in Scotland then it is more likely that the organisation will be able to find competences that are distinctive within this geographical area than if the goal is to be number one in the world. Also **help participants recognise that distinctiveness will be a relative concept** – in relation to other competences and in relation to the competences of the competition.

Review the Results

Once all the results are in, **compute rough average scores** (to determine distinctiveness) and **indicate rough degrees of consensus** (and the extent of the range of views). Review these results and in particular **discuss significant disagreements in terms of the scores allocated** as this may reveal differences in interpretation (see box 8.5). This activity therefore can potentially reveal new material as well as adding some humour and fun into the forum. It might be useful to have a coffee/tea/lunch break after the rating exercise to **provide some time to carry out the degrees of consensus and final rating scores**. When reviewing the significant disagreements **make sure that none of the participants feels exposed by the process**.

Box 8.5   Using Relative Distinctiveness Ratings to Gain Greater Clarity about Claims

One of the DCOs surfaced during the initial capture was 'high reliability'. However, the results of the rating exercise had revealed that there were different interpretations of (a) what was reliable and (b) how it might be achieved. The process of both refining the language (through elaboration) and exploring the competences supporting (laddering down) the outcome helped elaborate the emerging picture.

Inform participants that this activity aims not only to gain an idea of relative distinctiveness but also to **see where significant differences in opinion might lie and why**. The discussions emanating from reviewing competences with little consensus often give rise to participants getting a better understanding of the competence itself and its practice in parts of the organisation. The process often helps break down some of the silo thinking.

Deliverable: Categorised and refined picture of competences
Timing from forum start: 55 minutes minimum, expected 85 minutes

---

Distinctiveness Comes from Patterns

Discovering and exploring distinctiveness is very difficult. Rarely are individual competences distinctive.

Script for: Distinctiveness comes from patterns

Tasks:

1   'Drill down' from highly rated distinctive competences/outcomes: 20–30 minutes
2   Explore further links between competences, assets and outcomes and review the unfolding picture: 5–10 minutes
3   Identify distinctive competence bundles: 15–20 minutes

Deliverable: representation of categorised and refined competences
Script timing: minimum 40 minutes, expected 60 minutes

Task 1: Drill Down from Highly Rated Distinctive Competences and Distinctive Competence Outcomes

Identify the Most Distinctive DCO   Before participants can drill down (that is explore the underlying supporting competences) from the highly distinctive competence outcomes they should first identify the most distinctive DCO. The DCOs typically are identified from the earlier script on rating distinctiveness but where there hasn't been time to do this task, ask the group to use their judgement about which outcome is the most distinctive (see box 8.6).

Box 8.6 Drilling Down from DCOs

If we take Apple as an organisation, a possible DCO might be to *have an excellent reputation for producing personal electronic devices everyone wants*. To support this DCO, competences such as *ability to design user interfaces that are intuitive to use* and *ability to design devices that have not been considered before* can be linked into the DCO.

Search for Supporting Competences and Assets   **Ask participants 'which of the surfaced distinctive competences or assets might support the selected distinctive competence or competence outcome'?** This is easiest done by asking for the numerical tag, e.g. 45, rather than the text of the statement. **Move these suggested assets/competences so that they are beneath the DCO being considered.** Encourage participants to be as inclusive as possible and not to get too perturbed if an asset or competence appears to support more than one of the highly rated DCOs. This is because it helps identify those competences or assets that support a lot of competence outcomes and which are therefore more potent. **Keep laddering down to assets.** An alternative prompt is to ask **participants which of the surfaced competences are supported by the most distinctive asset.** For example, Strathclyde Police's distinctive asset of *being the largest police force in Scotland* helped support their *ability to carry out excellent forensic work*, one of their distinctive competences. However, this asset also supported a number of other important and distinctive competences, so be **alert for multiple consequences**.

Build a Causal Map Hierarchy   Try **to position the identified competences/assets in a hierarchical format so that the most subordinate statement is at the bottom of the tear drop with the focal distinctive competence outcome at the top**.

As participants discuss and agree on the assets, competences and distinctive competences that support the selected distinctive competence outcome, **note the supporting links with an arrow**. Arrows reflect support – causality – and thus help convert the mass of contributions into an emerging network by building a causal map hierarchy. Thus as implied above (and reflected in figure 8.4), assets are likely to be at the bottom of the hierarchy and competence outcomes at the top.

Identify New Material   While carrying out this task, encourage participants to **identify new material** and not feel constrained to just working with the material they have created from earlier tasks. This part of the forum can provide valuable learning to participants as they take a wider view of the organisation's resources. **Be alert to this material and capture it on the Decision Explorer® view along with allocating the appropriate category**. New material will emerge as participants realise that the arguments they use to create links suggest further competences and assets they hitherto have not considered explicitly – the act of structuring making divergence more apparent.

This part of the forum will help build up the hierarchy – an example is illustrated in box 8.7 and figures 8.4 and 8.5.

Box 8.7   Drilling Down to Manageable Competences

A small company in the business of laundering boiler suits (overalls used in factories etc.) was considering their strategy and in particular seeking to gain competitive advantage. One of the statements that they had generated in the forum was *ability to provide an excellent service*. However, further reflection had revealed that this was in fact a DCO rather than a DC. In the process of drilling down, one of the managers noted that one explanation was the *ability of our van drivers to be flexible and helpful* as this helped achieve the DCO. The facilitator asked the participant to say more about this. His explanation was that the van drivers knew that each day they had to visit a large number of companies both to drop off but also to pick up laundry. However, while many of these drivers had a designated route, frequently, in order to enable a company to finish a particular job, they would delay their arrival at the factory and instead pick up laundry from another company. Thus there was the *ability to tailor pick up times to suit the customer!* Another manager provided a similar example. Soon the map showed the DCO at the apex supported by a distinctive competence subsequently supported by further competences.

See figure 8.4 for a pictorial format.

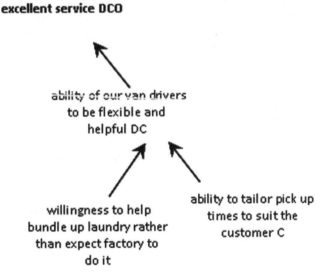

Figure 8.4   Illustrating the Link Between Competences, Distinctive Competences and Distinctive Competence Outcomes

Continue to Surface Support Relationships

Encourage participants to move up and down the hierarchy looking for support relationships. For example, when exploring which competences support a particular outcome, it might be that the group not only identifies a competence but, as with the example above, also reveals support for this competence. Thus a chain of argumentation develops. This might be further augmented by a participant noting that an asset links to this material – thus extending the chain and potentially prompting another participant to note that the asset additionally supports competences elsewhere on the overall map. Repeat this exercise until most if not all of the competences are linked.

Look for Links Between the Competences

To further refine the emerging structure, **look for links between the competences** on the map to see whether any of the competences support one another. This process helps build up the map illustrating how the DCO can be managed and protected (through protecting the competences supporting it).

Continue also to use the categories to help manage the growing body of material as well as ensure a high degree of understanding of each statement.

Task 2: Extend the Linking Process and Review the Unfolding Picture

Ensure All Links Have Been Captured

To widen the development of the unfolding network and thus ensure that all of the links between assets, competences and outcomes have been captured, ask participants to **explore whether there are any further links between material supporting the different distinctive competence outcomes**, but beware of links for their own sake where 'everything links to everything else' through the use of weak or summary links.

When discussing how competences can support outcomes, participants may note that while a competence isn't currently supporting either another competence or an outcome, it could be designed so as to provide this support thus gaining further leverage. **Capture these new potential links**. To help clarify that they are prospective rather than current, **use dotted arrow/links to differentiate them**. When checking links it is helpful to **provide participants with copies of the competence picture** so that they can examine the material and consider further links.

See Appendix: Using Causal Mapping Software: Decision Explorer®, 1.5 Linking Statements and 2.4 Creating and Using Styles

Check to **ensure that the assets, particularly those that are distinctive, are being exploited** as widely as possible.

Consider Other Viewpoints

Finally, **get the group to test whether they are taking a rose-tinted view of the material**. Consider the material from the viewpoint of customers, senior or junior management, other parts of the organisation. Are the competences worded as competences?

Appreciating systemicity!

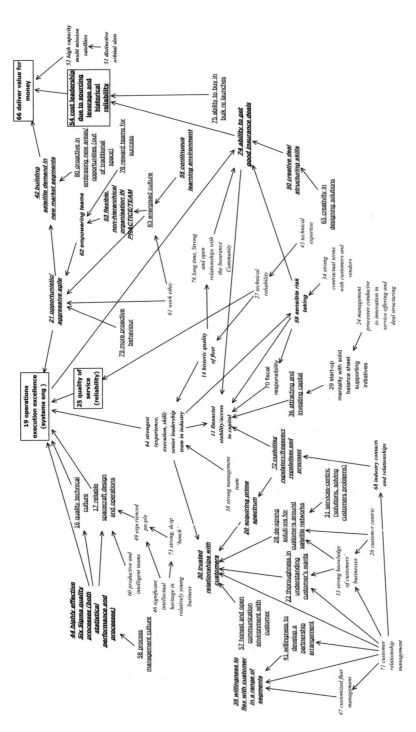

Figure 8.5 Distinctive Competence Network. Those statements in boxes represent distinctive competency outcomes, those in italics and Times Roman font are *assets* with **distinctive assets** in larger font and bold. Competences are in Tahoma font and underlined, <u>**distinctive competences**</u> are bold and underlined

Task 3: Identify Distinctive Competence Patterns/Bundles

Why Are Patterns Important?   Identifying individual distinctive competences and distinctive competence outcomes is important but rarely leads to high levels of distinctiveness. Another, and more promising, way of revealing distinctiveness is to **explore the network/map to determine whether there are any combinations of the contributions that are distinctive**. For example, it might be the case that each of the competences identified by the group is held – to a greater or lesser degree – by another organisation. However, none of the other organisations have the total portfolio of competences, nor do they have them working in concert (or in that particular structure). Thus the distinctiveness comes from both the competences *and* how they fit together (see box 8.8 for an example).

Box 8.8   Differentiation Through Bundles

During the forum, participants from a high quality stereo equipment company were aware that many of their company's competences were held by others, for example, one was *ability to design high quality equipment*, another was *willingness to install equipment* and a third was *ability to understand customer's needs*. However, what they believed was different is that no other single company had all these competences (the others just had two or three) and that they were actively ensuring that the competences supported one another – the pattern was unique.

Consider Distinctive Bundles   Competences and competence outcomes can combine to form two types of patterns. The first pattern is a portfolio or 'bundle' – that is where a group of competences/competence outcomes work together to reinforce the effect of one another (the 2+2=5 effect), create a critical mass or significant focus of energy, and therefore through the combination, be distinctive. It is possible that these patterns are particularly important as *the pattern* is the distinctive competence – nobody else could achieve the pattern even if they could acquire the competences and competence outcomes. Ask the group to **consider whether these distinctive bundles are capable of additional exploitation or could be the basis for new business** (see chapter 7).

Consider Feedback Loops   The second type of pattern relates to feedback loops – which are self-sustaining patterns of behaviour. These loops can have incredibly important implications for the organisation as they can sustain the organisation over the duration of the intended strategy where exploited and their self-sustaining and potentially distinctive nature will render them very difficult to replicate.

There are a number of different types of self-sustaining feedback loops:

- A feedback *loop of competences* where distinctiveness comes from the sustainable nature of the loop – nobody else can make them work together in this way.
- Similarly, a feedback *loop with at least one highly distinctive competence* in it – as this reinforces the power of the loop. Thus, the distinctive competence is reinforced by the loop as a pattern of competences.
- Loops *with the ability to resource a distinctive competence* makes the distinctive competence more powerful.
- Feedback *loops of distinctive competences* are particularly important because they reveal a self-sustaining nature. This is rare.

Explore the Network to See if there are Any Feedback Loops   This can be either identified through looking at the network and visually identifying the loop or using the analyses in Decision Explorer®. If the map is quite busy, it might be easier to use the analytical function to ensure all loops are detected.

> See Appendix: Using Causal Mapping Software: Decision Explorer®, 3.2 Identifying Feedback Loops

Check the Validity of Feedback Loops   Where feedback loops are identified **check their validity** – that is, are all of the links correct? A particular example of a potential invalid loop is where the feedback loop includes a distinctive asset that relates to history. All statements in a feedback loop must be variables because they must change over time. History cannot be a variable and so a distinctive asset of this sort must be reconceived, if possible, so that it is written into the future of the organisation and can change over time (see box 8.9 and figure 8.6).

Box 8.9   Identifying a Feedback Loop

An engineering organisation was considering its competitive advantage. The group had already completed the surfacing and categorisation stages and had linked up the model. They were now exploring the overall network – particularly a feedback loop that had been identified earlier relating to 'win the business'. In examining the loop in detail they realised that in fact there were two loops (potentially making a third that encompassed both). Each of the loops had at least two DCOs (supported by competences and in two cases by distinctive competences). They were aware that the loops were both positive and virtuous and that if protected would allow sustainable growth.

It is interesting to note the position of the asset in the loop (statement 24 in figure 8.6) as assets are typically at the bottom of the hierarchy. However, the financial stability gained from winning the business becomes over time an asset which can support the renewal of other competences and yield outcomes.

Establish the Nature of the Feedback of Genuine Loops   When genuine loops appear it is useful to **establish the nature of the feedback**. When the loop contains an odd number of negative links (assuming the negative links are accurate!), the loop is depicting self-control. That is, any change in the state of the issues in the loop will result in stabilising dynamics. Alternatively, an even number of negative (or all positive) links suggests regenerative or degenerative dynamics where changes result in exponential growth (virtuous cycle) or decline (vicious cycle). It is worth ensuring that there is time to **direct the attention of the group to exploitation of virtuous cycles or removal of vicious cycles (these rarely appear in a competitive advantage forum)**. It is important to note that all statements in a feedback loop must be capable of being viewed as variables – try putting increase/decrease in front of the wording.

Where the feedback loops are positive and virtuous, **encourage the group to consider how they might be protected and grown**.

Review the Final Network Map with the Group   **Check all of the links are valid, ensure all distinctive patterns have been identified, and confirm the categorisation**. This provides the group with a powerful image depicting the resources which can be used to achieve the organisation's intended strategic direction.

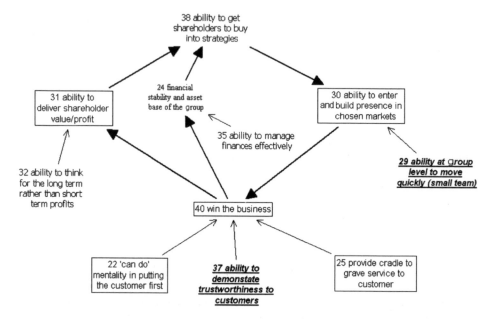

Figure 8.6 Illustrating a Feedback Loop

Note: Those statements that are underlined represent those that the participants considered distinctive. Those statements with boxes are distinctive competence outcomes, those in small Times New Roman are assets, those with italic are distinctive competences and the rest are competences.

Deliverable: representation of categorised and refined competences
Timing from forum start: 95 minutes minimum, expected 145 minutes

Creating the Strategy Deliverable

Script for: Writing up the statement of strategic intent

Tasks:

1   Create a first draft of the statement of strategic intent: 10–20 minutes
2   Review and refine the SSI with the group: 10 to 30 minutes

Deliverable: an agreed statement of strategic intent
Script timing: minimum 20 minutes, expected 50 minutes

Task 1: Write the Statement of Strategic Intent

It is important that the statement of strategic intent is produced either at the end of the forum or soon after (preferably the same day) and distributed to all participants. Writing it at the end of the forum acts as a take-away that gives a sense of closure to the forum.

Focus on the Most Distinctive Competence Outcomes

To start the process of writing the statement, **identify the most distinctive competence outcomes**, particularly if they stand out from the crowd as having a high degree of consensus among participants. **Take one of these and note the competences linking in to it**. Next formulate the text so that the distinctive competence outcomes appears after some introductory text, e.g. 'we intend to achieve competitive advantage through leveraging x'. This sets out a punchy beginning. Follow this with some discussion of the competences, particularly distinctive competences supporting this outcome. For example, 'this outcome is supported by leveraging our competences of xx and yy' (noting the competences that link into/support the outcome). Try to **use the minimum of connecting phrases**, so as to focus on the map's content.

Ladder Down to Cover All Distinctive Competence Outcomes

Depending on the hierarchical position of the distinctive competence outcomes, either take the next most distinctive (if they are similarly positioned in the map) and repeat the process. Alternatively, when laddering down through the map, reinforce the significance of any patterns that might have emerged. For example, 'by ensuring that these xx competences support one another … we will be able to achieve the distinctive outcome' which is seen as critical to our strategic success. Similarly it is worth commenting specifically when dealing with feedback loops reflecting their importance to the overall strategic direction.

Stay Faithful to the Competence Map

As much as is possible, try to **keep the language of the competence statements** and ensure that the linking text **reflects the causality** thus staying truthful to the overall structure and meaning of the map.

Consider Style and Presentation

To facilitate the process, **copy and paste bundles of statements from Decision Explorer® in a word processor**. They will appear in numerical order, rather than any chosen order, but can be re-sorted quickly. **Use bold and italic formatting for emphasis**. This helps with navigation around the text and highlights the key points.

See Appendix: Using Causal Mapping Software: Decision Explorer®, 4.2 **Copy and Paste Map Material into a Word Processing Document, or PowerPoint**

Try to **keep the text on one page** as this ensures that the statement is both concise and easily read.

Box 7.1 in chapter 7 shows the result of converting the competence map into a statement encompassing sentences and paragraphs.

Task 2: Validation with the Manager-client and Group

Validate the SSI

It is crucially important to **ensure both the manager-client and group sign off the SSI document**. Although, if written well, it will be a direct translation of an agreed competences map, the translation into sentences and paragraphs may indicate a different emphasis and meaning to participants.

Ensure the Language and Emotion Reflect the Competences Map Where possible meet with the group (perhaps after a break in the forum) and review the draft document. **Check with the group that the language is easily understood by all those in the department or organisation** and not just to the group. In addition make sure that the statement is not just a good reflection of what has been agreed in a simple easy to understand text format but also that it **gets at the emotion – the hearts and minds – of the intended audience**.

Box 8.10 Illustrating Ladders of Competences to Unfold Actionable Claims

An organisation that was in the business of providing satellite coverage for companies such as BskyB and other broadcasters was exploring its competitive advantage. Having brought together management team members from its three different operating sites they began to explore their resources. As seen in the small excerpt of their map below (figure 8.7), they identified a number of distinctive assets: for example, strong financial position, HQ in a neutral country and also assets, namely: the range of experience of all major competitors, diverse styles and nationalities, unique backgrounds and experience that can be tapped or called upon, stable shareholder structure and highly effective six sigma quality processes (both statistical performance and processes). One of the assets that was seen as particularly distinctive was having their HQ in a neutral country (which enabled the company to avoid being seen as a national threat by the countries around it) as this ensured that the organisation could work with and influence the administrations of all of the other countries (a competence that they believed was very distinctive) and do so in a way that was coordinated. This ability enabled them to be able to deliver high levels of performance and thus deliver reliability – illustrating the chain of argument from asset to competence outcome. In looking to understand reliability better (as this was seen by all to be difficult to manage) the group explored in more detail how they could deliver highest levels of performance and were pleased not only to identify other competences but also to detect a feedback loop that reinforced the performance levels.

Deliverable: an agreed statement of strategic intent
Timing from forum start: 115 minutes minimum, expected 195 minutes

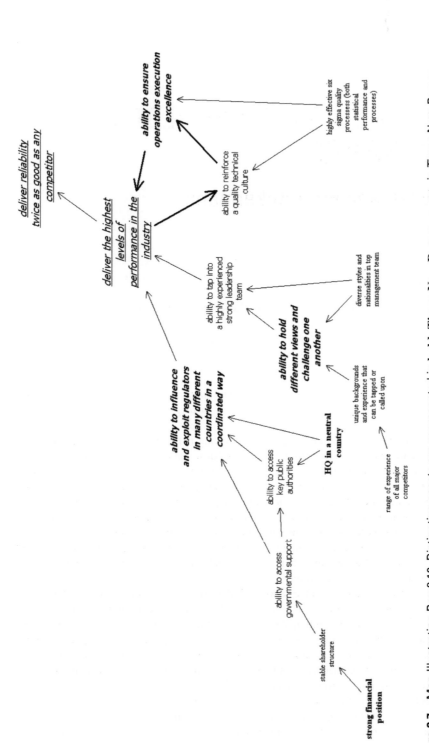

Figure 8.7 Map Illustrating Box 8.10. Distinctive assets are represented in **bold**, Times New Roman, assets in Times New Roman, competences in Tahoma with ***distinctive competences*** in Tahoma, bold, italic. ***Distinctive competence outcomes*** are bold, italic, with underlining. The feedback loop is represented with bold arrows

9

STRATEGY AS STAKEHOLDER MANAGEMENT

Colin Eden and Fran Ackermann

Actions of stakeholders, and the actions of others that unintentionally impact the organisation's environment, can destroy expected outcomes from a strategy.

One of the most important tasks during strategy making is the management of the interface between the many, and often competing, demands of different organisations, groups and people. In some instances an external organisation may develop an initiative that seeks to support or sabotage the strategic goals of your organisation, and in other instances the energy for support or sabotage will come from groups or individual people. In each case they are prepared to act because they have an interest, a stake, in the future direction your organisation wishes to take – they are 'stakeholders'. On some occasions these organisations, groups or individuals sabotage or support the intended strategies without any deliberate intention to do so. Instead they are protecting and developing their own interests and take action that unintentionally impacts the future of your organisation.

The actions of stakeholders, and the actions of others that unintentionally impact the organisation's environment, can destroy or reduce the efficacy of the expected outcomes from a strategy. Thus, there is a need to anticipate and *manage* these actions to ensure our own organisation's strategies can be realised. In some instances anticipating their actions leads to careful and strategic management of stakeholders, and in other instances it leads to adapting existing strategies so that the stakeholders are less likely to promote actions that sabotage the strategies (or more likely to promote actions for support).

This chapter takes the view that stakeholders should be considered in *relation to their impact on the goals of the organisation* as understood by the members of the top or middle management teams. The stakeholder management forum provides the means for a team to develop strategies for effectively managing their stakeholders and so realise their strategic goals.

Stakeholders have, over the past decade, become very topical – both in the academic and popular press.[1] However, there has been little attention paid to the processes for designing strategies to manage them. Rather, in the academic world, attention has been on developing stakeholder theory as a theory of the firm[2] – seeking to explain how a firm develops over time – and in the practitioner world attention has been placed on the perceived importance of *involving* stakeholders in strategy development – particularly in the not-for-profit sectors.

Each organisation has a unique set of stakeholders and how they can be managed will therefore differ.

Whatever focus is taken, it is taken for granted that it is possible and easy to identify who the stakeholders are. And yet, most organisations are faced with a plethora of stakeholders, each with different interests and a different potential to influence the future of the organisation. Moreover, the task of identifying stakeholders has been supposedly simplified by the identification of categories of stakeholder (as a means of both prompting and prioritising potential stakeholders).[3] However, this categorisation assumes that the same categories are equally applicable across all organisations and by implication treats them all as equally important. Additionally, the use of categories tends to result in identifying stakeholders at a very generic, broad level – implying that this is an appropriate level of disaggregation for permitting the development of effective stakeholder management strategies. But, each organisation has a unique set of stakeholders and how they can be managed will therefore differ.[4] This is, in a large part, due to the uniqueness of an organisation's goals and strategies as well as its unique internal and external context and history.

In this chapter we will suggest that it is crucial to identify the *specific stakeholders* for any particular organisation (or part thereof), as opposed to relying on generic lists of stakeholders. Uniqueness is thus seen to be related to the need to be clear about the *significance of stakeholders* for the future of the organisation and thus in relation to the strategy.[5] A management team needs to decide which of the many potential stakeholders identified are those they *must* consider and manage for the strategy to succeed. Given the numerous demands on managers and strategy making it is important to recognise the limited time team members have available. This time pressure implies focusing the energy of the managers and so concentrating on a manageable number of *key* stakeholders.

Furthermore, not all stakeholders are of equal importance and so it is essential to focus energy on the management of those that are most important – the key stakeholders. Gaining a deeper understanding of the stakeholder's power for, as well as interest in, influencing the direction of the organisation can be used as two significant dimensions of analysis for assisting this prioritisation process. From this examination of power and interest it is possible to determine when it is appropriate to develop or alter the bases of an individual stakeholder's significance.

WHO ARE THE STAKEHOLDERS?[6]

Stakeholders are those who have a stake in the future success or failure of the organisation – those who can deliberately 'make', 'break' or 'shake' the success of any strategic action. However, in developing successful strategy we must also consider those who, without deliberate or designed actions to support or sabotage, can also affect significantly the future of the organisation – these also need to be managed. Thus, we are interested in those who have the *power to affect what happens* – they can take actions that will affect the success of our strategic actions. We are also interested in those who have a *stake in the situation* – they will approve of some possible outcomes more than others.

In some of the earliest work on stakeholders an internal memorandum at the Stanford Research Institute conceptualised stakeholders as 'those groups without whose support the organisation would cease to exist'. However, other researchers suggest including as stakeholders those groups or individuals who are affected by the organisation as well as those who can affect it. Thus, *who* are stakeholders is related to the multifarious nature of the *demands* they can make of the organisation, regardless of whether they have the power to change things. The latter view provides the impetus to consider dimensions such as power, interest and urgency as possible key criteria when considering the relative priority (and subsequent management) of stakeholders.

> *It is the heterogeneity of organisational strategies and the organisation's environment that significantly affects who the stakeholders are.*

When considering who the stakeholders are, there are a number of frameworks that can act as useful ways of thinking about who might and might not be of importance. A number of these frameworks take a narrow view of who are stakeholders – for example, a market orientation (as seen by Michael Porter's five forces framework)[7] – or assume that an economic (input-output) view is sufficient. In both these instances the number of stakeholders is relatively bounded and appears, at least from the frameworks, to generate highly generic lists. There are other researchers who see stakeholders as being more heterogeneous, and that it is the heterogeneity of organisational strategies and the organisation's environment that significantly affects who the stakeholders are. Their view is that a generic level of analysis tends to lead to generic strategies that could be applied regardless of industry or sector or purpose. This slide into generic strategies is an important concern when strategies are expected to be organisation specific, business goals are specific, distinctive competences are specific and the context is specific. Consequently paying attention to, and managing, a *specific set of stakeholders* is most likely to have a powerful effect on the feasibility of the strategy and thus the long term viability of organisations.

Thinking about stakeholders from the perspective of interest and power prompts a two dimensional framework of analysis where power and interest are independent and so orthogonal – see figure 9.1. The framework, seen as a grid, reveals who is observing the organisation (has an interest), and who has the power to affect the success of the strategy.[8] If we imagine this grid as having four quadrants then we may describe those who are not stakeholders but who do have power, but no interest, as 'context setters'. These context setters may be a part of generating alternative scenarios in which our strategies must work. Often a power base is confused with interest – having an interest does not necessarily give power and powerful people may, or may not, be interested. It is essential to draw a clear distinction between influencers and stakeholders:[9] Some actors in the enterprise (for example large investors) may be both, but some stakeholders (for example job applicants) have no influence, and some influencers (for example the media) have no stake. There is nothing original about such a grid based on these dimensions; it builds on the work of others.[10] However, while the grid might be common, researchers use it for a range of different purposes. For example, the power–interest grid can be used as a basis for understanding the environment rather than for proactive stakeholder *management*.[11]

> *Often the stakeholders who can most powerfully and deliberately influence the strategic future of the organisation are specific individuals and groups.*

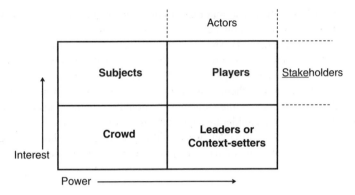

Figure 9.1 The Power–Interest Framework

Closely associated with determining power and interest in the identification of the unique set of stakeholders there will always be a question about the appropriate level of disaggregation of stakeholders.[12] When considering the management of stakeholders it is usually the case that negotiations be directed at someone, or at least a negotiating party, rather than a reified entity. Of course, in some instances, the negotiation will take place with a categorised mass of people (as with categories of consumers), but often the stakeholders who can most powerfully and deliberately influence the strategic future of the organisation are specific individuals and groups. This suggests that it is appropriate to encourage a management team to disaggregate to the level which they believe they could attempt to manage. 'What is important is developing an understanding of the real, *concrete* stakeholders who are specific to the firm'.[13] Disaggregation to an appropriate level is crucial – namely at what level can the organisation influence or manage the stakeholder. For example, it is rarely possible to manage strategically a government but it might be possible to manage the minister of a specific government department. Stakeholders and context-setters – the actors – are therefore individual people, or groups (e.g. committees) or organisations such as firms, governments departments or unions. Each actor will tend to have *his/her/its own idiosyncratic definition of the situation.* Identifying stakeholders at an appropriate level of disaggregation means that there is no common set of stakeholder categories. Working at an appropriately disaggregated level of stakeholder determines *who* the organisation's stakeholders are. It is only when addressing stakeholders at the appropriate level of detail that the management of the stakeholders becomes realistic.

The Strategic Context of Stakeholder Management: Seeing Patterns in the Power–Interest Grid

The grid (figure 9.1) will reveal the dominant categories. Where the grid is dominated by subjects – those with interest in the future of your organisation but little power to influence it – then the organisation is able to make a free strategic *choice* about whether to take any notice of their interests. For many not-for-profit, and public sector, organisations the choice will lead to a reaffirmation of organisational goals that express an aspiration to deliver outcomes that reflect the interests of particular groups of subjects – for example, goals relating to health will be observed by consumers and ministers. In some cases a goal may imply a strategy to increase the power of some of the subjects so that they become actors (players or context-setters). For example, in chapter 5 on organisational purpose, we show a goals system for an organisation aiming to relieve poverty (figure 5.4). Therefore those in poverty are presumed to have an interest in the organisation – they are taken to be stakeholders, stakeholders who see themselves as having little power to influence the organisation. However, the organisation has the aim to give them more power and encourage them to have a more powerful interest not only in the relief of poverty but also an influence on the strategies the organisation develops to relieve poverty. With respect to the grid the stakeholder management objective will be to move them from being subjects to becoming players. Moreover, we would expect to see as players specific policy-makers who are both interested in and have the power to influence the delivery of the goals of the organisation.

The organisation is at the risk of being subjected to the unintended consequences of actions taken by context-setters.

Where the grid is dominated by context-setters, different strategies are demanded. In this situation we see a number of stakeholders possibly having relatively little deliberate or designed impact on the strategic future of the organisation, but instead being able to influence their external world. This non-controllable behaviour of powerful players becomes the dominant interest for strategy making. In effect we need to become focused on understanding possible alternative scenarios that depend upon the decisions made by the context-setters; otherwise the organisation is at the risk of being subjected to the unintended consequences of actions taken by context-setters with respect to other organisations. When very powerful context-setters are revealed on the grid then their possible behaviours must become a part of any scenario planning that is undertaken as a part of strategy making[14] and seek to manage them through lobbying or indirect influences.

Stakeholder management is invariably more complex, problematic and uncertain in the public sector.

If the grid is dominated by actors then stakeholder management becomes possible, rather than being subject to the behaviours of context-setters as part of the environment. However, with a dominance of actors, stakeholder management is likely to be more complex because there are so many who might be of significance and need careful work on how to manage them. Indeed, the level of complexity of the grid overall typically provides some indication of the complexity of stakeholder management. In public sector and not-for-profit organisations over 100 appropriately disaggregated stakeholders and context-setters is usual, whereas for the for-profit sector 25 would be expected. Stakeholder management is invariably more complex, problematic and uncertain in the public sector.

Needless to say, some stakeholders (both subjects and actors) will take consistent positions with respect to the strategic aims of the organisation – they will always be negatively, or always positively, disposed to the organisation and consistently will take actions to sabotage or support the organisation. Others will take a position dependent upon their own goals and their interpretation of the specific strategies the organisation is seeking to implement. Consequently, the grid can be easily extended to provide an overview of the strategic context of support or sabotage – colouring those negatively disposed in red and those positively disposed in green. When the actor quadrant is dominantly red then managing the potential for sabotage becomes a crucial strategy making activity, whereas a dominant green suggests strategies to exploit support. Similarly when the dominant disposition of subjects is negative (red) then there may be more possibility of clusters of subjects forming a coalition in order to increase their likelihood of successful sabotage.

Each of these overviews of the map of stakeholders provides a crude analysis of the strategic context of stakeholders, but it is, at least, indicative of the extent and nature of the stakeholder management task. Most significantly the grid reveals a small set of key stakeholders that must be thought about in detail because they are both the most powerful and most interested – those stakeholders at the top right of the grid. However, the positioning of stakeholders on the grid suggests a static view of their position, and such a view can be dangerous. Stakeholders do not always remain static in their power or interests and the potential range of their position can be mapped onto the grid in a manner that shows their instability[15] – exhibiting a range of interest and power with respect to a range of strategies. The management of stakeholders who hold a fairly consistent power base tends to be easier.

Networks – Stakeholders Interact!

The power base of many stakeholders depends, in part, on their influence over other stakeholders.[16] There is a network of relationships, both informal and formal, that this power base may depend upon. Informal relationships are important and often can be more significant than formal relationships.[17] Formal relationships are usually well understood whereas informal relationships are more subtle and pervasive. Informal links can include those who are travelling companions on the home-to-work daily run, club membership, family ties, alumni relationships and social status ties (consider, for example, the impact of these types of informal relationships on the history of the Roman Empire). Formal relationships rely on traditional power relationships through the positional power in organisational structures, contractual arrangements, accreditation review and committee structures. Thus once the network has been constructed, it becomes possible to identify stakeholders that act as a nexus and so are more powerful than the management team initially anticipates.

> *When stakeholders take a position in response to a particular action, they do so with respect to other actors as well as the organisation.*

This perspective on stakeholders builds naturally from developing the power–interest grid by revealing further insights about power and interest (particularly in relation to potential coalitions). By implication when stakeholders take a position in response to a particular action, they do so with respect to other actors as well as the organisation.[18] Thus, the actions of one stakeholder could generate an unfolding dynamic of responses across a range of other actors (thus, context-setters as well as stakeholder may respond) dependent upon the nature of the influences.[19]

Thus, the relationship between stakeholders on the power–interest grid can be mapped out as a network (or directed graph) where links show either informal or formal influences and the direction of influence. This aspect of stakeholder analysis therefore aims to surface the formal, *and informal*, relationships that are the basis of the network.[20] The network is a form of social network analysis.[21]

Emergent Properties of the Social Network of Stakeholders

Each organisation will have a unique network of informal and formal relationships. Attention to the unique pattern[22] expects to provide insights as to where the organisation should devote strategic effort, effort designed to create and sustain winning coalitions.[23] Perhaps of greater significance is that the network gives a picture of power such that some stakeholders who were thought to be powerless are now seen to have significant power that, as we note above, derives from the central position in the network of influence. The power–interest grid changes as deeper understanding of power emerges.

Where there exists a high density (centrality) of stakeholders communication flows are considerable and stakeholder management options may be constrained by the norms established by the network.[24] Those stakeholders that are influenced by, and can influence, a large number of others become key stakeholders to monitor and where there are clusters of stakeholders there may be possibilities for coalition building.[25]

THE BASES OF INTEREST AND POWER

Perceptions about the bases of power and interest of key stakeholders are rarely well articulated.

The stakeholder grid and social network analysis only represent an initial step in stakeholder analysis and they do not address explicitly *how* to manage stakeholders. As a management team explores the output from, and discussions about, the grid and the social network map, a range of comments typically arise that suggests to participants that the discussion itself – *the strategic conversation* – is as highly valued as the actual outputs. Examples of this type of commentary include: 'I wish we'd noted down the discussion: that was where I found myself seeing new ways [of managing the stakeholders]'; 'I learned most from the argument about where to put them [the stakeholders on the grid] – the output itself was not much help'. In particular, discussions about where to place stakeholders on the power–interest grid yield insights into how to manage stakeholders. It follows that the bases of power *and* interest must be explored for, at least, the most significant stakeholders.

If these apparent side-comments are important, and they reflect important learning about how to manage stakeholders, then it is important to establish the content and *structure of the power and interest dimension* of possible actors. In the context of managing stakeholders through negotiation, a deep probing of stakeholder interests may emphasise their underlying interests[26] as distinct from the issues on the table and the positions taken, so that trade-offs can be evaluated. These explorations may directly imply actions to either change the basis of power and/or interests of an actor. Revealing a deeper appreciation of the manifest forms of power and bases of power is essential for stakeholder *management*.

Perceptions about the bases of power and interest of key stakeholders are rarely well articulated and the multiple ramifications of possible management options frequently have not been explored. Taken-for-granted understandings are different across members of a management team – and the aggregation of their views provides informal research agendas to resolve conflicting views and test those understandings that are critical to the effectiveness of proposed stakeholder management options.

What Are Stakeholders Interested In?

As we have suggested above, the *demands* of stakeholders can be understood with greater clarity through separating interests in the organisational strategies from power to influence the outcome of these strategies. The interests of stakeholders will relate to the 'spectacles' through which a stakeholder views the unfolding strategies (or perceives strategies will unfold). The spectacles are not so much ways of seeing but also ways of not seeing – a stakeholder focuses their attention on the things that matter to them, so they see a narrow view of the organisation and its strategies. As a result, the goals of the stakeholder have a great influence over what they are willing to see and accept as reality. Thus in considering interests we are particularly interested in the 'performance indicators' that are used by a stakeholder to evaluate success or failure of strategies. Inevitably, these will be driven by the goals of the stakeholder – what they see, or measure, depends on what they want to achieve.

What Is the Basis of Power?

Revealing a deeper appreciation of the manifest forms of power and bases of power is essential for stakeholder management.

The power of stakeholders derives from many sources. The power that derives from the network of relationships is an important consideration – it is the ability to transmit a perspective of the organisation to other powerful stakeholders. But this is only one form of power for a stakeholder. The frameworks of power presented in the relevant literature are important ways of thinking about what a management team has to say about ways of sabotage and support for the organisation. When thinking about stakeholder analysis the reason for unfolding dimensions of power in some degree of detail is that it will provide clues as to the best ways of managing and exploiting that power. Obvious aspects of power need to be made explicit – the ability of a stakeholder to withdraw significant levels of funding, to mount audits that can query the veracity of financial controls, the ability to raise questions about the role of the organisation, the initiation of major campaigns against major strategies – these are all sanctions that can impact the success of an organisation.

However, similarly, the power to provide significant support as an opinion leader, as the provider of resources to deliver strategy, to form a powerful coalition of support, and simply give permissions and approvals are all aspects of power that need to be explicated in detail.

Stakeholder Dynamics: The Unfolding Game?

Unfolding dynamics are a sort of multiplayer chess game.

Understanding the dynamic impact of stakeholder reactions to strategies is a critical part of ensuring the likelihood of success. It is important to acknowledge the multiple and *interdependent interactions between stakeholders* and potential stakeholders as noted above in the discussion about influence networks.

There is a tendency to consider stakeholders in a static manner. Stakeholders respond to the strategies of those organisations they have a stake in, and those responses are seen by other stakeholders, and depending on their spectacles, the responses made will in turn generate responses from them. A 'game' unfolds where positions and actions unfold over time, not just in response to the original strategy, but in response to the strategies of others who are responding to it. The unfolding dynamics are a sort of multiplayer chess game, but where the rules are not known by all.[27] The game is understood more or less fully by the stakeholders, and non-stakeholder participants. Some stakeholders are able to anticipate multiple dynamic responses

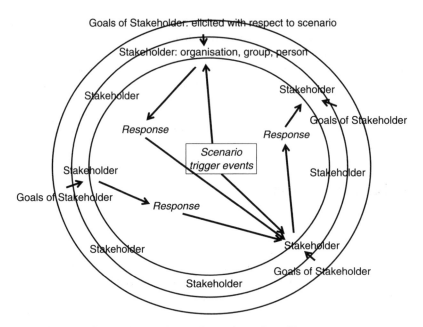

Figure 9.2 Mapping Out the Dynamics of Responses Over Time

and plan their own responses with respect to their own goals, whereas for others the responses are more simplistic.

From the perspective of the focal organisation we need an ability to understand and manage the unfolding game so that it gradually stabilises in support of the proposed strategies. Understanding and exploiting interactions can emerge from examining the social networks which focus on the relationships between stakeholders, and also the interests (goals) of the stakeholders. The network can thus be used potentially to reveal not only responses to organisational actions but also counter responses, thus expressing a dynamic orientation.

Figure 9.2 illustrates a build-up of dynamics following a 'trigger event' (in the middle of the diagram) caused by the focal organisation seeking to implement a strategy. In this illustration the trigger event causes initial responses from two stakeholders, and later involves four stakeholders. Each of their responses acts as a trigger to elicit further responses, which in the case of one stakeholder results in their subsequent response being to reinforce their initial response (see the stakeholder in the bottom right of figure 9.2).

The objective of understanding stakeholder dynamics is to judge the reaction of a range of stakeholders to strategy initiatives. In this process we are using our understanding of the interests (goals) of each stakeholder and considering that these are the drivers of responses. However, in some instances we might need to accept that reactions are not driven by stakeholder goals but by knee-jerk habit. Furthermore, the dynamics of stakeholder responses can cause possible escalation through feedback dynamics where the initial trigger leads to responses which contribute to the continuing failure of the strategy without any single stakeholder necessarily anticipating such a dynamic of responses. Until a formal explication of possible dynamics occurs, potential compensating feedback that destroys the effectiveness of options is unlikely to be revealed.

STAKEHOLDER MANAGEMENT

Each of the areas discussed so far: (1) the power–interest grid that helps sort out key stakeholders, (2) the analysis of social networks and stakeholder power, and (3) the more detailed exploration of the basis of power and the nature of interests, suggests ways of managing stakeholders. However, it is the last of these that provides the most help because it aligns the management of stakeholders with the notions of managing interests and power.

Typically it is the top management team that crafts the strategy and so needs to attend to the strategic management of stakeholders in order to ensure the robustness of the strategy. That said, stakeholder management can take place at any level of the organisation as departments and divisions work to ensure the greatest likelihood of a strategy's success. Middle managers will continually find themselves having to take account of both external stakeholders (which may be clients, competitors, regulators, etc.) as well as internal ones (in the form of other potentially competing divisions/departments, boards, other managers and staff).

As we noted earlier, the stakeholder environment consists of 'a series of multilateral contracts among stakeholders'.[28] Power is often derived from the influence of one stakeholder over another. Thus completing the influence network reveals a representation of the overall system of interactions and suggests one strategy of stakeholder management: use the network to influence and so change opinions and actions. As has been argued, 'stakeholder management suggests that stakeholder relationships can be created and influenced, not just taken as given'.[29]

THE STAKEHOLDER MANAGEMENT FORUM

Discovering Key Stakeholders: Developing a Power–Interest Grid

The power–interest grid technique puts into practice the requirement to identify (1) the degree of uniqueness and (2) the relative significance of potential stakeholders. This is achieved through positioning identified stakeholders on a grid with interest and power as the two axes. Although these two axes are well established in the literature, there is no consistent or precise definition of power provided. However, in helping a management team construct the power–interest grid a tight definition of power does not seem to be helpful. Deliberately not defining power will help give rise to more free-ranging conversations as subtle and broad dimensions of power are considered through members' experience and intuition.

The separation of power and interest as orthogonal dimensions enables an appreciation that those potential stakeholders with significant amounts of interest are not necessarily powerful and vice versa. Often a management team pays too much attention to those that 'shout loudest'. It is also possible to detect which of the stakeholders has both power and interest.

Disaggregation

One of the tensions likely to emerge for participants and facilitators is that of getting a sensible balance between attending to the need to recognise the uniqueness of each organisation's stakeholders (disaggregation) alongside being faced with an unhelpfully long list.[30] There is likely to be an initial tendency of the management team to surface highly aggregated stakeholders in order to avoid a long list. However, the use of the two dimensional grid helps groups deal with the longer list arising from disaggregation as the grid allows for categorisation. In addition, whereas short lists of generic stakeholders tend to produce a 'so what?' response from the team, the development of a unique longer list will usually provide the team with a sense that stakeholder analysis is likely to be of some use – they are being able to consider the whole panoply. Nevertheless, disaggregating to the appropriate level for management of the stakeholder is rarely an easy task.

In addition, the process of disaggregation reduces the extent of instability in the positioning of stakeholders, because a highly aggregated stakeholder may include a number of more discrete stakeholders who therefore will need to be positioned at different locations on the grid and whose dynamics (responses) will be different.

The four categories that naturally emerge from the two dimensions provide groups with additional structure which supports the process of disaggregation and discovery. For example, when positioning the highly aggregated stakeholder of 'competition' it is likely that power and interest varies significantly between different competitors. Some competitors might be seen as players with high power and interest, whereas others appear as subjects, and a smaller number seen as context-setters. In addition, separating players from context-setters effectively reveals to the management team the requirement for different types of management strategies, where the behaviour of context-setters requires some attempt at reacting to them as part of the environment – through, perhaps, scenario development (see chapter 12).

Creating an Actor-influence Network

A natural follow on from mapping potential stakeholders onto the power–interest grid is the need to surface and examine their relationships with one another. As participants debate the positions of stakeholders on the grid occasionally they will suggest that their power derives from the influence one stakeholder has over another. These comments naturally introduce the task of mapping out the network of influences.

The network is formed by each relationship between stakeholders being depicted by an arrow linking one stakeholder to another. The direction of the arrow (that is which stakeholder is at the tail of the arrow and which is at the head) provides an indication of the nature of the relationship (the direction of influence is from tail to head). Where stakeholders influence one another, a double headed arrow can be used.

To further extract insights and knowledge about relationships, formal and informal relationships are distinguished. The formal influences are those typically reflected in reporting lines – for example staff member and supervisor, agency and government department, subsidiary to corporate office, etc. – with informal relationships reflecting other, more social, links. This distinction is reflected in the nature of the links used; formal links are depicted as solid arrows and informal relationships as dotted arrows.

As with the power–interest grid, the conversation surrounding the process of surfacing the relationships acts as a rich dialogue for participants to learn more about the stakeholders. In some cases pairs of stakeholders are revealed to have both formal and informal links, possibly suggesting a strong enduring relationship. The resulting network is a complex web of relationships that can often look messy and complex to an outsider, although not to the group who has created it. Capturing the dialogue that provides the support for the relationship proposed ensures that the commentary is not lost. It also provides the beginnings of a rich reservoir of material for thinking about stakeholder management options.

Capturing the relationships graphically, in the form of a map or network, additionally allows for analysis of the network through enabling an exploration of patterns in the resultant structure. Thus, where there are stakeholders with lots of relationships linking into them then this suggests that they are likely to be seen as significant stakeholders by others. Their position at the receiving end of many relationships potentially enables them to gather considerable information and gain a more holistic view of strategies unfolding, and thus wield considerable power. These stakeholders may be potentially useful allies where they are positively inclined. Likewise, where a stakeholder has lots of links outwards then there is the potential for influencing a wide range of opinions or actions. These stakeholders are a powerful conduit to other parts of the network. As a result of reviewing the network, participants will often realise that a stakeholder is more powerful than they originally supposed.

As the positive or negative disposition of a stakeholder may have been noted as the power–interest grid was developed, potential dangers can be revealed. For example, if a perceived negatively disposed stakeholder is central within the structure (lots of links leading both in and out), and this stakeholder has the wherewithal to significantly influence others to the detriment of the organisation, then action may need to be taken to change the disposition or reduce the power of the influence. Sometimes these insights come as a shock resulting in participants commenting, for example, 'Oh [my goodness], that stakeholder which we put low down in power and interest is incredibly well networked and could do us all sorts of damage'. Likewise, those stakeholders that are positively inclined and central, but who have not previously been considered significant, must have their status changed on the power–interest grid as their support might provide greater benefits than originally conceived.

Invariably there are likely to be complex and extensive *informal* networks. These networks are rarely discussed or elaborated by a management team in a structured manner. Each of the managers often demonstrates a taken-for-granted way of managing his or her own informal network without appreciating the wider subtleties of the more complete and complex network that emerges as the knowledge from all of the team members comes together. In contrast, formal networks are better understood. The network frequently indicates the need to adapt the power–interest grid as the network analysis shows some actors to be more or less powerful than initially supposed. Often, and significantly, a management team notes that the newly discovered powerful actors are themselves unaware of their own power base. Not surprisingly, the changes in an understanding of power derive mostly from the analysis of the informal relationships. Similarly discovering the network will reveal new stakeholders or the requirement for further disaggregation.

Figures 9.3a and 9.3b show the development of the actor-influence network. Figure 9.3a shows the network developing on the power–interest grid, and figure 9.3b shows the network extracted and laid out to display the structure and character of the network. The process leads the group to have to consider (1) the disaggregation of business passengers (because of the informal link to the media not arising from all business passengers but rather a small group); (2) similarly the disaggregation of other hub airlines to reflect informal links; and (3) the disaggregation of airlines to unravel informal links. This requirement is a typical outcome from developing the actor-influence network. Figure 9.3b shows why views about the other hub airlines began to change as the management team realised the extent of informal influence they (or some of them) had – their power base was more significant than expected.

Manipulating Power and Interest: The Stakeholder Management Web

The first step is to select the key stakeholders from the power–interest grid (those in the high interest, high power quadrant) revised through the introduction of social network considerations.

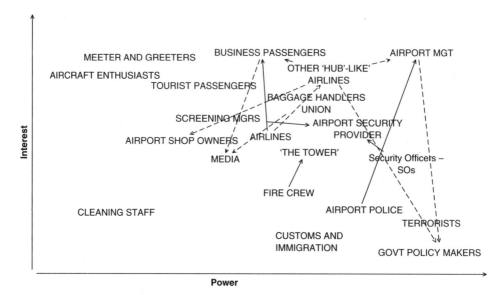

Figure 9.3a An Example of an Actor-influence Network (developed for the management team of a hub airline – modified to retain confidentiality)

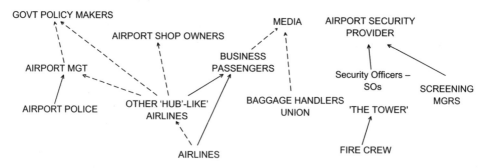

Figure 9.3b Mapping Out the Actor-influence Network to Unravel Unexpected Changes in Power

Recall from earlier material in this chapter that the reason for introducing the stakeholder management web is because the discussions emerging from both the power–interest grid and actor-influence network have not been formally recorded and understood as a system – and thus can be seen as a basis for analysis. The first stage of developing the web, therefore, is to represent explicitly on a web the notes from these discussions along with the key stakeholder and any other stakeholders directly connected to them. This pre-recorded material is then elaborated by exploring in greater depth the bases of power and interest. The use of power is sometimes seen as positive – that is, support tactics (processes or actions). It may also be negative – where the stakeholder could use sanctions or various other hostile actions to counter possible strategies. It is worth noting that a stakeholder might show support for some strategies while sabotaging others. In the process of developing the web, participants may find their thinking about management options triggers further discussion about the relationships between the stakeholders under scrutiny. Inevitably the interests of some stakeholders are influenced by the position taken by others, and this is taken as one basis of power.

The top part of the web diagram thus records several levels of causalities relating to the *bases of power* (different support and sanction options) and the bottom part of the web records the causalities relating to the *bases of interest*. By surfacing not just initial but subsequent consequences, additional subtleties may be detected, particularly revealing both supportive and detrimental behaviours. Gaining insights into what each stakeholder is expected to monitor is achieved through considering: 'what particular aspirations or goals (of the other organisation) will the strategy in question attack or support?' In other words, why would the strategy matter to the stakeholder? Note that it is what is *perceived* by this stakeholder that must to be explored, and the perception might not necessarily be what the organisation is actually intending or asserting in its public pronouncements. The stakeholder's perceptions drive their interpretation of a strategy and subsequent action in response to it. It is not uncommon when doing this activity to hear participants comment 'until we did the web I hadn't really thought through all the different ways these key organisations could sabotage what we want to achieve'. In addition, through working in a diagrammatic format – creating the web, rather than lists, it is possible to reveal ramified causal consequences of interest and subsequent actions. This elaboration of the different bases creates the stakeholder management web where further explorations radiate in and out from the stakeholder at the centre of the web. After considering the bases of power, the management team can consider how a particular strategy or strategic direction might be assessed through the chosen stakeholder's eyes (their spectacles or lens). Answers will be required to the following questions: *How* would they (the stakeholder) interpret the strategies proposed by the organisation? *Why* are the strategies, or some of them, being monitored? The answers elicit the specificity of the stakeholder perspective.

The stakeholder management web is designed to record, in a structured manner, information about the actions, objectives and motivations of specific groups/stakeholders. The specific power and interest bases suggest different options for intervening. More than the other techniques, the discussion that arises from explicating each of the bases of power and interest naturally suggests management options, as managers are incapable of divorcing their discussion about the possible actions and interests from means of managing the stakeholders. The enhanced understanding of how to manipulate key stakeholders usually results in a re-prioritisation of the key stakeholders and a fine tuning of the strategies in such a way as to reduce powerful negative responses.[31]

Figure 9.4 shows an example of an early draft of a stakeholder management web. The figure shows how the formal links between Helen and Graham represent a power base for Helen – one that reinforces the sanction she has in promoting 'Tmax producing an outsourced R&D unit'. Note that because the web is based on a real case, understanding the web is difficult for someone not a part of the team. However, Helen's interest in monitoring the possibility for potential future R&D business stands out in the web because of her interest in links with other R&D units and financial viability, both of which are indicators of future business.

The different responses, as seen when exploring the interest bases, reveal multiple and subtly interwoven consequences which are also influenced by, and influence, other stakeholders. Comparisons across stakeholder management webs are likely to reveal the relative priority of

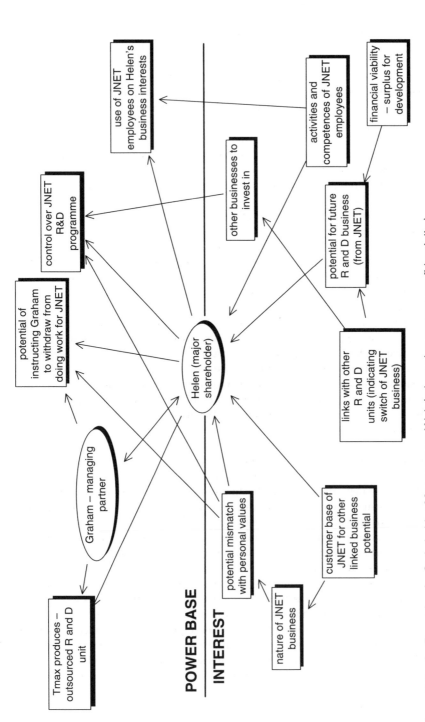

POWER BASE

INTEREST

use of JNET employees on Helen's business interests

activities and competences of JNET employees

financial viability – surplus for development

control over JNET R&D programme

other businesses to invest in

potential for future R and D business (from JNET)

potential of instructing Graham to withdraw from doing work for JNET

Helen (major shareholder)

links with other R and D units (indicating switch of JNET business)

Graham – managing partner

potential mismatch with personal values

customer base of JNET for other linked business potential

Tmax produces – outsourced R and D unit

nature of JNET business

Figure 9.4   An Example of a Stakeholder Management Web (adapted to protect confidentiality)

options. As a result, an unfolding 'game' can begin to be pieced together and through this enhanced understanding a more robust strategy designed. For example, common sanctions stemming from a similarity in interest bases across stakeholders can highlight potentially risky actions for the organisation as they can set up opposing coalitions. Where multiple stakeholders are being scrutinised and re-occurring patterns of sanctions, support mechanisms or aspirations appear, this will give the management team a clear indication about high leverage strategies for manipulating stakeholders. For example, where there is a cluster of stakeholders with similar aspirations, provided they are aware of this particular disposition, then the potential for *their* building a coalition increases. Alternatively, the creation of a coalition of support can be encouraged by the organisation.

Using Analysis Techniques to Identify Stakeholder Management Strategies

It is best to see the three techniques as a unified stakeholder management method. None of the techniques when taken on their own provides insights of great significance. Each of the individual techniques is *relatively* superficial in terms of the benefit yielded. For example, the power–interest grid *when taken on its own* reveals very little in terms of extending the proposition of intervention. Each of the techniques is informed by another, with the stakeholder management web pulling together insights from both the grid and from the network. However, the grid and the network can each be modified by work on the management web. The integration of the stakeholder management web (building upon the power–interest grid) and the actor-influence network enables a stakeholder (chosen through the power–interest grid results) to be considered not only in relation to their own actions but as a nexus in a shifting body of possible coalitions. A more robust and sustainable stakeholder management strategy thus could be developed.

THE STRATEGY DELIVERABLE: A *STATEMENT* OF STRATEGIC INTENT?

The output from a stakeholder management forum is problematic to deal with. The deliverable is usually powerful but a management team is typically uneasy about publishing it, even to themselves as the audience, because it is contains highly confidential data.

Most often the output is a confidential pack consisting of (1) a power–interest grid, (2) an actor-influence network, and (3) a stakeholder management web for each of the key stakeholders. Stakeholder management is regarded as highly manipulative (as if effective management was not a manipulative role!). However, in some instances confidentiality is possible across participants or a small group of them and a more normal statement of strategic intent can be a helpful record and guide to strategic action.

The two stakeholder management webs shown in figures 9.5 and 9.6 can be converted into an SSI. The first web relates to a sub-contractor and the second to a competitor. The SSI also contains commentary that derives from the power–interest grid and the implications for, and changes to, strategies agreed in other forums.

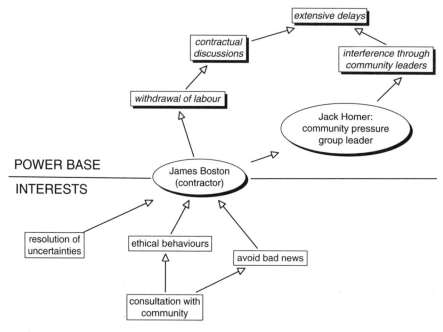

Figure 9.5   Stakeholder Web for a Key Stakeholder: James Boston

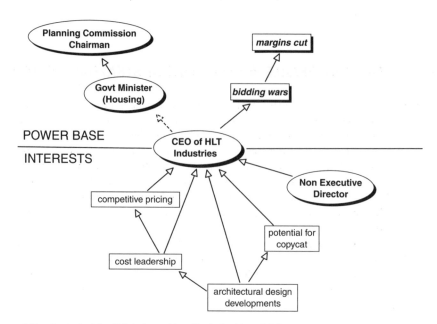

Figure 9.6   Stakeholder Web for a Key Stakeholder: CEO of HLT Industries

Statement of Strategic Intent

1   We have identified a small number of stakeholders who we believe have the power to influence the effectiveness of our strategic moves over the next few years. These stakeholders we must monitor very carefully and we must **understand better the power they have to affect our future and also the way in which they view us**. These stakeholders are:

SH1
SH2
SH3
etc.
James Boston (one of the contractors we depend upon)
The Chief Executive of HLT Industries (the current CEO)

2   In addition we have realised that there are a number of organisations that are following our progress very carefully and would very much like us to achieve our goals. Unfortunately they have too little power to help us. However, we believe that if they could be persuaded to work together then they might have considerable power to help us indirectly through the power they would then have to influence key aspects of the media. Therefore, **we intend to facilitate their working together through providing funding, administrative support and meeting facilities to form a 'club' committed to interests that will ultimately serve our strategic goals**.

3   Each of James Boston and the CEO of HLT we consider to be of particular significance because they both have very considerable power to affect our future in negative ways.

(a)   **James Boston** is a contractor we are perhaps too dependent on given the extent of their power to sabotage our core activities. We must look for another equally good contractor. However, we have no intention of losing the services of James Boston and so we must be careful, in our interactions with them, to focus on early partnering activities and ensuring that **(i) we work closely with them to manage their uncertainties in the contract; (ii) we involve them fully in consultations with the community and demonstrate our commitment to ethical behaviour throughout the contract; and (iii) we manage bad news very carefully and seek to avoid reactions from the community that would be construed by James Boston's senior management team as bad news**. Also we must be aware that the company has a very close relationship with Jack Homer who has the power to raise effective objections within the community and so increase the likelihood of considerable contract delays and so consequential liquidated damages. **Our own relationship with Jack must be developed**. It is possible that James Boston might consider withdrawing their labour if they are discomforted by our management of the three key factors above. **Our contracting with James Boston must improve**.

(b)   **The CEO of HLT** listens carefully to Ken Jennings (one of our non-executive directors) because of his position as a Regulator. **We will review his position as a non-executive at the earliest opportunity**. However, HLT's main focus of attention on our strategic developments lies in their particular interest in our architectural design developments. They are keen to match our cost leadership and we have evidence that they 'copycat' our approaches rather than seek their own developments as our other competitors do. It is of considerable importance that we do not allow them to develop more competitive

(Continued)

(Continued)

pricing as a result of their interests in us. **We must institute more careful procedures in protecting our ideas from the CEO of HLT. We must also take every opportunity to persuade him that his approach is unlikely to be successful.** His children go to the same school as the children of the current Government Minister for Housing and they meet often socially. He can therefore influence the Minister in decisions that will affect the success of our own intentions – **be aware of this in framing all proposals to the Minister.**

4   Some of our strategies have been modified so that they elicit more support from some stakeholders, and others have been adjusted so that they are (i) less likely to be noticed by those wishing to sabotage our ability to achieve our goals, (ii) less likely to produce responses from powerful stakeholders that will affect significantly our achievement of key goals. **Note the following changes:**
    Strategy 1: etc.
    Strategy 2: etc.

WHAT MIGHT BE WRONG WITH MAKING STRATEGY THROUGH STAKEHOLDER MANAGEMENT?

It's All Too Confidential to Be of Any Use as a Part of Strategy Development

All of the material (power–interest grid, actor-influence network and stakeholder management webs) will be very specific to the focal organisation and will be highly sensitive in content and so confidential to the managers developing the material. This is particularly the case when building the formal representation of networks – as often it is as discomforting as it is rewarding. The more specific and detailed each of the three sets of material, the more likely it is to be highly confidential. Thus, a strategy statement cannot be made public and cannot guide the organisation.

Although the work and output is usually confidential and cannot become known across the whole of an organisation, it is, nevertheless, crucial to the successful delivery of strategy. Thus, the statement of strategic intent with respect to management of stakeholders will often only sit within a management team and may often not appear on paper. The strategic conversation about the management of stakeholders may be the full strategy process – influencing the thinking and behaviours of each member of the management team and facilitating coherent and coordinated attitudes and actions with respect to key stakeholders.

It Is Too Manipulative – and so Managers Don't Like Doing It!

Being explicit and thoughtful about the power of stakeholders, and then continuing to plan how to manage them, is almost always seen as 'manipulative'. Managers are often discomforted by the designed process and some see it as inappropriate – as something that should just be done intuitively. Thus, the process of determining how to strategically manage stakeholders is not always seen as legitimate in the organisation.

It is also remarkable how many managers 'don't get it' at the beginning of the process because they do not easily see that stakeholders may see their world from a very different perspective to theirs. After a period of time, often when thinking about social networks, they do 'warm' to the activity. This is because they are fascinated about how much is revealed.

As noted above, general management is manipulative but seen as legitimate, considering how to manage stakeholders is simply an extension.

Not Well Established – It's Alright in Theory But There's Not Enough Practice?

The research on which this approach to stakeholder management is based sought to build on the work of others who have explored or suggested procedures. The discussion presented in this chapter, and the approach to practice presented in the next chapter, has been developed through working with a wide variety of management teams, where the theories expressed through the procedures are required to be workable in practice. Multiple case research was used and it sought to develop conceptual rather than statistical generalisation beyond the specific local conditions. Although Bryson argues, 'there is no overwhelming body of evidence indicating that stakeholder analyses do help produce desirable outcomes',[32] the analyses developed and tested through our research appear to provide the basis for creating such evidence.

It's Wrong to Ignore 'Subjects' Who *Should* Be Listened To

Some stakeholder management literature takes a liberalistic stance on who should be listened to, and so given power. An emphasis on corporate social responsibility focuses attention on stakeholders who may not have any power to disrupt or support the delivery of strategy. If corporate social responsibility is a goal of the organisation then it is the role of strategy development to provide a power base to chosen stakeholders with little power. The organisation must work out ways of moving some stakeholders from being subjects to being players. However, this is a strategic choice not a general requirement – unless there are regulatory constraints that require such outcomes. Otherwise stakeholders are important because of a strategic choice – for example, giving the impression of being an organisation attending to corporate social responsibility might provide more consumers.

Too Complex – Too Much Disaggregation

This book has devoted two whole chapters to stakeholder management and so given it equal status to developing purpose, exploiting competitive advantage, and determining and managing strategic priorities. The material in these chapters has argued for a detailed and three stage process that goes well beyond that proposed by most strategy books (some of which mention the power–interest grid only). Is this not overkill?

As we state above, these chapters on stakeholder management derive from 15 years of extensive research with over 200 organisations. The result of that work shows that (1) the power–interest grid alone takes a management team not much further than their intuitive sense of key stakeholders, but that this is partly because of too little appropriate disaggregation; (2) the grid *implies* stakeholder management but does not allow a team to agree coherent, coordinated and thoughtful action, but adding strategic conversation about the detailed bases of power (including from social network analysis) and interests reveals more thoughtful and robust strategies. In particular the three processes taken together make a sensible whole.

Stakeholder Dynamics Are Impossible to Analyse

Modelling, and so understanding, stakeholder dynamics is difficult. In the practice chapter (chapter 10) we do not propose that this process is included in a typical half-day forum. Undoubtedly the exercise may require off-line (outside forum) modelling that can be used to inform and so modify the outcomes from the stakeholder management forum.

In the same way as exploring alternative futures (scenario planning) is intended to tune thinking, then so is the *consideration* of stakeholder dynamics intended to alert the team to possibilities that need consideration in the strategic management of stakeholders.

NEXT STEPS – EXTENDING THE SCOPE OF THE STRATEGY: LINKING TO OTHER STRATEGY MAKING FORUMS

It is unusual for stakeholder management to be considered until there is some sense of an agreed strategy, either published or generally known. Often a management team will choose to undertake a stakeholder management forum as an adjunct to their published strategy. The team become aware that in devising their published strategy, often through the use of support staff, they have paid scant attention to stakeholders – at least in any formalised manner. At the end of a stakeholder management forum the team will usually react in one of the following ways: (1) with a greater sense of comfort in their published strategy; (2) with a significant discomfort in the published strategy and so a wish to revisit it; and/or (3) with a sense from the manager-client of how useful a team based designed strategy forum can be for gaining commitment from the team. In the latter two instances the manager-client becomes curious about how a strategy might be refined, or redeveloped, through the team rather than a planner.

The discussion with the manager-client about next steps can follow several avenues:

1 Developing a set of strategic priorities – *strategic issue management.* A central concern of the stakeholder management forum was the extent to which agreed strategies could be sabotaged or supported through the actions of stakeholders. Most strategies are less workable than might have been hoped once they are seen from the perspective of stakeholders. Alternatively they may be less ambitious than they might be because of the support that could be garnered from effective stakeholder management. In both cases the strategies need to be tweaked. However, in doing so the original context of the strategies is often lost, and so the tweaking loses some of the original purpose of the strategy. In addition, priorities might shift as ambitions change.

   A natural extension of the stakeholder management forum becomes the requirement to revisit strategic priorities. An issue management forum – strategy as the prioritisation and management of key issues – provides such an opportunity. Although it is tempting to simply readdress the priorities, and tweak the design, of the strategies it makes sense to start from scratch and revisit the new views of management team members about their overall sense of where priorities lie. The issue management forum is designed as a half-day episode, and so the extent of resource (time) required is not great, and there is usually some high degree of enthusiasm for continuing to a logical next step in strategic thinking – one that is informed by their learning from the stakeholder management forum.

   See chapters 3 and 4.

2 Revisiting purpose – *goals system* exploration. A stakeholder management forum is designed to be organisation specific. Rather than seeing stakeholders that need to be managed as a generic set of interested parties, the stakeholder management forum addresses those stakeholders that have the power to affect the future of the specific organisation. The forum focuses attention on the impact

of stakeholders on the attainment of the specific goal of the organisation – particularly business goals rather than generic goals (such as more market share, growth in revenue, more profit, etc.).

Thus, the next forum may be focused on exploring the nature of the existing goals system in the light of stakeholder management. The outcome of such a goals system exploration establishes a revised goals system that fully attends to the constraints placed on aspirations by key stakeholders, and the possibility for more ambitious aspirations.

See chapters 5 and 6.

3   Strategy making through managing *competitive advantage* and seeking out new business. Stakeholders and their management can affect, in significant ways, competitive advantage. The strategic management of stakeholders can be an aspect of competitive advantage – the ability to manage and exploit stakeholders through an ability to manage and grow coalitions of support may be a distinctive competence. Indeed, through the stakeholder management forum there may be a greater ability to sustain and develop such competences so that the ability becomes a highly distinctive competence. Similarly, the effective strategic management of stakeholders may be important for the successful exploitation of competitive advantage (suggesting that it might be more appropriate, when possible, to undertake a stakeholder management forum after a competitive advantage forum).

See chapters 7 and 8.

NOTES

1   For example, Donaldson and Preston (1995); Freeman and McVea (2001); Frooman (1999); Mitchell, Agle and Wood (1997).
2   See, for example, Jawahar and McLaughlin (2001) and Jensen and Meckling (1976).
3   For example, Freeman (1984) and Porter (1985).
4   Some have argued that the categorisation is too vague and that 'political, social and technological context must also be reckoned with if the firm is to incorporate the rate of institutions and actions – both public and private – that affect its operations (Cummings and Doh, 2000: 83). Others that argue for heterogeneity are Rowley (1997) and Wolfe and Putler (2002).
5   Bryson, Gibbons and Shaye (2000) argue that paying attention to a comprehensive set of stakeholders is likely to have a powerful effect on the feasibility of the strategy and thus the long term viability of the organisation.
6   Questions about stakeholders' identities and demands have been addressed before, but our specific focus is: *how can management teams manage their stakeholders effectively so as to realise their strategic goals?* The majority of the extant literature implies that stakeholders are managed by the whole organisation, rather than by a specific group of managers. But since (typically) it is the management team that crafts an organisation's strategy, it therefore also needs to attend to the strategic management of stakeholders if it wants to ensure that strategy's robustness. By anticipating and managing stakeholder responses to organisational strategies, actions can be put in place that either capitalise on potential positive responses or reduce or eradicate negative responses.
7   See Porter (1980).
8   Winstanley, Sorabji and Dawson (1995). It is also necessary to draw a distinction between influencers and stakeholders (Donaldson and Preston, 1995).
9   See Donaldson and Preston (1995).
10 Specifically the idea of a grid builds on Freeman (1984: 60).
11 See Freeman and Reed (1983) or Johnson, Scholes and Whittington (2005: 182–188) as examples of the development of the grid's dimensions, in particular their examination of power in detail (paying attention to formal voting power, economic and political power).

12 When working on disaggregating to the level of management 'what is important is developing an understanding of the real, concrete stakeholders who are specific to the firm' (Freeman and McVea, 2001: 4).

13 Freeman and McVea (2001).

14 Scenario planning often ignores context-setters and will focus more often on external events rather than the actors who generate them. See Kees van der Heijden (1996) for an excellent discussion of scenario planning and its role in strategy making.

15 Managing potential conflict stemming from divergent interests recognises that stakeholders are associated with interactions that are dynamic and possibly unstable (Frooman, 1999).

16 'Identification of both the stakeholders and the interconnections between them is a critical step' Freeman and McVea (2001: 191). Also see Cross and Prusak (2002), Nohria (1992: 1–22).

17 Krackhardt and Hanson (1993).

18 'Identification of both the stakeholders and the interconnections between them is a critical step' (Freeman and McVea, 2001: 191).

19 Some see the firm as a *nexus* of formal and social contracts with its stakeholders (Jensen and Meckling, 1976).

20 See Cross and Prusak (2002); Krackhardt and Hanson (1993); Maclean, Harvey and Press (2006); Nohria (1992).

21 See Karl Rethemeyer's extensive research (Hee Park and Rethemeyer, forthcoming) on social network analysis.

22 Cummings and Doh (2000) and Rowley (1997).

23 Preston and Sapienza (1990).

24 Rowley (1997).

25 Wolfe and Putler (2002).

26 Frooman (1999) and Sebenius (1992).

27 In game theory terms this is known as a hypergame – see Bennett (1980). Hypergame theory has now developed into drama theory – see Bryant (2010).

28 Freeman and Evan (1990).

29 Freeman and McVea (2001: 194).

30 An 'unhelpfully long list' (Wolfe and Putler, 2002: 65).

31 Mitchell, Agle and Wood (1997).

32 Bryson (2004: 47).

Further Reading

Freeman, R. E. and McVea, J. 2001. A Stakeholder Approach to Strategic Management. In Hitt, M., Harrison, J. and Freeman, R. E. (eds), *Handbook of Strategic Management*: 189–207. Oxford: Blackwell Publishing.

Frooman, J. 1999. Stakeholder Influence Strategies. *Academy of Management Review*, 24: 191–205.

Mitchell, R. K., Agle, B. R., and Wood, D. J. 1997. Toward a Theory of Stakeholder Identification and Salience: Defining the Principle of Who and What Really Counts. *Academy of Management Review*, 22: 853–886.

10

THE STAKEHOLDER MANAGEMENT FORUM

Fran Ackermann and Colin Eden

WHAT DOES A STAKEHOLDER MANAGEMENT STRATEGY FORUM LOOK AND FEEL LIKE?

What Does it Look Like to a Participant When You Walk in the Room?

We were seated in a semicircle facing a large projector screen and the facilitator was at the front to the right.

The facilitator was using a laptop computer that was connected to a projector displaying a blank white screen.

What Happened?

The forum started with us being asked to name as many groups, organisations, or individuals who could affect the organisation's strategic direction. While I knew of a fair few, I didn't expect so many to emerge – but in retrospect most were familiar, it was just that I hadn't considered them all at the same time. The extensiveness was also due to the fact that the facilitator encouraged us to disaggregate (breaking down large groupings) stakeholders where possible – for example, we split competitors into clusters where those within the cluster would be treated more similarly. This meant that by the time we had exhausted all we could think of (at the time) we had around 50 to 60 stakeholders in about 15 minutes! On the screen that we could all see, we then moved these stakeholders around a grid that had the axes of power along the bottom and interest up the side. As we did this we found ourselves having to disaggregate even further some of those we had originally mentioned, or we would have had to put the same organisation at two different places on the grid. The facilitator did a great job capturing some of the explanations given for why one stakeholder was more powerful or interested than another – this was great stuff. We then coloured the stakeholders according to their disposition towards us, that is, whether they were on the whole negatively or positively inclined towards the organisation. Of course, some had no clear disposition – it depended on specific circumstances.

The next task was to consider the relationships between stakeholders. We captured these relationships as either formal or informal using solid arrows for formal connections or dotted arrows for informal links. The arrows were intended to show who had influence over whom. In addition to this the facilitator encouraged us to think about the nature of the relationship – was it one way or bi-directional. I continually found myself surprised both by the extent of the networks that existed and also that we knew more than I knew we knew. I learnt more about some of the stakeholders in 45 minutes of doing this task than during the four years I had been working in the organisation! We next explored the networks – looking for well connected stakeholders and trying to determine those that were most significant to us. Of course, those with lots of power and who were very interested in what we are up to were chosen for more work, but we also were interested in some of the tightly knit networks where they could form themselves into a coalition and really affect us negatively. We were also really interested in one network of low interest stakeholders that we thought we might be able to encourage into a coalition of support for us.

Finally we chose just two of the most significant stakeholders and explored them in more depth. I could see now even more why the facilitator had tried to keep all the notes on the stakeholders – this provided us with valuable reference material as we sought to develop a picture illustrating both the sanctions and support mechanisms open to the focal stakeholder and also helped us better appreciate how they viewed us! It was interesting to see how this built very strongly on the earlier material. The detailed work forced us to be much clearer, in the case of the two stakeholders, about how they could affect us, and how they looked at us. We began to realise that if we did things a bit differently – but with the same intended outcomes – then they would be less inclined to stymie our strategy. In one case we reckoned that we could shift the presentation of one of our strategies so that a particular stakeholder would be more likely to support what we wanted to achieve (without realising they were doing so) than sabotage it. Furthermore, in one of the cases one of the stakeholders displayed had a particular power base that we felt we might be able to influence if we worked in an organised way. It was clear that too often we tended to try and manage these key stakeholders in a disorganised and random way – we needed to have a coherent approach.

What Did it Feel Like?

Surfacing the stakeholders was relatively easy but the results were a bit startling – I hadn't realised how many stakeholders mattered to us and could affect our success! However, when we then started to position the stakeholders against power and interest things got a little harder. We continually found ourselves realising that despite disaggregating them we still tended to think of them as bundles rather than as having importantly different intentions. I found this breaking down of large groups particularly helpful because it gave me a much better sense of how to handle some of the stakeholders that had a particular interest in my part of the business. The positioning task also meant that lots of interesting new information surfaced – as we sought to justify a position. The task of considering disposition was relatively easy with little disagreement; however, the resultant image depicted some interesting properties – lots of the stakeholders in the highly interested but low power quadrant were very supportive and so reinforced our view that we should be helping build coalitions.

The next task, that of thinking about the relationships, was really engaging. I found it was easy to come up with the formal relationships and I don't think we got anything particularly insightful from this (except to see them all in one place) but the outcome of revealing informal relationships was fascinating. I hadn't realised quite how many of the key folks in some of our key suppliers had studied together in the same place – this had created a very subtle but powerful network. It was also quite disturbing to see one of our biggest critics as being incredibly networked. As we developed this picture I did feel a bit nervous – lots of the material was pretty sensitive and I was nervous what might happen if someone outside of the group got hold of it.

The final stage of looking in detail at two of the most important stakeholders helped crystallise how we could manage them more effectively. I felt that very soon we must look in more detail at a few more of the critical stakeholders.

What Did I Go Away With?

The short answer is, with a lot better understanding of the range of stakeholders facing the organisation. I think we all had a clear idea of how we must work together in a coherent way if we are to stop some potentially disastrous interference. We also got printed copies of the material we had generated, but this was to be treated as highly confidential and to be shared only within the team. In any case, I am not sure that those who were not at the forum would find the power–interest grid all that clear – the wealth of material and all the links appeared very messy and complex.

Was it Worthwhile?

Yes – for a variety of reasons. One of the benefits is that we all now have a better understanding of the significance of some of our stakeholders (previously we had just responded to those who shouted the loudest and I am not sure they were the ones with power). Another benefit was that we now have a range of options which will help increase our chances of strategic success.

RESOURCES

- 1–2 hour meeting of facilitator and manager-client (to agree the design of the forum); this time is still necessary when the facilitator and manager-client are the same person as the design is still required.
- 1 hour setup by the facilitator.
- 1–3 hours of group work – it is usual to complete this forum in half a day but it can be done in as little as 2 hours.
- Decision Explorer® (the software that captures the views and links) loaded onto a laptop, and a small table positioned so that the facilitator can see the public screen and the group.

- 1280x1024 pixel data projector (this resolution works best, as it permits more material to be explored at one time).
- Large public screen.
- Room with chairs (preferably on castors) – one for each participant.

THE PRACTICE OF MAKING STRATEGY: STRATEGY AS STAKEHOLDER MANAGEMENT

Stakeholder Management Strategy Forum: Identifying and Prioritising Stakeholders

> There is nothing more difficult than to achieve a new order of things with no support from those who will not benefit from the new order, and only lukewarm support from those who will. (Machiavelli, *The Prince*, 1514)

Script for: Identifying and prioritising stakeholders: the power–interest grid

Tasks:

1 Introduce the stakeholder management forum: 5 minutes
2 Surface stakeholders: 10–15 minutes
3 Review emergent material: 5 minutes
4 Position stakeholders against the dimensions of power and interest: 15–30 minutes
5 Note the typical disposition of stakeholders: 10–20 minutes
6 Consider candidate management options: 5–15 minutes

Deliverable: a structured map illustrating stakeholder priority
Script timing: minimum 50 minutes, expected 90 minutes

Task 1: Introduce the Stakeholder Management Forum

Getting Started   Before starting the forum, **create a Decision Explorer® view with the axes of power (horizontal) and interest (vertical) marked** (see figure 10.1). This view can be revealed as part of the introduction.

Next **explain to the group the benefits of a stakeholder management forum focusing on the impact of key stakeholders on the strategic future of the organisation** (see box 10.1). Note that considering who the organisation's stakeholders are typically generates a large number of candidates and it is not uncommon in a public sector organisation to generate over 100 throughout the course of the forum. **Reassure participants that the resultant mass of stakeholders will be structured for easier management** through categorising them against power and interest and also (possibly) disposition.

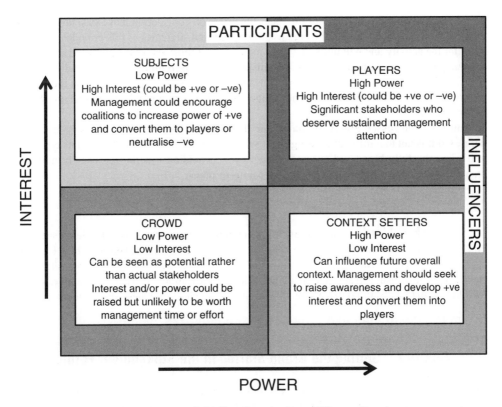

Figure 10.1   The Power–Interest Grid Showing the Four Different Quadrants

Box 10.1   Just Who Are our Stakeholders?

A CEO of a public sector organisation wished to test out the robustness of the newly generated potential strategies. He was concerned that not only would there be adverse reactions from some significant stakeholders but that there was a risk that by implementing the strategy his organisation could drive the negatively disposed stakeholders together to form a dangerous coalition. However, he was aware that he was not entirely sure who all of the stakeholders might be, let alone how they might respond. He needed to find some way of firstly identifying the different stakeholders and then prioritising them according to their power, interest and influence.

What Is a Stakeholder?   Stakeholders are those who have a stake (interest) in the organisation's future; however, there are others who, while not having much interest in the organisation and its actions, will still be critical to the success of the organisation. Explain that it will be important to **separate stakeholders (who have an interest) from those who have the power to unintentionally impact the future** as this will help manage the large number of potential stakeholders that must be identified.

When explaining the task and forum, focus the group on considering those stakeholders that would be relevant in relation to the organisation's proposed strategies as this provides a framework for the activity and will ultimately help increase the robustness of the proposed strategies. Encourage members to **name groups, organisations and individuals** who they believe have power to influence the delivery of the organisation's strategy, and/or an interest in the strategies of the organisation. In addition, **encourage participants to piggy back on one another's contributions**.

Don't get too fussed about the nature or definition of power. 'Power may be tricky to define but it is not that difficult to recognise' (Salancik and Pfeffer, 1974). Participants typically will take a usefully broad and encompassing view – providing a definition usually narrows responses and risks missing interesting dimensions of power.

Task 2: Surface Stakeholders

Identify Stakeholders   **Start by asking participants to surface stakeholders** (see box 10.2). To ensure that everyone has the chance to have their say **use a round robin**. Capture suggestions on the Decision Explorer® view. Don't worry at this stage about where to position the stakeholders, just ensure all are easily readable. Where abbreviations are used, for example, WHO (World Health Organisation) make sure all participants are clear who these stakeholders are.

Box 10.2   Getting the Group Started in the Stakeholder Forum

As part of a strategy exercise, a strategy forum comprising both issue and stakeholder management had been arranged. The morning and early part of the afternoon had concentrated on surfacing issues and designing a statement of strategic intent. The group had been energised and found the process transparent and effective. However, the move to the stakeholder foci saw a slump in energy. The group found themselves struggling to surface stakeholders. The facilitator found herself continually making suggestions and asking for elaboration. This endeavour proved fruitful because as the picture unfolded the added material allowed for further 'piggy-backing' and gave rise to a more comprehensive picture.

Consider Both Internal and External Stakeholders   **Encourage participants to consider both internal and external stakeholders** – don't just focus on external ones. Thus, suggest that they consider internal stakeholders such as the Board, other operating companies/divisions within the organisation, key staff, support staff, etc. It may also be worthwhile to **ask participants to think about who could 'make, break or shake' the success of the strategy**.

Don't be surprised at the extent of material and **continue to cycle around the group until participants are unable to generate further stakeholders**.

Task 3: Review Emergent Material

Once the initial generation of stakeholders has slowed down, review the resultant collection. First **check that all participants are clear who each stakeholder is, paying particular attention to acronyms**.

Disaggregate the Stakeholders   Next, **check whether there are some stakeholders that should be disaggregated when the responses of the specific individuals or departments would be different**. For example, considering the government or competition is usually unhelpful – ask participants to think about which departments/divisions of government (or ministers) would be either interested or powerful (departments are likely to be differently positioned depending on their goals and power). Likewise, with competition consider whether two or three are particularly significant and also whether there are sub-groupings of the rest. Sometimes this level of detail can result in the stakeholder being captured at the level of an individual, where that person stamps her/his personality/values on the position and their power is specific to the individual rather than their organisation.

Work hard at stakeholder disaggregation – Experience suggests that candidate stakeholders are usually not at the right level of disaggregation and so cannot be managed successfully.

Task 4: Position Stakeholders Against Dimensions of Power and Interest

This task will help with the apparent complexity of the large number of stakeholders surfaced as it provides some structure to the messy picture and also some indication regarding which of the many stakeholders identified are most important (see box 10.3).

Classify Stakeholders According to Power   To get started, **ask participants to examine the captured stakeholders and consider which of them are the most powerful in their ability to affect the success of the strategy**. Depending on the time available and the number of stakeholders generated, there are two ways of carrying out this task. The first way is to ask the group to identify the most powerful stakeholder and put that stakeholder at the right hand most position on the grid. Following this, ask for the next most powerful until two or three have been positioned. Then ask for those stakeholders that are the least powerful (noting that this does not mean they have no power) and position them at the left hand side of the power dimension. These two activities provide anchor points for the rest of the stakeholders to be positioned against.

Box 10.3   Working Out Which Stakeholders to Manage

A public sector organisation wanted to manage its stakeholders better. They were aware that there were a number of different stakeholders who were either influential over and/or interested in the success of the organisation but they didn't know which to focus on – they couldn't deal with them all. As a result they thought spending a couple of hours undertaking a stakeholder management forum might help them prioritise.

An alternative and quicker method is to ask the group to consider which stakeholders would be in the top band, the middle band, etc. (an analogy from sport would be to ask which of the stakeholders were in the premier division, first division, and so forth). This is less 'fine grained' than the first method, but usually provides enough differentiation. A combination of the two methods can also be employed – using the bands to manage those less powerful and the detailed method to examine those with power. In either case **move the stakeholders across the grid**

(left to right) according to the group's view of relative power. The positioning of each stakeholder need not be absolutely accurate, and so discourage extensive discussion about the precise location on the grid.

Classify Stakeholders According to Interest

Once positioning on the x axis (power) has been completed **ask participants to view the stakeholders and consider which of the stakeholders are the most interested in 'what we are up to'**. As with the power dimension using either anchor points or bands can help. Make clear to the group that one of the benefits of positioning stakeholders is that it can **reduce the risk of paying too much attention only to those stakeholders that shout loudest**.

Capture Insights About the Rationale Used

When positioning stakeholders against the dimensions, **capture notes about the rationale** participants give to explain the stakeholder's location on the grid (perhaps using the memo-card feature in Decision Explorer®). This can provide valuable material for the management of stakeholders as well as being a valuable knowledge source in its own right.

See Appendix: Using Causal Mapping Software: Decision Explorer®, 4.1 Using Memo Cards

Visualise the Grid as Having Four Quadrants

Ask the group to imagine the grid as four rough quadrants with those that are both powerful and interested (top right) called 'players', those that are powerful but not interested (bottom left) called 'leaders or context-setters', those who are interested but not powerful called 'subjects' and the remainder are seen as 'the crowd' (see figure 10.1). This helps with the management of the complexity inherent with generating large numbers of stakeholders.

Identify Volatile Stakeholders

Recognise that some stakeholders might be 'unstable' in their position on the grid and could move from one quadrant to another depending on which of the strategies (or other focal points) they are responding to. Reflect this in the diagram by showing this movement (see figure 10.2).

Task 5: Note the Typical Disposition of Stakeholders (optional)

An additional means of managing the potential complexity of the stakeholder grid is identifying and capturing the disposition of stakeholders. For example, are they positively inclined towards the organisation and its aims, negatively inclined, generally neutral or mixed?

Capture Stakeholder Disposition in Relation to Strategies

To carry out this task, **ask the group to determine the typical disposition of each stakeholder (or at least those in the player, context-setter, or subject categories) in relation to the strategies**. Using Decision Explorer® create styles recognising the different categories (for example, positive might be green, negative red) and **apply the styles to the selected stakeholders to show inclination for sabotage or support**.

See Appendix: Using Causal Mapping Software: Decision Explorer®, 2.4 Creating and Using Styles

Capture Any Further Disaggregation

This task may result in stakeholders being further disaggregated because they appear to be both generally positively and negatively disposed.

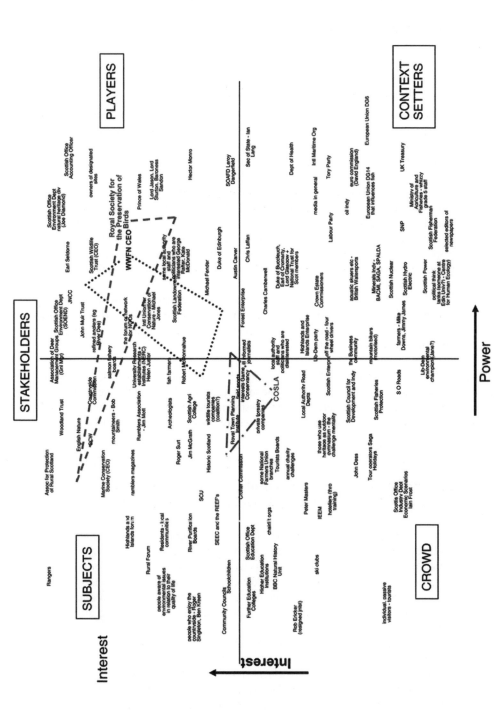

Figure 10.2 A Power–Interest Grid with the Four Quadrants and Two Dimensions Noted, Stakeholders Positioned, and Instabilities Highlighted (dotted areas)

For example, a newspaper which initially was viewed as having a mixed response was, on reflection, the result of the editor being positively inclined and the publisher being negatively inclined. **Capture this further disaggregation. Capture also any further information provided explaining dispositions** as participants are likely to surface potentially important context when arguing for a disposition.

Task 6: Consider Candidate Management Options

The final task in this script is to ask the group to begin to **consider candidate options for the strategic management of key stakeholders**. It is likely that some of these options have already appeared and have been captured in the memo-card or alternatively on flip-chart sheets. Make sure that participants are reminded of these.

Consider the Players **Encourage the group to attend to the management of, at least, stakeholders positioned in the high power and high interest (players) quadrant.** Where these key stakeholders are positively inclined, options to encourage support are appropriate. However, stakeholders that are powerful and interested but negatively disposed may lead to developing options for diminishing their interest (that is stopping them doing certain actions) or neutralising their power (that is breaking/influencing existing and potential coalitions).

Consider the Subjects Where stakeholders are positively inclined but not powerful (subjects), ask the group to examine them to determine whether there are any actions the organisation might take that can help the subject build their power base, for example by encouraging the formation of coalitions with other subjects.

Consider the Context-setters Alternatively those potential stakeholders that are powerful but not interested (context-setters), typically due to a lack of awareness of the organisation, but are perceived to have similar values, are reviewed. Possible means of increasing their interest so as to encourage them to support the organisation's objectives are considered (see box 10.4).

Box 10.4   The Danger of Only Focusing on Those Currently Having Most Power and Interest!

A Local Economic Development Company (LEDC) was considering its future. Their current strategy seemed to be working but the management team was nervously aware that the economic constraints and impending funding cuts would have serious implications for them. They were worried that their resources would diminish – just at a time when they needed them most (the financial situation was causing further job losses). They therefore needed to act proactively to manage key stakeholders. The leader decided they needed a stakeholder management forum.

The team of six got together with the facilitator and quickly began the process of surfacing stakeholders. After ten minutes they were impressed with the extensiveness of their work but somewhat overwhelmed too! They knew that there were a lot of stakeholders so which should they influence? They couldn't attend to all. However, after completing the prioritisation task they began to feel better. They could at least see the wood from the trees. Capturing the dispositions also helped.

(Continued)

(Continued)

It was becoming clear that two of the players (stakeholders in the top right quadrant) had significant influence over funding allocations. Perhaps focusing on these two would gain them maximum benefit with minimum effort. However, they were worried that maybe they had missed a trick. Was there anyone else they should be focusing on?

Deliverable: a structured map illustrating stakeholder priority
Timing from forum start: 50 minutes minimum, expected 90 minutes

---

Stakeholder Management Strategy Forum: Exploring Stakeholder Relationships

---

Script for: Exploring stakeholder relationships: the actor-influence network

Tasks:

1 Explore and capture the formal and informal relationships between stakeholders: 20–25 minutes
2 Examine the resultant 'influence network' to detect emergent properties and consider management options: 20–35 minutes

Deliverable: structured stakeholder map illustrating social networks and highlighting areas for management
Script timing: minimum 40 minutes, expected 55 minutes

Task 1: Explore and Capture the Formal and Informal Relationships Between Stakeholders

This task builds on the power–interest grid and recognises the fact that stakeholders don't act in isolation of one another. Instead they monitor not only the focal organisation's strategic actions but also the responses from other organisations to these strategic actions. Thus, this script in the forum pays close attention to the fact that the actions of one stakeholder could generate an unfolding set of responses across a range of other stakeholders which could have significant negative effects for the group, their organisation and possibly the industry.

Identify and Capture Formal and Informal Links   Start the task by asking the group to **identify formal and informal relationships that exist between all of the candidate stakeholders on the power–interest grid**. Formal relationships are typically reporting lines, for example staff member and supervisor, agency and government department, subsidiary to corporate office, etc. Informal relationships reflect other, more social links (who plays golf with whom, whose children go to the same school, who belongs to the same social club, etc.). Typically it is these informal links which reveal vital and significant insights (see box 10.5). **Capture the formal and informal links**.

Box 10.5   Identifying an Important Coalition

A small public sector body undertaking a stakeholder management forum was focusing on the relationships that currently existed between identified stakeholders. After around 10 minutes and around 20 to 25 links had been captured, it became very clear to the group that there was a tightly integrated network of key governmental decision makers they had to manage, and that what bound these stakeholders together was the fact that they had all done the same university degree.

Differentiate the Links   To recognise the different styles of links **create and use different styles of relationship arrow for each of the informal and formal links**. For example, use dashed arrows for informal relationships and solid arrows for formal relationships. Where the relationship works both ways (i.e. both stakeholders influence one another) a double headed arrow can be used. See Figure 10.3 for an example showing both formal and informal links.

Capture Insights About the Rationale Used to Explain Relationships   In addition, as participants suggest links and provide explanations for them, **capture this further information in the memo-cards (of Decision Explorer®)**. This task often provides participants with additional insights into their stakeholders – as each participant is aware of a few of the links, but not the totality. The task also facilitates learning about the stakeholders.

Be Aware of the Mood of the Group   As more and more relationships get noted, particularly informal relationships, and the detailed explanations provided help explain the links, **watch the group to see if there is any discomfort about the sensitivity of the unfolding picture**. Reassure the group that the unfolding picture is intended to support their thinking and that managing the confidentiality of this unfolding network can be undertake later (just before the forum is finished).

Task 2: Examine the Resultant 'Influence Network' to Detect Emergent Properties and Consider Management Options

Analyse the Network in Terms of Stakeholder Relationships   For example, look for where there are stakeholders with lots of relationships (formal and/or informal) as these stakeholders may be seen as significant by other stakeholders. A position at the receiving end of many relationships suggests that the stakeholder is the recipient of a considerable amount of information which may imbue them with more power than initially supposed. Likewise, where a stakeholder has many outwards links connecting them to lots of other stakeholders, their position in the network may provide them with the potential for influencing a wide range of opinions or actions. Finally stakeholders that have a large number of links both in and out of them are particularly critical as they dominate the network.

   Consider whether stakeholders should be moved, on the power–interest grid, in terms of the power dimension. Also encourage the group to **consider whether these stakeholders are potentially useful allies or powerful enemies**.

   All three of these analyses can either be carried out either by simply visually examining the network or through using the analysis built into Decision Explorer®. **Get the group to discuss the emergent insights**.

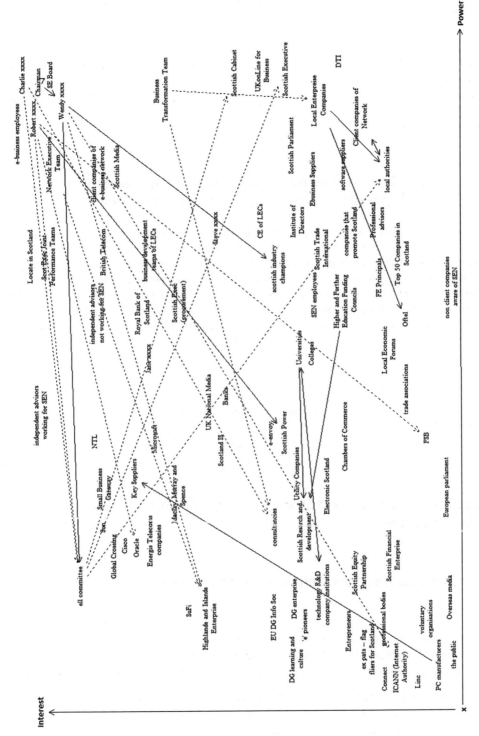

Figure 10.3 An Early Version of the Power–Interest Grid with Formal (solid) and Informal (dotted) Links Illustrated

See Appendix: Using Causal Mapping Software: Decision Explorer®, 3.3 Finding Busy and Central Statements

Analyse the Network in Terms of Stakeholder Disposition and Position   **Look at the well-networked stakeholders in relation to their disposition and position on the network**. Consider whether prioritisation of the key stakeholders needs adaptation. For example, consider those stakeholders that were identified earlier as having a negative disposition – what impact might their position in the network have (for example, see box 10.6). **Encourage participants to review each highly networked stakeholder and consider options**.

Box 10.6   A Rude Awakening, Discovering a Negatively Disposed Stakeholder Has Considerable Influence!

A management team of a small to medium sized organisation had just completed putting in the relationships between their stakeholders and were exploring the network's structure. The first thing to strike them was that one of their stakeholders, someone that they had not considered being particularly powerful, was very well networked. What made the situation worse was that this stakeholder had been categorised as being negatively disposed towards the organisation. In talking over this startling fact, the group believed that this stakeholder was currently unaware of her latent power. However, if she did begin to exploit the power, it could have severe repercussions for them. They needed to develop a strategy quickly.

Deliverable: structured stakeholder map illustrating social networks and highlighting areas for management
Timing from forum start: 90 minutes minimum, expected 145 minutes

---

Stakeholder Management Strategy Forum: Building Stakeholder Management Webs

---

Script for: Building stakeholder management webs

Tasks:

1   Select key stakeholder(s) to be examined: 5–10 minutes
2   Explore in depth the bases of power and interest: 15–50 minutes
3   Review the resultant different webs for commonalities of interests and power: 10–20 minutes

Deliverable: detailed understanding of key stakeholders and management options
Script timing: minimum 30 minutes, expected 65 minutes (for 3 webs)

Task 1: Select Key Stakeholder(s) to Be Examined

Identify Several Key Stakeholders   To start this task, **select two or three key stake-holders** depending on how much time is available. To choose the stakeholders, use the insights gained from positioning stakeholders on the power–interest grid (particularly considering those in the top right of the players quadrant), from considering stakeholder relationships (and thus network centrality) and also dispositions.

Focus on One Key Stakeholder   Next, take the first of the selected stakeholders and **bring this stakeholder onto the centre** of a new Decision Explorer® view. Explain to the group that this task will explore in more depth the *bases of power* (that is, what are the different support and sanction options) and the *bases of interest* (the 'lenses' being used). The top part of the unfolding picture – a form of 'spider web' – will represent several levels of causal argument relating to how the stakeholder's power may be manifested, with the bottom part of the web depicting causalities related to interest.

> See Appendix: Using Causal Mapping Software: Decision Explorer®, 2.1 Using Views and 2.2 Managing the Map

Task 2: Explore in Depth the Bases of Power and Interest

Retrieve Notes Captured in Preceding Tasks   Typically, during both the positioning of stakeholders on the power–interest grid and the surfacing of formal and informal stakeholders, valuable information is presented (as rationale for the positions). Where this has been captured – either in the memo-cards (in Decision Explorer®) associated with each stakeholder or elsewhere – **bring it on to the view** as this material provides a good starting point and avoids duplication.

Elaborate in Terms of Power Bases   Next, encourage the group to **elaborate on this material**. As with positioning stakeholders, it may be worth asking the group to **start with the power bases and to identify what responses might be open to the focal stakeholder**. These responses might be positive – manifested through different forms of support – or negative – manifested through sanctions (see box 10.7). Be alert to both forms of power expression rather than concentrating solely on positive or negative responses – stakeholders usually have access to both sanctions or various hostile actions as well as supporting strategies. When the power–interest grid shows instability then such diversity in how power is deployed is more likely. In addition, **encourage the group to consider how the other stakeholders related to the focal stakeholder might influence power options**, as inevitably the interests of some stakeholders are influenced by the position taken by others. **Capture the new material along with any associated causal links** on the Decision Explorer® view, checking with the group that it is both understood and correct.

Box 10.7   Identifying a Power Base

The group was exploring the power base of one of their prioritised stakeholders and asking themselves what different support mechanisms and sanctions they had. One of the first to be noted was the willingness of the stakeholder to attend their events as this would give the events prestige (and would show that the key stakeholder endorsed the organisation's work). Another form of support was in mentioning the organisation in key speeches. However, it was noted that if the stakeholder lost interest in their organisation then she could also divert interest and support.

Elaborate in Terms of Interest Bases   Once the group has completed a first attempt at elaborating the power bases, ask participants to **repeat the exercise considering the interest base**. This part of the task focuses on gaining insights into what participants perceive the focal stakeholder will monitor and therefore will take into account the particular aspirations or goals. This part of the task stimulates consideration of the current (and/or intended) strategy and how it will attack or support the aspirations of others (hence their interest). Thus, **request partici-pants to consider why would the strategy matter to the stakeholder?** Note that it is what is *perceived* by this stakeholder that is to be explored, and the perception might not necessarily be what their organisation is actually intending or asserting in its public pronouncements. It is the stakeholder's perceptions that drive their interpretation and subsequent action. **Capture the new material and position it beneath and linking into the focal stakeholder**. See figure 10.4 for an example of a web for Scottish Natural Heritage.

Review the Captured Material   Once a first pass has been undertaken of both the bases of interest and power, **review the captured material** as this might tease out subtle insights that have not yet been realised or captured. In addition, as this process usually triggers fur-ther discussion about the relationships between the stakeholders, **continue to modify the stakeholder relationship network** (see box 10.8).

Box 10.8   Recognising the Interactive Nature of Stakeholders

A police force was considering its strategy and was very aware that in order to best do their job they needed to consider in detail a number of the key stakeholders. They had generated a power–interest grid, thought about existing relationships and on the basis of this work identified the criminal justice service (CJS) as being one of the stakeholders of crucial importance. However, they were aware that the CJS had been going through some changes and they needed to pool what knowledge they had to understand how best to work with them. As a result of beginning the process of building the web it became clear to them that CJS's interest and power was highly dependent on two other key stakeholders – the government and also judges – and that if they were to work effectively with the CJS they would also need to build good relations with these other stakeholders.

Consider Appropriate Action   Finally it is important to **consider what actions, if any, need to be taken to increase the robustness of the strategy**. These actions might involve determining ways of ensuring that the likelihood of support is increased. Likewise, where negative responses have been noted – for example, sabotage is possible – get participants to determine what actions might prevent this action or, where this is impossible, what are some of the means for minimising the resultant impact? Keep in mind at all times the relationships between stakeholders, recognis-ing that the means of managing one stakeholder may have ramifications for others. **Consider creating a new style in Decision Explorer® to reflect this new material and its action status**.

Task 3: Review the Resultant Different Webs for Commonalities of Interests and Power

Once the stakeholder management webs have been completed for the selected stakeholders, a final task is to **examine the webs alongside one another**. This comparison may provide

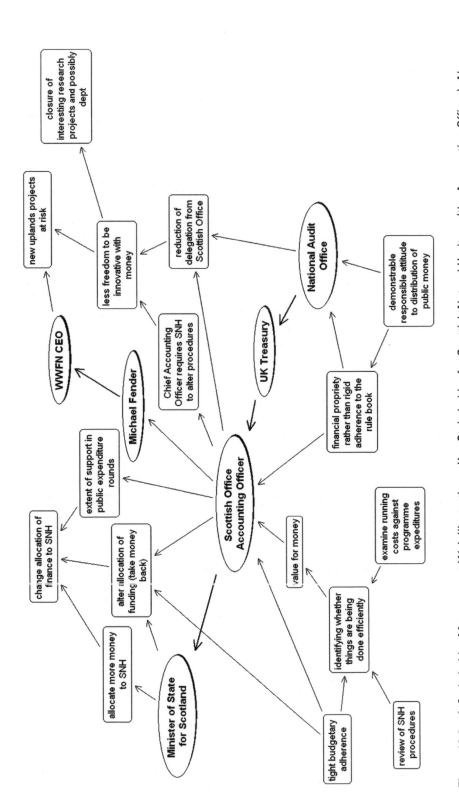

Figure 10.4 A Stakeholder Management Web Illustrating a Key Stakeholder for Scottish Natural Heritage (the Accounting Officer). Along with relevant related stakeholders (those statements in ovals) and the two levels of causality (power and interest)

important insights into common interest bases, similar power manifestations, or the use/impact of stakeholder relationships. As a result it may provide clues towards the relative priority of options. For example, common sanctions stemming from a similarity in interest bases can highlight potentially risky actions and result in triggering opposing coalitions (see box 10.9). The different responses, as seen when exploring the interest bases, may reveal multiple and subtly interwoven consequences which are influenced by and influence other stakeholders.

Box 10.9 Identifying a Potential Disastrous Coalition

The management team were just getting to the conclusion of their stakeholder management forum and were comparing the webs they had produced. To expedite the process they had broken into subgroups with each subgroup focusing on one of the selected key stakeholders. This was the first time therefore that they were looking at all of the webs and it soon became apparent that there was the potential for a very dangerous coalition. An action designed to manage one stakeholder could trigger a response from another, essentially driving them together. This, in the view of the team, would then result in the third stakeholder (featured in a web) joining the coalition as they had very similar aims and could see this as a powerful way of helping them achieve their goals. The resultant outcome could be extremely problematic for the team's organisation – different actions needed to be developed.

Deliverable: detailed understanding of key stakeholders and management options
Timing from forum start: 120 minutes minimum, expected 210 minutes

---

Stakeholder Management Strategy Forum: Producing the 'Statement of Strategic Intent'

Script for: Producing the statement of strategic intent

Tasks:

1 Discuss audience and content: 5–10 minutes
2 Produce pack of material: 15–25 minutes
3 Agree dissemination process: 5–10 minutes

Deliverable: brief document outlining actionable areas
Script timing: minimum 25 minutes, expected 45 minutes

Task 1: Discuss Audience and Content

Discuss Confidentiality   Having carried out the power–interest grid, the actor-influence network and the stakeholder management webs for the key stakeholders, it is worth asking the group to **discuss what to do next with the material**. As noted in chapter 9, producing a statement of strategic intent for the stakeholder management forum can be difficult due to the confidential nature of the material. **Start with asking the group whether they themselves wish to retain copies of the material** (see box 10.10). Where this is the case, next ask whether participants want copies of all of the work or a summarised version (focusing perhaps on just one or two of the webs). **Ask the group also whether they would be interested in producing a statement of strategic intent**. Producing an SSI can be helpful as it acts as a summary and helps the group focus on what activities they are going to invest cash and energy into. Having a record will not only help increase the likelihood of success but also help group members present a unified view to stakeholders (rather than be played off against one another).

Box 10.10   Not Losing the Good Work

The top management team of an organisation had just spent a morning undertaking a stakeholder management forum. They had found the process very insightful but also very uncomfortable. Being a public sector organisation – and vulnerable to those who funded their work – they knew that they needed to tread carefully. This was particularly the case because one of the strategies they were considering was likely to cause considerable resistance from one of their key stakeholders. Nevertheless they believed that if they managed the key stakeholders carefully then the benefit of achieving the strategy (which they felt was fundamental to the organisation's success) would be maximised. However, they felt that having any record of the work would put them in a vulnerable position and so did not produce an SSI.

Unfortunately, not having a record of the myriad and interconnecting stakeholders meant that they no longer were completely clear exactly how the subtle dance they needed to undertake would work – and were worried that they might get it wrong.

Consider Other Audiences   Where the group has agreed to produce some output and has agreed what they believe they want, **ask whether there is anyone else that might be considered as an audience**. Where there is, **agree what form of feedback they will receive** (will it be the same as the group or a reduced/abbreviated version).

Task 2: Produce Pack of Material

The simplest way for providing the group with material is to produce a pack which contains the power–interest grid with the results of the actor-influence network overlaid and copies of the webs. **Review each of these pieces of work**, discussing with the group whether any content needs to be hidden for confidentiality reasons.

Stay Faithful to the Material Captured   Where the group has agreed to produce an SSI then craft this document. As with the other forums, as much as is possible, not only **capture the key stakeholders** but also make sure that the text **reflects the links** – the relationships – as this information helps ensure that the SSI is extremely powerful. **Capture also the management options identified**. The SSI will therefore comprise a list of the key stakeholders that need to be managed, the management actions agreed upon, and any specific relationships or coalitions to be built or prevented. See the example of an SSI in chapter 9.

Consider Style and Presentation   To facilitate the process, **copy and paste bundles of statements from Decision Explorer® in a word processor**.

> See Appendix: Using Causal Mapping Software: Decision Explorer®, 4.2 Copy and Paste Map Material into a Word Processing Document, or PowerPoint

They will appear in numerical order, rather than any chosen order, but can be re-sorted quickly. Use **bold and italic formatting for emphasis**. This helps with navigation around the text and highlights the key points.

Try to **keep the text on one page** as this ensures that the statement is both concise and easily read.

Task 3: Agree Dissemination Process

Finally where further work needs to be done, consider how the material – particularly if a tidied version is to be produced – is provided to the group (see box 10.11).

Box 10.11   *Careful Management of the Material!*

The team had finished what they felt was a really useful session – they now had a clear idea of how to manage some of their key stakeholders. However, the manager-client wanted a little more analysis carried out of the network and also requested that the facilitator provide a set of tidied maps. He also wanted this material urgently and thus requested a copy faxed to him – but he added to the facilitator – please call him first so that he could be standing by the fax machine when the material was sent.

Deliverable: brief document outlining actionable areas
Timing from forum start: 145 minutes minimum, expected 255 minutes

11

FACILITATING GROUPS IN STRATEGY MAKING

Fran Ackermann and Colin Eden

As noted in the introduction to this book, a key element of making strategy that helps ensure that the deliverables are both desirable and politically feasible is to *undertake the strategy making with those who have to deliver the strategy*. These might be top management teams (TMT) or groups of middle or junior managers and their staff. By undertaking the four forums discussed in this book with a group, there is a greater likelihood of commitment at both an intellectual level and at an emotional level (from being involved). However, the difference between working with groups rather than on behalf of them is not trivial. This chapter aims to cover some of the key considerations necessary *to facilitate a forum* by providing practical guidance and examples. The chapter will include not only suggestions aimed to support the running of the forum but also the preparation before hand – preparation can be a significant contributor to facilitating a successful forum.[1] This preparatory work will include: how to manage the facilitator role, who to involve, where to run the forum, what is needed, and how to set the scene – including setting expectations.

This chapter therefore aims to present practical considerations in facilitating a strategy forum. The contents of this 'how to' chapter will be considerably enhanced by reading chapter 2 – Strategic Management Is a Social Process.

BEING A FACILITATOR

Before considering the practicalities, it is important to note that those facilitating a forum could be external to the group (but not necessarily to the organisation) or a manager-client who is facilitating and participating. While for the most part the facilitation practices are identical, there are some particularities that are associated with each of these two operating modes. When working as the manager-client (that is conducting the forum with your own team) think carefully about some of the social and political implications. For example, one key consideration for a manager-client is to **determine how those participating can be encouraged to have their say and contribute their views** rather than feel intimidated by the risk of potentially contradicting their boss. Participants' attention to social conformity pressures, a common phenomenon in many meetings, becomes exacerbated in situations where their manager/boss is leading the meeting as they seek to avoid potential political consequences.[2] **Reassure participants that it is an open forum and that all views are sought, no matter how divergent**. They may not believe this statement, but the objective is to draw out the best of the wisdom and experience of the participants, although regular encouragement might help this occur. Alongside the social pressures there are also content pressures – facilitating a group is hard work, making contributing difficult if not impossible. However, it is important to ensure that the manager-client is also able to have his or her say. **Make sure that there are opportunities to capture manager-client views, even if they have to take short 'time-outs' from their role as facilitator so they can participate in a round robin**.[3]

Building a Facilitator/Manager-Client Relationship

Where there is an external (to the group) facilitator then they will need to **build in time to understand the situation/context**. This activity may comprise becoming familiar with some of the jargon the organisation uses (particularly the acronyms) if from outside of the organisation, understanding a little about the particular group's wider remit, and seeking to detect some of the 'world-taken-for-granted's' around the organisation.

More importantly, when working as an external facilitator it is also important to **build a good relationship with the manager-client**. This means developing an open and trusting relationship, where both parties feel comfortable with sharing sensitive information. Help establish a good rapport by building in time before the forum to **explain both the content and process benefits of the forum, along with some of the possible 'downsides'**.[4] This can be achieved by spending time in a pre-meeting with the manager-client to **review some of the reasons for using participative methods and agreeing both invisible and visible outcomes**. Benefits can include widening the range of perspectives captured and thus helping *ensure that robust outcomes* result as a more comprehensive set of views are captured. Benefits may also encompass encouraging *participants to feel more engaged with the outcomes* through being involved (see the discussion on procedural justice in chapter 2). A forum may also help *build teams* as working together on the future is a powerful activity to stimulate a shared appreciation and those involved are potentially more likely to remain with the organisation. And finally, the process frequently encourages *individual learning, and sometimes the possibility of group learning*.

However, it is also important to spend time with the manager-client to **familiarise him or her with some of the possible negative impacts of participative methods**. These impacts include alerting the manager-client that, due to the participative nature of a forum, it is important that the manager-client **feels comfortable with opening up and raising issues – particularly those that either might be organisationally contentious or challenging of past decisions**. Hindsight is 20:20 vision – and this is sometimes forgotten. Furthermore, it is hard for a manager-client to ignore contributions once they have been made in the public arena of a forum. It is usually better not to have important issues raised than to have them raised and ignored. Being aware of the consequences of the participative nature of the different types of forum – regardless of whether an external facilitator or a manager-client is supporting the group as well as gaining ownership (from procedural justice) – is important.

Another related consideration for the external facilitator is to **develop a good level of trust with the manager-client**. One means of building this trust is through discussing the above benefits and disadvantages of participative methods. A second, and very important, means is to **provide the manager with an appropriate degree of control**. This means attending to the manager-client's concerns about opening up the arena, particularly in relation to topics that are not able to be discussed in the forum because of political pressures from above. Ensure that the manager-client is aware that he or she will be consulted as the forum unfolds, so that they can discuss progress and influence the next steps in the forum.

Finally, spend time with the manager-client to **determine the objectives of the forum from their point of view – both invisible as well as visible objectives (see, for example, box 11.1)**. This includes being clear about what will be achieved through the forum (in terms of the development of statements of strategic intent), how he or she views putting the resultant outcomes into action (is there a commitment to action?), and whether the resources are available for both running the forum (see below) and implementing it. It is also useful to **begin to sketch out a time plan** for the forum to help with both ensuring sufficient time is available and to help monitor progress during the forum. Each 'how to' chapter for each forum provides a rough timetable that can be used to guide this discussion.

Box 11.1 Examples of Visible and Invisible Objectives in Designing a Forum Agenda

Visible purpose: work up a selection of issues beyond 'motherhood'.
Invisible purpose: cross link thinking from politicos and the rest at a level of detail which shows the importance of working together.

Visible purpose: get some example of closure.
Invisible purpose: to show that more work on each area must be done and that it can produce action programmes and commitment.

WHO SHOULD PARTICIPATE IN A STRATEGY FORUM?

There is always a challenge when making sure that the forum includes those whose views will add depth of wisdom and experience and expertise, those whose direct support is required if a strategy is to be implemented, and those who can influence others to support the outcomes. The first task therefore is to **choose who will take part in the forum**.[5] When running a forum for the first time as a facilitator, it may be worth working to **keep the group to a small number – between 5 and 7 participants**. This will allow the surfacing of a diversity of views while also ensuring that the group dynamics are more easily manageable. Starting with this number will also **facilitate there being enough airtime for each participant to be able to both generate and review the unfolding material**. Typically in meetings the time available for discussion is unfairly divided with some participants dominating the forum and others having less of a say. Keeping the number of participants to between 5 and 7 and using the processes presented for each forum will help reduce those with a 'loud mouth' being domineering.

Spend time reviewing potential participants by considering their roles, knowledge bases and personalities. Groups that are more mixed (in terms of hierarchy) may be quieter than those

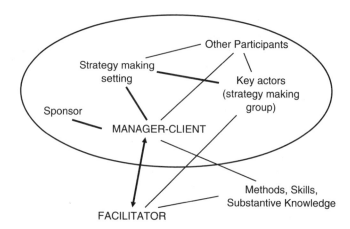

Figure 11.1 Conceptualising the Facilitator–Client Relationships

where the participants are all of roughly the same status. Mixing disciplines (for example, contributions from marketing, production, sales, etc.) may also result in more interaction than those within a single functional area of the organisation. It is also important to **consider which other powerful players might be monitoring the forum outputs and who could protect and generally support the outcomes – who could act as a 'sponsor' for the strategy making forums**. Figure 11.1 provides a picture of the facilitator-client interaction. Note that the facilitator and client could be the same person where the manager-client acts as a facilitator, and, as with an external facilitator they would bring knowledge of the methods outlined in this book, facilitation skills, as well as substantive knowledge about the organisation and industry. Nevertheless consideration of who are the *key* actors (those with the power to make, break or shake), the participants (with potential expertise), and who might be the sponsor can help ensure a group that increases both the substantive and processual benefits. See box 11.2 for some group choices.

Alongside this consideration of who to involve, **review the participants in terms of their personalities and dispositions to strategy making**. A useful checklist is to consider the potential participants through reviewing them against the following characteristics.

- Anticipated winners – those who believe that they will benefit from the outcomes of the forum and therefore will be supportive.
- Anticipated losers – those who believe that they will not benefit from the outcomes of the forum and therefore will seek to rubbish the forum and its outcomes.
- Saboteurs – similar to anticipated losers, these participants aim to ensure that the outcomes of the forum do not succeed and may use subtle but powerful means of undermining the event.
- Cynics – these participants have been involved in numerous strategy making exercises, have seen little or nothing change, and therefore are sceptical. However, if they can be persuaded of the usefulness of the activity then they can be powerful supporters.
- Ideas generator – similar to Belbin's 'plant'[6] – people who are creative and can generate creative options. They can, however, be difficult to manage as it is hard to keep them focused on the task at hand and to listen and attend to the views of others.
- Opinion formers – those participants whose views are taken seriously by others and therefore carry more weight.
- Fence-sitters – those who will watch, wait and see and will follow the prevailing direction.

Box 11.2   Choosing a Team

Example 1: You are the manager of a computer services department – a department that supplies a service to a large organisation with sites all around Europe. You may have some access to the senior management team of the whole organisation, to the extent that you report to one of the vice presidents. However, your ability to influence the senior management team with respect to their strategy making for the whole organisation is negligible. Your input to the strategic thinking of the whole organisation does not go beyond expressing a specialist view – you are a source of specialist information. You are also aware that there remains a continuing risk that the main organisation may choose to outsource computer services. As a services department, you put a strategy on paper a couple of years ago, and the senior management team accepted it.

In this case, we would expect you to take on the challenge of using strategy making as the basis for developing, reviewing and renewing a strategy for the computer services department. The strategy you develop may, or may not, replace your published strategy. At this stage your strategy making is designed to secure the strategic future of your department. We would not expect you to use this book to stimulate you facilitating the senior management team in their development of strategy.

Here, you are both facilitator of the strategy making and client. This dual role for yourself is likely to be problematic.

Example 2: You are a member of staff in a sales office consisting of eleven others including your local manager. You have reasonable access to your manager and are well regarded by most of your colleagues. Your colleagues know that you are undertaking studies in the field of business and management. Although you have met the sales manager to whom your manager reports, you are not well placed to persuade her that you could help her undertake strategy making for the whole of the sales team.

In this case, we would expect you to take on the challenge of developing and delivering a strategy for your sales office. Your client is likely to be your own manager. The manager has never thought about developing a strategy for her small team before, and is likely to resist the need for it. It is unlikely that you will be able to demand that the work is undertaken; rather you will need to work towards small gains in commitment to thinking about strategy. Your reasonable expectations are to gradually develop an enthusiasm and involvement in strategy making.

If working as an external facilitator, **ask the manager-client to provide you with brief outlines – 'pen portraits' – with respect to the above dispositions** as these can help in designing and managing the forum. However, **keep these safe!** While bringing them to the forum may seem a good idea so they are easily available as a reminder, if they were to be seen by any of the participants the forum's potential for success would likely be severely impaired.

Alongside choosing who to include, allocate time to **draft an invitation ('calling note') to the forum**. This invitation sets out, in broad terms, the objective(s) of the forum and what will take place, along with information on where and when the event will occur. While the aim is to **reassure those attending by providing some clarity with regards to the objectives,** it is worth avoiding providing too much detail in order to avoid participants spending a considerable amount of time reflecting in advance of the forum and thus developing firm (and potentially fixed) views.

GETTING THE ENVIRONMENT RIGHT

Choosing where to hold the forum is important, more important than is often initially conceived.[7] One option is to **find somewhere that is away from the day to day working** as this will encourage participants to view the forum as something that is different from the discussion of urgent operational issues and thus help engender a different focus and thinking. Additionally, it will send a clear signal (particularly if the forum is being carried out off site) that this activity is being taken seriously. Holding the forum away from the routine operation of the organisation will also discourage participants from returning to their offices and thus breaking the thinking/negotiation taking place. However, beware of the 'away-day' syndrome[8] where disengagement from the usual can lead to disengagement from the agreements made at a forum.

While the forums noted in this book don't demand any extravagant requirements, there are a couple of factors that are worth attending to and are rarely taken seriously. For example, **find chairs that are comfortable (but not too comfortable) so that participants are not distracted by physical discomfort**. If possible, choose chairs that are on casters as these allow participants to move their seats around in relation to other participants and may promote and change the dynamics within the group. Where possible, **remove tables or put them to one side** as this will help flexibility of seating arrangements. **Arrange the chairs initially into a semicircle to ensure all participants can easily see one another – even if tables are used**. Also, try and ensure that all chairs and other physical artefacts are the same in order to equalise impressions of power (some group leaders always try to take up a physical position that makes it difficult for others to participate effectively).

The most demanding requirement is to ensure satisfactory projection of the output from the modelling software (Decision Explorer®). A key recommendation is to **use a high quality projector (for example minimum of 1024×1400 pixels if possible and with high luminosity)**. This is to ensure that participants are easily able to view the material being projected and not have to strain their eyes. Where possible **choose a room that has natural daylight** as this is less tiring on eyes – but this requirement needs to be balanced with the brightness of the projector. In addition to this, **ensure there is a laptop with Decision Explorer® already loaded and set to work at the high resolution of the projector**. This will allow the contributions to be captured, and edited along with the relationships. It may be helpful to **ensure that an external mouse is used** as this makes operation of the software easier. Also **make sure of having a good screen** as this too will help participants read the material easily. As one of the key benefits from the forum is to facilitate social and psychological negotiation, being able to see all the contributions (without necessarily remembering who said them) allows for participants to change their mind without penalty and also be able to listen and absorb views more effectively and even asynchronously. Finally, if possible **make sure that there is a fast colour printer available** as providing participants with regular printouts of their work can be motivating. Furthermore, by generating in-progress products this reduces the possibility that the 'minutes' of the forum are less likely to be distorted after the event – in effect minutes are being produced in real-time. See Figure 11.2 for an example of room layout.

As a last task, **make arrangements for refreshments**. Where a forum starts in the morning, having coffee and tea available before commencing the forum can help participants relax by

Public screen

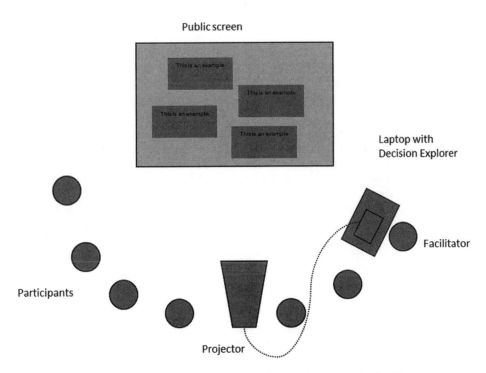

Laptop with
Decision Explorer

Facilitator

Participants

Projector

Figure 11.2   An Example of a Room Set Up with Six Participants, the Facilitator, a Laptop with Decision Explorer® Loaded and the Projector

chatting over a drink. Taking time out mid-forum can also allow a mental and physical break and supply the facilitator/manager-client with an opportunity for catching breath and preparing for the next part of the forum.

It has been argued that any form of meeting should comprise three stages: (1) an introduction, (2) the main body comprising the tasks/activities, and (3) time for closure.[9] Another tip is to ensure that both the facilitator and the manager-client **arrive early so as to get set up, check for any potential problems and confirm refreshments**. If using an unfamiliar room, it will be important to find the time to **check it meets the requirements noted above**. In particular, if using a hotel conference facility check that the layout is as required – conference facility managers are used to providing a boardroom layout, not the more unusual setup required for a strategy forum (a perfect setup the night before can often be rejigged by a new porter first thing in the morning!).

GETTING STARTED: INTRODUCING THE FORUM

Typically it is worth starting the forum by getting the manager-client to **provide a welcome to participants, thank them for their attendance and provide a brief introduction to the purpose of the forum**. If an external facilitator is being used (not the manager-client themselves) then

request that the manager-client introduces her or him to the group as this helps to justify their presence (see box 11.3).

Box 11.3   A Possible Script Introducing the Forum

'Good morning and welcome to the forum on xx, thank you for coming.

Today is an opportunity for us to take time out from our day to day concerns and to consider our strategic future – building together a direction. I hope we can make this forum an enjoyable and productive session. I know I am looking forward to both contributing and seeing what others have to say today.

Please do see this as an opportunity to voice your views – it is important that we make sure that the resultant direction is one that addresses all of our concerns and is something we all feel proud of.

I have asked xx to facilitate this forum and will now hand over to him/her to explain how the forum is going to unfold.'

It is also important to **put participants at ease**. This is because there may be some concern about how they should be expected to behave in what may be a new environment, what will be required from them, etc. – particularly as they will see the laptop computer and projector. While it is recognised that those in senior management teams have been exposed to a considerable amount of strategy making, the different nature of the forums noted in this book demand a different way of working (for example, using computer-based group support – the Decision Explorer® software) and thus participants may feel a little anxious.

Although all of the forums do use Decision Explorer®, at the beginning it is important to **acknowledge that there is computer support being used**, but without going into very much detail regarding exactly how the software works (as this will become transparent to participants as the different tasks are embarked upon) – see box 11.4 for a possible script.

Box 11.4   A Possible Script Introducing
the Software and Technology

'As you can see we will be using some computer technology to assist us in today's forum. It is here to help us capture and explore not only the different points of view, but also how these views relate to one another. By using the software we can make sure that all of your contributions are captured (rather than getting lost in the ether) and do so in a way that allows us to explore the diversity of views and get a big picture, rather than feel we have to work on chunks'.

Go through an un-timed agenda (possibly written up earlier on a flip-chart) so as to **provide an introduction to the tasks that will take place during the forum**[10] – but do so in very general terms (and let the detail of the tasks become clearer as each is embarked upon). Providing only a brief explanation to the tasks focusing more on the what and why (rather than the how) will enable participants to gain a degree of clarity regarding what will be covered without getting too concerned about the actual mechanics. While it is important to provide some indication of the finish time, **don't make public any timing for the tasks or breaks**. Avoiding presenting timings means that breaks can be, and typically are, taken contingently (for example, when a task has been completed and a product is evident). However, do **stick to the final finish time**. It can be very hard for participants, particularly when there are senior people involved in the forum, to reject a proposal for an extension to the forum's completion time – regardless of the fact that they have made prior engagements which are going to be affected. Instead, these participants might well remain in the forum as unwilling participants generating an unproductive atmosphere and potentially threatening all the good work already carried out.

Another part of an introduction that can aid the forum's smooth running is to **provide some ground rules for behaviour**.[11] For example, **ask participants to turn off their mobile phones** as this will allow all to concentrate on the task being addressed without interruption to themselves or others. While it is recognised that in many instances managers feel the need to keep in touch with their office, trying to keep this to a minimum (that is in the breaks) will help with achieving the aims of the forum and allow others to focus attention.

In addition, encourage participants to appreciate and value one another's contributions. Ensure participants **recognise that there will be differences in views, expertise, and experience and that these need to be sought and duly considered**. Participants, particularly the quieter ones, will feel more able to contribute their different points of view. Diversity, particularly at the beginning of the forum, is to be valued.

Carry out the introduction in a gentle, relaxed manner. Speaking slowly and quietly will not only settle participants but also provide an air of competence and confidence (for both yourself and the group). Sometimes settling the group can be facilitated by sitting down during the introduction – reducing the impression of 'conducting' the group.

MANAGING THE PARTICIPANTS

As noted above, in all four of the forums the process typically starts by seeking contributions from participants and it is important that this is as productive and comprehensive as possible. One way of doing this is to **regularly carry out round robins** (where each participant's view is sought in turn). However, do recognise that there will be times when participants genuinely have nothing to add to the discussion (perhaps because it is on a topic they know less about) and therefore must be comfortable in not offering any views. The important objective is to give them the chance to have their say. Continuously returning to a repeat of the ground rules can help legitimise this activity. As the views are surfaced **capture them using the software** (see below and also the Appendix: Using Causal Mapping Software: Decision Explorer®).

When working to elicit and then structure views from participants, as a facilitator, try to continuously **use language that is encouraging and non-judgemental** (see box 11.5). This is because by phrasing questions in a manner that allows for contradiction and change, participants are more able to change their mind – the equivocality (fuzziness) aids the negotiation process (see chapter 2 regarding face saving for more detail). Recognise that at times the role of the facilitator can feel like that of an umpire where you are working to ensure everyone has a chance to be heard and fair play – procedural justice – is seen and appreciated.

Box 11.5 Sample Scripts Illustrating Encouraging, and Non-judgemental, Language

'Can I just check that I have captured what you said accurately.'

'If I understood something said earlier … one of the main topics was ….'

'Could we just do a quick check using a round robin that we have captured all the material relating to xx – if all your views have already been captured, that is great.'

Alongside this use of gentle phrasing to encourage contribution and change, **check that all of the contributions have been captured so that ownership is maintained**. Using the participants' own language (while following the conventions set in the forum) will not only increase ownership but also will ensure that the diversity of views is represented. This is particularly important if the facilitator is the manager-client.

Watch for non-verbal forms of communication. These might be participants continuously trying, and failing, to get their contributions heard (evidenced through getting ready to speak but not finding the opportunity). Alternatively these might also illustrate when participants have finished with the task (some participants will finish earlier than others and will therefore sit back). Remember that two-thirds of communication is through non-verbal behaviours, and so simply recording what is said may miss what was meant – a good facilitator will seek to record what was meant rather than precisely what is said. Expressions of puzzlement (such as frowning) might suggest that the participant does not understand the task being undertaken and/or the material being surfaced (see box 11.6).

Box 11.6 Watching for Non-verbals

A middle management team were surfacing issues facing their organisation as part of an issue management forum. One of the contributions concerned a particular technical consideration – something that judging from the quizzical looks on a number of participants' faces was not well understood. The facilitator wasn't sure she understood it either! She therefore asked the participant who had raised the issue if they would mind – for her benefit – explaining the issue in a little more detail. The participant was happy to oblige and soon it was clear to the whole group exactly what the issue entailed. In the break, however, two of the participants independently came up to her and thanked her for doing this – they had never really understood the issue but now, due to her request, they did!

Carefully manage those participants that are apparently being difficult. This behaviour might entail participants making comments that continuously contradict those being made by others. It might be participants who don't believe that the direction being taken is the appropriate one and vociferously comment on this. **Try to find out what the problem**

might be (perhaps using a coffee break to create the opportunity) as this might provide clues as to how best to manage the situation. Another approach is to **ensure that their views are captured and captured publicly** (see box 3.5) as this allows the participant to move on from their frustrations. However, it is important that in the situations where, despite efforts being made to support the participant, no improvement to their behaviour is made that the problem participant is to some extent ignored allowing others to progress. There is the real danger that the forum can be derailed by the objections of a single participant. It may be helpful to engage with the manager-client before isolating a problem participant as there may be other considerations to take into account (for example, extenuating circumstances, power bases, etc.).

KEEPING THE GROUP ON TRACK

Throughout the forum, it is important to build in time to **review progress**. This tends to work best if done on an approximate 20 to 25 minute cycle – that is opening up the forum for the generation of contributions (allowing divergence) and then exploring what has been surfaced and checking understanding of that material (convergence). As in all of the forums, there are a number of tasks that work on an approximate 25 minute cycle time. The overall process can be helped by the facilitator frequently reminding the group of the nature of the task they are working on, how it fits into the overall direction, and commenting on the progress at the end of each cycle . The facilitator's view of progress can help participants gain a sense of being in joint control. A sense of progress within the overall plan helps participants work with the unfolding complexity and absorb the material being generated. As a part of the reviews, **regularly reward the group by highlighting the milestones they have achieved**. These milestones might be the completion of a number of tasks and deliverables, the generation of material, negotiating agreements, etc. A good way of showing the delivery of a milestone is to **provide participants with a printout of the work they have done to date**.

In addition, in all of the forums there are particular conventions regarding the generation and capture of material. Continually **remind participants of the conventions for working successfully with their views** – particularly at the beginning of the forum. Explain to participants that the computer software acts as a means of not only capturing the contributions but also supporting their analysis of the material, keeping 'minutes', allowing continual changes as their views develop, and signalling agreements. As such it acts as a 'transitional object', allowing the views of each to be explored alongside one another, allowing changes to be made (to help comprehension) in real time, and allowing the unfolding map to shift from a set of individual views to a view held by the group.

It can be helpful to put time aside periodically to **'check the pulse' of the group**. This might be carried out by simply asking the group whether the progress and direction being taken makes sense to them. Alternatively it might take the form of assessing the level of ownership and commitment participants have to emerging directions – particularly towards the completion of the forum. Consider whether it is worth spending some time asking the participants to **rate or rank the particular options already captured in order to establish a rough measure of the degree of consensus**. This could be done by printing off a list or picture of the work undertaken and asking participants to note which of the contributions they would rate or rank as most important/urgent/easy-to-deliver (etc.) – perhaps over a coffee break.

PROVIDING GROUP SUPPORT USING THE SOFTWARE[12]

While more in-depth information regarding the use of the software Decision Explorer® is given in the appendix to the book, when facilitating using the software the following hints will help:

- **Set up styles (categories) in advance of the forum**. This avoids having to create them in front of the participants, potentially distracting the group and wasting valuable time. **Use fonts such as Times Roman and Arial** when projecting onto a screen as they are the easiest to read. It is also recommended that borders (in styles) are not used as they take up screen room and therefore reduce the amount of material that can be easily viewed. Also it is more difficult to use effectively the selection of statement command – the selection box becomes confused with the border box. (They are, however, very useful for distinguishing different categories when printing off final maps using black and white printers.)
- **Capture all of the contributions being made** – using and encouraging participants to use the 'formalisms'/rules appropriate for a particular forum. Recognise that when using Decision Explorer® there may be difficulty in keeping up with the rate at which participants are making contributions – particularly if working with a large group. Carrying out round robins can help as they limit the amount of material being generated at any one time. Appreciate that the group will be aware that it is important to get the statements captured and that it takes time to type them in and will therefore be willing to wait until they are captured. That said, on topics where there is considerable emotion, and therefore possibly a lot of material being generated at the same time, regularly review progress and encourage participants to declare missed contributions.
- **Avoid moving statements around the screen too much or too quickly**. There is an inherent desire to make the picture as tidy as possible and so to continually reposition statements. However, not moving statements around too much is important as it is very distracting for participants. Participants manage the complexity of the unfolding picture by remembering where statements are located on the screen. **Use the views (tabs) to manage the amount of material the group is working on**. As with avoiding the temptation of moving statements around as a means of managing the growing complexity, using views to focus on particular themes or clusters can help participants navigate the material. (There are 32 views available and each of these can be labelled, as with an Excel Spreadsheet, for easy reference.)
- **Move statements into bundles (themes) where appropriate**. In a number of the forums this is a designated task, but where this is not mentioned it can be helpful to cluster contributions according to their content. This helps participants manage the complexity of the content generated.
- **Create the links in front of the group explaining carefully their meaning**. Typically the linking formalisms are easily understood and adopted by groups; however, when capturing the first few links it is worth spending time explaining their meaning. This helps participants appreciate that they represent causality and not chronology.
- **Use refreshment breaks to tidy up the material and experiment with analysis prior to undertaking analysis with the group**. This recommendation corresponds with the advice provided about not moving statements around too much. Using the break to produce a tidied version (preferably on a different view) can help manage the complexity of the unfolding picture while also retaining an original and recognisable picture.

PROVIDING CLOSURE

This is probably the part of a forum that is most often neglected as time is tight and there is a real temptation to keep working on the data until the posted end time. However, it has been found by many experienced facilitators to be a crucial part of the forum – spending time reflecting on what has been achieved, what is to happen next, and checking participants' comfort with the resultant products and agreements will pay dividends.

Therefore **build in at least 15 minutes to enable a period of closure to the forum**. During this period review the tasks undertaken (going back to the original agenda), the progress made (possibly noting the number of contributions, reviewing each map/tab, etc.), and provide participants with printed copies of the final material. This last action can be very helpful as it provides participants with a tangible artefact from the forum and something to refer to at a later date. As noted above, **do not run the forum past the published completion time unless you are really sure everyone is comfortable with this**.

When there is time, consider whether it is possible to **draft a first version of the statement of strategic intent** as these statements are an integral part of all four of the forums and are best done with the group (for ownership) at the time (while it is clear in participants' minds what has been covered). **Provide printed copies of this document**.

Finally **discuss what might be the next steps following on from the forum**. This might include deciding who is going to refine the statement of strategic intent should that be considered desirable; who will take responsibility for the agreed actions (where appropriate); and also agreeing what is going to be said to others who might be curious about outcomes. This latter step is important as it ensures that a consistent representation is provided to others avoiding the risk of different perceptions being gained and worries unfolding.[13]

Finally, regardless of whether an external facilitator or the manager-client is running the forum, **thank the group for their time and effort**.

NOTES

1 For good overviews of facilitation of groups see Ackermann (1996); Phillips and Phillips (1993) and also Schwarz (1994, 2002).

2 For a discussion on role ambiguity in terms of the potential lack of clarity experienced – both in terms of the manager-client's role (participant or facilitator) and also how participants 'should' behave see McGrath (1984).

3 A round robin is an important tool for reinforcing procedural justice (see chapter 2) and involves each participant making one contribution in turn, and then a second in turn, and so on. The process is designed to ensure everyone has their full say, can anticipate when they will be given airtime to say it, and so can devote time to listening to what others say rather than fighting for airtime. The round robin process will be an important process to be used in each of the four forums.

4 For a good discussion on the advantages and disadvantages of participative methods of working when working with clients see Eden and Ackermann (1998).

5 For a range of different views on considering who to involve in a strategy making team see Ackermann and Eden with Brown (2005); Eden and Ackermann (2004); Mason and Mitroff (1981).

6 Belbin's team roles, Belbin (1981).

7 See Hickling (1990), and also Huxham (1990) on the 'trivialities' of group support.

8 More information on strategy workshops can be found in Hodgkinson, Whittington, Johnson and Schwarz (2006).

9 For more information on addressing the three stages of a facilitated group meeting see Ackermann (1996); Bostrom, Anson and Clawson (1993); and McFadzean and Nelson (1998).

10 For further information regarding the role and importance of producing and using an agenda see Friend and Hickling (1987).
11 A good discussion on ground rules can be found in Schein (1988).
12 For further information on the use of group support systems when working with groups see Ackermann and Eden (1997); Clawson, Bostrom and Anson (1993); McGoff and Ambrose (1991); Nunamaker, Dennis, Valacich and Vogel (1991); and Vogel, Nunamaker, Martz, Grohowski and McGoff (1990).
13 Getting the end of the workshop right is critical – for further discussion see Friedman (1989).

Further Reading

Eden, C. and Ackermann, F. 1998. *Making Strategy: The Journey of Strategic Management.* London: Sage, chapter P5.
Schwarz, R. M. 2002. *The Skilled Facilitator: A Comprehensive Resource for Consultants, Facilitators, Managers, Trainers and Coaches.* San Francisco: Jossey-Bass.

12

THE CONTINUATION AND CLOSURE OF THE STRATEGY MAKING JOURNEY

Fran Ackermann and Colin Eden

INTRODUCTION

The introduction to this book stated that one of our objectives was to provide the designs for four facilitated strategic conversations – designs that are *bite-sized*, and *accessible* to anyone wanting either to carry out a strategy making journey or to teach strategic management. It was suggested that these designs would be applicable to small owner-operated firms as well as large multinational organisations, to senior management teams as well as middle management teams, and could be carried out by managers themselves as well as by internal facilitators or external consultants.

As well as being stand-alone strategic conversations with clear deliverables each of the forums is designed to be undertaken in as little as three hours. Providing strategy making forums that can be completed in half a day seeks to increase the likelihood of use as such timing recognises the practical challenges of getting a management team together. Each forum is expected to provide valuable outcomes, with respect to content (what needs to be done) and also process (building commitment). Each forum, in its own right, can provide a *robust strategy*, and the strategy will be something that people *want to implement* and can be immediately acted upon. However, we also note in the introduction that these separate forums when integrated (either in pairs, triplets or all four) can lead to an *increasingly robust and coherent strategy*.

The book also sets out to reinforce the belief that developing strategy *with groups*, rather than on behalf of groups, is a key element in the pursuit of creating implementable strategy – as such strategy making takes into account social processes as well as analysis. Thus, we have included one chapter on group process (chapter 2) and another on facilitation (chapter 11), but additionally, for each of the forums we have provided a chapter that explicitly discusses in detail how to carry out the forum. The academic credibility of these practical chapters is provided through the inclusion of an associated chapter that addresses the conceptual and/or theoretical elements underpinning the design. Thus readers can explore not only how to carry out the forum, but also what theories, concepts and assumptions underpin it.

There are three further aspects of strategy making. These will be explored in more depth below. The first is exactly why and how the forums should be integrated. This consideration goes beyond the possible 'next steps' sections discussed at the end of each of the theory chapters and comprises the next section of this chapter. The second consideration concerns what might be missing even if all forums were undertaken – in essence how could the strategy's robustness be further increased? However, it is important to note that it is not the aim of this section to address everything that could be done to increase the robustness of any strategies developed. Instead, this section addresses activities and analyses that we have found, in our practice, to be of significant use to strategy making groups and which complement the four forums. The final consideration relates to some of the implementation issues beyond those considered in the group processes chapter (chapter 2). This section on implementation issues is divided into two. The first part of the section presents a discussion relating to the impact of systems (for example, costing and transfer pricing systems) upon strategy delivery. The second part of the section presents material relating to monitoring and controlling implementation: identifying performance indicators, deciding when to stop the strategy making process, and agreeing closure and monitoring progress.

INTEGRATION: COMBINING THE FORUMS – EXTENDING ROBUSTNESS AND COHERENCE

While each of the strategy forums produces, in its own right, a statement of strategic intent that the management team will want to implement, an obvious way of combining the forums is to link the SSIs into a single document. However, as it is the material that underpins the SSIs that is more important, increased robustness will come from the linking together of this material (integrating the causal maps from the different forums). Working at this lower level of detail not surprisingly demands more work than simply forming one SSI from several SSIs. However, it is in our opinion, a worthwhile activity. The order, and the particular combinations, of the forums are determined by the particular demands facing the management team. However, there is an ideal logic (scheme) that might be considered when there is an *a priori* agreement to undertake all four forums. Prioritising strategic issues naturally leads to exploring purpose and stakeholder reactions to implementing priorities. Exploring competitive advantage leads to exploitation of advantage with respect to purpose and so naturally leads to questions about purpose. Figure 12.1 shows this scheme for the ordering of the forums.

That said, often forums are undertaken necessarily without an overall plan. It may be that the management team decide to augment their initial strategy making by undertaking a second of the forums, and then a third, in an incremental pattern (implied by the discussions about next steps at the end of each theory chapter). The decision to do more than one forum is often not taken early on but can depend on the team's view at the end of a forum of the benefits of undertaking more. In figure 12.2 we present the interactive logic that links the forums and so show how the different forums might be combined.

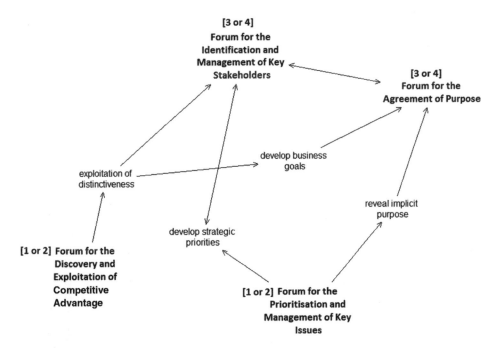

Figure 12.1   The 'Ideal Logic' Ordering of the Forums

Combining the Strategy as the Prioritisation and Management of Key Issues Forum with Other Forums

As we noted above (and see in figure 12.2) one obvious form of integration comprises combining how to prioritise and manage key strategic issues (chapters 3 and 4) with the forum on
strategy as purpose (chapters 5 and 6). In the process of surfacing and prioritising strategic
issues the team is very likely to reveal some emergent goals (an issue will only be an issue if
it attacks or supports a goal or negative goal). These emergent goals can provide a good starting
point for the strategy as purpose forum as they can be evaluated with respect to the view the
team have of their aspirations for the future. However, strategic issues and thus emergent
goals are often based on the past, and so need to be revisited with respect to developing a
more idealised strategic future. Moreover, as the emergent goals system is modified through
the strategy as purpose forum, the team should re-evaluate the strategic issues network as the
new goals are likely to subtly but significantly shift priorities. This interaction between the
prioritisation of strategic issues and the development of the goals system continues until
agreement is reached. Agreement demands that the strategy making team are clear that they
have a realistic and distinctive goals system, and have been able to prioritise strategic issues
based upon their interaction with each other and, most importantly, based upon their impact
on goals.

Likewise, when undertaking the forum detailing how to prioritise and manage key strategic issues (chapters 3 and 4), the surfacing of issues might reveal key stakeholders who
need to be attended to because they are causing the issues (for example, a competitor has

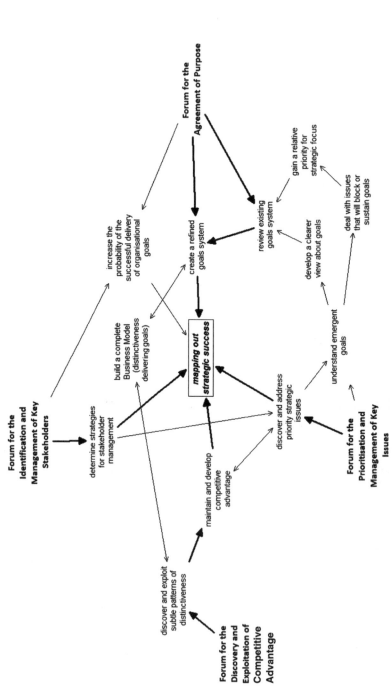

Figure 12.2 The 'Interactive Logic' that Links the Forums. The four forums are identified using bold text with the overall objective in bold italic (successful strategic future). The thick links illustrate how the forums on their own contribute to mapping out strategic success with the thin links illustrating how combining forums can increase the robustness

just launched a new product). As such, this 'starter pack' of stakeholders that arise within issue statements will help group members quickly get started when embarking upon a forum on how to strategically manage stakeholders (chapters 9 and 10). However, as with the combining of the issues and goals forums, linking issues with stakeholder management is also cyclical. Through examining stakeholders and determining strategies for their management the priority strategic issues might need to be reviewed. New issues might emerge that need to be taken account of, as well as other issues potentially being downgraded. As with all combinations of forums, it is also possible, although less logical, when undertaking this pair of forums, to start from the stakeholder forum and as a result of this consideration discover a wider range of issues concentrating not only on those that are stakeholder based.

The issue management forum, due to its tendency to focus on areas of concern, may limit group members' appreciation of some of the positive aspects or abilities within the organisation as managers get caught up with the negative demands of future pressures. As such, following the issue management forum with the forum concentrating on competitive advantage is likely to provide group members with a more upbeat sense of the potential for strategic success. Taking the reverse scheduling, candidate distinctive competences and competence outcomes can be viewed against the realities that are raised in the issue management forum. It is not untypical to discover that a distinctive competence outcome – for example, concerning 'excellent reputation for high quality service' – is in serious jeopardy as one of the issues surfaced relates to 'falling service level quality'. This apparent contradiction needs to be highlighted and discussed. Often in these circumstances the statements are not contradictory; rather, the potential for distinctiveness has been identified but is currently weak. Therefore, by identifying a significant strategic priority for redevelopment, the extent of distinctiveness might be reinforced. As with the links between the goals and issues, considering together both issues and competences increases the robustness of the strategy, particularly when cycling between them.

Exploring Purpose and Competitive Advantage

Moving from the agreement of purpose forum to the forum for the discovery and exploitation of competitive advantage provides another means of increasing robustness. Starting with an agreement of purpose forum allows the group to determine an agreed goals system. This can be used as a powerful means of assessing the distinctiveness of assets, competences and outcomes. For example, if the goal is 'be the best XYZ in Europe' then having a competence that is distinctive in relation to this aspiration is more difficult than 'be the best XYZ in Bruges'. This can be very helpful when group members are struggling to determine distinctiveness because the goals system provides an initial benchmark. However, an agreed goals system can also be constraining on the exploitation of distinctiveness because it can discourage the development of new business (and so new business goals). Where distinctive competences (individually or in patterns) and distinctive competence outcomes support the realisation of at least one goal then the rationale for their exploitation becomes clearer. As with the other pair combinations, cycling between the outputs of these two forums will help refine the goals system and also assist in discovering and exploiting subtle patterns of distinctiveness. The two forums, taken together, help maintain and develop competitive advantage and also introduce possible new business opportunities.[1]

Other Powerful Forum Combinations

Figure 12.3 shows three other powerful combinations where robustness is increased. These are: exploring purpose alongside stakeholder management, exploring stakeholder management alongside exploiting distinctiveness, and developing the business model.

Exploring Purpose and Stakeholder Management

Combining the forum for the agreement of purpose with that concentrating on the identification and management of stakeholders can provide useful insights about which stakeholders to focus attention on. For example, when an agreement of purpose forum has revealed a goals system this can act as a useful focal point when considering the importance of stakeholders through their position on the power–interest grid. Some goals will be of more interest than others, and some stakeholders will have more power than others to support or sabotage the achievement of the goals.

In addition, the impact of considering stakeholder management is the determination of whether the goals system can be made more aspirational or needs some adaptation. This is achieved through reviewing the stakeholder responses (potential or realised) to assess the viability of the goals; for example, it may be that aspiring towards a particular future might cause sufficient stakeholder backlash that the organisation is at risk.

Exploring Stakeholders and Competitive Advantage

The focus on stakeholders helps refine an appreciation of competitive advantage as competences and competence outcomes, particularly those that are distinctive, are assessed against those held by others – for example the competition – and a finer appreciation of distinctiveness is acquired. Additionally, the strategic management of stakeholders can be an aspect of competitive advantage – managing and exploiting stakeholders through an ability to manage and grow coalitions of support may be a distinctive competence.

Developing and Exploring the Business Model

Possibly the most significant integration of forums is recognising that developing a business model can itself contribute to mapping out strategic success. The process of linking competitive advantage to purpose – the business model – can ensure that the goals system is realistic and the distinctiveness exploited. Additionally, the business model development can reveal which competences are particularly significant, are core to the strategic success, and so are core competences, or preferably core distinctive competences. Essentially what this means is that those distinctive competences that support a number of goals are central or core to the overall network of competences and goals and thus provide a more indisputable sense of a core (distinctive) competence.[2]

The building of the business model also enables the explicit consideration of how competences and competence outcomes support the goals and thus avoids the goals from the risk of being perceived as unattainable. It also reveals whether the goals are aspirational enough – for example, where a goal is supported by a number of distinctive competences

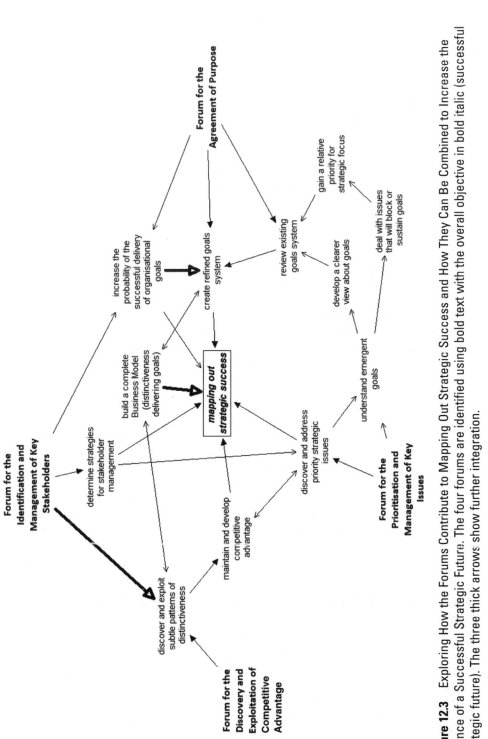

Figure 12.3 Exploring How the Forums Contribute to Mapping Out Strategic Success and How They Can Be Combined to Increase the Chance of a Successful Strategic Future. The four forums are identified using bold text with the overall objective in bold italic (successful strategic future). The three thick arrows show further integration.

its scope can be extended. As a result the business model attaining strategic success should be coherent and internally consistent. The development of the business model will follow the logic:

> 'I aspire to . . .'
> 'I have competences to do so which are distinctive to me.'
> 'They match my aspirations.'
> 'Or, if they don't, I will develop distinctiveness, or modify my aspirations.'
> 'I am assured that there is someone who will: (for commercial organisations) buy my product or service because I provide customer value; (for public or not-for-profit organisations) legitimise my aspirations by providing a mandate and finance.'
> 'This support will provide a continuing surplus or profit, or my right to sustain a continuing livelihood.'

Thus the business model highlights where sustenance, protection and development of existing patterns of core distinctive competences should be focused and will most likely change strategic priorities in general. It may also reveal where continual sustenance is required for the operational requirements of marketing, sales, production and the facilitative demands of management accounting, and HR (sustenance of core threshold competences). It will also have revealed those competences and distinctive competences that are no longer important for the future of the organisation. Competences which don't support the goals may be judged to be unimportant and thus may no longer need sustenance, releasing energy and resources – sometimes whole departments may be released or outsourced. This release of energy provides important strategic slack[3] that enables new strategies to be delivered effectively. However, this downgrading of a competence does need to be done carefully – paying attention to both its consequences (links) within the overall model and the emotional attachment (particularly if the competence was significant in the growth of the organisation). In addition there is a danger that threshold competences might be lost (see figure 7.3 for ways of thinking about outsourcing).

Finally, as a means of exploring in further depth and testing out the robustness, the business model can also act as the structure for a computer simulation (for example, System Dynamics[4] or using Discrete Event simulation methods)[5] enabling the simulation model to show numerically graphs of behaviour over time of how the causal relationships will work over a strategic future. This can be extremely useful where a dip in performance might be experienced before the benefits accrued (the so-called 'J-curve').[6]

WHAT ELSE IS MISSING? HOW CAN ROBUSTNESS BE INCREASED FURTHER?

There are a large number of further analyses that can be carried out to refine the statements of strategic success (there are large compendiums articulating a wealth of different means of assessing market positions, competitive positions, product portfolios, etc.).[7] However, we have found some activities to be particularly helpful in assisting management teams in increasing the robustness of their strategy: (1) the development of action programmes, (2) considering alternative futures, (3) undertaking a quick 'resource' check.

Development of *Action Programmes*

For all of the strategy forums presented in this book (alone or in combination), spending some time laddering down to actions and so creating action programmes that support strategies can be essential to the implementation of strategy.[8] This laddering down activity requires taking each of the strategies identified (whether it is a stakeholder management strategy, a strategy for protecting/growing a distinctive competence, or a strategy for managing a prioritised strategic issue) and discussing the means by which this might be achieved – the means-ends causality shown by arrows on a causal map. The laddering down activity therefore extends the causal map by providing a further level of action-oriented detail.[9]

Each of the forums will have surfaced a range of detailed options that will have been recorded as part of a causal map, and so there will be candidate actions and their implications among the material already recorded. These represent a good starting point because they are psychological links to previously conducted forums. Recall that in the introduction we argued for operations and strategy to be integrated and laddering down is a mechanism directed towards the achievement of this proposition.

Once the management team has considered each of the strategies in turn, exploring potential synergies can help ensure that an efficient as well as effective set of options is generated. For example, if a particular action, maybe with a little adaptation, could also support other strategies and goals then this increases its potency and attractiveness as an effective strategy. It is important, at all times, to work with the causal maps (rather than lists) as this ensures that the action possibility is always explored in relation to the strategies and goals it is aiming to support (that is, its causality).

One of the most likely reasons for a lack of appropriate implementation of strategy arises from *actions being agreed and implemented but for the wrong reasons* – the causal link has been forgotten or ignored, so developing a 'tick-box' mentality. Taking action is not an end in itself, *actions are designed to cause change and so deliver strategies*, which in turn deliver goals.[10]

Considering Alternative Futures – 'Wind-tunnelling' Strategy

Some acknowledgement of the external world will have been undertaken during all of the forums. Considering strategy as the prioritisation and management of key strategic issues will always raise issues that derive from the external world – shock events, trends reaching critical stages, etc. Through the identification and management of key stakeholders, alternative futures will have been invaluable in the assessment of action possibilities and strategy viability. The possible behaviours of competitors will have been considered as a part of evaluating distinctiveness during the competitive advantage forum.

A focus on further exploring alternative futures – alternative scenarios – will help the management team consider the impact of different futures and assess ('wind tunnel') the strategies against these futures. The future cannot be forecast with a high enough degree of certainty for precise strategic plans to be constructed that are guaranteed to succeed. A management team needs, therefore, to understand the structure and character of possible futures rather than predict them. By understanding the nature of multiple possible futures, the team will be in a position to act thoughtfully, within a strategy framework, as the external world unfolds. More importantly, it may be able to do so faster than its competitors,[11] or fast enough to avert disasters, or fast enough to lever aspirations more efficiently. An organisation that is able to change its strategy, within the context of a strategic framework of intent, in response to changes in the environment, tends to outperform those that do not (and research supports this view).[12] Thus explicitly and carefully exploring alternative futures is an important part of strategy making.

Strategy is about managing and controlling the future, and so forecasting based on trend projection, where the future is a function of time rather than events, is not overly relevant in strategy making. The future is a function of events – external events and events created through strategic action. Thus, the future is subject to a stream of possible events rather than trends (although trends reach critical stages where events must follow). Considering alternative futures must therefore be about exploring streams of critical events, and these are often 'flip-flops' where the future bifurcates. As individuals, most people's lives are significantly influenced not by trends but by key events, and so it can be for organisations.

In recent years the approach to scenario planning originally developed and implemented by Shell[13] has gained popularity, albeit often in adapted forms. The Shell approach is all encompassing and expected to be the driver for strategy development, rather than just an important part of strategy making. It is our view that strategy should not be driven by the external world, rather it should be informed by it. A part of the pay-off from good strategy making is increasing the degree of control and management of the future – becoming proactive rather than reactive.

The Shell approach is highly qualitative and depends upon extensive interviewing and workshops. It is, therefore, often considered to be too sophisticated and expensive for many organisational settings. The principles of exploring alternative futures are, nevertheless, important to scenario planning. However, there are quicker and less expensive approaches that reflect these principles.

Our experience has shown that a *half-day alternative futures forum* generally provides significant added value to the strategy making group (see box 12.1). This depends upon their involvement in the generation of the alternative futures and their evaluation of the considered options with respect to their developing strategy. Most scenario planning approaches do not involve directly the management team (as a group) in their development – except as interviewees and as an audience for the exposition of the scenarios.

Box 12.1   Vignette Exploring the Significance of Scenarios

A management team had worked hard on its strategy, undertaking all of the forums and arriving at a set of strategies they felt happy with. However, they did feel that they should consider these against the possibility of different futures just in case.

They started by considering all of the different triggers (events over which they had no control) that might occur within the next five years (their agreed time horizon). Each of these was captured on a screen in Decision Explorer® allowing team members to 'piggy back' off one another's contributions. After about 10 minutes, and having exhausted all of the events they could think about, they began to assess each of the events against their impact and probability as this would allow them to determine which were the most significant. This resulted in some fairly heated conversations as participants sought to convince their colleagues that a particular

(Continued)

(Continued)

trigger was much more impactful/predictable than others. The facilitator was seen working hard to capture all of the ensuing rich material.

Finally (after a vigorous 20 minutes) the positioning against the dimensions of impact and predictability was complete and the team began to review the results. They noticed that one of the triggers in the high impact/very unpredictable quadrant was 'government agrees a ceasefire with paramilitary prisoners'. Everyone agreed that if it happened it would be very significant but were exceedingly sceptical it would ever happen. Still as it potentially had the greatest impact they decided to explore the consequences further. At this stage they saw the event as being mostly positive but as they began to consider the various ramifications they realised it could also result in a large number of negative consequences. In the short term there would be problems with an excess of prison estate which would have effects on both staff but also the communities around the prisons. In the longer term the nature of the prison population would change – seeing increases in 'ordinary decent criminals' and away from paramilitaries – and a rising drug problem. The entire scenario alarmed them but in discussing the situation they realised that if the event was to occur, they could use the short term excess to their advantage, updating prisons, training staff, etc. so that they could be better prepared for the other long-term consequences (see figure 12.4).

There are three important considerations when undertaking the construction of scenarios. The first relates to building on the work already done in other forums. For example, as we commented above, in the issue management forum it is very likely that some of the issues relate directly to expected future events – for example, 'cope with the increasing costs of oil' or 'manage the impacts of economic cutbacks'. Likewise, in the stakeholder management forum, those stakeholders located in the bottom right quadrant (see figure 9.1 in the chapter on stakeholder management) – 'context-setters' – will also significantly impact the strategic future of the organisation (for example, a particular part of government bringing in new regulations). This material must not be ignored for both efficiency and coherency reasons. A second consideration concerns changing the thinking of the management team as much as it concerns arriving at clear scenarios.[14] This is because their mental models are extended as they become aware of events and their significance, and so they will be more likely to spot earlier a new and different future arising (seeing 'weak signals').[15] Finally, the third consideration, that of learning, is about being alert to possibilities so that managers will be able to act more opportunistically. Scenarios help managers widen their scope of awareness.

Therefore developing scenarios can help management teams in a number of key ways. The first, and possibly foremost, is to increase the robustness of their strategy through 'wind-tunnelling' as managers expose their nascent strategy to alternative circumstances. This process of wind-tunnelling helps reveal where potential weaknesses might lie and helps prompt either adaptations to the strategy to enable it to perform more successfully or conceive actions that can mitigate or capitalise upon the future should it emerge. This leads on to the second benefit – that is the exploration of different futures that gives rise to new possible strategies. As management teams debate the different events that lead to changing circumstances they cannot help but think about the means to manage these futures and thus they surface options. These options become extremely useful either for immediate or subsequent use should the scenario come to pass. Finally, there is also the benefit gained from changing managers' mental models – and thus extending the lenses through which they view their world.

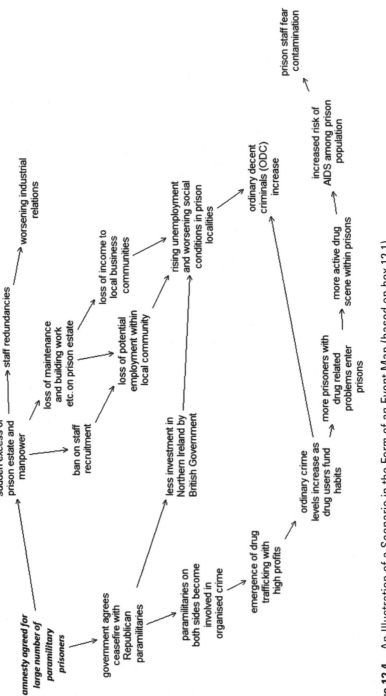

Figure 12.4 An Illustration of a Scenario in the Form of an Event Map (based on box.12.1)

The Resource Feasibility of Strategy: 'Back of the Envelope' Spreadsheet Analysis

Calculating the rough costs of the intended strategies can provide a useful reality check. This assessment does not have to be in the form of a detailed financial model but can be relatively crude – in essence – a 'back of the envelope' type costing. The costs and revenues following strategic change are very difficult to predict with any accuracy and detailed analysis is inappropriate.

A good place to start the process is from the strategy maps produced as these provide the basic structure for a spreadsheet model. Each causal link implies a possible arithmetic relationship. Each node implies a possible revenue or cost. Indeed, one of the earliest forms of spreadsheet software (*Javelin*) allowed causality – words and arrows – to be the basic structure for building the spreadsheet. It would have been a very useful product to help in the evaluation of a business model, had Microsoft not dominated the marketplace with *Excel*!

Of course, difficulties arise in using spreadsheet analysis when there are feedback loops. A feedback loop depicts a dynamic outcome, where the nodes are variables that will change over time in an accelerating and exponential manner when there is positive feedback – sometimes this dynamic has an undesirable outcome (vicious circle) and sometimes a desirable outcome (virtuous circle). The loop may also be a negative feedback loop where the impact is controlling. Without the use of specialist computer software[16] it is difficult to anticipate the behaviour of feedback loops as often there are counter-intuitive aspects.[17] For the purposes of a 'back of the envelope' check on the business model then the first step will be to establish whether the first period of analysis can be estimated to show positive results. However, it is worth recalling that often a strategy is expected to trigger the feedback loop, and in doing so, demands a cost before revenue follows. Thus, the strategy is expected to have a long term positive impact alongside a short term negative impact. In these circumstances, an evaluation of the best-case and worst-case outcomes, both in terms of time to deliver and revenue, must be undertaken.

The spreadsheet is best constructed interactively with the strategy making management team. Indeed, it is crucial that those who have formulated the strategy provide estimates of revenues and costs as they have intimate knowledge of the possible behaviour of the nodes and will have made the intuitive judgements that will have influenced agreements.

Nevertheless, for many strategy making management teams the construction of a spreadsheet is seen often as a backroom activity that is of a specialist nature. In these circumstances there is likely to be resistance to the idea of building a spreadsheet interactively and the facilitator (manager-client or external) needs to be skilled in the fast construction and manipulation of the spreadsheet. They also need to be able to build the spreadsheet in a transparent manner and at a level of detail that is appropriate. The basic structure of the spreadsheet can be constructed off-line, as long as it can be shown to represent faithfully the structure of the maps, and is reviewed with the group.[18]

As noted above, in order to adequately test the robustness of the strategy it is important to consider best-case and worst-case situations. However, in doing so, it is important to remember that it is extremely unlikely that all worst-case revenues and costs will occur at the same time. Also, each member of the strategy making group is likely to have differing views about costs and revenues. It is often helpful, therefore, to encourage each member of the group to make independent estimates and then pull these together, as a probability distribution, as a basis for both discussion and final estimation of the expected outcomes and possible variance from these expectations. The process for doing this type of analysis is outlined in box 12.2.

Box 12.2   A Quick Calculation of Expected Values and Variance in Estimates

Expected = Sum(L+4M+H)/6

  M = most likely, L = low surprise limit, H = high surprise limit
  Variance = average((b−a)/3)^2

In our experience it is rare for the spreadsheet analysis to imply that the strategy and business model are unrealisable or incredible, rather judgements become more robust. However, it is extremely common for the outcomes of the strategy to be evaluated as overly optimistic. In these circumstances, it is likely that strategies will need to be refined. However, on some occasions the quantitative modelling has reduced aspirations that have subsequently been attained, and so apparent realism can be at odds with aspirational judgements.[19] Over-delivery may not be a concern if it occurs, but the reduction of aspiration makes under-achievement more likely.

THE IMPACT OF SYSTEMS AND STRUCTURES

One of the important considerations for the effective implementation of strategy is the impact of systems and structures, both formal and informal. Here we consider their role as we move the discussion towards closure and strategy delivery.

Our experience suggests that there are two very important systems that impact the reality of strategy delivery: reward systems (both formal and informal), and costing or transfer pricing systems. Others that are often significant are: information systems, architecture (and its influence on social processes), and budgeting procedures. Each of these are important contributors to emergent strategising,[20] in that they have a powerful influence on strategic futures but not a deliberate or designed impact. Below we shall discuss both costing and transfer pricing systems. However, as reward systems are directly related to the appropriate development of performance indicators they are considered later in this chapter.

Costing Systems

Costing systems are usually designed by cost accountants and reflect the traditions of their profession or of industry practices (they are often a part of the 'industry recipe').[21] They are rarely designed to support the delivery of a particular strategy, and yet their role can be profound. In all organisations costs are the result of subjective judgements, not objective analysis. For instance, overheads can usually be allocated in many different ways, each of which is seen as rational by the proponents of the method. For example, in a consultancy business the overhead costs of marketing staff, the salaries office and facilities management can be allocated by proportion of customer revenue generated, by headcount, by different product types, and so on. Each method will show different levels of profit for business units and so significantly influence motivations of staff, and ultimately budgeting, and so strategic futures.

All organisations, from community groups seeking to offer a community hall for use by residents to small consultancies or software houses to large multinationals, will be making operational and strategic decisions significantly determined by the particular nature of their way of understanding their costs – often explicated as a costing 'system'. The costing system itself may be carefully constructed, possibly – but unusually – to reflect the strategic intent of the organisation, or may simply be an informal set of obvious assumptions believed to be 'matters of fact', which are taken to be the cost of undertaking activities. However, this system, or set of assumptions, will be one of many ways of determining the cost of a service or product, each of which will importantly suggest very different strategic futures. Often such costing systems are designed with no regard to their strategic impact, but rather are designed by staff who have in mind the creation of a system which is closest to the 'truth' – a notion of the 'real cost'.

The impact of different ways of understanding cost cannot be underestimated (see box 12.3); indeed academic accountants are recognising that concepts of cost and profit should be accepted as social constructions rather than matters of fact, including social accounting, accounting for corporate social responsibility, etc.[22] In particular, it is important to recognise the strategic impact of apparently obvious decisions about distributing overheads.

Box 12.3   Illustrating the Impact of a Costing System on Strategy

A new chief executive of a magazine publishing company decided that central overheads needed to be fully distributed to the business units, in order to make the managers of these units more accountable. The basis for distribution was that of headcount, as this seemed to be a realistic reflection of the use of overheads since the business was people intensive. The managers concerned were awarded bonuses as a function of yearly profits. On reflection it was not surprising that these managers looked for ways of reducing their headcount to reduce overheads relative to other units, and so make higher profits than their colleagues, and so be rewarded with a higher bonus. The simplest and fastest way of reducing headcount was to invite journalists to become freelance. The process was successful, the headcount was reduced and the company's total overheads were genuinely reduced as well as those for the particular unit concerned. However, some years later it emerged that freelance journalists had, quite reasonably, been servicing other organisations with the same expertise that had once belonged to the original company. This company gradually shared what had been a significant and distinctive competence.

Journalists were doing well and were reticent to move back onto the payroll as a normal employee. Meanwhile the strategic future of the company was, perforce, shifting from selling information to packaging information belonging to others. A procedure for keeping managers aware of costs had resulted in important emergent strategic consequences.

The Role of Transfer Pricing in Determining a Strategic Future

The second significant and related system is that of transfer pricing. As with costing systems these systems are often seen as simple operational considerations that are determined by cost accountants who have not been required to deliberate in the light of strategic intent but rather develop objective views about costs. Transfer pricing systems are common to many organisations, particularly those that have gone down the devolved 'independent' strategic business unit route. It is obvious that the managers of these units will want to demonstrate prowess in relation to their own unit. In order to do so transfer pricing becomes a political football driving a considerable amount of manoeuvring and short term decision making. This form of decision making builds patterns of behaviour, and so an emergent strategy, which can be difficult to break and can determine strategic futures in many unintended ways (see box 12.4).

Box 12.4   Illustrating the Strategic Impact of a Transfer Pricing System

In many educational institutions the unit of trading is that of the number of full-time equivalent students that attend a class. Thus, transfer pricing is based upon a charge per student per class. Here many products (the degree programme spanning several years) become highly distorted because the providers focus upon those classes which attract maximum students rather than those which act as key elements within the context of the whole educational experience of the degree programme. The transfer pricing mechanism gradually reduces the quality of the product. This, in turn, determines a strategic future that is about servicing a particular market of degree awarding institution, rather than being an educational experience focused institution. The institution may choose either route, but the point here is that it is very likely that the chosen structure determines an emergent strategic future not a deliberate strategic intent.

As illustrated in boxes 12.4 and 12.5, these simple examples demonstrate how powerful reasonable notions of costs can be in determining a strategic future, even if the costing system or transfer pricing system was designed to have operational impacts only. Our experience suggests that sometimes it is only an outsider who can detect these emergent consequences, for the systems tend to have become a part of the 'world-taken-for-granted' of the management team. Spending time considering not only the impact of the current transfer pricing system or costing system on the strategies but also what an alternative might be, and how it might affect the strategies, can illustrate how the systems impact organisational life.

Typically investment decisions and effort are organised according to the understanding of costs and so relative profits. Sales staff may put their effort into those products or product types that show the most apparent profit (according to the current costing system). Consider how investment and effort will push the organisation in a particular strategic direction, and how this might be different for the alternative costing system.

Box 12.5   Illustrating the Impact of Transfer Pricing

Consider a small printing firm with three printing machines and operators (one that is capable of undertaking specialist high quality work and the other two ordinary jobs) and a process planner

(Continued)

(Continued)

who optimally prepares jobs so that they take the least amount of time and are printed to the best quality. The firm carries overheads for management, for selling, and for the cost of space, and it also worries about retaining access to funds when it is required to replace printing machines.

If we take two plausible, but extreme, systems for costing jobs, for the purpose of illustration, then we see two different strategic futures unfold.

In the first case overheads are spread across each of the four resources and profit margins are expected to provide a source of funding for replacement printing machinery when required. Jobs are costed according to the time each resource is used, and this cost is a consideration in pricing the job. In the second case the overheads are distributed unevenly so that the machines carry a greater proportion because it is believed that the extent and type of space they occupy costs more than the cost of employing the process planner. The cost of the higher quality machine is greater than for the other machines and so the depreciation costs are now included in the hourly cost rate and are higher for the more expensive machine.

Given that each of the systems is designed to reflect expected utilisation of the resource, and that the aggregate cost recovery in either case will be the same, then the impact of each system will be different. In the second case the higher quality jobs will carry a relatively higher cost, and jobs with a relatively lower proportion of process planning will cost relatively more. In the second case the firm will find it easier to bid for jobs with a relatively higher proportion of process planning, indeed these jobs will probably begin to look more profitable than if the first system was used. If there are other firms using the first system then they will believe they make more profit from low proportion process planning and high quality jobs. The marketplace is likely to become differentiated, with each of the firms beginning to specialise by focusing their selling efforts and expanding accordingly. Each firm is likely to believe their strategic growth is successful and will ensure that their systems become self-fulfilling. Indeed it is possible that for the first case the firm will emerge with a production-oriented strategic future, where they are not oriented to product type but more concerned about selling production resource. Growth is more likely to be by expansion in accordance with bottleneck relief. In the second case it is probable that the firm emerges with a product orientation, given that it has a greater capability of identifying costs by product.

MANAGING IMPLEMENTATION

It is important to recognise that strategy making involves change that might not be palatable to everyone (see chapter 2). For example, some much-prized competences thought to be distinctive will have been seen to be unimportant depending on how they support the goals identified. Other competences need to be given more resources, and entirely new directions may have emerged through an awareness of the outside world. All these things may affect managers and staff, sometimes negatively, and therefore the *management of implementation* is an important factor in the delivery of strategy.

In many respects, shared understanding among the management team about strategic intent will make things happen differently – this has been the essence of our case that the most successful strategic change will come from managers making sense of their world in new ways and so acting differently. However realistic this approach to organisational change may be, it does not satisfy the need a person and an organisation has for an artefact, something concrete, which signifies that the task of strategy development has been completed and, later, that progress in strategic change has been made.

Closure

When considering closure, the creation of performance indicators, reward systems and strategic control processes becomes relevant. Determining when to move from the development of strategy making to closure can vary. The ideal point in strategy making to develop closure is when the most appropriate balance between emotional and cognitive commitment and strategic analysis has occurred. For the facilitator or manager-client driving strategy making, it can sometimes be frustrating when the strategy making team are clear in their own minds that they have a robust strategy and yet they have not undertaken all of the analysis that would seem to the facilitator to be sensible. However, it is better to have a strategy that is less well thought through but will be delivered, than a strategy that has been fully developed but will not be delivered because there is no commitment to it from those who must deliver it. Strategy delivery must be politically feasible (see chapter 2).

Closure is a problematic notion because for many management teams strategy making will be *continuous* (rather than as something cast in stone). To some extent strategy making is itself part of a continuous improvement process in organisations (see chapter 2), and certainly can be an important part of organisational learning and team building (see chapters 2 and 11). Nevertheless a clear articulation of what has been decided and how it is to be achieved is important.

Closure may also imply consideration of the best methods for project managing the delivery of strategy, for example whether and what performance indicators are necessary. However, it is not uncommon for one outcome of a successful forum to be that some members of the team start implementing the consequences of the forum before the series is complete. This means that strategy delivery will have commenced before the strategic thinking is complete. When this occurs it should be a cause for satisfaction rather than frustration for the facilitator and team – it means the team are convinced by and have engaged with the strategy making and have been able to translate it into action.

The strategy making outcome will always be contingent upon the particular circumstances of the organisation. There is a spectrum running from agreement to a deliberate emergent strategy; through to the development of a statement of strategic intent encompassing a detailed explication of the strategies through to a published strategy that may often contain a clear system of distinctive goals, and a set of interacting strategic programmes (supporting the management of stakeholders, issues and protecting distinctiveness); through to a detailed strategy involving carefully evaluated budgets, project teams, responsibilities and control systems.[23] The choice again will be dependent on the organisation.

A good starting point for closure therefore is to consider whether a more detailed action programme is required, including determining performance indicators and the production of a strategy delivery support system (SDSS).

The Implementation of Action Programmes

Depending on what form of strategy deliverable is to be presented, it is likely that further consideration of both the strategic actions and the means of their assessment is required. As noted above, in the section on extending the robustness of the strategy, drilling down to strategic actions can help in ensuring a successful implementable strategy.

Drilling down to the actions also allows not only the means for achieving the strategies to be revealed but also a further method for ensuring that all the team understand what the strategy entails (see box 12.6). Fleshing out the actions to strategies to goals hierarchy thus helps clarify the meaning of actions. It also helps review the viability of the strategic direction. For example, once the strategic actions have been agreed, it can be valuable to begin to allocate names against responsibilities for their implementation.[24] This might be one of the management team themselves or it might be that the action will be delegated further down the organisation but under the auspices of one of the management team. It is crucial that every strategy has the ownership of one member of the strategy making team with respect to responsibility and accountability in relation to other team members.

Box 12.6   Developing the Action Programmes

The management team of a medium sized engineering organisation were feeling pleased with themselves. They had completed three of the four forums (missing out only on the stakeholder management one – due to time pressures) and had agreed upon a strategic direction that all felt was robust but also exciting. They were now keen to start putting the strategy into action. However, on looking at what they had produced, they realised that it was still very high level – they needed to put some more flesh on the bones.

It occurred to them that a nice way of doing this was to have a couple of meetings whereby those reporting to them (and who would be responsible for the actions) would be involved in helping consider the right actions to support the strategies. Using this process would not only help gain ownership for what was proposed but it would also act as an effective way of ensuring that this important tranche of managers understood the intended direction.

By having some of the management team at both of the meetings, they could ensure that any synergistic benefits (where an action supporting one strategy could be designed to support another) could be capitalised upon. They also felt that they needed to keep an eye on ensuring that no one person ended up with too much on his or her plate!

As with the forums, using Decision Explorer® to support the action programming effort means that the actions agreed upon can be captured in the causal context of the remainder of the material and that it is possible to show not just what has been agreed but also why (the links, as always, playing an important role).

Performance Management System and Strategy Delivery Support System (SDSS)

The development of key performance indicators (KPIs) plays a role in the delivery of a strategy. Establishing appropriate performance indicators can take an organisation some way towards combating the problems of strategic control outlined later on in this chapter. The development of performance indicators additionally tends to help develop strategic options. Often the creation of

KPIs will lead a team to say 'never mind measuring it that way, let's just do it' – the performance indicator becomes a part of the action programme.

The greatest danger in establishing performance indicators is a strong temptation to establish only quantitative performance indicators. The old adage 'what gets measured gets done' is a great danger for strategy delivery. As Einstein noted, 'Everything that can be counted does not necessarily count; everything that counts cannot necessarily be counted'. Similarly, Steven Kerr [25] argues that a 'fascination with an "objective" criterion' causes goal displacement. It is therefore important to undertake the process of agreeing performance indicators (or critical success factors) carefully and thoughtfully as it is important not only to get a good balance between qualitative and quantitative indicators but also to make sure that the indicators are clearly understood by all (see box 12.7).

Box 12.7   Revealing a Key Misunderstanding!

The local economic development company management team were considering the performance indicators for their set of strategies and had arrived at a set of between three or four for each of the strategies. As a way of both testing these (and their understanding of the strategy) as well as determining a benchmark (so that when they came to review progress they would have something against which to compare) the team agreed that it would be good to see how they currently did. Thus using flip-chart sheets, they noted along the top of each (in landscape) the strategy, and then listed the performance indicators along the left-hand side – allowing for a scale from 0 to 100 to be on the right hand side. Each team member then assessed the current position using 'sticky dots'.

On reviewing their work, they were a bit taken aback. One of the performance indicators had a remarkable range showing – with the rankings ranging from 10 per cent progress to 70 per cent. How could this be? However, it soon became clear that they had very different understandings of the performance indicator. The strategy was 'develop a highly skilled and flexible workforce (in the area – Govan)' and the indicator in question noted 'increase the number of completed training programmes'. And so, for some they had considered those who lived in Govan and had completed training programmes, for others they had considered those who worked in Govan and for the third set, they had considered both populations! No wonder there was so much variety.

Progress towards most goals can only be established by creating a portfolio of qualitative and quantitative performance indicators. The now well-established balanced scorecard approach offers some assistance.[26] Through directly considering four dimensions (financial, customer, internal processes, and innovation and learning) the organisation is moved away from a focus only on the traditional bottom line of short term profit. Moreover, the scorecard recognises the interactivity of the measures. This direct acknowledgement of the impact of measures on one another is also carried through, in terms of mapping measures, onto the organisation's strategy map. Here obvious measures could be derived but for them to be exploited fully a set of qualitative as well as quantitative measures are necessary (to ensure the integration of the goals system). However, keep in mind the need to ensure that the data are available for assessing performance and that it is not prohibitively costly to collect. Where performance measurement systems have been seen to fail is where the cost of undertaking the activity far outweighs the benefits accrued. The other main cause for poor adoption comes from the measures not being developed by those who will be using them.

A final consideration, and one that ties in with earlier comments regarding the building of quantitative simulation models, is recognising that often performance drops for a time as new strategies are put in place (as staff become accustomed to the new ways of working). Frequently there is the temptation to assume that the strategies aren't working and so change direction before the expected benefits can be realised.

Communicating the Strategy: Double Messages

For senior managers and the management team it can be clear what actions need to be taken in relation to a strategy. However, apparent resistance at lower levels in the organisation may occur. This may be as much to do with a lack of clarity about what is expected and when than an outright disagreement with the course of action. Thus, what is an actionable statement for one person may remain ambiguous or meaningless for another. The confusion can be further exacerbated when senior managers, who believe they are acting consistently within a world of complex multiple goals, are perceived to be acting inconsistently by others who are more singularly focused in their tasks. Double messages can abound, particularly where a senior manager demands one thing from subordinates but appears to pay lip service to it him or herself, by doing the opposite.

Considering how to present the strategy to the rest of the organisation can therefore be a good way of stopping the continuous development process explaining the details and moving towards closure. This might be in the form of road shows where members of the management team (in turn) present the strategy to different parts of the organisation – see box 12.8.

Box 12.8   An Example of a Road Show's Benefit

The management team were just about to carry out their first road show. Two (out of the team of eight) had agreed to do the first of a series of six and were nervously reviewing the presentation. While they strongly believed that the strategy that they were presenting was powerful – they were a little worried about how it might be received. They knew in the audience that there were a number of staff who had on previous occasions expressed some cynicism regarding the strategic direction of the organisation (and they had had good reason to!). Both team members were hoping they weren't going to be too dismissive this time.

Just as they finished, one of the most vociferous of the union members stood up – their hearts sank – and to their great amazement congratulated the team! For once, the union member said, she understood not only where they were heading but why!

Production of an artefact – whether it be a glossy document or the material posted on the web page of the organisation – ensures that all can become aware of the strategy, or at least the statement of strategic intent.

The Impact of Reward Systems on the Realisation of Strategy

An important aspect of communicating strategy lies in the nature of reward systems used in the organisation – both informal and formal. Regardless of the number of forums undertaken, ensuring successful delivery of the strategic intent requires that the management team understands the potential impact of existing reward systems and adapts them where necessary. Probably one of the most difficult parts of strategic management is the identification of appropriate reward systems. This is because reward systems can often stymie successful implementation through their unintended dysfunctional effects (in a manner not dissimilar to those of control systems). Paying attention to the reward system suggests reviewing the performance measurements as they are closely linked.

What frequently happens is that double messages emerge – where the strategy argues for one set of activities and effort but the reward system incentivises another set of activities. Examples of these double messages include:

- The desire of the strategy for long term growth but the reward system in place incentivises short term progress. For example, bonuses (quarterly or annually) usually engender a very short term perspective. Sadly, short term and easily measurable performance indicators often dominate organisations.
- Where the strategy focuses upon the realisation of goals but the reward system incentivises activities without reference to their role in delivering the goals. Thus for example, the goal 'ensure commitment to total quality' is measured by the performance indicator of 'shipping on schedule' *but with the risk of defects.*
- The strategy seeks to develop a culture of innovative thinking and risk taking so as to remain competitive but the reward system encourages sticking with proven methods and punishes entrepreneurial, and intrapreneurial, failures.[27]

There is often a focus on action (doing something – the node on the causal map) rather than on what the strategic action is designed to achieve (and therefore not leveraging the benefits nor achieving the strategy – the arrow on the causal map). By using lists of actions as a check for strategy delivery there is a danger of encouraging a 'tick box' mentality that ignores the reason *why* the action must be taken. The use of causal maps to monitor strategy implementation encourages attention to causality and so increases the probability that the actions are implemented so that they contribute towards the achievement of the appropriate goal(s).[28]

It is important to explore what types of (rational) behaviour are currently rewarded and consider what manipulative behaviour can gain rewards. It is also important to note that 'all organisational behaviour is [not] determined by formal rewards and punishments'.[29] Another key consideration is reflected in the fact that there are going to be cases where 'the rewarded is not causing the behaviour but is only a fortunate bystander'.[30] For example, the dilemma of bonus payments to all for the behaviour of a few; rewarding the good performers but not being seen by the good to punish the bad. Developing an appropriate control or reward systems for delivering strategy is immensely difficult, and so needs constant attention.

With these warnings in mind we must devise processes for monitoring, reviewing and strategic control, which in themselves promote organisational learning, do not stultify strategy, and yet provide respect for a carefully developed strategy and enable operational effectiveness and efficiency to develop. This means we must attend to the causes of reward systems being dysfunctional, by addressing the following:

- Use of qualitative as well as quantitative measures.
- Application of specificity only when appropriate.

- Reward for managing causality.
- Explicit recognition of systemicity (the inter-relationship between strategic actions, strategies, goals).
- Process management as well as content management.

Strategic Control and Review

The process of reviewing progress typically occurs some time after the strategy has been agreed upon and efforts towards its implementation are in place. The first, and most obvious benefit, is that the review can highlight deviations from the anticipated progress. These deviations can be both positive (in which case there is cause for celebration) and negative (and thus some remedial action is required). In situations where more progress has been made than initially aspired towards, those responsible can be suitably rewarded. It might also suggest judicious reallocation of effort towards those areas where less than hoped for progress has been made.

A second benefit from the process of review is that of reminding and re-energising staff. This comes from the fact that, as those involved in the review reflect on what progress has been made, this reveals to them that the strategy is making a difference to the organisation's direction. This sense of 'it being for real' helps renew the energy that is clearly visible at the end of each forum. The review also acts as a useful reminder of the strategy – providing a stimulus to look at the whole picture rather than just a small part. This leads to the further benefit of organisational learning. During the review process areas that have made good progress can be examined to understand why this is the case, what lessons can be learnt and whether the progress can be replicated elsewhere.

Reviews can be carried out after six months – particularly if the team want to remind and re-energise the staff – or after a year. The decision is based around a number of factors. These include whether enough progress has been achieved to make the effort worthwhile. In some situations it might be that no real progress will be evident until at least six to eight months have passed as it takes a period of time before any clear progress can be seen. Avoiding too long a break ensures that problematic behaviour gets picked up (measurement after all is to ensure deviations can be understood and managed, and also to capitalise on any best practice that can be shared). A final consideration is that the timing of the review might be dependent on the nature of the organisation and its industry – for example, in the public sector there are particular times of the year when progress reports are required.

In addition to more formal reviews, regular progress assessments are very important. This might be done on a monthly basis where one strategy is reviewed at each regular meeting of the management team, and so may just involve the management team. However, making sure that progress is fed back to other staff is important as otherwise they may believe that like many of the strategies they have seen come and go, this one also leaves no trace.

Ensuring in the design of the action programmes that there are a few 'quick win's' can facilitate this – as progress can be communicated early on. Having regular formal and informal meetings also allows continual updating, enabling staff to feel progress is being made and enabling a wider audience (which might be staff and stakeholders) to appreciate what has happened subsequent to the promulgation of the strategy.

One helpful device for carrying out a review is to focus on the strategies and their performance indicators. Following the procedure noted above regarding the development of performance indicators, progress can be easily identified. Again where there is variation in opinion (perhaps someone thinks more progress has been made than someone else) this can be identified and

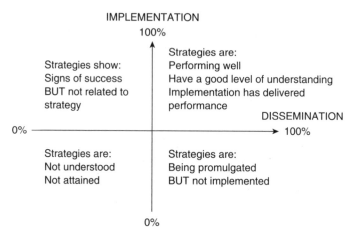

Figure 12.5 Reviewing Strategy

discussed. This process then allows the strategies to be assessed against one another. Using a two-dimensional matrix (see figure 12.5), where the two axes are achievement and awareness, each strategy can be plotted. The results of this matrix will be an insight into those strategies that are well understood and are being well executed – progress is being made. There will also be those that are making good progress, but there is some uncertainty as to why – there is not much awareness among staff. This might suggest more information is required to make the strategies more visible. The third quadrant shows those strategies that are well understood but aren't making much progress. Here effort can be spent discussing and debating why progress is not forthcoming, and what action might need to be taken. Finally there are those strategies that are both poorly understood and showing little progress. It is this final tranche where time is required to understand why and what can be done. This might be simply that the world has moved on and the actions originally agreed upon are no longer viable. New actions are therefore required *but* within the context of the old. What this means is not just looking at the other options available but doing so with regards to the intent, that is, what the action was seeking to achieve. The strategy therefore becomes dynamic and adaptive. Feeding the progress back to staff can act as a useful reminder of the strategy's salience, a powerful way of rewarding those who have worked hard to make it a success (see box 12.9 and figure 12.6).

Box 12.9   Keeping the Strategy Alive

It had now been a year since the strategy had formally been presented to staff and the management team were keen to update everyone on the progress made. They had noticed that the initial enthusiasm and engagement had waned a little and felt that sharing the success stories would be a good way of regenerating the energy.

The team had already carried out an assessment of each of the strategies against their performance indicators (in the same manner as they had done a year ago) and were delighted to notice a range of particular successes. These they thought would make a good basis for an update report.

(Continued)

(Continued)

The resultant document showed the strategy at the top of each page, the performance indicators beneath along with the progress made for each. As much as possible they tried to link the progress to particular members of staff to ensure that their efforts were seen by all.

Bring investment into Govan

Performance Indicator: The upgrading and development of derelict land

> There are currently around 418 acres of derelict land in the Greater Govan area. This adversely affects the image of the area and dissuades private investment.
>
> Govan Initiative aims to proactively address infrastructural constraints and facilitate the direct provision of space. The redevelopment of vacant land and property, particularly at key locations, will then provide the opportunity for inward investment and location.

Analysis

(Covers *physical development* work which was *completed* during 1997)

The amount of land improved may be detailed under the different roles which Govan Initiative may play:

- Direct Implementation – includes all work which Govan Initiative has carried out either on its own or as part of a joint venture.

Amount of land improved	4.5 acres	Moorpark

- Advisory role – Includes all work to which Govan Initiative has given support through the provision of advice and guidance.

Amount of land improved	2 acres	Festival Court

This advisory role includes financial assistance in the form of extensive environmental upgrading programmes, carried out to properties and the public realm, which in turn have improved the marketability of adjacent sites and thus initiated new development.

> **Conclusion**
>
> Govan Initiative will be involved in a partnership project with a local company to develop an area of derelict land into an office and industrial park of around 4.5 acres. Although beginning in 1998, it is not due for completion until early 1999.
>
> The amount of land improved through indirect involvement should be greater than in 1997. This is as a result of areas beginning to benefit from the upgrading of adjacent sites and routes, e.g. Neilstra development in Drumoyne Road – 1 acre.
>
> In addition, there will be various other developments in the Ibrox, Drumoyne and Kinning Park areas as a consequence of the substantial environmental improvements carried out by Govan Initiative.

Figure 12.6   An Example of Reporting on Progress Against a Performance Indicator

SUMMARY

This chapter has provided a very brief introduction to aspects of making strategy that go beyond the initial strategy development process which is the main focus of this book. These extensions to strategy making are important additions. It is rare for us to be involved in strategy making that does not encompass at least some work on a quantitative analysis of the viability of the business model, alternative futures, and/or the development of performance indicators (albeit these activities sometimes appropriately are very rough and ready).

Nevertheless there have been many management teams of large organisations who have been extremely satisfied with developing a robust SSI with its clearly articulated strategies and business model. They have determined that they have considered stakeholders and alternative futures adequately enough through working on their own independent views of the future. They have been committed to mapping out strategic success that shows clearly why things need to be done and how they are to be done. They have used the causal arrows as the basis for project management of their strategy, and in many cases they have used Decision Explorer® as the basis for that project management. Establishing whether strategies have been implemented is one thing, establishing whether they have been implemented for the right reasons is almost more important.

Nevertheless, one of the reasons that change will have been successful will be because the new ways of doing things appear obvious and the old ways have been forgotten. Thus, as we said above, the more successful the change process then the less easy it is to recognise it. It is similar to the dilemma for the facilitator who manages successfully the process of a team of managers genuinely changing their mind (rather than being compromised into agreement). A genuine change of mind will have been largely imperceptible for the person who has changed their mind and so the role of the facilitator in the process will be difficult to acknowledge. The facilitator who is acknowledged as successful is often forced to use performance measures that can be counterproductive to the reality of success where hidden and subtle objectives may be paramount (and only sometimes known to the single client rather than to the management team as a whole). In the same way an organisation and its managers need to create success measures which, when properly constructed, can encourage rather than inhibit the strategic change required.

NOTES

1 The provision of what is often called a 'Blue Ocean strategy' (Kim and Mauborgne, 2005).
2 See Eden and Ackermann (2010a) for an extended discussion the nature of 'coreness'.
3 Bourgeois (1981) argues that a strategic function of slack is to provide resources for the delivery of new strategies.
4 SD modelling Vensim (www.vensim.com, accessed January 2011) is particularly suited to such modelling because it allows causality to be represented using word and arrow diagrams that are close to causal maps (see Ackermann, Eden and Williams, 1997; Andersen, Richardson, Ackermann and Eden, 2010a; Eden, 1994; Howick, Eden, Ackermann and Williams, 2008 for a link between causal maps and simulation modelling). See also Howick, Ackermann and Andersen (2006) for a description of the use of System Dynamics modelling as a part of strategy making.
5 Discrete event simulation using a visual interactive software package such as *Simul8* (www.simul8.com, accessed January 2011).

6 Pettigrew, Whittington, Melin, Sanchez-Runde, Van den Bosch, Ruitgrok and Numagami (2003: 129).

7 See for example Johnson, Scholes and Whittington (2005) for a compendium of analyses.

8 See Eden and Ackermann (1998: 9) for a discussion on the spectrum of possible strategies from deliberate emergent strategy to strategic planning.

9 See Eden and Ackermann (1998: 438–445) for detailed examples of the development of action programmes.

10 See Eden and Ackermann (2001b).

11 De Geus (1988).

12 For research on the relationship between the environment and strategic success see Cameron, Sutton and Whetten (1988); Hambrick and D'Aveni (1988); Haveman (1992); and Smith and Grimm (1987).

13 For examples of the use of the Shell approach see Ringland (1998); van der Heijden (1996); Wack (1985a); and Wack (1985b). However, other methods include Brightman, Eden, van der Heijden and Langford (1996); Eden and Ackermann (1998 :153); Eden and Ackermann (1999); Georgantzas and Acar (1995); Godet (1987); Howick, Ackermann and Andersen (2006); O'Brien and Meadows (1998).

14 Suggesting the reaction of a rabbit in the headlights of a car – paralysed. See Staw, Sandelands and Dutton (1981).

15 See Haeckel (2004) and Saul (2006) and for an original reference see Ansoff, Declerk and Hayes (1976).

16 Specialist software such as Vensim (www.vensim.com) and see note 4 above.

17 Counter-intuitive outcomes are an important discovery from the use of System Dynamics simulation model: see Andersen (1990); Forrester (1971); Richardson, Andersen and Wu (2002).

18 The construction of a spreadsheet or simulation model through 'visual interactive model-ling' is demanding for facilitators, who have to be highly skilled in the use of the software. See Eden, Ackermann, Bryson, Richardson, Andersen and Finn (2009).

19 See the case in Ackermann, Eden and with Brown (2005: 156) where subsequent to the strategy making episode the actual outcome was very close to the original aspiration even though it had been reduced through crude spreadsheet modelling.

20 See Eden and Ackermann (1998: 79–101); Eden and van der Heijden (1995); Mintzberg and Waters (1985).

21 Spender (1989).

22 See, for example, Hines (1988) and Hopwood and Miller (1996).

23 See Eden and Ackermann (1998: 9) for a discussion on the spectrum of possible strategies from deliberate emergent strategy to strategic planning.

24 For a more detailed example of action programming see Eden and Ackermann (1998: 260–261).

25 Kerr's classic article (Kerr, 1995).

26 Kaplan and Norton (1992); Kaplan and Norton (1993); Kaplan and Norton (1996a); Kaplan and Norton (1996b); Kaplan and Norton (2000).

27 See Provera, Montefusco and Canato (2010) for an interesting discussion of the impact of a 'no blame' culture.

28 Telford, Cropper and Ackermann (1992).

29 Kerr (1995: 13).

30 Kerr (1975: 781).

Further Reading

Eden, C. and Ackermann, F. 1998. *Making Strategy: The Journey of Strategic Management.* London: Sage. pp 424–474.

Kaplan, R. S. and Norton, D. P. 1996b. Using the Balanced Scorecard as a Strategic Management System. *Harvard Business Review,* 74: 75–85.

Kerr, S. 1995. On the Folly of Rewarding A, While Hoping for B. *Academy of Management Executive,* 9: 7–16.

Van der Heijden, K. 1996. *Scenarios: The Art of Strategic Conversation.* Chichester: Wiley.

APPENDIX
USING CAUSAL MAPPING
SOFTWARE: DECISION EXPLORER®

Fran Ackermann and Colin Eden

This resource is written as a guide to facilitator/manager-clients who are using the Decision Explorer® software to support the four forums presented in this book. It does not therefore encompass all of the commands in the software; instead it concentrates on those that are directly relevant to the strategy forums. The resource is divided into four sections dealing with 'Getting Started', 'Working with Maps', 'Analysis of Maps' and 'Further Useful Commands'.

The resource is in partnership with an on-line video showing Decision Explorer® in use. Where possible, we would recommend using the video for an initial experimentation with the software, and this text-based resource as a portable brief guide.

Please note that for many of the commands there are two or three different methods for undertaking the operation. When using the software for the first time using the drop down menus is recommended, but as familiarity is gained using the short cut keys can assist the facilitator/manager-client (as it is quicker) and the group is not distracted by the menus dropping down across the screen.

Further information about the software can be accessed by visiting Banxia Software – (www. banxia.com/dexplore/index.html) – including full user and reference guides.

These instructions assume the use of a PC, rather than an Apple Mac.

The codes used in this resource are:

Bold = an objective the facilitator is aiming for.
Underline = menu in Decision Explorer®.
Italics = using the mouse.
>italics = using the command line/keyboard. The text in italics is typed, and first key stroke will cause the > to appear.
nn = any statement number (in Decision Explorer® each statement is referred to as a 'concept').

Short cut commands such as *Alt* = involves depressing the *Alt* key and with it the = key is depressed, similarly *Ctrl B* involves depressing the *Ctrl* key and with it held down the *B* key is depressed.

1 GETTING STARTED

1.1 Opening and Closing a Model

A model is a single file that stores all of the data about a causal map, even though the whole of the map may not be viewed at any one time.

When Decision Explorer® is opened the program automatically starts with either an empty model (if this is the first time the program has been used) or the model last used.

To **create a new model**, select the file menu and chose the option new model. To select an existing model, again use the file menu but this time choose open model and then locate and select the desired model (models are, by default, saved in the folder c:\program files\dexplore\model).

The software undertakes an automatic save every one minute (unless this is changed by the user). This feature is not enabled until the model is saved for the first time against a specific name, for example, strategy.mdl (where mdl is the file extension automatically used – in the same way as .doc is the default file extension for a Word file). It is therefore recommended that soon after creating a new model, the **model is saved**. Saving a model can be carried out either by using the file menu and selecting the save model option or by selecting the icon representing a disk (as for Word). The backup feature of the software produces additional files beyond the readable file .mdl; these are .mlk, .mdk, .mdb. These additional files cannot be opened and are not required for future use of the model, or when sending a copy of the working model to others – just send .mdl file.

It is possible to have up to four models open at the same time.

To **close a model**, select the file menu and the close model option. This will automatically prompt a request to save the model. To **exit** from Decision Explorer® return to the file menu and select exit.

The autosave that occurs every one minute is reassuring for the facilitator, as it is very unlikely that a computer crash will cause the loss of much data – an important consideration for a strategy making forum!

1.2 Capturing Statements

As the main purpose of the software is to support the exploration of views from participants in the forums, capturing the contributions made by them is a key feature. There are two means of **entering statements** into Decision Explorer®.

- The first and simplest is to *move the mouse* to a desired position on the screen (the position of the mouse is usually represented by an arrow) and then *double clicking with the left hand button*. At this point a number will appear and the cursor will change to a single flashing vertical line indicating that the software is now in text entry mode. Type in the text and press the enter key, or *click the left mouse button*.

Note: the numbers that appear at the beginning of each statement are reference tags and predominantly are used to manipulate the data. However, they can be useful for auditing purposes (see additional features below).

- The second means of entering material into Decision Explorer® is to use the command line which is activated by pressing any of the alphanumeric keys (an > appears). To inform Decision Explorer® that a statement is about to be entered, precede the statement with an = symbol. In this case the software will place the statement in a random position on the screen. However, when a specific location is desired select a statement close to the desired location before carrying this process. Select a statement by *moving the mouse onto the statement and click once* (left button). This triggers a box to be placed around the statement. The new statement appears close to the one selected.

When using either mode of entry, it is also possible to enter statements with a predefined 'number tag'. This can be useful when text is being captured within the model – as with the strategy as purpose forum (when building the goals system from existing documents). In this case the number required is placed before the = symbol, e.g. 23=some statement; and as long as there is not already a statement numbered 23 then the new statement will appear on the screen.

1.3 Editing Statements

Editing statements is a crucial aspect of the map being in continual transition as negotiation occurs throughout a forum.

Editing material can be carried out by *double clicking the left button on the statement to be edited*. The cursor will again change to a flashing vertical line and it is then possible to make the necessary changes.

Hint: standard Word keystrokes allow movement between words and using the *end* key allows rapid movement to the end of each line; *pressing the end key twice* moves the cursor to the end of the statement.

Note: the software allows multiple views of the material (see section 2.1 for a discussion on the use of views/tabs) and when the text or links are edited in one view then the statement will be changed in any view that displays the statement.

1.4 Moving Statements

There are two methods to move statements.

- The easy way is to select a statement by *moving the mouse onto the statement and click once* (left button). This triggers a box to be placed around the statement. *Click with the right mouse button* to access a menu. Select move concept and the cursor will now change to a hand icon. Move the statement to a desired location and *click once with the left mouse button* to drop the statement in the new position.

- An alternative, quicker but not so simple method is to use a combination of the mouse buttons. Select the statement to be moved and *depress and hold down the left mouse button.* While *holding the left button down hold down the right button* so both buttons are depressed. The hand icon once again appears. Move the hand to the desired location and *let go of the two mouse buttons.*

    This mode of moving statements can be done on multiple statements. Select the statements in question and then *hold down the shift key, move the mouse* to one of the statements and *use the left/right combination* noted above.

1.5 Linking Statements

As with capturing material there are two different means of **linking statements** together.

- The first method is to *move the mouse onto the statement* that is to be linked to another statement, i.e. the arrow will go from the selected statement to its consequences statement. *Holding the left mouse button down move from the first statement to the second releasing the mouse button once the intended target has been selected* (a dotted box appears around the second statement). A link will automatically appear.
- The second method works through the command line. Here it is possible to link not only pairs of concepts but also entire chains. To link a pair, *type the number of the supporting statement and then the + symbol followed by the number of the second, consequential statement.* Thus a link from statement 34 to statement 33 would be entered as 34+33, and the arrow points from statement 34 to statement 33.
- To link an entire chain the process follows the same logic. For example 45+23+55+12 would show a causal chain of argument from 45 to 23 to 55 to 12. Where there are a lot of statements linking in or out of a statement the < or > symbols can be used. For example where statements 1, 43 and 87 all link into 66 then typing 66<+1+43+87 would allow these links to be captured.
- To **change a link**, *double click with the left mouse button on the arrow.* This will cause a dialog box to appear. It is then possible to **delete, reverse** or **edit the link**. It is also possible to **create a negative link** using this dialog box. Reversing a link can be done by *clicking on the arrow in the dialogue box.*

2 WORKING WITH MAPS

2.1 Using Views in Decision Explorer®

Decision Explorer® in essence works as an enhanced relational database – storing statements and links, and other data such as the style of the data (see section 2.3). As maps can contain up to several hundred statements and links, the software provides a number of user controlled views through which the material can be explored in different ways.

> Note: when the text or link is edited in one view then the statement or link will be changed in any view that displays the statement or link. The software is not like a series of Powerpoint slides where each view is independent of others.

The most common task in dealing with views in a forum is to **rename** the views (from the default View 1, View 2, etc.) to something more meaningful to both the facilitator and the group. *Click on one of the view tabs* with the right hand mouse button and this will cause a pop up menu to appear. Choose the <u>rename</u> option.

It is also possible to **add up to 28 new views as required**. *Click with the right hand mouse button on any of the four view tabs* along the bottom of the screen (in the same way as renaming a view) and then <u>insert</u>. Views can also be **re-ordered** (allowing for those views that are most frequently used to appear at the beginning of the list) and **deleted** using the same menu.

In addition to creating and renaming views, the amount seen on a view can be adjusted. For example, if there is a lot of information to display (perhaps as a result of surfacing a large number of issues when carrying out the forum dealing with issues) it might not be possible to see all of the material at once (as the screen is full). To manage this situation, change the screen setting from normal mode (where the text appears in normal size) to the fit to window mode. Select the <u>view</u> menu followed by the <u>display scale</u> option and then <u>fit to window</u>. Alternatively, select the fit to window icon on the toolbar (fifth from the right).

Alternatively use *Alt* = (this involves depressing both the alt key followed by the = key in combination) for fit to window or *Alt* < for normal view. Fit to window causes the text to be shrunk so that all of the material on the view can be seen. This might result in the statements being so small they are unreadable but it does provide a good overall image of all of the material on that view. For example, an unreadable view might reveal patterns within the network. When the text is very small, *clicking the mouse on any of the statements* causes the text to be shown in the command line and the text can be then edited.

2.2 Managing the Map

Bringing layouts from one view to another. The image depicted on one view (tab) can be brought onto another view (tab). This facility is useful to allow the map to be tidied in the new view without losing the original structure in the other view.

Bringing layouts from one view to another might also be useful when a busy map is to be presented to a group and the facilitator wishes to **slowly build up the map** using a series of pre-prepared views. Starting with the last version subsequent views can reduce the material displayed while ensuring that statements remain in the same 'geographical location'.

To build a series, *create or select a blank view* where the repeat of the map is to be brought and, using the *right click on the tab*, select <u>bring layout from</u>. A list of the available views is then presented and the user can choose which view to transfer.

Toggling between displays. In addition to having 32 views, each view can be toggled between a map display and a text display (use *Ctrl M* for map view and *Ctrl T* for the text view). Text displays may comprise different lists, including:

- **List heads**. This provides a list of all of those statements that have no out-arrows. To produce a list of heads either type >*LH* or select the <u>list</u> menu and select <u>heads</u>.
- **List all the statements**. This provides a list of all of the statements in the model. To get this list either type >*L* or select the <u>list</u> menu and choose <u>all concepts</u>.
- **List all the statements on a particular view**. This can only be carried out by typing >*l onmap*.

- **List selected concepts.** Type _>/ sc_.
- The list which results from some analytical routines.

Views provide a useful way of managing the growing model. However, there are a number of commands that are useful for managing the material on each view.

Selecting statements. There are two means of identifying specific statements for further examination:

- One means for selecting a statement is to _move the mouse onto the statement and click once_ (left button). This triggers a box to be placed around the statement. If more than one statement is to be selected, hold down the shift key while clicking on each statement. Alternatively, swipe across the statements with the mouse. _Hold the left button down and move the mouse across all the statements to be selected, then let go of the mouse button._
- Another means is to use the command line. Here specified statements can be selected, for example, typing _sc = /43#44#32_ causes the three statements to be selected (the # symbol separates the different number tags).

Bringing statements from one view to another. Because Decision Explorer® acts as a relational database with the views as windows onto the model, bringing a statement from one view onto another must be done using the _bring_ command. Beware, if copy is used then a duplicate statement is created. This will not only affect the analyses but might also result in the statement being missed or not recognised for its importance. There are a number of different means for bringing statements onto views.

- Using the command line, type _bring_ followed by the statement number. For example _bring 32_ brings statement 32 onto the current view. Should more than one statement be brought on, then separate each number using the # symbol, for example _bring 43#15#78_ will bring all three statements onto the view.
- For examining those statements directly related to a statement already on the screen, _select this statement and then press Ctrl B_. To bring just those statements linking in, use _Ctrl I_ and for those linking out, use _Ctrl O_.
- An alternative means of bringing on statements in and out of a specified statement is to _select it, and then using the pop up menu_ (accessed by clicking with the right mouse button) select bring unseen.

Hiding statements (rather than deleting them). As with bringing material, it is possible to hide statements from a map without deleting them from the model:

- Select the statement to be hidden and press _Ctrl H_.
- Using the command line type hide and the statement number, for example, _hide 32_ will cause statement 32 to disappear from the map (but not from the whole the model).
- An alternative means of hiding statements is to _select the statement_, and then using the pop up menu (accessed by _clicking with the right mouse button_) select hide concept.

Working with hidden links. Because the views are usually used to show only part of the total map, often those statements currently being displayed on a map have links to other statements not on the current view. These hidden links can either be viewed for all statements on a map view or just statements selected. To view hidden links either:

- Use the tool bar and *select the right hand most icon* to show all links or the icon to the left of this to show the hidden links of selected statements.
- Type >*sul* on the command line (sul is a shorthand for Show Unseen Links) (this will just show those hidden links for selected statements).
- Select the <u>property</u> menu and select <u>model display</u>. Then choose the option to show unseen for all or just selected statements.

It is when hidden links are displayed that *Ctrl I* and *Ctrl O* are most useful – they allow a gradual build-up of a map by bringing additional context as required and with knowledge of the amount of material that will appear (indicated by the number of hidden arrows).

Finding statements with specific text in them. Either move to the <u>list</u> menu and select <u>find text in concepts</u> or type >*find xxxx* on the command line (where xxxx is the specific text to be found). In both cases it is possible to search using a wild card, for example the command >*find mark~* will produce a list containing any statement with a word commencing with mark in it, for example marketing, marketer, markets, marking schedule.

2.3 Managing the Material Captured

Exploring the material around statements. One way of gently exploring the context of statements is using the >*xnn* (eXplore) command. Varieties of this command can be used (as illustrated in figure A1.1). To elicit an understanding of those statements that both support 1 and are supported by 1, the X command is used: >*x1*.

Should further detail be required about the consequences of statement 1 (that is two levels out) then >*xc1* (eXplore Consequences) is used. Similarly >*xe1* provides two levels of explanatory text (eXplore Explanations). See figure A1.1a.

If, however, only explanations or consequences are required – for example, only those statements supporting statement 1 then >*xi1* (eXplore In) is used. Likewise >*xo1* allows one level out to be displayed. See figure A1.1b.

Finally, if two levels in and out are desired the map command can be used: >*map 1*. See figure A1.1c. However, this command can often produce very detailed images as displaying two levels in and out of the focal statement can result in the map comprising 40 or 50 statements.

2.4 Creating and Using Styles

Styles are used to distinguish between different categories of statements, for example, issues, goals, competences, strategies, distinctive competences, etc. As a result they can assist in reducing complexity as it becomes easier to navigate the material by recognising the status of statements using colours and fonts.

Creating styles. To create a style use the <u>property</u> menu and select <u>concept style properties</u>. This will cause a dialog box to be opened providing the facility to create and edit not just one, but a number of styles. Select the <u>new style</u> button and enter a name for the new style. Use single words (do not use spaces – computer software sees a space as ending a command) and keep as short as possible, for example, use 'dc' for a distinctive competence style. The longer the name, the more typing is required each time styles are used. Once the style name has been generated, it is possible to choose fonts by *pressing the font button*. Fonts, style, size and colour can be chosen. *Press the ok* <u>button</u> to return to the original dialog box and *press ok* again to exit from the style properties dialog box.

> Hint: Times Roman, Arial and Tahoma fonts work best. It is also possible to generate borders for the styles. Only use borders (ovals, rounded rectangles and rectangles) for monochrome printing, where properties other than colour need to be used to differentiate styles. Borders take up a lot of space on the screen and make it more difficult to see selected statements (those that have a box around them).

Using styles. Having created styles, they are then available for application to statements.

- Select the <u>property</u> menu and then choose the <u>show style selector</u>. This will cause a dialog box to appear at the top right of the screen (it can be moved). Select the statement(s) to be attributed the style, move the mouse to the dialog box and select the desired style.
- Alternatively, use *Alt Y* and then select the statement(s) to be attributed the style and then select the style. *Alt Y* will act as a toggle to display or remove the dialog box.
- Alternatively, use the statement pop up menu (accessed by *clicking the right mouse button when on top of the selected statement*) and select the <u>style</u> option. Then select the preferred style.

Once styles have been created and applied then their contents form an 'intrinsic set' allowing further exploration. For example, it is possible to examine all of the goals by typing *map goal* (where the style is called goal).

In addition to providing styles for statements, it is also possible to **create styles for links**. For example, in the strategy as the discovery and exploitation of distinctiveness forum, it is useful to identify feedback loops and make the links contributing to the loop distinguishable (for example, use a thick red arrow). To create the link style, select the <u>property</u> menu and choose the <u>link style property</u> option. Press the *new style* button and provide a name for the new link, for example, feedback. Then provide the link with particular attributes (for example, thick arrow, red colour and solid head) and then press the *ok* button. Next move to the link that is to be changed and using the *left hand mouse button double click on it* (a dialog box appears). *Click on the small scrolling arrow* and *choose the style to be used*. Press on the *ok* button to confirm the action. It is also possible to create dotted links showing potential but not yet confirmed links.

3 ANALYSING CAUSAL MAPS[1]

3.1 Listing Heads

Listing heads reveals those statements with no links out of them (they are in essence at the head of the whole map). In, for example, a strategy as prioritisation of key issues forum this might suggest candidate goals. To list the heads click on the *list* menu and select <u>heads</u>. Alternatively, type *>lh*.

> Note: statements that are not yet linked will also appear in this list as they too are heads. Statements with no links, in or out, can also be detected by typing >*orphan* on the command line. It is recommended that these are linked into the rest of the model where appropriate.

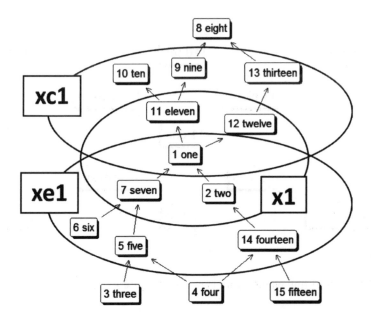

Figure A1.1a   >x1, >xe1 and >xc1 (the whole figure is shown is figure A1.1d)

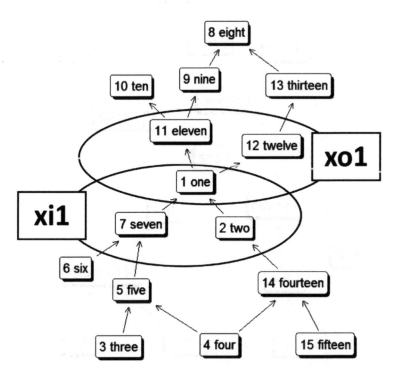

Figure A1.1b   >xo1 and >xi1 (the whole figure is shown is figure A1.1d)

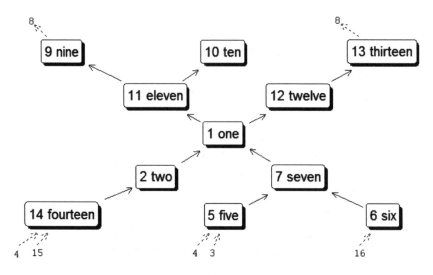

Figure A1.1c >map1 (the whole figure is shown is figure A1.1d)

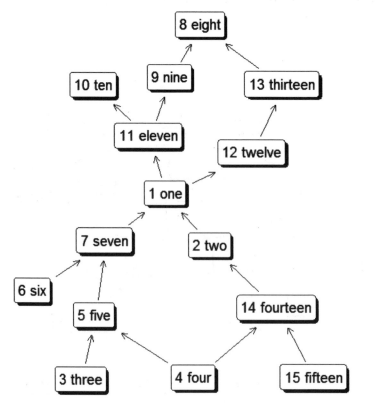

Figure A1.1d The Whole Map

3.2 Identifying Feedback Loops

Feedback loops are important for all of the forums (but particularly the forum on competitive advantage) and they play a major role in the development of strategy. To identify loops, move the mouse to the <u>analysis</u> menu and select the <u>loop</u> option. This will result in a box appearing, asking the user to confirm the running of the analysis (press the *ok* button) and the result of the analysis will then be listed when they exist. If nothing is listed then there are no loops in the model. Where there are loops listed then these can be explored further either by:

- Typing >*map loopnn* to produce a map in a view.
- Typing >*l loop1* to see a list of the loops' contents.

Where two or more loops appear to be similar it is possible to map them on the same view. To do this, start by typing >*map loop1* to show the first loop and then >*bring loop2* (which allows the second loop's contents to be added to the view). It will be necessary to move statements around a little to tidy up the loops making the loop more easily distinguishable (the software is designed to display an hierarchy and so has difficulty with a loop). Alternatively swipe across all of the loops of interest to select the statements of interest and then >*map sc*.

3.3 Finding Busy and Central Statements

There are two ways of considering issues.

- The first is **domain** analysis. This examines each statement and calculates the number of links in and out (essentially determining how busy it is). To carry out this analysis move the mouse to the <u>analysis</u> menu and select <u>domain</u>. As noted in the forum on strategy as the prioritisation of issues, this analysis can be helpful in detecting potential key issues. Alternatively type >*domt 20* to get the top 20 busy statements. Similarly, identifying those statements with the most in-arrows is possible by typing >*domi* and for the most out-arrows typing >*domo*.
- A second way of considering issues (and one that both reinforces the domain analysis as well as suggesting new key issues) is to review the overall model's structure to see which statements are central. To understand this analysis, consider the structure of a molecule (for example, water). Here elements are connected to one another with bonds – with some of the elements being relatively peripheral with few bonds connecting them while others are more central. By identifying those statements that are both busy and central a greater sense of confidence in revealing the key issues is acquired. This analysis is usually impossible to do without the software. To use this analysis move the mouse to the <u>analysis</u> menu and select <u>central</u>. The software will prompt once to confirm whether the analysis is to be run and once to inform the user that when working with large models, it might take a little while to run the analysis.

  Note: the central analysis is best used for 'backroom' work.

Those issues identified as highly central or with a high domain score can be attributed with a specific style (a typical key issue style might be italic, purple, 12pt). While domain analysis can often easily be conducted visually rather than having to use the software, it is harder accurately

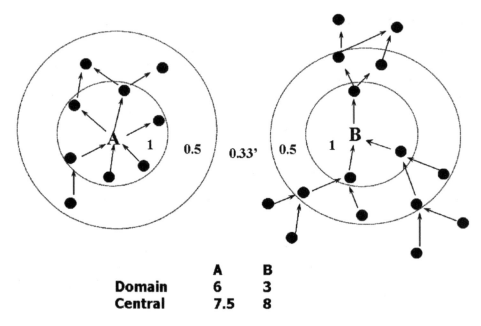

	A	B
Domain	6	3
Central	7.5	8

Figure A1.2 Domain and Central Analyses (when calculating the domain score, each statement linking either in or out of the focal statement counts as one (hence A receiving a score of six). However when calculating the central analysis, in addition to statements linking either into or out of the focal statement being allocated, one subsequent bands out continue to add to the score but with a distinished weighting. For example, 0.5 for two bands out and 0.33 for three bands out (hence B being allocated eight)).

to predict the results of the central analysis. The software provides a list of the top scoring statements and so it is possible to identify appropriate 'break-points' between a 'top' busy group compared to others, and this is not easy to spot visually. Figure A1.2 shows how the scores differ for each of domain and central analyses.

3.4 Slicing the Model into 'Chunks'

There are two methods for slicing the model.

- The first explores **clusters** ('islands' with a minimum of 'bridges' to other islands) which can be detected visually, particularly when using the fit to view mode. However, it can also be useful to explore clusters using the analysis available in the software. To use the cluster analysis, move the mouse to the <u>analysis</u> menu and select <u>cluster</u>. Once the analysis is complete, one way of viewing the clusters is to move to the <u>list</u> menu and select <u>sets</u>. This will result in a list of all the sets being displayed (showing the cluster number, date, number of statements in the cluster). As with the loop analyses these can then be further explored by either:

- ○ Typing >*map cluster1* to produce a map (please note this command requires the number of the cluster to be included).
- ○ Typing >*l cluster1* to see a list of the cluster contents.

- An alternative method for slicing the model is to **create hierarchical sets**. Hierarchical sets – as their name suggests – takes each member of the seed set (for example key issues) and drills down the chains of argument all the way to the base of the chain of argument. Each of the statements linking into the seed (see figure A1.3 below) along with all of the material that links into them are captured producing a tear-drop shaped set.

    To use this analysis first move to the <u>analysis</u> menu and then select <u>hieset</u>. This will cause a dialog box to appear allowing the analysis to be focused upon a particular seed set. For example, when carrying out the strategy as the prioritisation of issues forum the seeds might be the candidate key issues or the heads; alternatively when running the strategy as competitive advantage forum this might focus on the distinctive competence outcomes. As with the cluster analysis a number of sets will be produced and they can be viewed by moving the mouse to the <u>list</u> menu and selecting <u>sets</u>. This will result in a list of the sets being displayed (showing the hiesets by hierarchical number, date, number of statements in the cluster). As with the loop analyses these can then be further explored by either:

- ○ Typing >*map hieset1* to produce a map (please note this command requires the number of the hieset to be included).
- ○ Typing >*l hieset1* to see a list of the hieset contents.

3.5 Identifying Potency of Statements

Only once a hierarchical set analysis has been carried out, is it possible to determine which statements are potent (that is, those that have consequences for a large number of the seed statements). This is one means of prioritising statements as actions or strategies. See figure A1.3 that shows those statements in the light shaded area having an impact on three of the key issues. To undertake a potent analysis select the <u>analysis</u> menu and <u>potent</u>. The output from a potent analysis is listed in descending order of potency, with those supporting the highest number of seed statements used in the hieset analysis at the top of the results.

3.6 Producing an Overview of the Model's Content: Collapsing the Model

Constructing an overview road map of the model during a break in the forum is often helpful. This process is similar in concept to the production of a road atlas, where the front cover depicts the whole country with the major cities/towns and their summary road connections. This picture typically shows routes between the major cities (for example, a direct route between Glasgow and Edinburgh) which when examined in further depth, within the atlas, proves not to be the case (for example, the Glasgow to Edinburgh route actually runs through other towns such as Linlithgow, Falkirk, etc.). The same process is possible with the map, resulting in a collapsed picture of, for example, the goals and key issues (cities and towns) with the various chains of argument (routes) between them (both those that are direct as well as those that traverse additional argumentation).

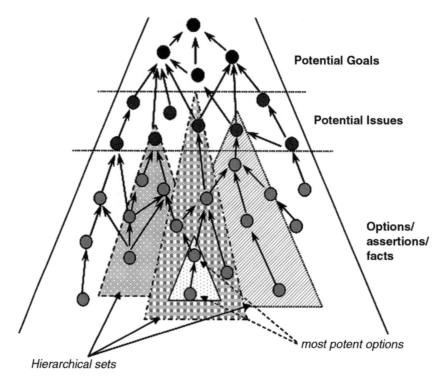

Figure A1.3 Illustrating Hierarchical Sets Based on Three Potential Key Issues

To produce an overview map, bring the statements to be focused upon (the major cities) onto a view (this might be goals and key issues, or distinctive competences and distinctive assets). Thus, for example, this could be done by typing >*bring goal* and then >*bring key* (providing these are what the styles are named). Next type >*col onmap*. This will now show any routes between the statements on the view that are both direct and indirect (that is, connected through other statements not currently on the view). This may make the view fairly messy but often reveals which of the statements are very potent or busy. To return to the full model where all the statements can be seen, type >*coloff*.

> Note: when in a collapsed mode, any statements that are not included in the focal view will no longer be able to be viewed on other views until the collapse has been turned off. The signs on arrows cannot be relied upon as they are usually the result of the last route explored by the software. *Do not* try analyses when the collapse is turned on, or add links.

All of the above analyses appear only to pay attention to a model structure and not to content. However, the causal map was constructed with respect to content and so the analyses are of both structure and content.

4 OTHER USEFUL COMMANDS AND FEATURES

4.1 Using Memo Cards

These can be useful when carrying out the strategy as the management of stakeholders forum as explanations regarding the power or interest bases can be retained in the background. To use the memo card *click with the right hand mouse button on the statement* and then select <u>view memo card</u>. It is possible to provide both a title and detailed text. To close the memo, *click on the small horizontal line* at the top left of the card and select *close*. The statement will now depict a paper clip with a red T (for text).

4.2 Copy and Paste Map Material into a Word Processing Document, or PowerPoint

In all of the forums it is recommended that a statement of strategic intent be produced from the maps. Thus copying and pasting the statements into a word processor is an efficient means of starting the process. The first requirement is to select those statements that are required to be copied. This may be done either through >*sc = l goal* (if all of the goal statements are to be copied – as in the strategy as purpose forum) or through dragging the mouse with the left button depressed across all of the focal statements. Then select <u>copy</u> from the <u>edit</u> menu. Pasting in Word follows the normal conventions.

4.3 Copying a Map into a Word Processing Document, or PowerPoint

Often participants will want a record of all of the final maps, but will not want to use (or have the use of) Decision Explorer®. To copy a map, go to <u>edit</u>, and then select <u>copy</u>; pasting follows the normal conventions.

> Note: when copying maps it is possible to copy using alternative forms of image – scalable or bitmap, and with colours, link arrows, selections, etc. To make these choices select <u>control</u> and then <u>map copy options</u>. A bitmap image may be useful when a printer is unable to cope satisfactorily with a scalable image.

4.4 Use the Software Short Cuts/Hot Keys

This is perhaps the most difficult of the suggestions as it does depend on a degree of familiarity with the software. However, as more experience is gained, start to use some of the more frequent short cuts as doing so will not only speed up operations (they are short cuts after all) but also disrupt the group less as intrusive drop down menus can be avoided. The most useful hot keys are:

- *Ctrl M* and *Ctrl T* – each flip between a map view and text view.
- Select a statement(s) and use *Ctrl I* to bring all of the statements that have arrows into the statement, or *Ctrl O* for those out of the statement(s) selected.
- *Ctrl B* will bring both in and out statements.

- *Alt Y* toggles the styles selector box on and off the screen.
- *Alt =* enables a fit to view mode.
- *Ctrl H* hides a selected statement(s).
- *Alt S* is the fast way of saving the model.
- *F5* will refresh the screen – sometimes the screen can become muddled because it has not been refreshed for a while.

> Note: it is very important to regularly save the model: use *Alt S*. It is often useful to save a copy of the model at different stages of the forum – that is the equivalent of a photocopy of work to date that is filed away for future reference (this file will not be opened rather the original file remains as the working document). When doing this select <u>file</u>, followed by <u>save copy as</u> and provide a new name for the file.

NOTE

1   See also Bryson, Ackermann, Eden and Finn (2004) Resource B, Eden (2004), and Ackermann and Eden (2010b).

BIBLIOGRAPHY

Ackermann, F. 1996. Participants' Perceptions on the Role of Facilitators Using Group Decision Support Systems. *Group Decision and Negotiation*, 5: 93–112.

Ackermann, F., Andersen, D. F., Eden, C. and Richardson, G. P. 2010a. ScriptsMap: A Tool for Designing Strategy Workshops. *Omega*, 39: 427–434.

Ackermann, F., Andersen, D. F., Eden, C. and Richardson, G. P. 2010b. Using a Group Support System to Add Value to Group Model Building. *System Dynamics Review*, 26: 335–346.

Ackermann, F. and Eden, C. 1994. Issues in Computer and Non-computer Supported GDSSs. *International Journal of Decision Support Systems*, 12: 381–390.

Ackermann, F. and Eden, C. 1997. Contrasting GDSSs and GSSs in the Context of Strategic Change: Implications for Facilitation. *Journal of Decision Systems*, 6: 221–250.

Ackermann, F. and Eden, C. 2001a. Contrasting Single User and Networked Group Decision Support Systems for Strategy Making. *Group Decision and Negotiation*, 10: 47–66.

Ackermann, F. and Eden, C. 2001b. SODA – Journey Making and Mapping in Practice. In Rosenhead, J. and Mingers, J. (eds), *Rational Analysis in a Problematic World Revisited*. London: Wiley: 43–61.

Ackermann, F. and Eden, C. 2010a. The Role of Group Support Systems: Negotiating Safe Energy. In Kilgour, D. M. and Eden, C. (eds), *Handbook of Group Decision and Negotiation*. Dordrecht: Springer: 285–299.

Ackermann, F. and Eden, C. 2010b. Strategic Options Development and Analysis. In Reynolds, M. and Holwell, S. (eds), *Systems Approaches to Managing Change: A Practical Guide*. London: Springer and the Open University Press: 139–190.

Ackermann, F. and Eden, C. 2011. Negotiation in Strategy Making Teams: Group Support Systems and the Process of Cognitive Change. *Group Decision and Negotiation*, 20: 3.

Ackermann, F. and Eden, C. with Brown, I. 2005. *The Practice of Making Strategy*. London: Sage.

Ackermann, F., Eden, C. and Williams, T. 1997. Modeling for Litigation: Mixing Qualitative and Quantitative Approaches. *Interfaces*, 27: 48–65.

Ackermann, F., Franco, L. A., Gallupe, B. and Parent, M. 2005. Group Support Systems for Multi-organizational Collaboration: Reflections on Process and Content. *Group Decision and Negotiation*, 14: 307–331.

Ackoff, R. L. 1974. *Redesigning the Future: A Systems Approach to Societal Problems*. New York: Wiley.

Ackoff, R. L. 1981. The Art and Science of Mess Management. *Interfaces*, 11: 20–26.

Agor, W. H. (ed.). 1989. *Intuition in Organizations*. Newbury Park, CA: Sage.

Allison, G. T. 1971. *Essence of Decision: Explaining the Cuban Missile Crisis*. Boston, MA: Little Brown.

Ambrosini, V., Bowman, C. and Collier, N. 2009. Dynamic Capabilities: An Exploration of How Firms Renew Their Resource Base. *British Journal of Management*, 20: 9–24.

Amit, R. and Schoemaker, P. J. 1993. Strategic Assets and Organizational Rent. *Strategic Management Journal*, 14: 33–46.

Andersen, D. F. 1990. Analyzing Who Gains and Who Loses: The Case of School Finance Reform in New York State. *System Dynamics Review*, 6: 21–43.

Andersen, D. F., Richardson, G. P., Ackermann, F. and Eden, C. 2010. Using a Group Support System to Add Value to Group Model Building. *System Dynamics Review*, forthcoming.

Andersen, T. J. 2000. Strategic Planning, Autonomous Actions and Corporate Performance. *Long Range Planning*, 33: 184–200.

Anderson, P. F. 1982. Marketing, Strategic-planning and the Theory of the Firm. *Journal of Marketing*, 46: 15–26.

Ansoff, H. I. 1980. 'Strategic Issue Management'. *Strategic Management Journal*, 1: 131–148.

Ansoff, H. I., Declerk, R. P. and Hayes, R. L. (eds). 1976. *From Strategic Planning to Strategic Management*. London: John Wiley & Sons.

Ansoff, I. 1965. *Corporate Strategy*. New York: McGraw-Hill.

Argyris, C. and Schon, D. A. 1974. *Theories in Practice*. San Francisco, CA: Jossey-Bass.

Argyris, C. and Schon, D. 1978. *Organizational Learning: A Theory of Action Perspective*. Reading, MA: Addison-Wesley.

Augier, M. and Teece, D. J. 2009. Dynamic Capabilities and the Role of Managers in Business Strategy and Economic Performance. *Organizational Science*, 20: 410–421.

Axley, S. R. 1984. Managerial and Organizational Communication in Terms of the Conduit Metaphor. *Academy of Management Review*, 9: 428–437.

Ball, D. W. 1972. 'Definition of the Situation': Some Theoretical and Methodological Consequences of Taking W.I. Thomas Seriously. *Journal for the Theory of Social Behaviour*, 2: 61–82.

Balogun, J. and Hope Hailey, V. 2004. *Exploring Strategic Change (2nd edn)*. Englewood Cliffs, NJ: Prentice Hall.

Balogun, J., Huff, A. S. and Johnson, P. 2003. Three Responses to the Methodological Challenges of Studying Strategizing. *Journal of Management Studies*, 40: 197–224 .

Bansal, P. 2003. From Issues to Actions: The Importance of Individual Concerns and Organizational Values in Responding to Natural Environmental Issues. *Organization Science*, 14: 510–527.

Barney, J. B. 1986. Organizational Culture: Can It Be a Source of Sustained Competitive Advantage? *Academy of Management Review*, 11: 656–665.

Barney, J. B. 1991a. Firm Resources and Sustained Competitive Advantage. *Journal of Management*, 17: 99–120.

Barney, J. B. 1991b. The Resource Based Model of the Firm: Origins, Implications, and Prospects. *Journal of Management*, 17: 97–98.

Barney, J. B. 2002. *Gaining and Sustaining Competitive Advantage*. Englewood Cliffs, NJ: Prentice Hall.

Beer, S. 1966. *Decision and Control*. London: Wiley.

Belbin, R. M. 1981. *Management Teams: Why They Succeed or Fail*. Oxford: Heinemann.

Belton, V., Ackermann, F. and Shepherd, I. 1997. Integrated Support from Problem Structuring through to Alternative Evaluation Using COPE and V.I.S.A. *Journal of Multi-Criteria Decision Analysis*, 6: 115–130.

Belton, V. and Stewart, T. J. 2002. *Multiple Criteria Decision Analysis*. Norwell, MA: Kluwer.

Bennett, P. G. 1980. Hypergames: Developing a Model of Conflict. *Futures*, 12: 489–507.

Berger, P. L. and Luckmann, T. 1966. *The Social Construction of Reality*. New York: Doubleday.

Bies, R. J. and Moag, J. S. 1986. Interactional Justice: Communication Criteria of Fairness. In Lewicki, L. R., Bazerman, M. and Sheppard, B. (eds), *Research on Negotiation in Organizations*. Greenwich, CT: JAI Press: 43–55.

Bittner, E. 1973. Objectivity and Realism in Sociology. In Psathas, G. (ed.), *Phenomenological Sociology: Issues and Applications*. New York: Wiley.

Bobocel, D. R. and Zdaniuk, A. 2005. *How Can Explanations Be Used to Foster Organizational Justice?* Hillsdale, NJ: Lawrence Erlbaum.

Bogner, W. C. and Thomas, H. 1994. Core Competence and Competitor Advantage: A Model and Illustrative Evidence from the Pharmaceutical Industry. In Hamel, G. and Heene, A. (eds), *Competence Based Competition*. Chichester: Wiley: 111–143.

Bostrom, R. P., Anson, R. and Clawson, V. K. 1993. Group Facilitation and Group Support Systems. In Jessup, L. M. and Valacich, J. S. (eds), *Group Support Systems: New Perspectives*. New York: Macmillan: 146–168.

Bougon, M. G. 1992. Congregate Cognitive Maps: A Unified Dynamic Theory of Organization and Strategy. *Journal of Management Studies*, 29: 369–389.

Bougon, M. G. and Komocar, J. M. 1990. Directing Strategic Change: A Dynamic Holistic Approach. In Huff, A. S. (eds), *Mapping Strategic Thought*. New York: Wiley: 143.

Bougon, M. G., Weick, K. and Binkhorst, D. 1977. Cognition in Organizations: Analysis of the Utrecht Jazz Orchestra. *Administrative Science Quarterly*, 22: 609–632.

Bourgeois, J. B. 1980. Performance and Consensus. *Strategic Management Journal*, 1: 227–248.

Bourgeois, L. J. 1981. On the Measurement of Organizational Slack. *Academy of Management Review*, 6: 29–39.

Bourgeois, L. J. 1985. Strategic Goals, Perceived Uncertainty, and Economic Performance in Volatile Environments. *Academy of Management Journal*, 28: 548–573.

Brewer, G. D. 1981. Where the Twain Meet: Reconciling Science and Politics in Analysis. *Policy Sciences*, 13: 269–279.

Brightman, J., Eden, C., van der Heijden, K. and Langford, D. 1996. The Development of an Industry Futures Bulletin. In Langford, D. and Retik, A. (eds), *The Organisation and Management of Construction, Shaping Theory and Practice*. London: E & FN Spon: 129–139.

Bryant, J. 2010. The Role of Drama Theory in Negotiation. In Kilgour, D. M. and Eden, C. (eds), *Handbook for Group Decision and Negotiation*. Dordrecht: Springer.

Bryson, J. M. 1995. *Strategic Planning for Public and Nonprofit Organizations*. San Francisco: Jossey-Bass.

Bryson, J. M. 2004. What to Do When Stakeholders Matter: Stakeholder Identification and Analysis Techniques. *Public Management Review*, 6: 21–53.

Bryson, J. M., Ackermann, F. and Eden, C. 2007. Putting the Resource-based View of Strategy and Distinctive Competencies to Work in Public Organizations. *Public Administration Review*, 67: 702–717.

Bryson, J. M., Ackermann, F., Eden, C. and Finn, C. 1995. Using the 'Oval Mapping Process' to Identify Strategic Issues and Formulate Effective Strategies. In Bryson, J. M., *Strategic Planning for Public and Nonprofit Organizations*. San Francisco, CA: Jossey-Bass: 257–275.

Bryson, J. M., Ackermann, F., Eden, C. and Finn, C. 2004. *Visible Thinking: Unlocking Causal Mapping for Practical Business Results*. Chichester: Wiley.

Bryson, J. M. and Crosby, B. C. 1992. *Leadership for the Common Good: Tackling Public Problems in a Shared-power World*. San Francisco, CA: Jossey-Bass.

Bryson, J. M., Gibbons, M. and Shaye, G. 2000. Enterprise Schemes for Nonprofit Survival, Growth, and Effectiveness. *Nonprofit Management and Leadership*, 11: 217–288.

Bryson, J. M. and Roering, W. 1988. The Initiation of Strategic Planning by Governments. *Public Administration Review*, 48: 995–1004.

Cameron, K., Sutton, R. and Whetten, D. 1988. *Readings in Organizational Decline*. Cambridge, MA: Ballinger.

Campbell, A. and Tawadey, K. 1990. *Mission and Business Philosophy*. Oxford: Heinemann.

Chaffee, E. 1985. Three Models of Strategy. *Academy of Management Review*, 10: 89–98.

Checkland, P. 1981. *Systems Thinking, Systems Practice*. Chichester: Wiley.

Chia, R. and Holt, R. 2006. Strategy as Practical Coping: A Heideggerian Perspective. *Organizational Studies*, 27: 635–655.

Chia, R. and MacKay, B. 2007. Post-processual Challenges for the Emerging Strategy-as-practice Perspective: Discovering Strategy in the Logic of Practice. *Human Relations*, 60: 217–242.

Child, J. 1997. Strategic Choice in the Analysis of Action, Structure, Organizations and Environment: Retrospect and Prospect. *Organizational Studies*, 18: 43–76.

Clawson, V. K., Bostrom, R. P. and Anson, R. 1993. The Role of the Facilitator in Computer-supported Meetings. *Small Group Research*, 24: 547–565.

Cohen, M., March, J. and Olsen, J. 1972. A Garbage Can Model of Organization and Choice. *Administrative Science Quarterly*, 17: 1–25.

Collins, James C. and Porras, Jerry I. 1995. *Built to Last: Successful Habits of Visionary Companies*. London: Century.

Collinson, D. 2009. Rethinking Leadership and Followership. In Clegg, S. R. and Cooper, C. L. (eds), *The Sage Handbook of Organizational Behavior*. London: Sage: 251–264.

Collis, D. J. 1994. Research Note: How Valuable Are Organizational Capabilities? *Strategic Management Journal*, 15: 143–152.

Collis, D. J. and Montgomery, C. A. 1995. Competing on Resources: Strategy in the 1990s. *Harvard Business Review*, July–August: 118–128.

Colquitt, J. A., Greenberg, J. and Zapata-Phelan, C. P. 2005. What Is Organizational Justice? A Historical Overview. In Colquitt, J. A. and Greenberg, J. (eds), *Handbook of Organizational Justice*. Mahwah, NJ: Lawrence Erlbaum: 3–56.

Coyne, K. P., Hall, S. J. D. and Clifford, P. G. 1997. Is Your Core Competence a Mirage? *The McKinsey Quarterly*, 40–54.

Cropanzano, R. and Mitchell, M. S. 2005. Social Exchange Theory: An Interdisciplinary Review. *Journal of Management*, 31: 874–900.

Cross, R. and Prusak, L. 2002. The People Who Make Organizations Go – or Stop. *Harvard Business Review*, June: 105–112.

Cummings, J. L. and Doh, J. P. 2000. Identifying Who Matters: Mapping Key Players in Multiple Environments. *California Management Review*, 42: 83–104.

Cyert, R. M. and March, J. G. 1992. *A Behavioural Theory of the Firm (2nd edn)*. Englewood Cliffs, NJ: Prentice Hall.

Daft, R. L. and Weick, K. E. 1984. Toward a Model of Organizations as Interpretive Systems. *Academy of Management Review*, 9: 284–295.

Datar, S. M., Garvin, D. A. and Cullen, P. G. 2010. *Rethinking the MBA: Business Education at the Crossroads*. Boston, MA: Harvard Business Press.

Day, G. S. 1994. The Capabilities of Market-driven Organizations. *Journal of Marketing*, 58: 37–52.

De Dreu, C. K. W. and West, M. A. 2001. Minority Dissent and Team Innovation: The Importance of Participation in Decision Making. *Journal of Applied Psychology*, 86: 1191–1201.

De Geus, A. 1988. Planning as Learning. *Harvard Business Review*, March–April: 70–74.

Denis, J. L., Lamothe, L. and Langley, A. 2001. The Dynamics of Collective Leadership and Strategic Change in Pluralistic Organizations. *Academy of Management Journal*, 44: 809–837.

Denis, J. L., Langley, A. and Rouleau, L. 2007. Strategizing in Pluralistic Contexts: Rethinking Theoretical Frames. *Human Relations*, 60: 179–215.

Dess, G. G. 1987. Consensus on Strategy Formulation and Organizational Performance: Competitors in a Fragmented Industry. *Strategic Management Journal*, 8: 259–277.

Dickens, L. and Watkins, K. 1999. Action Research: Rethinking Lewin. *Management Learning*, 30: 127–140.

Dierickx, I. and Cool, K. 1989. Asset Stock Accumulation and Sustainability of Competitive Advantage. *Management Science*, 35: 1504–1511.

Donaldson, T. and Preston, L. E. 1995. The Stakeholder Theory of the Corporation: Concepts, Evidence and Implications. *Academy of Management Review*, 20: 65–91.

Doran, G. T. 1981. There's a S.M.A.R.T. Way to Write Managements's Goals and Objectives. *Management Review (AMA Forum)*, 70 : 35–36.

Dutton, J. E. 1986. The Processing of Crisis and Non-crisis Strategic Issues. *Journal of Management Studies*, 23: 501–517.

Dutton, J. E. and Ashford, S. J. 1993. Selling Issues to Top Management. *Academy of Management Review*, 18: 397–428.

Dutton, J. E., Ashford, S. J., O'Neill, R. M. and Lawrence, K. A. 2001. Moves That Matter: Issue Selling and Organizational Change. *Academy of Management Journal*, 44: 716–736.

Dutton, J. E. and Duncan, R. B. 1987. The Creation of Momentum for Change Through the Process of Strategic Issue Diagnosis. *Strategic Management Journal*, 8: 279–295.

Dutton, J. E., Fahey, L. and Narayanan, V. K. 1983. Understanding Strategic Issue Diagnosis. *Strategic Management Journal*, 14: 307–323.

Dutton, J. E. and Ottensmeyer, E. 1987. Strategic Issue Management Systems: Forms, Functions and Contexts. *Academy of Management Review*, 12: 355–365.

Dutton, J. E., Walton, E. J. and Abrahamson, E. 1989. Important Dimensions of Strategic Issues: Separating the Wheat from the Chaff. *Journal of Management Studies*, 26: 379–396.

Easterby-Smith, M. and Lyles, M. (eds). 2003. *The Blackwell Handbook of Organisational Learning and Knowledge Management*. Oxford: Blackwell.

Eden, C. 1993. From the Playpen to the Bombsite: The Changing Nature of Management Science. *Omega*, 21: 139–154.

Eden, C. 1994. Cognitive Mapping and Problem Structuring for System Dynamics Model Building. *System Dynamics Review*, 10: 257–276.

Eden, C. 2004. Analyzing Cognitive Maps to Help Structure Issues or Problems. *European Journal of Operational Research*, 159: 673–686.

Eden, C. and Ackermann, F. 1998. *Making Strategy: The Journey of Strategic Management*. London: Sage.

Eden, C. and Ackermann, F. 1999. The Role of GDSS in Scenario Development and Strategy Making. In *6th International SPIRE/5th International Workshop on Groupware Proceedings, Cancun Mexico*: California: IEEE Computer Society Los Alamitos.

Eden, C. and Ackermann, F. 2000. Mapping Distinctive Competencies: A Systemic Approach. *Journal of the Operational Research Society*, 51: 12–20.

Eden, C. and Ackermann, F. 2001a. Group Decision and Negotiation in Strategy Making. *Group Decision and Negotiation*, 10: 119–140.

Eden, C. and Ackermann, F. 2001b. A Mapping Framework for Strategy Making. In Huff, A. and Jenkins, M. (eds), *Mapping Strategy*. London: Wiley: 173–195.

Eden, C. and Ackermann, F. 2001c. SODA – The Principles. In Rosenhead, J. and Mingers, J. (eds), *Rational Analysis in a Problematic World Revisited*. London: Wiley: 21–42.

Eden, C. and Ackermann, F. 2004. Use of 'Soft-OR' Models by Clients – What Do They Want from Them? In Pidd, M. (ed.), *Systems Modelling: Theory and Practice*. Chichester: Wiley: 146–163.

Eden, C. and Ackermann, F. 2007. The Resource Based View: Theory and Practice. Presented to Academy of Management Conference, Philadelphia 3–8 August.

Eden, C. and Ackermann, F. 2010a. Competences, Distinctive Competences, and Core Competences. *Research in Competence-Based Management*, 5: 3–33.

Eden, C. and Ackermann, F. 2010b. Decision Making in Groups: Theory and Practice. In Nutt, P. and Wilson, D. (eds), *Handbook of Decision Making*. Oxford: Blackwell: 231–273.

Eden, C., Ackermann, F., Bryson, J., Richardson, G., Andersen, D. and Finn, C. 2009. Integrating Modes of Policy Analysis and Strategic Management Practice: Requisite Elements and Dilemmas. *Journal of the Operational Research Society*, 60: 2–13.

Eden, C. and Huxham, C. 2001. The Negotiation of Purpose in Multi-organizational Collaborative Groups. *Journal of Management Studies*, 38: 351–369.

Eden, C., Jones, S. and Sims, D. 1979. *Thinking in Organisations*. London: Macmillan.

Eden, C., Jones, S. and Sims, D. 1983. *Messing About in Problems*. Oxford: Pergamon.

Eden, C., Jones, S., Sims, D. and Smithin, T. 1981. The Intersubjectivity of Issues and Issues of Intersubjectivity. *Journal of Management Studies*, 18: 37–47.

Eden, C. and Spender, J. C. 1998. *Managerial and Organizational Cognition*. London: Sage.

Eden, C. and van der Heijden, K. 1995. Detecting Emergent Strategy. In Thomas, H., O'Neal, D. and Kelly, J. (eds), *Strategic Renaissance and Business Transformation*. New York: Wiley.

Eisenhardt, K. M. 1989. Making Fast Strategic Decisions in High Velocity Environments. *Academy of Management Journal*, 32: 543–576.

Eisenhardt, K. M. and Martin, J. A. 2000. Dynamic capabilities: What are they? *Strategic Management Journal*, 21: 1105–1121.

Feldman, M. S. and March, J. G. 1981. Information in Organisations as Signal and Symbol. *Administrative Science Quarterly*, 26: 171–186.

Fisher, R. and Ury, W. 1982. *Getting to Yes*. London: Hutchinson.

Floyd, S. W. and Woolridge, B. 1992. Managing Strategic Consensus: The Foundation of Effective Implementation. *Academy of Management Review*, 6: 27–39.

Floyd, S. W. and Woolridge, B. 1994. Dinosaurs or Dynamos? Recognizing middle management's strategic role. *Academy of Management Executive*, 8: 47–57.

Floyd, S. W. and Woolridge, D. 2000. *Building Strategy from the Middle: Reconceptualizing the Strategy Process*. Thousand Oaks, CA: Sage.

Folger, R. and Bies, R. J. 1989. Managerial Responsibilities and Procedural Justice. *Employee Responsibilities and Rights Journal*, 2: 79–90.

Forrester, J. 1961. *Industrial Dynamics*. Cambridge, MA: MIT Press.

Forrester, J. 1971. Counter-intuitive Behaviour of Social Systems. *Technology Review*, January: 53–68.

Franco, A. L. 2009. Problem Structuring Methods as Intervention Tools: Reflections from Their Use with Multi-organisational Teams. *Omega*, 37: 193–203.

Freeman, R. E. 1984. *Strategic Management: A Stakeholder Approach*. Marshfield, MA: Pitman Publishing.

Freeman, R. E. and Evan, W. M. 1990. Corporate Governance: A Stakeholder Interpretation. *The Journal of Behavioural Economics*, 19: 337–359.

Freeman, R. E. and McVea, J. 2001. A Stakeholder Approach to Strategic Management. In Hitt, M., Harrison, J. and Freeman, R. E. (eds), *Handbook of Strategic Management*. Oxford: Blackwell: 189–207.

Freeman, R. E. and Reed, D. L. 1983. Stockholders and Shareholders: A New Perspective on Corporate Governance. *California Management Review*, 25: 88–106.

Friedman, P. G. 1989. Upstream Facilitation – A Proactive Approach to Managing Problem Solving Groups. *MIS Quarterly*, 3: 33–50.

Friend, J. and Hickling, A. 1987. *Planning Under Pressure: The Strategic Choice Approach*. Oxford: Pergamon.

Frooman, J. 1999. Stakeholder Influence Strategies. *Academy of Management Review*, 24: 191–205.

Frost, P. 1987. Power, Politics and Influence. In Tablin, F., Putnam, L., Roberts, K. and Porter, L. (eds), *Handbook of Organizational Communications: An Interdisciplinary Perspective*. London: Sage: 229–295.

Galbteath, J. and Galvin, P. 2008. Firm Factors, Industry Structure and Performance Variation: New Empirical Evidence to a Classic Debate. *Journal of Business Research*, 61: 109–117.

Galer, G. and van der Heijden, K. 1992. The Learning Organisation: How Planners Create Organisational Learning. *Marketing Intelligence and Planning*, 10: 512.

Gallimore, K. 2008. *A Developing Framework for Strategic Thinking*. University of Strathclyde: PhD Thesis.

Gallimore, K. 2010. Developing a Tentative Framework for Strategic Thinking. *British Academy of Management Conference, Sheffield*.

Garrett, B. 1990. Creating a Learning Organization: A Guide to Leadership, Learning, and Development. Cambridge: Simon & Schuster.

Garud, R. and van de Ven, A. H. 2002. Strategic Change Processes. In Pettigrew, A., Thomas, H. and Whittington, R. (eds), *Handbook of Strategy and Management*. London: Sage: 206–231.

Garvin, D. A. 1993. Building a Learning Organization. *Harvard Business Review*, July–August: 78–91.

Georgantzas, N. C. and Acar, W. 1995. *Scenario-driven Planning: Learning to Manage Strategic Uncertainty*. Westport, CN: Quorum Books.

Gill, R. 2006. *The Theory and Practice of Leadership*. London: Sage.

Gioia, D. A. and Chittipeddi, K. 1991. Sensemaking and Sensegiving in Strategic Change Initiation. *Strategic Management Journal*, 12: 433–448.

Godet, M. 1987. *Scenarios and Strategic Management*. London: Butterworth.

Goffee, R. and Jones, G. 2006. *Why Should Anyone Be Led by You?* Boston, MA: Harvard Business School Press.

Goleman, D., Boyatzis, R. and McKee, A. 2002. *Primal Leadership*. Boston, MA: Harvard Business School Press.

Gopinath, C. and Becker, T. E. 2000. Communication, Procedural Justice, and Employee Attitudes: Relationships Under Conditions of Divestiture. *Journal of Management*, 26: 63–83.

Guth, W. D. and MacMillan, I. C. 1986. Strategy Implementation Versus Middle Management Self Interest. *Strategic Management Journal*, 7: 313–327.

Haeckel, S. H. 2004. Peripheral Vision: Sensing and Acting on Weak Signals Making Meaning Out of Apparent Noise: The Need for a New Managerial Framework. *Long Range Planning*, 37: 181–189.

Hall, R. 1992. The Strategic Analysis of Intangible Resources. *Strategic Management Journal*, 13: 135–143.

Hambrick, D. and D'Aveni, R. 1988. Large Corporate Failures as Downward Spirals. *Administrative Science Quarterly*, 33: 1–23.

Hamel, G. 1994. The Concept of Core Competence. In Hamel, G. and Heene, A. (eds), *A Competence-based Competition*. Chichester: Wiley: 11–33.

Hamel, G. and Heene, A. 1994. *A Competence-based Competition*. Chichester: Wiley.

Hamel, G. and Prahalad, C. K. 1989. Strategic Intent. *Harvard Business Review*, May–June: 63–77.

Hannan, M. T. and Freeman, J. 1989. *Organizational Ecology*. Cambridge, MA: Harvard University Press.

Harary, F., Norman, R. and Cartwright, D. 1965. *Structural Models: An Introduction to the Theory of Directed Graphs*. New York: Wiley.

Harvey, J. 1988. The Abilene Paradox: The Management of Agreement. *Organizational Dynamics*, Summer: 17–34.

Haveman, H. 1992. Between a Rock and a Hard Place: Organizational Change and Performance Under Conditions of Fundamental Transformation. *Administrative Science Quarterly*, 37: 48–75.

Hayes, R. H., Wheelwright, S. C. and Clark, K. B. 1988. *Dynamic Manufacturing: Creating the Learning Organization*. New York: Free Press.

Hee Park, H. and Rethemeyer, R. K. forthcoming. The Politics of Connections: Assessing the Determinants of Social Structure in Policy Networks. *Journal of Public Administration Resaerch and Theory*.

Hickling, A. 1990. 'Decision Spaces': A Scenario About Designing Appropriate Rooms for Group Decision Management. In Eden, C. and Radford, J. (eds), *Tackling Strategic Problems: The Role of Group Decision Support*. London: Sage: 169–177.

Hindle, G. and Franco, L. A. 2009. Combining Problem Structuring Methods to Conduct Applied Research: A Mixed Methods Approach to Studying Fitness-to-drive in the UK. *Journal of the Operational Research Society*, 60: 1637–1648.

Hines, R. 1988. Financial Accounting: In Communicating Reality, We Construct Reality. *Accounting, Organisations and Society*, 13: 251–261.

Hodgkinson, G. P., Whittington, R., Johnson, G. and Schwarz, M. 2006. The Role of Strategy Workshops in Strategy Development Processes: Formality, Communication, Coordination and Inclusion. *Long Range Planning*, 35: 479–496.

Hogarth, R. M. 1987. *Judgment and Choice: The Psychology of Decision*. New York: Wiley.

Hopwood, A. and Miller, P. 1996. *Accounting as Social and Institutional Practice*. Cambridge: Cambridge University Press.

Howick, S., Ackermann, F. and Andersen, D. 2006. Linking Event Thinking with Structural Thinking: Methods to Improve Client Value in Projects. *System Dynamics Review*, 22: 113–140.

Howick, S. and Eden, C. 2010. Supporting Strategy in the Public Sector: Issues for OR. *Journal of the Operational Research Society*, forthcoming.

Howick, S., Eden, C., Ackermann, F. and Williams, T. 2008. Building Confidence in Models for Multiple Audiences: The Modelling Cascade. *European Journal of Operational Research*, 186: 1068–1083.

Huff, A. S. (ed.). 1990. *Mapping Strategic Thought*. New York: Wiley.

Huff, A. S. and Eden, C. 2009. Managerial and Organizational Cognition. *International Studies of Management and Organization*, 39: 3–8.

Huff, A. S. and Jenkins, M. (eds). 2001. *Mapping Strategy*. London: Wiley.

Huxham, C. 1990. On Trivialities in Process. In Eden, C. and Radford, J. (eds), *Tackling Strategic Problems: The Role of Group Decision Support*. London: Sage: 162–168.

Huxham, C. (ed.). 1996. *Creating Collaborative Advantage*. London: Sage .

Isenberg, D. J. 1987. The Tactics of Strategic Opportunism. *Harvard Business Review*, March–April: 92–97.

Janis, I. L. 1972. *Victims of Group Think*. Boston, MA: Houghton Mifflin.

Jarzabkowski, P. and Fenton, E. 2006. Strategizing and Organizing in Pluralistic Contexts. *Long Range Planning*, 39: 631–648.

Jawahar, I. M. and McLaughlin, G. L. 2001. Toward a Descriptive Stakeholder Theory: An Organizational Life Cycle Approach. *Academy of Management Review*, 26: 397–414.

Jenkins, R. 2008. *Social Identity*. Abingdon: Routledge.

Jensen, M. C. and Meckling, W. H. 1976. Theory of the Firm: Managerial Behavior, Agency Costs and Ownership Structure. *Journal of Financial Economics*, 3: 305–360.

Johnson, G. and Scholes, K. 2002. *Exploring Corporate Strategy (6th edn)*. Hemel Hempstead: Prentice Hall.

Johnson, G., Scholes, K. and Whittington, R. 2005. *Exploring Corporate Strategy: Text and Cases (7th edn)*. Harlow, Essex: Prentice Hall.

Johnson, P., Daniels, K. and Asch, R. 1998. Mental Models of Competition. In Eden, C. and Spender, J. C. (eds), *Managerial and Organizational Cognition*. London: Sage: 130–146.

Kaplan, R. S. and Norton, D. P. 1992. The Balanced Scorecard – Measures that Drive Performance. *Harvard Business Review*, 70: 71–79.

Kaplan, R. S. and Norton, D. P. 1993. Putting the Balanced Scorecard to Work. *Harvard Business Review*, 71: 134–147.

Kaplan, R. S. and Norton, D. P. 1996a. *The Balanced Scorecard*. Boston, MA: Harvard Business School Press.

Kaplan, R. S. and Norton, D. P. 1996b. Using the Balanced Scorecard as a Strategic Management System. *Harvard Business Review*, 74: 75–85.

Kaplan, R. S. and Norton, D. P. 2000. *The Strategy-focused Organization*. Boston, MA: Harvard Business School Press.

Kaplan, R. S. and Norton, D. P. 2004. *Strategy Maps: Converting Intangible Assets into Tangible Outcomes*. Boston, MA: Harvard Business School Press.

Kelly, G. A. 1955. *The Psychology of Personal Constructs*. New York: Norton.

Kelly, G. A. 1991. *The Psychology of Personal Constructs Volume 1: A Theory of Personality*. New York: Routledge.

Kepner, C. H. and Tregoe, B. B. 1965. *The Rational Manager: A Systematic Approach to Problem Solving and Decision Making*. New York: McGraw Hill.

Kerr, S. 1975. On the Folly of Rewarding A While Hoping for B. *Academy of Management Journal*, 18: 769–783.

Kerr, S. 1995. On the Folly of Rewarding A, While Hoping for B. *Academy of Management Executive*, 9: 7–16.

Kets de Vries, M. F. R. and Engellau, E. 2010. A Clinical Approach to the Dynamics of Leadership and Executive Transformation. In Nohria, N. and Khurana, R. (eds), *The Handbook of Leadership Theory and Practice*: Boston, MA: Harvard Business School Press.

Kilgour, M. and Eden, C. 2010. *Handbook for Group Decision and Negotiation*. Dordrecht: Springer.

Kim, W. C. and Mauborgne, R. A. 1991. Implementing Global Strategies: The Role of Procedural Justice. *Strategic Management Journal*, 12: 125–143.

Kim, W. C. and Mauborgne, R. A. 1995. A Procedural Justice Model of Strategic Decision Making. *Organization Science*, 6: 44–61.

Kim, W. C. and Mauborgne, R. A. 1996. Procedural Justice and Managers' In-role and Extra-role Behavior: The Case of the Multinational. *Management Science*, 42: 499–515.

Kim, W. C. and Mauborgne, R. A. 2005. *Blue Ocean Strategy: How to Create Uncontested Market Space and Make Competition Irrelevant*. Boston: Harvard Business School Press.

King, A. W., Fowler, S. W. and Zeithaml, C. P. 2001. Managing Organizational Competencies for Competitive Advantage: The Middle-management Edge. *Academy of Management Executive*, 15: 95–106.

King, W. R. 1982. Using Strategic Issue Analysis. *Long Range Planning*, 15: 45–49 .

Knight, D., Pearce, C. L., Smith, K. G., Olian, J. D., Sims, H. P., Smith, K. A. and Flood, P. 1999. Top Management Team Diversity, Group Process, and Strategic Consensus. *Strategic Management Journal*, 20: 445–465.

Kolb, D. and Rubin, I. M. 1991. *Organizational Behaviour: An Experimental Approach*. Englewood Cliffs, N.J. Prentice Hall.

Kotter, J. 1995. Leading Change: Why Transformation Efforts Fail. *Harvard Business Review*, 73: 59–67.

Kraatz, M. S. and Zajac, E. J. 2001. How Organizational Resources Affect Strategic Change and Performance in Turbulent Environments: Theory and Evidence. *Organization Science*, 12: 632–657.

Krackhardt, D. and Hanson, J. 1993. Informal Networks: The Company Behind the Chart. *Harvard Business Review*, July: 104–111.

Langley, A., Mintzberg, H., Pitcher, P., Posada, E. and Saintmacary, J. 1995. Opening Up Decision-making – The view from the Black Stool. *Organization Science*, 6: 206–279.

Leana, C. R. and van Buren, H. J. 1999. Organizational Social Capital and Employment Practices. *Academy of Management Review*, 24: 538–555.

Lewin, K. 1951. *Field Theory in Social Science: Selected Theoretical Papers*. New York: Harper & Row.

Lewis, L. F. 1993. Decision-aiding Software for Group Decision Making. In Nagel, S. (ed.), *Computer-aided Decision Analysis: Theory and Applications*: Westport, CN: Quorum Books.

Lewis, L. F. 2010. Group Support Systems: Overview and Guided Tour. In Kilgour, D. M. and Eden, C. (eds), *Handbook of Group Decision and Negotiation*. Dordrecht: Springer: 249–268.

Lewis, L. F., Garcia, J. E. and Hallock, A. 2002. Applying Group Support Systems in Social Work Education and Practice. *Journal of Technology in Human Services*, 20: 201–225.

Lindblom, C. E. 1959. The Science of Muddling Through. *Public Administration Review*, 19: 79–88.

Lindblom, C. E. 1980. *The Policy Making Process (2nd edn)*. Englewood Cliffs, N.J.: Prentice Hall.

Louis, M. R. and Sutton, R. I. 1991. Switching Cognitive Gears: From Habits of Mind to Active Thinking. *Human Relations*, 44: 55–74.

Maclean, M., Harvey, C. and Press, J. 2006. *Business Elites and Corporate Governance in France and the UK*. Basingstoke: Palgrave Macmillan.

Mangham I. L. 1978. *Interactions and Interventions in Organizations*. London: Wiley.

Mangham, I. L. and Overington, M. A. 1987. *Organizations as Theatre: A Social Psychology of Dramatic Appearances*. New York: Wiley.

Mason, R. O. and Mitroff, I. 1981. *Challenging Strategic Planning Assumptions: Theory, Cases and Techniques*. New York: Wiley.

McFadzean, E. S. and Nelson, T. 1998. Facilitating Problem Solving Groups: A Conceptual Model. *Leadership and Organization Development Journal*, 19: 6–13.

McGill, M. E., Slocum, J. W. and Lei, D. 1992. Management Practices in Learning Organizations. *Organizational Dynamics*, 21: 5–17.

McGoff, C. J. and Ambrose, L. 1991. *Empricial Information from the Field: A Practioner's View of Using GDSS in Business, Proceedings of the 24th Annual Hawaii International Conference on Systems Sciences*. Los Alamitos, CA: Society Press.

McGrath, J. 1984. *Groups: Interaction and Performance*. Englewood Cliffs, NJ: Prentice Hall.

Meacham, J. A. and Kuhn, D. 1983. *On the Development of Developmental Psychology*. Basel: Karger.

Miller, C. C. and Cardinal, L. B. 1994. Strategic Planning and Firm Performance: A Synthesis of More Than Two Decades of Research. *Academy of Management Journal*, 37: 1649–1665.

Miller, D. 2003. An Asymmetry-based View of Advantage: Towards an Attainable Sustainability. *Strategic Management Journal*, 24: 961–976.

Miller, G. A. 1956. The Magical Number Seven, Plus or Minus Two: Some Limits on Our Capacity for Processing Information. *Psychological Review*, 63: 81–97.

Mingers, J. and Rosenhead, J. 2004. Problem Structuring Methods in Action. *European Journal of Operational Research*, 152: 530–554.

Mintzberg, H. 1975. The Manager's Job: Folklore and Fact. *Harvard Business Review*, July–August: 49–61.

Mintzberg, H. 1978. Patterns in Strategy Formation. *Management Science*, 24: 934–948.

Mintzberg, H. 1987. Crafting Strategy. *Harvard Business Review*, July–August: 66–75.

Mintzberg, H. 1990. Strategy Formation: Schools of Thought. In Frederickson, J. W. (ed.), *Perspectives on Strategic Management*: New York: Harper & Row.

Mintzberg, H. 1994. The Fall and Rise of Strategic Planning. *Harvard Business Review*, January–February: 107–114.

Mintzberg, H. and McHugh, A. 1985. Strategy Formation in an Adhocracy. *Administrative Science Quarterly*, 30: 160–197.

Mintzberg, H. and Waters, J. A. 1985. Of Strategies, Deliberate and Emergent. *Strategic Management Journal*, 6: 257–272.

Mitchell, R. K., Agle, B. R. and Wood, D. J. 1997. Toward a Theory of Stakeholder Identification and Salience: Defining the Principle of Who and What Really Counts. *Academy of Management Review*, 22: 853–886.

Morgan, G. 1983. Rethinking Corporate Strategy: A Cybernetic Perspective. *Human Relations*, 36: 345–360.

Nahapiet, J. and Ghoshal, S. 1998. Social Capital, Intellectual Capital and the Organizational Advantage. *Academy of Management Review*, 23: 242–266.

Neisser, U. 1976. *Cognition and Reality*. San Francisco: Freeman.

Nohria, N. 1992. Is a Network Perspective a Useful Way of Studying Organizations? In Nohria, N. and Eccles, R. C. (eds), *Networks and Organizations: Structure, Form and Actions*. Boston, MA: Harvard Business School Press: 1–22.

Normann, R. 1985. Developing Capabilities for Organizational Learning. In Pennings, J. and Associates (eds), *Organizational Strategy and Change*. San Francisco, CA: Jossey-Bass.

Nunamaker, J. F., Dennis, A. R., Valacich, J. S. and Vogel, D. R. 1991. Electronic Meeting Systems to Support Group Work. *Communications of the ACM*, 34: 40–61.

Nutt, P. C. 2002. *Why Decisions Fail: Avoiding the Blunders and Traps that Lead to Debacles*. San Francisco, CA: Berrett-Koehler Inc.

Nutt, P. C. and Backoff, R. 1992. *Strategic Management of Public and Third Sector Organizations*. San Francisco, CA: Jossey-Bass.

O'Brien, F. A. and Meadows, M. 1998. Future Visioning: A Case Study of a Scenario-based Approach. In Dyson, R. G. and O'Brien, F. A. (eds), *Strategic Development: Methods and Models*: Chichester: Wiley.

Ocasio, W. 1997. Towards an Attention-based View of the Firm. *Strategic Management Journal*, 18: 187–206.

Ozbekhan, H. 1974. Thoughts on the Emerging Methodology of Planning. *Fields Within fields*, 10.

Penrose, E. T. 1959. *The Theory of Growth of the Firm*. London: Basil Blackwell.

Perrow, C. 1986. *Complex Organizations (3rd edn)*. New York: Random House.

Peteraf, M. A. 1993. The Cornerstones of Competitive Advantage: A Resource-based View. *Strategic Management Journal*, 124: 179–191.

Pettigrew, A. 1977. Strategy Formulation as a Political Process. *International Studies of Management and Organization*, 7: 78–87.

Pettigrew, A., Whittington, R., Melin, L., Sanchez-Runde, C., Van den Bosch, F., Ruitgrok, W. and Numagami, T. 2003. *Innovative Forms of Organizing*. London: Sage.

Phillips, L. and Phillips, M. C. 1993. Facilitated Work Groups: Theory and Practice. *Journal of the Operational Research Society*, 44: 533–549.

Porter, M. E. 1980. *Competitive Strategy: Techniques for Analysing Industries and Competitors*. New York: Free Press.

Porter, M. 1985. *Competitive Advantage*. New York: Free Press.

Prahalad, C. K. and Hamel, G. 1990. The Core Competences of the Corporation. *Harvard Business Review*, May–June: 79–91.

Preston, L. E. and Sapienza, H. J. 1990. Stakeholder Management and Corporate Performance. *The Journal of Behavioural Economics*, 19: 361–375.

Priem, R. L. and Butler, J. E. 2001. Is the Resource-based 'View' a Useful Perspective for Strategic Management Research? *Academy of Management Review*, 26: 22–40.

Provera, B., Montefusco, A. and Canato, A. 2010. A 'No Blame' Approach to Organizational Learning. *British Journal of Management*, 21: 1057–1074.

Quinn, J. B. 1978. Strategic Change: Logical Incrementalism. *Sloan Management Review*, 20: 7–21.

Quinn, J. B. 1980. *Strategies for Change: Logical Incrementalism*. Homewood, IL: Irwin.

Raimond, P. and Eden, C. 1990. Making Strategy Work. *International Journal of Strategic Management*, 23: 97–105.

Regner, P. 2008. Strategy-as-practice and Dynamic Capabilities: Steps Towards a Dynamic View of Strategy. *Human Relations*, 61: 565–588.

Richardson, G. P. 1991. *Feedback Thought in Social Science and Systems Theory*. Philadelphia: University of Pennsylvania Press.

Richardson, G. P., Andersen, D. F. and Wu, Y. J. 2002. Misattribution in Welfare Reform: a Stock-and-flow Archetype. In Davidsen, P. I., Edoardo, M., Diker, V. G., Langer, R. S. and Rowe, J. I. (eds), *Proceedings of the 2002 International Conference of the System Dynamics Society, Palermo, Italy, July*. Albany, NY: System Dynamics Society.

Ringland, G. 1998. *Scenario Planning: Managing for the Future*. Chichester: Wiley.

Rittel, H. W. J. and Webber, M. M. 1973. Dilemmas in a General Theory of Planning. *Policy Sciences*, 4: 155–169.

Rosenhead, J. 1989. Diverse Unity: The Principles and Prospects for Problem Structuring Methods. In Rosenhead, J. (eds), *Rational Analysis for a Problematic World*. Chichester: Wiley: 341–358.

Rosenhead, J. 2006. Past, Present and Future of Problem Structuring Methods. *Journal of the Operational Research Society*, 57: 759–765.

Rosenhead, J. and Mingers, J. (eds). 2001. *Rational Analysis in a Problematic World Revisited*. Chichester: Wiley.

Rowley, T. J. 1997. Moving Beyond Dyadic Ties: A Network Theory of Stakeholder Influences. *Academy of Management Review*, 22: 887–910.

Rughase, O. 2006. *Identity and Strategy: How Individual Visions Enable the Design of a Market Strategy that Works*. Cheltenham: Edward Elgar.

Rumelt, R. P. 1984. *Towards a Strategic Theory of the Firm*. Englewood Cliffs, N.J.: Prentice Hall.

Salancik, G. R. and Pfeffer, J. 1974. The Bases and Use of Power in Organizational Decision-making: The Case of Universities. *Administrative Science Quarterly*, 19: 453–473.

Sanchez, R. 2002. Understanding Competence-based Management: Identifying and Managing Five Modes of Competence. *Journal of Business Research*, 57: 518–532.

Sanchez, R. and Heene, A. 2004. *The New Strategic Management: Organizations, Competition and Competence*. London: Wiley.

Saul, P. 2006. Seeing the Future in Weak Signals. *Journal of Futures Studies*, 10: 93–102.

Schein, E. H. 1988. *Process Consultant (Vols 1 & 2)*. Reading MA: Addison-Wesley.

Schein, E. H. 2004. *Organizational Culture and Leadership*. San Francisco, CA: Jossey-Bass.

Schoemaker, P. J. H. 1992. How to Link Strategic Vision to Core Capabilities. *Sloan Management Review*, 34: 67–81.

Schwarz, R. M. 1994. *The Skilled Facilitator: Practical Wisdom for Developing Effective Groups*. San Francisco, CA: Jossey-Bass.

Schwarz, R. M. 2002. *The Skilled Facilitator: A Comprehensive Resource for Consultants, Facilitators, Managers, Trainers and Coaches*. San Francisco, CA: Jossey-Bass.

Schwenk, C. R. 1995. Strategic Decision Making. *Journal of Management*, 21: 471–494.

Sebenius, J. K. 1992. Negotiation Analysis: A Characterization and Review. *Management Science*, 38: 8–38.

Selznik, P. 1957. *Leadership in Administration: A Sociological Interpretation*. Evanston, IL: Row Peterson.

Senge, P. M. 1990. *The Fifth Discipline: The Art and Practice of the Learning Organization*. New York: Doubleday.

Senge, P. M. 1992. *The Fifth Discipline*. New York: Doubleday.

Shaw, D., Ackermann, F. and Eden, C. 2003. Sharing and Building Knowledge in Group Problem Structuring. *Journal of the Operational Research Society*, 54: 936–948.

Shaw M. E. 1961. Group Dynamics. *Annual Review of Psychology*, 12: 129–156.

Silverman, D. 1970. *The Theory of Organizations*. London: Heinemann.

Simon, H. A. 1957. *Administrative Behaviour*. New York: Free Press.

Simon, H. A. 1964. On the Concept of Organizational Goal. *Administrative Science Quarterly*, 9: 1–22.

Simon, H. A. 1976. From Substantive to Procedural Rationality. In Latsis, S. J. (ed.), *Method and Appraisal in Economics*: Cambridge: Cambridge University Press.

Simons, R. 1995. *Levers of Control*. Cambridge, MA: Harvard Business School Press.

Smith, K. and Grimm, C. 1987. Environmental Variation, Strategic Change, and Firm Performance: A Study of Railroad Deregulation. *Strategic Management Journal*, 8: 363–376.

Spender, J. C. 1989. *Industry Recipes: An Enquiry into the Nature and Sources of Managerial Judgment*. Oxford: Basil Blackwell.

Stacey, R. 1993. Strategy as Order Emerging from Chaos. *Long Range Planning*, 26: 10–17.

Stacey, R. 1995. The Science of Complexity: An Alternative Perspective for Strategic Change Processes. *Strategic Management Journal*, 16: 477–495.

Stalk, G., Evans, P. and Schulman, L. E. 1992. Competing on Capabilties: The New Rules of Corporate Strategy. *Harvard Business Review*, 70: 57–69.

Starbuck, W. H. 1983. Organizations as Action Generators. *American Sociological Review*, 48: 91–102.

Stasser, G. and Titus, W. 1987. Pooling of Unshared Information in Group Decision Making: Biased Information Sampling During Discussion. *Journal of Personality and Social Psychology*, 1467–1478.

Staw, B. M., Sandelands, L. E. and Dutton, J. E. 1981. Threat-Rigidity Effects in Organizaional Behaviour: A Multi Level Analysis. *Administrative Science Quarterly*, 26: 501–524.

Sterman, J. D. 2000. *Business Dynamics: Systems Thinking and Modeling for a Complex World*. New York: McGraw-Hill.

Tajfel, H. 1981. *Human Groups and Human Categories*. Cambridge: Cambridge University Press.

Teece, D. J. and Pisano, G. 1994. The Dynamic Capabilities of Firms: An Introduction. *Industrial and Corporate Change*, 3: 20.

Teece, D. J., Pisano, G. and Shuen, A. 1997. Dynamic Capabilities and Strategic Management. *Strategic Management Journal*, 18: 509–533.

Telford, W., Cropper, S. and Ackermann, F. 1992. Quality Assurance and Improvement – The role of Strategy Making. *International Journal of Health Care Quality Management*, 5: 5–11.

Thomas, J. B., Shankster, L. J. and Mathieu, J. E. 1994. Antecedents to Organizational Issue Interpretation – The Roles Of Single-level, Cross-level, and Content Cues. *Academy of Management Journal*, 37: 1252–1284.

Thomas, W. I. and Thomas, D. S. 1928. *The Child in America: Behavior Problems and Programs*. New York: Knopf.

Tyler, T. R. and Blader, S. L. 2000. *Cooperation in Groups: Procedural Justice, Social Identity, and Behavioural Engagement*. Oxford: Psychology Press.

Van der Heijden, K. 1996. *Scenarios: The Art of Strategic Conversation*. Chichester: Wiley.

Van de Ven, A. H. 1992. Suggestions for Studying Strategy Process: A Research Note. *Strategic Management Journal*, 13. Special Issue, Summer: 169–188.

Van Velsor, E., Taylor, E. S. and Leslie, J. B. 1993. An Examination of the Relationships Among Self-Perception Accuracy, Self-awareness, Gender, and Leader Effectiveness. *Human Resource Management*, 32: 249–263.

Vogel, D., Nunamaker, J., Martz, W., Grohowski, R. and McGoff, C. J. 1990. Electronic Meeting System Experience at IBM. *Journal of Management Information Systems*, 6: 25–43.

Vygotsky, L. S. 1978. *Mind in Society: The Development of Higher Psychological Processes*. Cambridge, MA: Harvard University Press.

Wack, P. 1985a. Scenarios, Shooting the Rapids. *Harvard Business Review*, November–December: 131–142.

Wack, P. 1985b. Scenarios, Uncharted Waters Ahead. *Harvard Business Review*, September–October: 73–90.

Walsh, J. P. 1988. Selectivity and Selective Perception: An Investigation of Managers' Belief Structures and Information Processing. *Academy of Management Journal*, 31: 873–896.

Walsh, J. P., Henderson, C. M. and Deighton, J. 1988. Negotiated Belief Structures and Decision Performance: An Empirical Investigation. *Organization Behavior and Human Decision Processes*, 42: 194–216.

Warren, K. D. 2002. *Competitive Strategy Dynamics*. Chichester: Wiley.

Weick, K. E. 1979. *The Social Psychology of Organizing*. Reading, MA: Addison-Wesley.

Weick, K. E. 1983. Managerial Thought in the Context of Action. In Srivastava, S. (ed.), *The Executive Mind*. San Francisco, CA: Jossey-Bass: 221–242.

Weick, K. E. 1995. *Sensemaking in Organizations*. Thousand Oaks, CA: Sage.

Weick, K. E. 1999. Theory Construction as Disciplined Reflexivity: Tradeoffs in the 90s. *Academy of Management Review*, 24: 797–806.

Weick. K. E. and Roberts, K. H. 1993. Collective Mind in Organizations: Heedful Interrelating on Flight Decks. *Administrative Science Quarterly*, 38: 357–381.

Wensley, R. 2003. Strategy as Intention and Anticipation. In Cummings, S. and Wilson, D. (eds), *Images of Strategy*: Oxford: Blackwell.

Wernerfelt, B. 1984. A Resource Based View of the Firm. *Strategic Management Journal*, 5: 171–180.

Wernerfelt, B. 1989. From Critical Resources to Corporate Strategy. *Journal of General Management*, 14: 4–12.

Whittington, R. 2001. *What is Strategy – And Does it Matter? (2nd edn)*. Andover: Cengage Learning EMEA.

Whittington, R. and Cailluet, L. 2008. The Crafts of Strategy: Special Issue Introduction by the Guest Editors. *Long Range Planning*, 41: 241.

Whittington, R., Molloy, E., Mayer, M. and Smith, A. 2006. Practices of Strategising/Organising – Broadening Strategy Work and Skills. *Long Range Planning*, 39: 615–629.

Winnicott, D. W. 1953. Transitional Objects and Transitional Phenomena: A Study of the First Not-me Possession. *The International Journal of Psych-Analysis*, 34 Part 2: 89–97.

Winograd, T. and Flores, F. 1986. *Understanding Computers and Cognition*. Norwood, NJ: Ablex.

Winstanley, D., Sorabji, D. and Dawson, S. 1995. When the Pieces Don't Fit: A Stakeholder Power Matrix to Analyse Public Sector Restructuring. *Public Money and Management*, April–June: 19–269.

Winter, S. G. 2003. Understanding Dynamic Capabilities. *Strategic Management Journal*, 24: 991–995.

Wolfe, R. and Putler, D. 2002. How Tight Are the Ties that Bind Stakeholder Groups? *Organizational Science*, 13: 64–80.

Woolridge, S. W. and Floyd, B. 1990. The Strategy Process, Middle Management Involvement, and Organizational Performance. *Strategic Management Journal*, 11: 231–241.

Yerkes, R. M. and Dodson, J. D. 1988. The Relation of Strength of Stimulus to Rapidity of Habit-formation. *Journal of Comparative Neurology and Psychology*, 18: 459–482.

Zagonel, A. A. 2002. Model Conceptualization in Group Model Building: A Review of the Literature Exploring the Tension Between Representing Reality and Negotiating a Social Order. *Proceedings of the 20th International Conference of the System Dynamics Society, Palermo, Italy, The System Dynamics Society*.

INDEX

AUTHOR INDEX

HOW TO ACCESS DECISION EXPLORER® AND ADDITIONAL RESOURCES

In order to access Decision Explorer® and other additional resources for the book please follow the instructions below:

1. Go to the SAGE website: www.sagepub.co.uk
2. Use the toolbar to search for **Ackermann** or **Eden** to find the webpage dedicated to the book (see below)
3. Click on the tab labelled Additional Resources.

Additional Resources

The Additional Resources for **Making Strategy: Mapping Out Strategic Succes**s include the following:

• Link to the special FREE edition of **Decision Explorer®**
• Additional teaching material including video material and PowerPoint slides

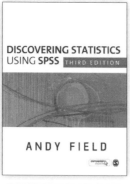
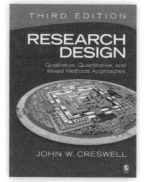
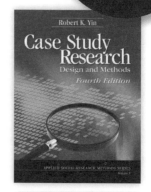

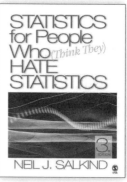

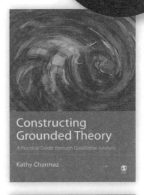

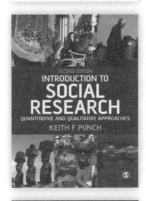
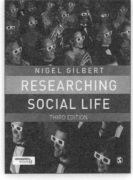

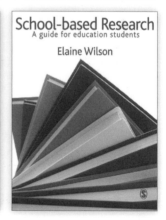